THE NAKED GUIDE TO
BRISTOL

By Gil Gillespie

First published in 2004 by Naked Guides Ltd. Second Edition
published 2006 by Tangent Books. This Edition published 2011 by
Tangent Books

Tangent Books, Unit 5.16 Paintworks, Bristol BS4 3EH
www.tangentbooks.co.uk
Tel: 0117 972 0645

Publisher: Richard Jones
Additional research, editing and writing: Richard Jones,
Marc Leverton, Nicky Johns, Darryl W Bullock
Design/cover artwork: Joe Burt
Maps/street art: Trevor Wyatt

ISBN: 978-1-906477-50-9

3nd Edition
Copyright Tangent Books Ltd 2011
All rights reserved

Printed by Mid Wales Litho, Pontypool

Tangent Books is a member of the Bristol Books and Publishers group

The Naked Guide to Bristol's cover stars

A	Tony Benn	H	Onnalee (Reprazent)	O	Brunel
B	Sapphire	I	Darth Vader (D Prowse)	P	Cary Grant
C	Ian Holloway	J	Tricky	Q	Gromit
D	Roni Size	K	Cops by Banksy	R	Paul Stephenson
E	Robert Del Naja	L	Alfred	S	Jane Couch
F	Grant Marshall	M	Bear by Banksy		
G	Ray Mighty	N	Concorde		

THANKS TO...

Contributors: Ian Bone, Mark Fletcher, John Hudson, Leonie Campbell-King, Caitlin Telfer, Mena Telfer, Mike Goldsmith, Will Scott, Gideon Kibblewhite, Claire Morgan, Steve Faragher, Anne Smith, Joe Burt, Trevor Wyatt, Johnny Ball, David Cann, Ella Voke, Finn Hutchinson, Darryl W Bullock, Marc Leverton, Nicky Johns, Jonathan Lewis, Beezer

Print management: Jonathan Lewis (EPM jonathanlewis.print@googlemail.com)

Inspiration: Steve Faragher, Gideon Kibblewhite

Photography: Richard Jones, Joe Burt, Trevor Wyatt, Maggie Telfer, Mena Telfer and Kate McDonnell

Picture credits: Arnolfini, p4 (Jamie Woodley); Stokes Croft riots, p25 (Alex Cater); drawing of Medieval Bristol, p87 (courtesy of Memories, St Nicholas Market); Brunel, p110 (Institute of Civil Engineers); Casualty, p110, p119 (courtesy BBC Press); David Neilson, p111 (courtesy ITV Press); Teachers, p111 (courtesy C4 Press); Jane Couch, p115 (Nigel Turner); Roger Cook and Roger Greenaway, p114, p115 (courtesy Charlie Dobson); Adam Hart-Davis, p116 (Chris Rydlewski/Andy Green); Ian Holloway, p118 (Empics); Precious McKenzie, p121 (courtesy Precious McKenzie); Wallace & Gromit, p122 (Aardman Animations Ltd/Wallace and Gromit Ltd 1989); Tony Robinson, p124 (courtesy C4 Press); Babyhead, p1, p138 (Robin Muscat); DJ Die, p141, MC Dynamite, p144, Krust, p150, Roni Size, p155 (courtesy Heavyweight Management/Alexis Maryon); John Parish, p152 (Ralph Enard); Hazel Winter, p156 (Jacqueline Glynn); Experimental Pop Band, p157 (Sebastian Mayer); At-Bristol, p169 (courtesy At-Bristol); ss Great Britain, p178 (ss Great Britain Trust, Mandy Reynolds). Graffiti street art pictures: Anne Smith, Jack (www.bristolgraffiti.com), Sarah Connolly, Ikue Uyama (relaxmax), Cheba, Iyers.

Cover artwork: Joe Burt. Pictures credits for images used on cover: Clifton Suspension Bridge (Anne Smith), Ian Holloway (Empics), Onallee and Roni Size (courtesy Heavyweight Management/Alexis Maryon), Massive Attack (Mark Simmons), Gromit (Aardman Animations Ltd/Wallace and Gromit Ltd 1989), Brunel (Institute of Civil Engineers), Jane Couch (Nigel Turner).

Gil Gillespie would like to dedicate this book to the beautiful Lulu and little Mister Joe Mancini Addison Gillespie, even though he's been absolutely no help whatsoever. Immeasurable gratitude to Mum, Dad, Meriel, Rhian, Phil Parkinson, Borja, Megan, Morgan and the Pant and Merthyr three. Significant nods also go out in the direction of Gary Tipp, Dav Ludford and all the never-say-die *Total Football* boys. Additional thanks to Cris Warren, Dan Slingsby, Borders bookshop and *The Guardian* for being rungs on the ladder of recognition. Cheers just for being around to Patrick Duff, Dodge Holme, the Martindales, Corrina Rowell, Moti Gokulsing, Matt and Aime, Devron, and Neil Whitcombe. Along the way I also wouldn't have made it without Antonio Gramsci, Franco Baresi, Johnny Owen, the Moonlight Mile, Roberto Mancini, Michael Foot, Fidel Castro, Hugo Chavez, Cutshaw (the astronaut), AC Milan 4 Barcelona 0, Giancarlo Gallivoti, Gabriel Marcotti, atheists everywhere, Stan Laurel and Oliver Hardy, David Bowie, Bobby Gillespie, Conor Oburst, LCD Soundsystem, the World Cup winning Azzurri '06 squad and about one million others whose names I can't remember right now.

Richard Jones would like to thank Maggie, Caitlin and Mena. Leonie and the girls for their contribution to Children's Bristol, all the contributors for their patience, but most of all Gil for his vision of Bristol.

Also thanks to: Precious McKenzie, Charlie Dobson, John Parish, Steve Symons, Robin Muscat, Catherine Mason at Broadcast Books, John and Angela Sansom of Redcliffe Press, Carolyn Jones, Charly Paige, Beast, Kate Pollard, Francine Russell, Dav Ludford and Rono Kahumbu Turner.

WELCOME

Hello and welcome to the third edition of *The Naked Guide To Bristol*. Almost seven years have passed since the first book hit the streets and the response, both in terms of feedback and sales, has been overwhelming. Thanks. For this new edition, we have retained the original Naked Guide template and packed in even more straight-talking, off-beat and occasionally off-the-wall observations. We've also added a handful of new features, here and there, just for the hell of it, and updated information where necessary. The music chapter has been extensively re-written to accommodate the recent explosion of genuinely exciting new bands currently perched on the edge of something very significant indeed. And we have, of course, kept an eye on the ever-multiplying number of new bars and restaurants that seem to spring up from nowhere every time you turn a corner. Well, that's just about it. Please turn the page in order to continue the reading process.

Gil Gillespie

CONTRIBUTE TO THE NAKED GUIDE TO BRISTOL

We have done our best to check all addresses, telephone numbers and other contact details, but these details often change. If you would like to update a contact, add your comment to a listing, or tell us about somewhere new, go to **www.tangentbooks.co.uk** or call us on **0117 972 0645**.

ABOUT THE AUTHORS

Gil Gillespie first started going out in Bristol when he was 14 and has enjoyed or endured many thousands of evenings in the pubs, bars, restaurants and clubs of the city ever since. Remarkably, he has also found the time to carve out a career as one of the most outstanding and outspoken magazine writers in the country and has sounded off about subjects including music, football, television, movies, technology, politics and culture for magazines such as *Total Football, Venue, Select, Football Italia, Big Issue, .net Directory, Connect, Focus* and *Comedy Review*. He lives in Bishopston with his long-term girlfriend Lucy and their son Joe.

Richard Jones first came to the public's attention as the fresh-faced pop page editor of the previously unhappening *Bristol Evening Post*. From here, he introduced the city to exciting new beat combos such as Massive Attack and Smith & Mighty and was one of the first to document the arrival of the so-called Bristol Sound. It wasn't long before he was headhunted by Future Publishing and, despite being a lifelong Rovers fan, offered a dream appointment as the editor of *Total Football* magazine. He now runs his own publishing company. His passions include roots reggae (1973-1985) and making cider. He lives in Totterdown with his partner Maggie and their two children Caitlin and Mena.

Area Map

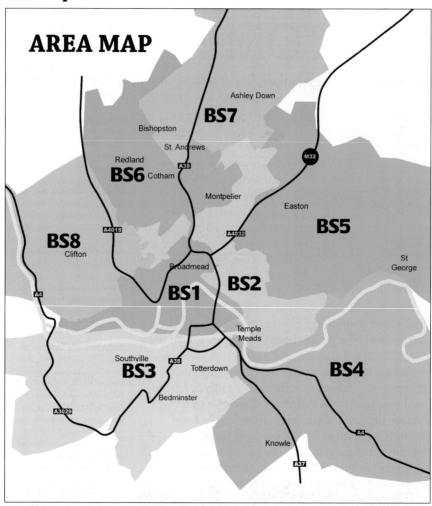

INDEX OF PLACES WITHIN AREAS

CONTENTS

AREA GUIDE P2 From Christmas steps to Picton street, discover the city.

UP CLOSE P86 Go under the skin of Bristol and discover what makes it tick.

LISTINGS P188 Find out where to party, shop, drink and eat.

BS1 The Centre and Old Bristol

Step back in history or step into a theme bar.
The choice is yours in Bristol's Old Town

Earthquakes, floods, riots, slavery, bandits, bombs and the most severe traffic congestion anywhere outside London. The square miles that make up Bristol's heartland have seen it all since their Saxon beginnings. Little pieces of history lurk in every corner…

THE CENTRE

The Centre (so named because it used to be the old tram centre) was once a jumble of concrete and burger bars clustered around the landmark Bristol Hippodrome. The Hippodrome was built by Oswald Stoll in 1912 and is one of the largest stages in England outside of the West End. Cary Grant worked there before he joined a travelling troupe and went to America to seek his fortune. Years ago, the Hippodrome used to have an illuminated board on the roof that displayed messages. So it was traditional to arrange for your Uncle Bill to be on the Centre while 'Happy Birthday Uncle Bill' was displayed on top of the Hippodrome. Oh, for the simple pleasures…

The Centre is now a semi-pedestrianised playground, complete with cobbles, sculptures and a collection of not-very-convincing fountains. Even the Lord Mayor described these dribbling aqueducts as being: 'Like a bunch of old men peeing.' And while we're on the subject of peeing, the notorious cab queue on St Augustine's Parade should be avoided at all costs.

Past Notes

▶ **1140** Building of St Augustine's Abbey, later to become Bristol Cathedral.

▶ **1239** River Frome diverted to increase trade at the port.

▶ **1654** Destruction of Bristol Castle by Cromwell.

▶ **1702** Queen Square built.

▶ **1831** Riots in Queen Square. Mansion House and Customs House destroyed.

■ The Bristol Hippodrome, designed by Oswald Stoll in 1912, is now the natural home for big musicals and pantomimes starring Jim Davidson.

■ John Cabot statue outside the Arnolfini. He sailed Bristol ship The Matthew to Newfoundland in 1497.

The Centre, as you see it today, is one of the most controversial developments in Bristol's recent history. Until 1892, the River Frome flowed through the Centre and into the Floating Harbour. It still does, but the Centre was built over it. The City Council decided to redevelop the Centre for the millennium and considered bold plans to re-open the Frome and ban cars. Instead, they opted to redirect traffic around the Centre, making it a car-snarled bottleneck. Several pedestrians were knocked over by cars and buses after the redevelopment because the traffic came from the opposite direction from before and it's not entirely clear where the pedestrian bit ends and the road starts. The fountains, which dribble so unconvincingly, are supposed to provide a cascade of water dancing in coloured lights. Two years after they were installed, the City Council claimed that the constructors had still not provided the software package to create this effect. The large 'ornament' in the middle is symbolic of Bristol's maritime history. Obviously.

The best thing about the Centre is the excellent Falafel King van which is parked up near the Harbourside most evenings and is a favourite snack haunt of clubbers.

> **Naked Truth**
>
> **Edmund Blanket**
> ❝The tomb of linen merchant Edmund Blanket, the 'inventor' of the blanket, who died in 1371 lays in St Stephen's Church, St Stephen's Street. The church has Merchant Venturer connections and a good cafe for rolls, soup, tea and cake.❞

> **QUICK PINT?**
> Try the **White Lion** on the Centre. Mind the steps to the toilet!

THE HARBOURSIDE

Fountains and dickheads apart, the whole Harbourside has been transformed in recent years as part of the area's massive regeneration programme. The Harbourside is certainly a whole lot better than it used to be – and you'd have a right to expect that because the 11-acre redevelopment will eventually cost more than £450 million. At-Bristol, The Aquarium and M Shed showpieces are the main attractions in the tourist brochures (see Children's Bristol). But At-Bristol wasn't an immediate financial success and had to ask the City Council for a £500,000 sub in 2003, so let's not forget about the other places that have propped up the Harbourside for so long.

Five places...

Top take-aways in BS1

❶ Lamb stew and mash from **Portuguese Taste** stall in St Nicholas Market.

❷ Curry with watercress bhaji from **Spice Up Your Life** in St Nick's Market.

❸ Falafels from **Yorm Adani's Falafel King** van on the Centre.

❹ Fish and chips from the **Rendevous** in Denmark Street.

❺ Tagine from **Al Madina** in St Nick's Market.

■ Once a working port, the Harbourside in the centre of Bristol now houses pleasure boats and bars.

There are those old favourites, the Watershed, Architecture Centre, YHA and the refurbished Arnolfini which are linked by the 'ear-trumpeted' Pero's Bridge. Designed by Irish artist, Eilis O'Connell, the bridge is named after a slave who was brought to Bristol from Nevis Island in the 17th Century. If it's heritage you're after, the ss Great Britain, The Matthew, and the £27 million M Shed (the old Industrial Museum) which opened in June 2011 will plunge you deep into the depths of Bristol's maritime past. If this doesn't satisfy your lust for the sea, try a guided tour offered by the Bristol Ferry Boat Company and Bristol Packet.

■ Pero's Bridge is named after the slave Pero who was the personal servant of John Pinney at his home in Great George Street.

BITE TO EAT?

The Watershed has an extensive menu, a well-stocked bar and it's kid friendly. It is still one of the coolest places in town.

The Harbourside is one of the best things about Bristol, not so much for the corporate regeneration, nor the profusion of theme bars and clubs, but because it's a lovely place to stroll around the water. On warm evenings, drinking outside the Arnolfini is still the venue of choice for Bristol's budding bohemians and artists.

CORN STREET

The rebirth of a city was never going to work on the strength of a few flashy multimedia projects alone. It's the sudden explosion in the centre's nightlife that has really put the spring in its heels. Now dizzy with pseudo-sophisticated style-bars, Corn Street used to be the place where most of the city's business dealings were conducted before the Corn Exchange was built. Transactions were carried out on four flat-topped bronze pillars called the nails. The bronze pillars still stand in Corn Street today and are the origin of the phrase 'to pay on the nail'. Bath, and

■ After a major refit, the Arnolfini is now up and running again. The perfect spot for some summer evening drinking by the water.

Eddie Cochran's death

☀ Eddie Cochran played his last ever show at the Bristol Hippodrome. And when the Ford Consul taxi carrying the rebel rocker slammed into a lamp post at Rowden Hill on 17 April 1960, Chippenham got its one and only rock 'n' roll story.

One of the most defiant young voices of the 1950s, Cochran was famous for anti-establishment classics such as *Summertime Blues*, *C'mon Everybody* and, most brilliantly,

the snarling proto-punk burn-up *Something Else*. He was in Bristol with Gene Vincent for a week-long rock 'n' roll extravaganza at the Bristol Hippodrome. On the last night of their residence, the two legendary greaseballs and Cochran's squeeze, Sharon Sheeley, made the fatal decision to get a cab up to Heathrow instead of taking the late train. Vincent and Sheeley survived the crash on the A4, but sadly Eddie Cochran died later in a Bath hospital. Chippenham has been etched forever on his soul.

some other towns with nails, also claim ownership of this phrase. Two of the nails on Corn Street are Elizabethan (1594). The others date from 1625 and 1631.

More recent history can be found on Broad Street, home to the Thistle Hotel which has never lived down the day in 1964 when it refused entry to The Rolling Stones because they weren't wearing jackets and ties. 'I realised the young gentleman was something of a celebrity,' said headwaiter Dick Court of Mick Jagger, 'but I would feel compelled to refuse anyone – even a king – if he did not dress correctly'. Mick and the boys probably headed off to King Street, an ancient pub-strewn badlands with many a story to tell.

Naked Truth

The Redcliffe Stocks
66 The last use of the public stocks on Redcliffe Hill was in 1826 when two men were put in the stocks for two hours for holding a drunken party in a nearby churchyard.99

■ The Edward Everard printers in Broad Street: the tiled facade was inspired by William Morris's Arts and Crafts movement.

ST NICHOLAS MARKET

QUICK PINT?
The Old Fish Market on is a Fuller's pub – quite a rarity in Bristol.

St Nick's Market dates back to 1743 and looks even older. It is divided into three parts – Exchange Hall, Glass Arcade and Covered Market. You'll find vegetables, flowers, Beast's Bristol T-shirts, Wanted Records, excellent take-away food, vintage clothes, jewellery, second-hand books, crockery, sweets, a milliner, many cafes, old prints, a computer repair unit and a resident psychic. The market is undergoing a resurgence – particularly for food. The Spice Up Your Life curry cafe in All Saints Lane is outstanding, the Moroccan Al Madinha does tasty tagines, and the selection of lamb or pork stew, chicken piri-piri and other delights served up with a helping of mashed potato at the Portuguese Taste stall is one of the best value meals in Bristol.

The market was originally built to get traders off the cluttered streets and has been added to over the years. Its last renovation in 2003 cost more than £300,000.

■ St Nicholas Market off Corn Street has stalls selling delicious Indian, Italian, Portuguese and Caribbean food.

KING STREET

King Street runs parallel to Baldwin Street, next to Queen Square. It's now Bristol's theatreland but once led down to the thriving docks at Welsh Back. The Llandoger Trow pub dates from 1664 and used to be the sort of ★ **Turn to p8**

5

A TOUR OF OLD BRISTOL

THE MEDIEVAL CITY REVEALED

1. St Nicholas Church, St Nicholas Street
Site of an odd annual ceremony in which school girls pay homage to their 17th Century male benefactor. The pupils from Red Maids School hold a service in front of an effigy of John Whitson in the church's medieval crypt. Whitson, merchant, Mayor and Member of Parliament for Bristol, died in 1629 after falling off his horse. He bequeathed cash for a hospital for '40 poor women children' to be 'apparelled in Red Cloth'.

2. Victoria Fountain, St Nicholas Street
Designed by the Coalbrookdale Iron Company of Shropshire in 1859 to commemorate Queen Victoria's 40th birthday.

3. Veiled Lady, St Nicholas Street
If you face the Elephant pub and look at the shop to the right, you'll spot a row of four figures on the wall. The second from the right appears to have no face. In fact, this is the Veiled Lady. Nobody knows who she is or what she signifies.

4. Corn Exchange and nails, Corn Street
John Woods designed the Palladian-fronted Corn Exchange in 1743, when the corn trade was at its height. The bronze pillars outside are the nails. Traders did business over the nails before the Corn Exchange was built. When the deal was done, the merchants handed over their groats and guineas and literally 'paid on the nail.'

5. Commercial Rooms, Corn St
It was in the Commercial Rooms that the merchants flexed their political muscle. In 1811, John McAdam (who invented Tarmac) became the first president of the Commercial Rooms. The three statues outside represent the City, Commerce and Navigation; the relief over the door shows Britannia with Neptune and Minerva receiving tributes.

6. Lloyds Bank, Corn Street
Opposite the Corn Exchange, the bank was built in 1857 and is based on the Library of St Mark's in Venice. It is the best example in Bristol of the Victorian High Renaissance style. Check out the frieze on the wall. It is believed that the bank was on the site of the Bush Inn as portrayed by Charles Dickens in *The Pickwick Papers*.

7. All Saints Church, Corn Street
One of three churches at the crossroads of the Medieval city. There has been a church here since 1066. The tower and cupular were built between 1712 and 1717. All Saints is now a Diocesan Education and Resource Centre and is not usually open to the public. The church houses a monument to Bristol slave trader Edward Colston, sculpted by Rysbrack, who did the William III statue in Queen Square.

8. Christ Church, Broad Street
The original Christ Church St Ewan was first mentioned in the 12th Century, but the current one was built in 1790 by William Paty. The church is best known for its clock (Henry Williams, 1883) where two quarterjacks dating from 1728 strike the bells every 15 minutes.

9. High Cross
The site of the original Medieval High Cross. A replica of the High Cross now sits in Berkeley Square, off Park Street (see History, p82).

10. Old Guildhall, Small Street
This was the site of one of Judge Jeffreys' Bloody Assizes, held after the Monmouth rebellion of 1685. Six people were hanged and Judge Jeffreys called the Bristol rebels 'mere sons of dunghills'.

11. Edward Everard Building, Broad Street
The former Edward Everard building is a burst of tiled Art Nouveau colour and oddity. The facade of Carrera marbleware was inspired by the William Morris arts and crafts revival.

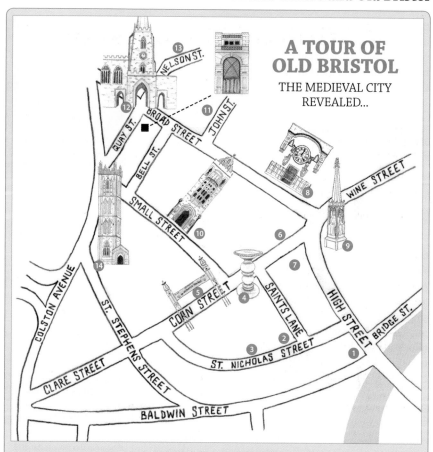

A TOUR OF OLD BRISTOL

THE MEDIEVAL CITY REVEALED...

It was built in 1900-1901 to house the works of Edward Everard. Figures on the front are of Gutenburg, who invented a printing process in the 15th Century, and Morris, who in the 19th Century helped to revive fine printing.

12. St John The Baptist, Tower Lane

The church of St John the Baptist or St John on the Wall incorporates the only surviving Medieval gateway on the city walls. The existing church dates back to the 14th Century. Inside, there's an Upper Church and a Crypt. The figures on the outside wall are Brennus and Belinus, legendary founders of Bristol. The church is no longer used for regular services and is part of the Churches Conservation Trust.

13. St John's Conduit, Nelson Street

On the other side of the gate is St John's Conduit, a 14th Century water supply which carried water from Brandon Hill to a Carmelite friary. The parishioners of St John's were allowed to use the overflow from the system. For a short time in World War Two, this was the only water supply for the city centre.

14. St Stephen's Church, St Stephen's Street

The magnificent 152-foot Gothic perpendicular tower dates back to 1470. It has been restored three times following storm damage in 1703, 1914 and 1970. Sadly the view of the tower is obscured by large, modern buildings.

Area Guide

place you went to if you were fond of wearing eye patches and carrying parrots on your shoulder. Originally, the pub occupied one of five buildings on the current site and was built on marshland that covered the area between the Centre, Welsh Back and Queen Square.

The pub's odd name comes from Captain Hawkins who retired to run it after sailing a trow – a flat-bottomed sailing barge – between South Wales and Bristol. The Llandoger part comes from Llandogo, a village on the Wye, perhaps Hawkins' home. Robert Louis Stevenson apparently used to drink there and it's also likely that Edward Teach of Redcliffe (aka Blackbeard) may have been a regular when he wasn't pirating. Certainly, Woodes Rogers, the privateer, explorer and colonial governor who lived in Queen Square, popped in for a quick grog. There was a network of tunnels leading to the waterfront that would have been used by smugglers, or by customers fleeing the press gangs. The remains of one tunnel were found but destroyed during refurbishment in 1962. Legend has it that the original pub's ceiling was painted with scantily-clad women but no evidence of this has been found.

King Street is also home to the Theatre Royal and the Bristol Old Vic. The Theatre Royal was opened on 30 May 1766 and survived plans in World War Two to turn it into a fruit warehouse. In 1946, the Old Vic Theatre Company made its home there and the entire theatre complex is now known as the Old Vic, encompassing the Theatre

BITE TO EAT?

Renato's in King Street is a legendary Italian restaurant much loved by the theatre crowd.

■ From pirates to revellers, King Street has a long history of boozing. And what a spot for it...

■ The impressive Queen Square is home to this famous statue of William III.

On the streets of Bristol...

1. Johnny Ball Lane: Not, as most people think, a misplaced homage to Zoe's dad. This dodgy looking alleyway near Christmas Steps is actually named after an 18th-Century local character of the same name.

2. Nelson Street: Found itself the subject of a campaign by *Venue* magazine who wanted it restored to its original medieval name: Gropecunt Lane.

3. Pitch and Pay Lane: Used as a line of segregation between the infected city and the countryside during the Black Plague. Villagers threw their produce over to the townsfolk who threw back their coins in payment.

4. Wade Street: Named after an extremely unpopular bloke called Nathaniel Wade who was a conspirator with the Duke of Monmouth in the rebellion of 1685.

5. There and Back Again Lane: Appropriately blunt name for the pointless little cul-de-sac opposite Pizza Express just off Park Street. Also the title of a Bristol-based Sarah Records compilation album featuring such luminaries as the Field Mice and the Sea Urchins.

Royal and the New Vic Studio. It is the oldest continuously working theatre in England and one of the first theatres to be based on a horseshoe-shaped auditorium.

King Street also has a rich musical heritage. Not only is it home to legendary jazz venue The Old Duke but the old Granary nightclub used to attract names such as Muddy Waters, Thin Lizzy and Led Zeppelin. It also had the worst toilets this side of Glastonbury – dimly lit and wet, with a door that stuck.

While King Street has hardly changed since its ooh-ar-Jim-lad days, Welsh Back now boasts a raft of new hotels, bars and restaurants.

Naked Truth

The Three Kings

❝The Chapel of the Three Kings of Cologne at the top of Christmas Steps is so called because the Three Wise Men of the Bible are said to all be buried at Cologne Cathedral in Germany.❞

Step out of the stylish Brigstow Hotel opposite the Glass Boat restaurant and stroll along the cobbles until you get to Aqua and the Spyglass barbecue and grill. Now take a right turn and walk through the restored and now traffic-free Queen Square. Check out the equestrian bronze statue by Rysbrack of William III, which dates from the 1730s.

QUICK PINT?

Mr Wolf's in St Stephens Street is a lively bar with music and noodles.

During World War Two, it was removed for safety to Badminton Park, home of the Duke of Beaufort. It was replaced in the Square after repairs in 1948. Head through the gap in the buildings and you'll come face to face with hip dockside eateries Riverstation, Severnshed and the award-winning Mud Dock Cafe or the still-floating Thekla nightclub. The Thekla has a glorious past. Ki Longfellow-Stanshall and her surrealist performer husband Viv Stanshall (of Bonzo Dog Doo Dah Band and Sir Henry Rawlinson fame) found the German-built boat in a dockyard in Sunderland.

Ki restored her and sailed her round Britain to Bristol with a rookie crew and no insurance. The Thekla (which had been renamed the Old Profanity Showboat) was opened in 1983 as a music venue. In December 1985, the couple staged the English comic opera *Stinkfoot* on board the Thekla. This truly remarkable piece of theatre was described by *Evening Post* theatre critic, the late David Harrison, as: 'a wondrous collection of bizarre characters, eccentric ideas, and at least one top ten contender among

Five places...

To go if you're loaded

① **Alfred Chillcott & Co. jewellers,** Park Street.

② **Hotel du Vin**, Lewin's Mead.

③ **Guilgert's Handmade Chocolates**, Leonard Lane.

④ **Crystal Cars** (chauffeur driven), Stillhouse Lane.

⑤ **Champagne & Cocktail Bar, Goldbrick House,** Park Street.

■ This is Brennus, allegedly the co-founder of Bristol. His brother Belinus is on the other side of the St John's Arch, the only remaining Medieval gateway to the city.

the songs'. Stanshall's daughter Sydney promoted at the Thekla into the 1990s. Viv Stanshall died in a fire at his London home in 1995 and the rest of the family now live in America. The Thekla remains a cutting-edge music venue.

ST THOMAS

BITE TO EAT?
Riverstation, Mud Dock and **Severnshed** in The Grove bring trendy dining to the dockside.

The area on the other side of Bristol Bridge from Baldwin Street has long been a barren collection of half-finished developments, corner shops, billboards and bathroom showrooms. Since the 1990s, the old dockside warehouses have been developed into (even more) posh apartments. The old Courage Brewery that looks over the Floating Harbour to Castle Park now houses 38 apartments and one- and two-bedroom flats – the 'prem lofts' would set you back about £500,000 when they went on the market in 2004, but a one-bed apartment was a mere £170,000. Local CAMRA real ale activists from the *Pints West* publication suggested the site be converted into a museum and visitor centre celebrating the tradition of beer-making in the city. The Council decided flats were a better idea.

There are several decent pubs in St Thomas. The Shakespeare (78 Victoria Street) claims to be one of the oldest (built in 1636) and The Fleece and Firkin (12 St Thomas Street) has been one of Bristol's leading live music venues since the early 1980s. The Seven Stars next door to The Fleece was the setting for a series of hearings held by anti-slaver Thomas Clarkson in 1787 that helped lead to the abolition of slavery. St Thomas is also home to the fantastic Kin Yip Hon Chinese supermarket (16a St Thomas Street) which is next door to the highly-rated Dynasty Chinese restaurant.

REDCLIFFE

Redcliffe now comprises a towerblock development, St Mary Redcliffe Church, a couple of hotels, three pubs, a school and traffic-snarled dual carriageways. The church was effectively put in the middle of a roundabout, flanked on all sides by major roads, as part of the dreadful outer circuit scheme of the early 1970s (see BS3, p36). In the Middle Ages, Redcliffe was outside the city walls and there

■ St Mary Redcliffe Church looks so good, the city planners decided to build a dual carriageway around it.

■ The famous Thekla was brought to Bristol in 1983 by Ki Longfellow-Stanshall.

was great rivalry with the port of Bristol on the opposite side of the river. The area is steeped in history but sadly, apart from the church, very little remains thanks to a combination of the Luftwaffe and the city planners. The church is still one of the finest sights in Bristol. The present building was founded in 1292 by Simon de Burton, three times Mayor of Bristol, although there was an earlier church on the site. William Canynges Senior completed the building of the church, which was then known as St Mary de Radeclive, back in the late 14th Century.

In 1446, the church was struck by lightning and badly damaged. Canynges' grandson, William, was responsible for funding much of the necessary rebuilding. His first celebration of mass at the church in 1468 is still commemorated annually. At this ceremony, called the Rush Service, the church floor is strewn with rushes and rosemary in memory of those ancient times. There is a richly-decorated Canynges tomb where his wife is buried and also a simpler one showing him in his priest's robes.

We will resist the temptation to mention the over-used quotation by Queen Elizabeth I about St Mary Redcliffe and instead mention some more recent history. During an air raid in 1941, a bomb threw a tram rail into the air and it became embedded in the churchyard turf. It remains there today, complete with a plaque.

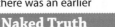

Naked Truth

The Church Cat

66Tom, the St Mary Redcliffe Church cat, who used to sit on the organist's knee while he played, was given a grand funeral in 1927. His grave is on the Bedminster side where he waited to be let in.99

QUICK PINT?

The Fleece and Firkin is the place to go to watch live music while you drink.

■ This tram rail was thrown over adjacent buildings during a WW2 air raid and remains embedded in the ground at St Mary Redcliffe.

■ The Fleece and Firkin has a long history of being one of Bristol's best music venues.

The Georgian House Museum

Seven Great George Street is unlike any of its neighbours' houses. There are no Habitat sofas, no washing machines, not even a dimmer switch. This place remains exactly as it was when it was built in 1790. And if you think this is taking retroism too far, fear not, it's a museum, not a deliberate attempt to live uncomfortably. And like its first resident, Bristol slave trader and sugar merchant John Pinney, you can call in and wander around four of the six storeys from kitchen to bedroom as if you own the place. Austerity dominates throughout but there are a few elegant pieces of furniture and some detailed plasterwork to admire, if you like that sort of thing. The Georgian House was home to Pero, a black slave Pinney brought back to Bristol from the Montravers Plantation on Nevis in the West Indies. The bridge over the Floating Harbour is named after Pero.

■ **Open all year round, Sat-Wed (closed Thurs, Fri), 10am-5pm, admission free.**

BROADMEAD

If all the new buildings around Welsh Back point to a brighter future for the Centre, the dreary 1950s-built Broadmead was an unwelcome stroll down a far less attractive past. But in 2006 work began at the bottom of the M32 on realising the planners' vision for 21st-Century shopping in Bristol. Concrete crumbled, bridges were dismantled, carpet showrooms sacrificed, all in the name of the new Broadmead (or the Merchants Quarter, as it was going to be called, until the developers eventually admitted it was a crap name and called it Cabot Circus).

BITE TO EAT?

Have a tasty, locally-sourced, organic and fairtrade snack at **The Folk House** on Park Street.

■ The statue of Charles Wesley sits in the courtyard of the Methodist New Rooms in the middle of Broadmead.

Cabot Circus opened in Autumn 2008 – just in time for the credit crunch. The £500 million makeover attracted more than 100 new shops, a state-of-the-art cinema complex, as well as student housing, bars, restaurants and thousands of parking spaces. Harvey Nicks is the flagship store which nestles under a 17-storey apartment block somewhere near where the Western Star Domino Club used to be.

The Broadmead redevelopment sparked a fierce debate that typifies criticism in some quarters that Bristol City Council has handed the city over to developers at the expense of the interests of long-standing residents. In December 2002, the City Council gave the go-ahead for the regeneration of the area promising a '24-hour living city'. The plan relied on rerouting the bottom of the M32 to allow Broadmead to expand towards St Paul's. The Council would claim that this is an example of visionary inner-city regeneration in partnership with blue-chip developers. In reality, however, it means that people who live in rented homes in St Paul's (the largest concentration of rented

John Wesley's Chapel

Built in 1739, John Wesley's Chapel is the oldest Methodist building in the world. The building is an oddity in the middle of the concrete surroundings of Broadmead – everything around it was destroyed in the Blitz – and is one of the most interesting places to visit in Bristol. Above the chapel are the rooms where Wesley and his brother Charles lived. Check out the chair carved from tree roots, the graffiti scratched into the glass panes and Wesley's private rooms. Fascinating. Admission is free.
■ The Horsefair ■ Tel: 926 4740
■ www.newroombristol.org.uk

homes in Bristol) could be kicked out to accommodate well-heeled newcomers if the area becomes prime real estate. The population of St Paul's has already seen much of its community destroyed to build the M32. Now the developers seem intent on dismantling still further a well-established community that has been responsible for fostering some of the most creative forces in Bristol.

BUS STATION

The redeveloped Bristol Bus Station was an indication of what we could anticipate from the rest of the Broadmead redevelopment – something functional and characterless where you have to pay 20p to take a leak. Admittedly, the bus station, which was completed early in 2006, now boasts some natural light and doesn't stink of piss. This is a significant improvement on the previous terminus which was built in 1958 and, it is popularly believed, wasn't properly cleaned between 1959 and 2004 when it was probably deemed cheaper to knock it down than to buy enough air fresheners to get rid of the rank urine odour.

The old bus station, y'see, was probably the most unpleasant first impression of a city anywhere in Europe. The new one is deeply uninspiring, but clean and functional. Its functionality is only marred by the fact that it doesn't have a car park. Don't expect to get a spot in the small lay-by on the side road, head to the NCP instead.

During the rebuilding of the bus station, the City Archaeological Unit uncovered part of the cloister and other original remains of the Benedictine Priory of St James. Founded in 1129 by Robert, Earl of Gloucester (the natural son of Henry I of England), the Priory is almost as old as the city itself and appears in the earliest maps of 'Brigstowe'. When St James' Priory was excavated in 1995, part of the original east end of the church was revealed along with more than 200 human remains from the adjoining burial ground. This site is now covered by an office block on Cannon Street right next to the bus station.

Naked Truth

Hole In The Wall, The Grove
❝Reputedly, the Spyglass in Treasure Island is based on this pub. It certainly has a spyglass which anxious sailors would peer through to spot approaching press gangs and hen parties.❞

QUICK PINT?

The **Mud Dock** on The Grove is a perfect spot for some water-side drinking.

■ The view across the water from the Riverstation and Severnshed makes it the perfect spot for a relaxing drink.

■ The new bus station no longer smells of wee and has numerous clocks so people know just how late the buses are running.

A CIRCUS CALLED CABOT

GIL GILLESPIE GOES DOWN THE SHOPS...

When it finally landed in the late summer of 2008, the corporate dragons in charge of unveiling Cabot Circus to a sceptical Bristol public proudly boasted that it had nearly 100,000 metres of retail space and had cost somewhere in the region of £500 million.

"Cabot Circus will provide city centre visitors with over 120 new shops... bringing the city back up the hierarchy to where it belongs," said chief ringmaster Richard Belt.

So has the region's retail mainstream been dragged kicking and screaming into a new blindingly modern and ultra European dawn? Not exactly, no. Y'see the trouble is that doing something so bold in a country that slaves under the ridiculous notion that the market is a force for progress which cannot be questioned is quite simply impossible. Cabot Circus is not about you, the citizens of this city, it is about making as much profit as possible for an increasing shrinking number of giant multi-national companies, a fact made more cruel when you consider its closeness to down-at-heel St Paul's.

The response from the ideologically narked off has been a couple of zombie marches where the visually undead stomp their way around the new cathedral in that tried and tested, but really not very insightful, eighties cinema trick of accusing consumers of being mindless. This is not a consumer issue, it is a government one, the zombies really are wailing in the wrong direction with this decidedly sixth form kind of protest.

But they are right about one thing: Bristol doesn't need any more versions of shops we have already got. You may already be familiar with one or two of the retail outlets available under the glass ceiling of downtown BS1. There's French Connection, H&M, Topshop, Oasis, Burton, Wallis, Orange, PC World, the Disney Store and a whole load of other well-lit joints that you will have wandered into before. What essentially we have is a sharper and more polished update on The Mall at Cribbs Causeway, which was itself built as a replacement for the dowdy, hot

dog munching concrete no space that is Broadmead.

And on your first visit, there is no denying its hyper-modernity, at least for the first ten minutes. If you go by car you will enter the place via the sleek white and neon curves of the car park and ascend into the heavens like a toy car climbing a helter skelter. You then follow one of the many yellow pedestrian pathways all the way to the twisted glass bridge which hovers over the grumbling stop-start traffic on Bond Street. Then, finally, you arrive on the third tier of the mighty monolith, just outside the House of Fraser. But as you walk around the circular path that takes you to the elevators and the escalators, you suddenly have the distinct sensation of being not a million miles away from what you imagine Taunton town centre must be like. It's all a bit grey concrete and steel really, there's even copious amounts of that most undesirable of architectural materials, Asda-style red brick. And although its shape and flow give the place elegance and the meandering glass roof means it is almost entirely light and airy, it's bloody freezing in the middle of winter.

However, the strangest and most over-powering thing about visiting Cabot Circus for the first time is just how unsettling it is to be in a oddly unfamiliar environment in an area that you used to know so well. You are suddenly as unsettled as a tourist, you don't know north from south and have no idea where the rest of Bristol city centre is, if it is there at all. Even the shoppers seem different, as if they have been dropped into the place from Regent Street in London. Where are the divs in trackies? Where are the screaming Hengrove mothers and their dangerous under-five crews? Where are the drunks, the crustys and the manic street preachers? Honestly, it is an unnerving and upsetting experience and you probably left in a bit of a huff. No? Just me then.

After the initial shock of the new, however, Cabot Circus can be a pleasurable all-shopping, all-eating, all-drinking, all-going-to-

the-cinema kind of experience. It feels more real, less plastic, than The Mall and especially in summer has a relaxed and comforting air about it. And if you are the sort of person who gets turned on by shelling out £295 for a very unspectacular Moschino T-shirt or still think it is fashionable to walk around with Bench written across your chest, then it could be the place for you.

In the early evening in the summer, by the way, when the late shoppers are still buzzing around and the aromas are exploding from the bars and restaurants, Cabot Circus starts to feel more than a little cosmopolitan, like you could be in Barcelona or Nice or Milan, or somewhere where tacky booze-belching stag and hen do's don't exist. It doesn't last long, though, because the shops shut at 8pm and the place goes back to being a bit of a deserted wasteland again.

5 BEST SHOPS IN CABOT CIRCUS

1. H&M, Brigstowe Street
It's the IKEA of high street fashion. Four floors of hip, heavily-rotated clothing for boys, girls and kids. Beware of taste horrors such as the lime green Bruce Forsythe shorts.

2. American Apparel, Concorde St
Walking into one of this ethically-leaning company's' stores is a bit like being battered around the head with a luminous kaleidoscope. This is basic cotton clothing gone freakin' Day-Glo.

3. Urban Outfitters, Concorde St
Okay, so it's not half as interesting as it promised to be but at least they have the guts to celebrate a less travelled lifestyle, until it comes to the embarrassingly crude novelty items at least.

4. Schuh, Concorde Street
An excellent range of the slightly more original end of the trainers market, as well as quirky woman's designers like Irregular Choice, Rocket Dog and Iron Fist. Crap men's shoes, though.

5. Hotel Chocolat, George White St
We are not talking Curly Wurly's here. This UK-based company scour the European peninsula to find the finest cocoa-based sweet stuff on the planet and bring it to us.

• Cabot Circus quickly acquired the nickname Carboot Circus which is not just a simple play on words but a historical reference to the bizarre car boot sale that used to be held on the indoor slopes of the multi-storey car park that used to welcome visitors entering Bristol from the M32.

COLLEGE GREEN

College Green at the bottom of Park Street is where the skateboarders congregate after tearing down the hill. It's also a pleasant spot to enjoy a lunchtime sandwich. It's dominated by the Cathedral, Central Library and the Council House ('Counts Louse' in Bristolese) which was commissioned in 1935 when the local authority outgrew its Corn Street base but, because of the war, was not finished until 1956. Check out Brunel House behind the Council House. Originally called the Royal Western Hotel, it was constructed by Brunel as a hotel for passengers disembarking from the Great Western Railway to stay overnight before boarding the ss Great Britain to sail to America. A proposed station near the Cathedral was never built and the hotel eventually became council offices.

> **BITE TO EAT?**
>
> **Byzantium** in Portwall Lane is a stylish Middle Eastern eaterie with belly dancers, DJs and a 2am licence.

■ The Ostrich has more picnic tables than you've ever seen, and it's right on the water too.

There has been a religious building on the site of the Cathedral for more than 1,000 years. The history of the existing cathedral dates back to 1140 when wealthy merchant Robert Fitzhardinge invited monks to set up residence in what was then known as St Augustine's Abbey. Since then, the history of the Cathedral has been one of gradual religious and aesthetic progression. The Cathedral itself was established in 1542 and finished by architect George Edmund Street in 1868.

Just along from the Cathedral sits the Central Library,

■ College Green is home to the Cathedral, as well as Bristol's skateboarders and students.

Wills Memorial Building

☀ If you've never set foot inside the skyscraper-high building at the top of Park Street, you really should take a detour next time you're walking by. Push open the huge double doors and you will be greeted by a sight so opulent it would make a peacock blush. There are two sweeping stone staircases which drop elegantly from the cavernous ceiling, while the grandest wooden entrance hall you've ever seen stretches out beneath. You don't get this sort of learning environment at Soundwell Tech.

Cigarette tycoon Henry Overton Wills put up £100,000 for the building in 1908 and over the years the Wills family donated the equivalent of £100m to the University. The Wills Memorial Building was opened by King George V and Queen Mary in 1925. The final cost was £501,566 19s 10d. At 215 feet tall, it is twice the height of the Cabot Tower.

The Wills tower, designed by George Herbert Oatley, is constructed from Bath and Clipsham stone. It has been called the last great Gothic building to be constructed in England. The bell inside the tower is called Great George and strikes every hour. It weighs over ten tons and is the fourth largest bell in Britain. The tower, which is covered in grotesque carved heads, was constructed to amplify the sound of the bell striking.

one of the greatest public buildings in the country. The first recorded public library in Bristol was founded in 1613 when a merchant called Robert Redwood gave his home in King Street to the city for conversion into a library. In 1740, a new Library was built on the same site and, in 1906, the Central Library was moved to its current site next to the Cathedral. There is a room at the library called the Bristol Room which is a copy of the old King Street library. It is not open to the public, but you can request a visit.

The library was designed in 1902 by Charles Holden, who later gained fame as the architect of many London Underground stations. The library was funded by a bequest of £50,000 from Vincent Stuckey Lean. Although its influences are Medieval/Tudor, this stunning building is regarded as an example of the early modern movement. The three large windows at the front hold sculptures by Charles Pibworth and depict Chaucer with the Canterbury Pilgrims, The Venerable Bede with Literary Saints and King Alfred.

Inside, the theme is more classical and the most immediately striking feature is the grand staircase which is made of white Sicilian marble from Carrara. The staircase sweeps you up to the reference library, one of the must-visit places in the city. The tunnel-vaulted skylight ceiling filters through a mellow light onto the original teak, leather-topped reading desks and white pillars. The room's design was inspired by the high chambers of the bath buildings of imperial Rome and its most spectacular features are the two great oriel windows at either end of the north wall, ornamented with heraldic panels commemorating figures from Bristol's past.

College Green is also home to the Lord Mayor's Chapel, an ancient house of worship, formally known as St Mark's Church and originally as the Chapel of the Hospital of the Gaunts. It was founded in 1220 by Maurice and Henry de Gaunt, grandsons of Robert Fitzhardinge who, in 1140, built the Abbey of the Black Canons of St Augustine, where

Naked Truth

The Louisiana Tunnel

❝There are many ancient tunnels underneath Bristol. One from the Louisiana pub in Wapping Road (the old Sheriff House), is said to have led to the old city jail opposite and was used by the hangman to avoid angry crowds.❞

QUICK PINT?

Why not combine pool and beer in the **Elbow Room** on Park Street?

Five things...

To keep an eye out for on Park Street

1 Random skateboard freaks bombing down the hill at speeds of 50mph.

2 Westworld staff doing their best to appear cool and detached at all times. You work in a shop, for Christ sakes!

3 Saturday parking opportunities.

4 Brilliant albums at amazingly low prices in Rise on The Triangle. '1970s Venezuelan Jazz-Funk Odyssey Volume 3 for £5? Got to get it! Bill Nelson Sings the Commodores for only £3? Silly not to!'.

5 Making sure you don't walk into one of those Christian bookshops by mistake.

the Cathedral now stands. The tower was a later addition in 1487. The building was originally built as a hospital. The nephew of the de Gaunts, Robert de Gournay, also had a hand in its endowment. Visitors should look out for the grotesque carvings that decorate the exterior of the tower and nave.

PARK STREET

It may have lost some of its appeal since the compact formula multinational convenience stores decided to move in, but Park Street is still one of the most elegant places to shop in the land – and one of the steepest. Standing at the top, looking down, you can't help but be impressed. We might take these things for granted, but this is one of the reasons so many visitors fall in love with Bristol. To the right, as you descend Park Street, is Brandon Hill and on top of that is Cabot Tower. It's hard to believe it now, but both have had their moments of controversy. A century ago, the breathtakingly landscaped hill was criticised by a local councillor as being 'a resort of lazy, idle, loafing persons' while the 105-foot tall monument to the explorer was described as 'a complete waste of money'. With this in mind, every visitor should climb up the spiral staircase and take a look at the most spectacular view Bristol has to offer. (Do not attempt this on very windy days or when drunk.) As inspiring as this sounds, however, it's not the reason the crowds flock to Park Street every Saturday. Unlike the Mall and Broadmead, many of the shops here are still independent and variety is still an option. DNA, The Boot Room, Uncle Sam's, the 50:50 skate shop, Weapon of Choice gallery, BS8, Love From Random and Bristol Guild all operate, to varying degrees, outside

■ The Red Lodge (box below) was built in 1590 and is home to The Bristol Savages.

■ Park Street has got to be one of the steepest shopping streets in the country.

The Red Lodge

☀ If you thought the Georgian House was ancient, you won't believe the state of this place. Built in 1590, this Elizabethan home was originally a Tudor lodge and home to a number of families over the years. Fortunately, the last people to live here seem to have gone in a hurry and left their furniture exactly as it was. As you tiptoe around, you half expect them to come bursting through the door at any minute demanding to know what you are doing in their house. A paternalistic group of artists, musicians and writers called The Bristol Savages (formed in 1894) hold their club nights in the gardens of the Red Lodge in a building called The Wigwam.
■ Park Row ■ Tel: 921 1360

the mainstream. In under half an hour, you could sign up for a water divining talk at the Folk House, buy an 'Enjoy Milk' baby top at Khoi, replace your cutlery at Bristol Guild and invest in a pair of dainty embroidered girlie shoes from The Boot Room. It's also worth mentioning that a more leftfield shopping experience can be unearthed on Park Row. To go from the glassy-eyed optimism of the Crystal Shop at the top of Lodge Street to the full metal hardware of Militaria on Lower Park Row takes only a handful of paces but is one hell of a cultural leap. (See Shopping Listings).

Naked Truth

Quakers Friars
66The city registry at Quakers Friars, Broadmead, is on the site of a Quaker meeting house that was built in 1667 on land that was the garden of the old Dominican Friary. Hence the name.99

If you take another small detour off Park Street onto Great George Street, you will find the popular venue of St George's (see Nights Out Listings).

QUICK PINT?

The Bunch of Grapes in Denmark Street is a long-time fave!

CHRISTMAS STEPS

There is a plaque at the top of Christmas Steps that reads 'This streete was steppered done in 1669' but anyone using it back in those days took their life in their hands. Old public records tell of a dangerously steep and muddy path that sent pedestrians hurtling down towards the Centre at breakneck speeds.

And if the conditions underfoot didn't get you, the dagger-wielding muggers would. It used to be known as Knifesmith Street, though this was because the city's knife makers worked here. It was also referred to as Cutellare (cutlery) Street in records dating back to 1389, but by the end of the 16th Century, it had become Christmas Street and Christmas Steps when the steps were built in 1669. Condemned prisoners were dragged up the 49 steps from Bristol gaol to be hanged on St Michael's Hill.

Christmas Steps is home to the mighty Bristol Cider Shop and at the top on Colston Street, there's a thriving community of independent shops. Booty has is great for second-hand books and records, locally produced cards and, er, hats. Bloom & Kurll is a lovely second-hand bookshop and you can get a haircut in Mack Daddy's before buying a bike at the Bristol Bicycle Workshop.

Five ancient...
City centre alehouses

❶ **The Hatchet**
Frogmore Street, 1606.

❷ **Ye Shakespeare**
Victoria Street, 1636.

❸ **Llandoger Trow**
King Street, 1664.

❹ **Kings Head**
Victoria Street, 1660.

❺ **Naval Volunteer**
King Street, 1673.

■ **Christmas Steps was the final walk for prisoners from Bristol gaol before they were taken to St Michael's Hill to be hanged or burned.**

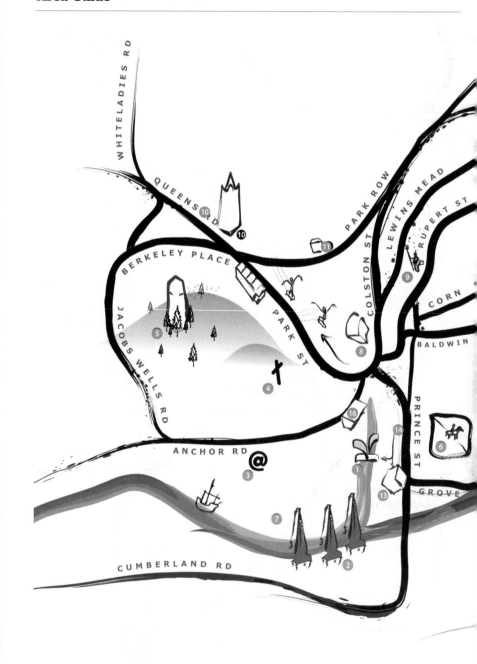

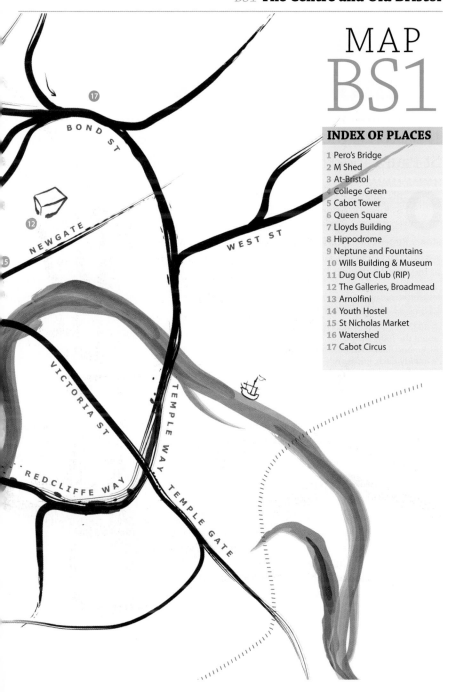

MAP
BS1

INDEX OF PLACES

1 Pero's Bridge
2 M Shed
3 At-Bristol
4 College Green
5 Cabot Tower
6 Queen Square
7 Lloyds Building
8 Hippodrome
9 Neptune and Fountains
10 Wills Building & Museum
11 Dug Out Club (RIP)
12 The Galleries, Broadmead
13 Arnolfini
14 Youth Hostel
15 St Nicholas Market
16 Watershed
17 Cabot Circus

BS2 **Montpelier to Temple Meads**

. . . .

If Easton is the new Montpelier, where does that leave
St Paul's and The People's Republic of Stokes Croft?

. . . .

O nly an estate agent would describe Montpelier
as Bristol's Notting Hill but this is where the city's
leafier crowd hang out. Don't be fooled by the five-
storey Regency terraced houses, Montpelier is full of what
we used to call Jitters. Linking this counter-culture enclave
to the world outside is Picton Street.

■ 'The people down on Picton
Street already are superstar,'
sang local boy Patrick Duff on the
Strangelove track Superstar.

Past Notes

▶ **1873 Residents complain
about the filthy state of
Richmond Road.** One talks of
'a muddy ditch, impassable
for pedestrians.'

▶ **1874 The Cheltenham
Road Viaduct, better known
as The Arches, is built.**

▶ **1882 The Montpelier
Hotel begins its 100 year
lifespan.**

▶ **1993 Dozens of 'Picton
Street Against The War'
posters fail to prevent the
invasion of Iraq.**

MONTPELIER

It's fitting that Montpelier's
main artery is a Georgian
raggle-taggle, car-unfriendly
lane where it's easier to buy
a 'Say No To Esso' T-shirt
than a top-up card for your
mobile phone. The following
organisations are, or have
been, located in Picton Street:
the British Association of Fair
Trade Shops, Eco-Logic Books,
Worldly Goods, Bristol Friends
of the Earth, Community

■ Bell's Diner is hidden away on
the end of York Road. It's well
worth searching it out.

Recycling Network and Apple Day Resources, a pressure
group that champions the rights of apples and orchards.
Luckily, there are a few wonderful places to eat and drink
too: Bell's Diner (1-3 York Road) is one of Bristol's most
inspirational restaurants, the One Stop Thali Cafe (12 York
Road) is renowned for its veggie Indian street food, Mela
(19 York Road) is an excellent Indian take-away, Licata (36
Picton Street) is an authentic Sicilian deli, Herbert's Bakery
(Wellington Avenue) is one of Bristol's finest bread-makers,
Radford Mill Farm Shop (41 Picton Street) is a top organic
and community wholefood shop while the Wai Yee Hong

Supermarket (4 Station Road) is a warehouse full of unusual delights from the Far East.

If you want a drink stop, why not savour the friendly local atmosphere of the Star and Garter or The Beaufort. For a livelier time, then head up the unassuming Richmond Road until you come to the legendary Cadbury House.

Until 2003, when the New Prince of Wales on Gloucester Road took the honours, *Venue* magazine readers voted the Cadbury House the best pub in Bristol for something like the previous ten years running. And it's easy to see why. It's one of just a handful of unique local landmarks that give underground Bristol its identity. You won't find anywhere like it in any other city.

Naked Truth

E W Godwin

❝The derelict buiding taken over by street artists next to Cafe Kino is the old Perry's Carriage Works. It is one of the finest examples of the work of Victorian architectural genius Edward William Godwin.❞

QUICK PINT?

The Bell in Jamaica Street is a Butcome pub with DJs most nights.

STOKES CROFT

The long, skinny stretch of tarmac that runs from City Road down to The Bearpit might have the highest percentage of drink-related broken limb hobblers in the city but this hasn't prevented Stokes Croft from significantly re-inventing itself.

When Chris Chalkley and a group of like-minded adventurers set up The People's Republic of Stokes Croft, they could hardly have realised the local, national and international impact that PRSC would have. Yet Stokes Croft has retained its character typified by Rita's still essential late-nite take-away, the Blue Mountain club and the universally-loved Pieminister. Crusts, it seems, have replaced crusties.

At least anyone fortunate, or gullible, enough to buy into the leisure lifestyle development at the bottom of Stokes Croft has something to do other than staring out of the window watching drunks drifting around The Bearpit.

PRSC, based in the Jamaica Street gallery with a shop next door, started the ball rolling by inviting artists to create visual art for the streets. The visual impact of this was massive, effectively turning the whole area into an outside gallery. There's now a buzzing, alternative art and cafe culture in Stokes Croft giving the area a modern

Four old...
Places in Stokes Croft

1 **Lifestyle Foodstore:** High-price, no-nonsense convenience store.

2 **Citi Centa Sauna:** Does anyone actually ever go in?

3 **Discount Heating Supplies:** Hardcore grates and radiators. Not for shoplifters.

4 **Fred Baker Cycles:** They have sold bikes since 1935!

■ **You can't miss Herbert's Bakery, – if you don't spot the graffiti the size of a house, just follow your nose.**

THE BATTLE AGAINST TESCO

WHEN STOKES CROFT RIOTED IN 2011 IT CAME AS NO SURPRISE THAT TESCOS GOT TRASHED

The battle against the siting of a Tesco's Metro store in Stokes Croft was long and acrimonious and culminated in a riot on the evening of Thursday April 21st, 2011. For those who had followed the No Tesco campaign closely, the trashing of Tesco's was entirely predictable. For more than a year 24-hour security guards had sat behind razor wire on the flat roof of the Tesco store to protect the site from protesters and squatters.

It was terrible PR for the supermarket giant who seemed completely unaware that its brand contradicts everything that is good about Stokes Croft – independence, support for local businesses and a readiness to wave two fingers at any form of authority should it dare to cross Turbo Island. The opposition to Tesco in Stokes Croft is overwhelming.

For over a year the majority of the local community worked hard to peacefully campaign to stop Tesco from opening – 2,500 people sent postcards to the Bristol City Council objecting to Tesco, thousands more signed petitions and 96 per cent of 700 people surveyed said they don't want a Tesco in Stokes Croft – technically the store (on the old Jesters' Club site) is just outside Stokes Croft, but because this is an argument used against the No Tesco Campaign by the very small number of people who support the store, we'll ignore it.

Throughout the campaign against Tesco, some of the organisers felt they were given assurances by councillors that the planning application would be refused. On planning grounds alone, the No Campaigners had a strong case. The Tesco store would require at least 42 lorry deliveries a week and the only place a lorry can park is across a cycle lane and a bus lane close to a busy junction on one of the main routes into the city. Of course, with 96 per cent of local people objecting to the Tesco application, those little things called Democracy and Accountability might also have had a role to play. But this is Bristol City Council. Many campaigners felt cheated by two-faced councillors and disenfranchised by the democratic process when the City Council planning committee voted 4-3 in favour of the wealthy and influential retail giant that spends millions on advertising in the local and national press and which has oodles of money to spend on planning appeals. And then came the riot.

As with the St Paul's riots 30 years earlier, cack-handed policing was the immediate cause of the unrest. Although there has yet to be issued a definitive account of exactly what happened in the hours before the first bricks were thrown, the word on the street its that it all went something like this.

At some point in the day, a squatter in Telepathic Heights directly opposite Tesco let it be known to staff at Tescos that he had made petrol bombs and they had Tesco's name on them. At the time of writing there is no evidence that any petrol bombs actually existed. It has been suggested that the squatter was a person with some form of learning difficulty. Whatever, concerned Tesco staff understandably called the Old Bill.

This is where the police had to make a decision. The information in front of them is that a person living in a squat opposite Tesco has petrol bombs and has threatened tio chuck them at Tesco. Given the strong tension in Stokes Croft and the feeling that the democratic process had betrayed the local community do you…

a) Send in plain clothes officers in ummarked cars, snatch the person in question grab the alleged petrol bombs and get the hell out of Stokes Croft.

b) Send in 16 riot vans packed with coppers from South Wales and Wiltshire who don't know the area and storm Telepathic Heights? Oh and let's stick a helicopter directly above Tesco, just in case people on the other side of town don't know what's going on.

Picture: Alex Cater

So the riot vans packed with coppers from outside Bristol cut through the early evening crowds of people gathering in Stokes Croft for an evening out before the Easter weekend. Other people were still returning from work. Stokes Croft was busy. Naturally, the 16 riot vans and helicopter attracted a crowd, the police started hitting people and the crowd fought back on a battleground that the police had decided should be directly outside Tesco.

At some point the police thought it would be a good idea to send in horses and to charge the crowd. Again it's a question of choices.

a) Do you charge the crowd into St Paul's which has a history or rioting and into Montpelier, home of many of the people most narked off with the whole Tesco thing.

Or

b) Try to disperse the crowd into the leafy residential areas of Redland and Cotham.

So then it kicks off in St Paul's and in Picton Street in Montpelier. It seems that one of the main issues once the police had decided on option b) above, was that people coming out of their homes in St Paul's and Montpelier to see what all the fuss was about

quickly found themselves on the wrong side of police lines and unable to return home. Requests to be allowed home were allegedly met with violence as the police successfully opened a second front of unrest.

There have been many complaints made against the police and one friend of the Naked Guides who was trying to negotiate with officers to allow people home was among a group near Picton Street who were charged by police horses without warning. He was then brought down by two police Alsatians and a dog handler also unleashed a Rottweiler on him. Unlike the Alsatians, the Rottweiller went bonkers and tore a chunk of flesh from under his arm.

Having by now seriously pissed off large parts of the community in Stokes Croft, St Paul's and Montpelier, the police eventually made the right decision and retreated leaving 'our popular local store' to quote a Tesco spokesperson, to be trashed.

At the time of writing the No Tesco campaign has been granted a judicial review into the process that led to Bristol City Council granting planning permission for the Tesco Metro store.

bohemian European feel in the evenings when politicos, artists, poets and passers-bye spill out onto the streets from the bars and cafes no doubt plotting revolution and burning their Tesco Club Cards, no matter what the consequences for their points tally. People's perceptions of this long-neglected part of town have changed, and it is now an example to radical communities around the world of how local people can take control of their own futures. Like so many of the best things in Bristol, Stokes Croft has thrived because creative, free thinkers have stepped into the vacuum left by years of civic apathy and neglect.

■ The People's Republic of Stokes Croft HQ next to the Jamaica Street studios.

BITE TO EAT?

Take 5 Cafe on Stokes Croft does curries and weekend breakfasts for a fiver. All prepared by Cosmic Jake.

Nowadays pop-up art galleries abound in Stokes Croft, PRSC produce Stokes Croft china (which is excellent) and restore furniture found in skips or abandoned in the streets. The Museum of Stokes Croft (opposite Canteen) should be on all visitors' must-see list of things to do in Bristol.

Developers and franchise stores are desperate to get a piece of the action in the hippest and fastest changing part

St Paul's Riots, 2 April 1980

The riots that broke out on Grosvenor Road 'Front Line' in 1980 were the most serious in modern British history and the precursors of the summer riots that swept through Britain's inner cities in 1981. A lot has been written about the social causes for the disturbances and certainly the riots had a lot to do with the black and the white community of St Paul's expressing its anger at heavy-handed policing, unemployment and poor housing. And yet the immediate cause of the riots, according to Bristol urban legend, was all to do with a ripped pair of trousers.

The riots started at the Black and White Cafe in Grosvenor Road. The Black and White was run by Stephen Wilks and his partner Shirley Andow. Wilks was a Jamaican national who came to Britain in the early 1960s, settled in Oxford and then moved to Bristol where he took over the Black and White in 1971. The cafe was well known as a haven for drug dealers. Some would say that it was fairly harmless – a few people indulging in small-time marijuana dealing. But others claimed it was actually the base for one of Britain's most serious drug operations.

What is beyond doubt is that the Black and White was a significant centre for a section of the black community. Detectives raided it on 2 April 1980, but had failed to warn either local uniform police or community leaders. Police met such violent resistance that they were forced to withdraw entirely for several hours and 19 officers were wounded. However, according to the rumours in the following weeks, in the process of searching for drugs, police ripped one of the customer's trousers. He demanded immediate compensation, the police refused, a scuffle followed that spilled out onto Grosvenor Road and… Bingo! Within hours, several thousand people were fighting a pitch battle with police. There were further riots in St Paul's in January 1982.

The Black and White Cafe was closed in 2003 and replaced with housing.

of Bristol, but fail to realise that if they move in they will destroy the very thing that makes Stokes Croft special.

But Stokes Croft isn't all about these bold nouveau enterprises, y'know. Some things have been around since the first alarm clock went off on the morning of the dawn of time. Take the heroically-named Everest Secretarial Services, for example. If you need a dissertation, CV, business proposal, manuscript or shopping list typed then look no further. Founded by Mrs Everest, yes really, it is a beacon of traditionalism where typists sit in a pool and quite possibly still buy their nylons off the black market. And their shoes in KBK.

Naked Truth
Faggot anyone?
66 St Paul's was the centre of Bristol's faggot industry. The company that became Brains, formed by A Smith in 1906, had a factory and shop in Upper York Street. Herbert Hill Brain took over in 1927. 99

QUICK PINT?
Canteen on Stokes Croft is the place to go to establish your boho credentials.

One site of historical importance is the building opposite the Here shop at the top of Picton Street. In the early 1980s, this was the legendary Demolition Diner, an anarcho-punk, peace-crazies squat and a centre for unruly music and even unrulier politics. The night when it was first squatted, police took dogs onto the roof to try and oust the new residents by entering via a skylight. But the dogs got scared and couldn't get down. After some hard bargaining, the police and their dogs were escorted through the skylight and allowed to leave via the front door.

ST PAUL'S

In the 1980s something remarkable happened in St Paul's, the consequences of which we are still experiencing today in the continued success of Massive Attack, Banksy, Tricky, Portishead and the hugely successful New Circus movement of which Bristol could lay a justifiable claim to being the international capital. Until recently, whatever cultural collision took place in St Paul's after the cold punches of Thatcherism resulted in the riots was almost entirely unrecorded. There wasn't a plan and there were no leaders. Its only real voice were the long-gone pirate radio stations such as FTP, Emergency Radio and others.

In their book *Art & Sound of the Bristol Underground*

Five places...
To visit in Stokes Croft

❶ **Pieminister:** Delicious pies from this local success story.

❷ **People's Republic of Stokes Croft:** Shop and gallery next to the Jamaica Street studios. The Museum of Stokes Croft opposite Canteen is an essential desination.

❸ **Canteen:** Thriving boho bar with good value-for-money food.

❹ **Here:** A little shop with some very big ideas.

❺ **Niche Frames:** Blimey, they take framing very seriously in here.

■ **Tesco provided a focal point for community protest in Stokes Croft when they opened a store on Cheltenham Road.**

(Tangent Books) Chris Burton and Gary Thompson pinpoint the birth of the movement in the free party scene driven by the arrival of hip-hop from New York. Punk and reggae had become mainstream. Black and white kids across town wanted a new beat for the sub-culture and it came in the form of hip-hop which Bristol embraced like no other UK city. To be a viable hip-hop crew you needed the four disciplines of a DJ, MC, break-dancers and a graffiti writer. Enter The Wild Bunch, a loose collective of young men that included DJ Milo (Miles Johnson), DJ Nellee (Nellee Hooper), graffiti artist and MC 3D (Robert Del Naja), MC Daddy Gee (Grant Marshall) and an associated crew of breakdancers. The Wild Bunch weren't the only exponents, FBI, UD4, City Rockas and others were just as popular, but it was Wild Bunch who formed the basis of Massive Attack with the arrival of Mushroom and the departure of Milo and Nellee.

> **BITE TO EAT?**
>
> **Cafe Kino** on Stokes Croft is a vegan gaff with a load of cosy extra seating downstairs.

■ The Black and White cafe in Grosvenor Road was closed down early in 2003 and demolished.

The young crews typically played house parties, often

St Paul's Carnival

Bristol's biggest street party is usually held on the first Saturday in July. It aims to promote and celebrate the culture and community of St Paul's – home to much of the city's African-Caribbean population.

The Carnival started in 1968 and has been held every year since, apart from 2002 and 2006. In 2002, it was cancelled following pressure from the police who were concerned about crack gangs looking for revenge for some non-fatal shootings after the 2001 event. There were certainly problems after the 2001 event, but in many quarters it was considered a disgrace that one of Bristol's longest-established, most vibrant and creative community-based cultural events was banned at the height of Bristol's bid to become European City of Culture in 2008. In 2006, it took a year off to undergo a major revamp.

St Paul's Carnival attracts thousands of people to Grosvenor Road and the surrounding streets. Everybody in Bristol who likes partying turns up and increasingly those from much further afield make the trip.

During the day Red Stripe, jerk chicken, fried fish and goat curry abound; after dark the music party moves up a few notches. Cultural events throughout June lead up to the Saturday event at which you'll find costume processions by local schools, community groups and anyone else with access to a float, as well as DJs, sound systems and bands, all blasting out reggae, hip-hop and dub.

For kids, there are two parks (St Agnes and St Paul's Adventure Playground) where they can see puppet shows, do face painting, listen to story-telling, join in drumming workshops and jump up and down on bouncy castles. Carnival has changed very little over the years. It's got bigger, but essentially the form on Carnival day remains the same: watch the procession, eat, drink, listen to music and walk up and down Grosvenor Road until it's time to go home.

St Paul's Carnival is one massive party for all ages and consequently gets very busy, so not one for claustrophobics.

■ **St Paul's Carnival runs from 1pm to 2am and is usually held on the first Saturday in July. Tel: 944 4176**

breaking into derelict buildings or being invited into squats, sometimes hooking up power from neighbouring buildings and hiring PAs from the reggae sound systems.

The parties were publicised by flyers in the New York tradition, designed by young wannabe artists such as 3D, Inkie, Nick Walker FLX, Chaos and others. The link from Banksy to 3D is well established and recorded in Felix (FLX) Braun's book *Children of the Can* and in *Banksy's Bristol* by Steve Wright (both Tangent Books).

New Circus entered the mix when travellers tired of battling the police in the countryside (most notably in The Battle of The Beanfield) and retreated into the inner city where they quickly became part of free party scene.

■ The bust commemorating playwright Alfred Fagon off Grosvenor Road, St Paul's.

> ### Naked Truth
>
> **The Gin Palace**
>
> ❝The Palace Hotel (Gin Palace) in Old Market was built as a plush hotel in the 1860s by speculators. They were convinced Bristol's main railway station would be built in Old Market, not Temple Meads.❞

QUICK PINT?

Join Dutty Ken at **The Star and Garter** in Brook Road for a late night drink.

Although it was based in St Paul's the scene attracted like-minded kids from across Bristol including Fresh 4 from Knowle West and Krissy Kriss and his comrades from Southmead.

For an area that has given Bristol more than any other in terms of music and character, St Paul's doesn't seem to get a lot in return. The Western Star Domino Club? Closed. Ajax Blues Bar? Shut down. And what happened to the club nights at the Malcolm X Centre? Early in 2004, the community was attempting to make the Black and White cafe the centre of a regeneration programme. Steve Wilks, owner of the Black and White, told a public inquiry that closing the cafe wouldn't solve the St Paul's drug problems. Wilks, 34, whose father opened the Black and White in 1971 said: 'We want the cafe to stay. We want it to be part of the rejuvenation programme for St Paul's'. However, the cafe was closed and has now been demolished and replaced with low-cost homes.

In the early 1990s, St Paul's was beginning to buzz again. Anyone looking for after-hours activity of the alcoholic kind would head down to the Jamaican Good Food after midnight and choose from the vast array of Red Stripe on offer. Or you could get a late one in the Criterion

■ A mural on the wall of Tony's Caribbean Foods on Grosvenor Road, St Paul's.

on Badminton Road. And just around the corner from there is the defiantly original Star and Garter, still shaking its floorboards after all these years.

The underground sub-culture that St Paul's nurtured has now moved a few hundred yards to Stokes Croft where it has a far more visible presence. Although St Paul's now lacks some of the energy of the 1980s it remains the area that shaped much of Bristol's contemporary culture.

ST WERBURGH'S

Narroways Hill, the area of steep wasteland that separates St Werburgh's from Ashley Hill, has a history that far exceeds its humble appearance. In the early part of the last century, for example, it was the scene of a terrible murder of a woman called Ada James by her boyfriend Ted Palmer. Once carved into pieces by railway tracks, its junction was a target for Nazi bombs during the war. More recently, British Rail put the land up for sale and local residents decided to raise the money to buy it. Finally, Avon Wildlife Trust registered the land as a nature conservation site. This is in keeping with the character of the people of St Werburgh's; why else would the suburb have been chosen as the site for the St Werburgh's City Farm? The Farm pub is a welcoming place with good food and hip-hop and beats DJs on Friday and Saturday nights and occasional sets from the legendary ska spinner DJ Derek. The Miners' Arms in Mina Road is the favoured watering hole of middle-aged musos and the Duke of York (Jubilee Road) is difficult to find but worth the effort for its homely atmosphere and excellent selection of real ales and ciders.

The other St Werburgh's pubs resemble hostels for mostly drunk but mostly amiable old fellas. St Werburgh's has a strong sense of community and the arrival of the uber-organic Better Food Company at the bottom of Ashley Down Road coupled with a retail revamp on Mina Road have added interest to the area. That said, there isn't all that much to get excited about. St Werburgh's is Montpelier with a motorway running past it really.

■ You can't miss the Duke of York in St Werburgh's – it is covered with graffiti on all sides.

SMITH & MIGHTY

THE STORY BEHIND BRISTOL'S MOST INFLUENTIAL AND RESPECTED DANCE DUO FROM ST PAUL'S

■ Rob Smith and Ray Mighty in Bristol in 1988, the year their label Three Stripe Records was born.

Rob Smith and Ray Mighty are the masters of the Bristol Beat, the street sound of St Paul's. They've also been hailed as the originators of drum 'n' bass. Rob and Ray are from radical funk and roots reggae backgrounds; they became Smith & Mighty after meeting up in a funk outfit called Sweat in 1986. They built a studio above a Blues Club just off Ashley Road and, by 1988 (when the picture above was taken), Three Stripe Records had been born.

After a brief collaboration with Mark Stewart from The Pop Group, Smith & Mighty released their sublime broken beats version of Burt Bacharach and Hal David's Dionne Warwick classic *Anyone Who Had a Heart*. This was followed in 1988 by the excellent ultra-mellow, bass-bubbling Jackie Jackson version of *Walk On By*.

They then teamed up with singer Carlton and the people who were to become Massive Attack when they remixed The Wild Bunch's cover of the Bacharach classic *Any Love* – a hauntingly minimalist counter to the richness of their Three Stripe work. Rob and Ray were gods of the nascent dance scene, their *Steppers' Delight* 12-inch is credited as being the birth of Jungle. They teamed up with Fresh Four for the Knowle West outfit's Top

10 version of *Wishing on a Star* (see BS3, p30). Although this track is their only commercial success to date, it's hardly representative of the depth and diversity of their outstanding work. The major labels were on the prowl for Smith & Mighty. Virgin got short shrift when Ray Mighty said of Richard Branson: 'We just don't like his style and the way Margaret Thatcher portrayed him as the ideal business mogul. Maybe it's got something to do with the fact that we used to be punks.'

Smith and Mighty eventually signed to ffrr (London Records) in 1990 but then hardly released a beat for five years. Sadly their legendary *Bass is Maternal* album was never released in its original form; it remains one of Bristol's lost musical treasures. Outtakes from those sessions revealed a work of sparsely interwoven beats, dub, soul and space (silence). A dub reggae version of the album was eventually released, but not until several years later.

After sitting out their contract and then parting company with London, Smith and Mighty added Peter D Rose as a third member and introduced the world to their More Rockers project. Their first album in this new formation was *Dub Plate Selection Volume 1* which is an uplifting gathering of dub and drum 'n' bass. More Rockers went further down the dub reggae path in their work with Henry and Louis (lovely stuff) and continued to record and tour in their own right. After the disappointment of the London deal, Smith & Mighty regrouped around the More Rockers posse and in 2003 were working again with Suv and Krust (originally from Fresh Four) on the outer fringes of hip-hop.

Rob Smith released his first solo album, *Up on the Downs*, in 2003. This was a heavyweight drum 'n' bass performance of great depth that retains the accessibility and hooks that are Rob Smith's trademark. After that he produced tracks as RSD (Rob Smith Dub) and still occasionally plays out with Ray Mighty. Catch them if you can.

OLD MARKET

I first went to Old Market aged 15 in 1979 to see two-tone band The Selecter at Trinity Hall. The mod revival was fresh in its sta-prest and the air was full of tension and excitement. As soon as Pauline Black and her speedy ska band plugged in, the place exploded. By the end of their set, the stage was bouncing with 15 or 20 uninvited mods. Stuff started to get broken, then someone threw a pint glass across the room; it smacked into the side of mod god Kev Rogers' head and almost took his ear right off. Although a river of blood was ruining his white Fred Perry, Rogers said he was fine, it was an accident, an in-house mod thing.

BITE TO EAT?
Whole-Baked Cafe in Lawford Street, Old Market is a good lunch option, but is only open weekdays.

The Trinity wanted us all out as soon as possible but there seemed to be a universal reluctance to go home. Everyone began loitering outside. Then some of the notorious Barton Hill mod squad began spotting non-mods and the fists and brogues started to fly. This wasn't playground fighting, this was ultra-violence. It had a cause and there was no bottling out. Yeah, scary. Really scary. As you may know, Trinity Church is opposite one of Bristol's largest police stations and it didn't take long before they noticed what was going on. They stepped outside and charged. Most of us legged it, others picked up bricks. There might have been a riot going on out there but we still had to get home. For what seemed like hours, we ducked in and out of the shop doorways all the way down West Street trying to avoid arrest. And ever since then, I have always had a fear of ever going back to Old Market again. Not least because it has always had a seedy feel to it at night. Blame the sex shop, nearby Stapleton Road and the constant stream of traffic from the busy Barton Hill roundabout.

Now Old Market is Bristol's 'gay village' with loads of pubs, clubs and even a gay sauna (see Lesbian and Gay Listings). The closure of the well-known Gin Palace during the Cabot Circus redevelopment meant that Old Market lost a famous old institution, but then it reopened again.

■ Punch Bowl beer garden: it may be concrete but it is still a garden – a haven in Old Market.

■ The Temple Quay development may be impressive but where is the low-cost housing?

Old Market, once the main shopping centre for Bristol, is still a dark edge of town.

TEMPLE QUAY

What was traditionally one of the city centre's most miserable areas is now a modern office development and the site of continuous building. Granted, it is still impossible to ignore the Old Market roundabout end-of-the-world concrete underpass and its broken-elevator, cold-bridge, back-of-the-NCP multi-storey brutality, but as you approach the roundabout where the Redcliffe flyover used to be, the new buildings of the £300 million Temple Quay development look pretty impressive.

Naturally, this being Bristol, Temple Quay is an entirely corporate office environment that piles thousands more cars onto the already gridlocked roads. The planners also resisted the opportunity to introduce low-cost housing, or build a community in the heart of the city, so, after 6pm, the streets and plazas of Temple Quay are windswept and deserted, and the only company is the scores of CCTV cameras. There was once a plan to turn Temple Quay into an official red light area. The sex workers, it was argued, would be well protected by CCTV, there's loads of parking after dark and excellent rail links. Bizarrely, the first new shops to service the hundreds of office workers in Temple Quay were a Lloyds Chemist, a mini-market and a Starbucks. Presumably these cater for every need of the 21st-Century office drone. The Knights Templar Weatherspoon's pub is the best option if you are meeting someone from Temple Meads.

Work on the next stage of this business centre development, the £200 million Temple Quay 2, started in the spring of 2003 to the north of the Floating Harbour. The developers claim Temple Quay 2 will include affordable homes in the area of Bristol called the Dings. This was once Bristol's working-class heartland – one theory about the name is that it comes from the railway sidings – but has remained a semi-derelict home to industrial estates and car breakers since World War Two. The definition of 'affordable housing' remains to be seen.

QUICK PINT?

Knights Templar in Temple Quay is a Wetherspoons pub dead handy for the train.

Five crews...
Who used to play house parties in St Paul's

1 **Wild Bunch:** Went on to become Massive Attack.

2 **FBI:** The initials stand for Funky Beats Incorporated.

3 **UD4:** DJ General was famed for his 'transformer' scratch.

4 **Def Con:** John Stapleton and Ian Dark pushing back the boundaries.

5 **City Rockas:** B-Boy crew who specialised in classic funk.

TEMPLE MEADS

On the other side of Temple Way from Temple Quay is the Mint Hotel, which has a good restaurant, and right in the middle of all this growth, is Brunel's stylish and underrated Temple Meads railway station. It's just a shame that nobody will ever be able to wave anyone goodbye from the platform ever again because First Great Western has installed ticket barriers – don't get us started on those ticket barriers. Suffice to say that if you crave a definition of the words 'feeble-minded' and 'management', just spend 10 minutes watching the barriers in 'operation'.

BITE TO EAT?

Try the little **Taxi Driver Cafe** on the left hand side as you approach Temple Meads for a cuppa and a sarnie.

■ Temple Meads linked London to Bristol and the ss Great Britain linked Bristol to America.

If your train is cancelled and you fancy a drink, the obvious choices are the station bar or the Reckless Engineer opposite the main entrance. Both of these are much improved with the Reckless Engineer offering a selection of real ales. If you fancy a sandwich, the unmarked little cafe on the right-hand side of the Approach as you walk away from Temple Meads is better value than the station shops.

MAP
BS2

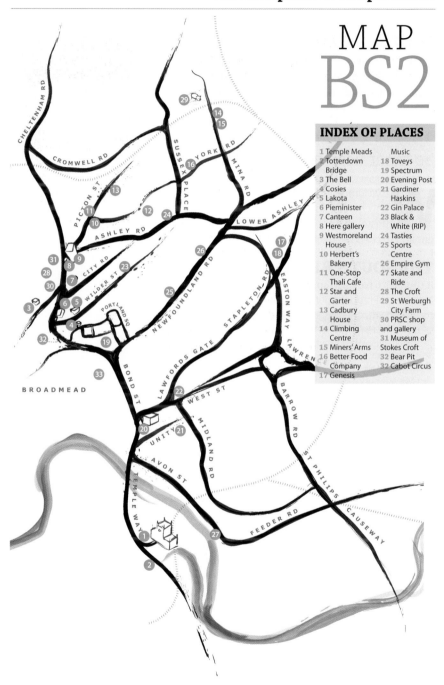

INDEX OF PLACES

1 Temple Meads
2 Totterdown Bridge
3 The Bell
4 Cosies
5 Lakota
6 Pieminister
7 Canteen
8 Here gallery
9 Westmoreland House
10 Herbert's Bakery
11 One-Stop Thali Cafe
12 Star and Garter
13 Cadbury House
14 Climbing Centre
15 Miners' Arms
16 Better Food Company
17 Genesis Music
18 Toveys
19 Spectrum
20 Evening Post
21 Gardiner Haskins
22 Gin Palace
23 Black & White (RIP)
24 Tasties
25 Sports Centre
26 Empire Gym
27 Skate and Ride
28 The Croft
29 St Werburgh City Farm
30 PRSC shop and gallery
31 Museum of Stokes Croft
32 Bear Pit
32 Cabot Circus

BS3/BS4 **Arnos Vale to Southville**

They've been trying to posh up South Bristol for years. So far, it hasn't worked

We've lumped BS3 and BS4 together because we'll only cover a little bit of BS4. This is the South Bristol chapter. If you're feeling adventurous enough to cross the river, read on…

THE SOUTH BRISTOL STORY

It could all have been so different… If, in 1835, John Miller, Vice-President of the Society of Florists, had gone ahead with his plan to build Bristol Zoo on land at Arnos Vale, then Totterdown and Knowle could now be affluent, sophisticated, leafy suburbs with the zoo and its magnificent gardens at their centre. A bit like Clifton perhaps. It seemed certain that the zoo would be built on the site that Arnos Vale Cemetery now occupies: in March 1835, *The Bristol Journal* reported that 'the planting of the Zoological Gardens, eight acres in extent on Pylle Hill near this city has just been commenced by Mr John Miller.' But the Zoo was built on its current site at Summer Trenmoor near Clifton Down. It now seems an obvious location for such a major project, but back in 1835, Arnos Vale was a pleasant and unspoilt area of open countryside, whereas the Downs were populated by vagabonds and highwaymen swinging in the wind from gibbets. South Bristol lost out. In fact, South Bristol always seems to lose out. One suspects that

> ## Past Notes
>
> ▶ **1080** Bedminster is listed as a royal manor in the Domesday Book.
>
> ▶ **1748** An angry agricultural mob stomp northwards to smash the new Totterdown toll gate.
>
> ▶ **1900** First section of the Totterdown YMCA is opened. The Village People's great grandfathers rumoured to be 'delighted'.
>
> ▶ **1988** Someone calls Southville 'Lower Clifton' in an attempt to make the area more appealing.

■ **The mural at South Street School, Southville reinforces the area's 'Lower Clifton' references much loved by estate agents.**

when the Romans arrived in Bristol, they decided to make Knowle West and Hartcliffe the leisure capital of their European empire. The first stone was probably about to be laid when a breathless centurion jogged up Hartcliffe Way and gasped: 'Hang on a minute, I've found this place called Aquae Sulis down the road. You should have a look there first.' Successive attempts to make South Bristol trendy have failed. One theory for the lack of anything much happening in South Bristol is that the secondary schools perform badly in the league tables, so parents who can afford it move to different catchment areas where the schools are better when their children reach Year Six, leaving behind those families who aren't in a position to evacuate the area.

Naked Truth

Vale Street

66 Vale Street in Totterdown is one of the steepest residential streets in Britain. Local residents hold an egg-rolling competition there on Easter Sunday. 99

And yet… along with Easton and St Paul's, South Bristol has one of the strongest and friendliest communities in the city.

QUICK PINT?

The Shakespeare in Henry Street is famous for its Sunday lunches.

TOTTERDOWN

Totterdown is split in two by the Wells Road. On the left going out of Bristol is Arnos Vale; on the right is the area most Bristolians would call Totterdown. The Arnos Vale side is residential but there is a bohemian element to the community which blends in with the established South Bristol vibe. There have been several welcome arrivals on Wells Road including the Al Waha take-away, the Assilah Moroccan restaurant, A capella deli and cafe and the marvellous Farrows chip shop. Down the hill on the Bath Road the Thunderbolt is an excellent live music venue,

The other side of Wells Road is a far livelier proposition and features some of Bristol's best pubs The Shakespeare, The Oxford, the Star and Dove gastropub as well as the excellent Thali restaurant and the old Lloyd's bank/YMCA building which houses the Banco Lounge. There's also a mosque on this side of Totterdown: the Bristol Jamia Mosque in Green Street.

In the 1980s and 1990s, The Shakespeare was run by Mad Ern (Vernon Somers) and his wife Sane Joan. Ern was one of Bristol's greatest characters and The Shakespeare

Five phrases…
You might hear in BS3

❶ **Thazza grey tide eel** (That's a great idea).

❷ **Oim goin ter Asdur in Bumster** (I'm going to Asda in Bedminster).

❸ **Soider oi up lanlawd** (Can I have a pint of cider please).

❹ **Awrite me babber. Ain't sinew frages** (Long time no see).

❺ **Surely, the secondary schools can't be that bad** (Skoolz roundyear are gert crap).

■ The Shakepeare is one of the nicest pubs south of the river, not that there's a great deal of competition, of course.

WILD WESTERNERS

THE LOW DOWN ON THE BRISTOL FACES WHO HAIL FROM THE DEPTHS OF KNOWLE WEST

■ Lizz E and famous Knowle Westerners Fresh Four: Suv Krust, Judge and Flynn.

You have to climb a hill from anywhere in Bristol to get to Knowle West. High above Victorian Bedminster on the southern fringes of the city, where the wind draughts in from the Dundry Beacon, it's always one or two degrees colder than the rest of town. The irony is that the families who were transplanted to Knowle West in the 1920s were brought from the slums behind Bristol Temple Meads railway station, which were built so close together that the area was always several degrees warmer than its surroundings.

They built Knowle West like a spider's web. Or so it appears from the map, and so it appears from the road. Every street and avenue looks the same and they're all littered with speed bumps. This is where BMX meets joyriding. Certainly, the natives seldom venture out of the estate for any length of time, except to go to Weymouth for their annual Courage Best and Ambre Solaire shandy – or to make it cautiously into the town centre for a little light pillaging, for the crime rate here is high.

At the middle of the web lies Filwood Broadway. Shut-down shops and boarded-up windows face a prevailing wind so strong you can hardly walk against it. Downtown Beirut it's called. Tricky grew up here, as did Julian Dicks. They say the reason Tricky never lifts his head from his microphone is a childhood fear of having his hat blown off. Then there's the graffiti: Sharon-4-Chris, Steve+Tracey4Ever, PIGS (defiantly), and Bruno. He gets everywhere does Bruno. If it's flat, Bruno has signed it. With spray paint and some jumbo markers.

At the edge of the web are the ex-council houses bought by Thatcher's property-owning democrats. All have storm porches. Some have stone cladding. A few have stone-clad storm porches. Here they have trees, and shelter. And hedges. And double-glazing. Elsewhere they have poverty and drugs, and stripped down Capris in the garden. And utter, utter hopelessness. I don't know where Julian Dicks would have gone to learn how to play football around here. In the street? On the rare patches of green? Or in the park at the end of Broadway? There's not much in the way of leisure facilities for the young in Knowle West.

But Filwood is on the up. The developers are moving in and parts are looking better. The double-glazing is on its way – new flats, new community spirit, rumours of a supermarket to replace the derelict shell at the end of the road, and new shop fronts. New flat surfaces. Bruno will like that.
Don Robbin

Four Famous Westerners
1) Tricky
2) Julian Dicks
3) DJ Krust
4) Suv (Full Cycle)

This piece first appeared in Total Football magazine as part of a profile of the footballer Julian Dicks who is from Knowle West.

exuded his extravagant personality. The walls and ceiling were completely covered with postcards, posters, witticisms and house rules. You never needed to take anything to read: you could just work your way around the walls and ceiling. In the midst of this chaos, Ern built himself a DJ den from where he and his mates would treat customers to an eclectic mix of tunes. Ern left in 2000 and a pub full of tat left with him. But under the stewardship of Warwick and Emma, The Shakespeare maintained its slightly eccentric character. There's a good range of beers, lovely organic Sunday roasts (booking essential), and DJs (in Ern's booth).

■ **Totterdown people love a party: in fact, they do it in the street.**

Naked Truth

Knowle West's Royal visit

❝King Edward VIII visited a council house in Lurgan Walk, Knowle West on 26 November 1934, when he was the Prince of Wales. He met unemployed labourer William Bailey, his wife and eight children.❞

QUICK PINT?

The **Thunderbolt** on Bath Road has a large garden for an al fresco tipple.

The Star and Dove used to be called the Cumberland and had a good music club upstairs called Coup d'Etat run by much-respected local muso Dave McDonald who is now at the Thunderbolt. PJ Harvey played Coup d'Etat once when she used to live in Totterdown. It is rumoured that Polly enjoyed her 'creative liaison' with Nick Cave in a house in Stevens Crescent. PJ Harvey producer and guitarist John Parish (see Bristol Beat) still lives in the area.

■ **Totterdown is very hilly, much like the rest of Bristol.**

Totterdown is now making a national name for itself for its Front Room Art Trail which began in 2000 and, by 2010, featured about 100 artists, 50 houses, three pubs and attracted around 4,000 visitors to Totterdown over two days in November. Basically, artists display their work in houses and members of the public wander in, admire, buy and go for a pint in The Shakespeare. It's a great event – up there with St Paul's Carnival and Brisfest in terms of a weekend to make sure you're in town.

KNOWLE WEST

There's absolutely no reason to visit Knowle West. It's a rough South Bristol council estate with enough drug and crime problems to rival anywhere else in Britain. And yet Knowle West has produced three of Bristol's best-known characters: footballer Julian Dicks, hip-hop maniac Tricky

(Adrian Thaws) and drum 'n' bass supremo Krust (Keith Thompson). Knowle West was also home to the band that achieved the highest ever chart position by a pre-Massive Attack Bristol outfit when Fresh Four reached number 10 in 1989 with *Wishing on a Star*.

There's certainly a link between Dicks and Tricky: they're both hard bastards. Dicks (whose nickname is the Terminator) was the most feared left-back of his generation at Birmingham City, Liverpool and, most famously, West Ham United; while Tricky was responsible for the most hard-edged, dysfunctional, alienated sounds of the 1990s. Krust too shows glimpses of the urban chaos that surrounded him in Knowle West in his breathtaking *Coded Language* album.

■ The water maze in Victoria Park marks the site of one of Bristol's original water supplies.

BITE TO EAT?

The **Banco Lounge** on Wells Road in Totterdown is a great place for a quick snack or dinner.

Tricky was christened 'the YTS Kid' by Massive Attack when he worked on their classic *Blue Lines* debut album because he was on a retainer of £25 a week. He was a feature at all the parties in town in the early 1990s and was known to one and all as 'the stoned kiddie from Knowle West'. Tricky's mother Maxine Quaye (after whom his 1995 debut album was named) died when he was four. His father had already left, so Tricky spent his childhood living with relatives around Bristol. He worked briefly with Krust in Fresh Four before moving into a squat with ex-Pop Group main man Mark Stewart, who at the time was working with On-U-Sounds producer Adrian Sherwood and Barton Hill hard case Gary Clail on a series of heavyweight dub reggae projects. In an interview with *Venue* magazine to promote his album *Never Trust a Hippy*, Sherwood claims that Tricky lived in a cupboard under the stairs in Stewart's squat. It may be coincidence, but Kat

■ The only two places you will find sheep in South Bristol are the Windmill Hill City Farm and on this house overlooking Victoria Park.

The Smythes

☀ John Smythe bought the Ashton Court Estate and large areas of South Bristol in the 16th Century. He is usually referred to as 'a successful Bristol merchant'. However, there is some evidence that he was actually a smuggler. The Smythes commissioned a survey to see if there were coal deposits in Bedminster. There were, and the first pit opened in South Liberty Lane in 1744. By 1830, there were 18 pits in Bedminster, the biggest of which was in Dean Lane. This can still be seen in Dame Emily Park (named after Sir Greville Smythe's wife), where a set of railings (and formerly a bandstand) marks the covered top of the area's biggest pit. The last Bedminster pit closed in 1924.

Day, guitarist with Bristol's finest guitar band of the early 1990s, the Seers, is also from Knowle West. Like Tricky, he sometimes wore a dress on stage. A trend that didn't catch on, luckily.

Fresh Four comprised Knowle Westerners Judge, Suv (now part of Roni Size's Full Cycle crew), his brother Flynn (of Flynn and Flora) and Krust. Their singer was Lizz E, a Bristol teacher. Tricky was in the same class as Flynn at Knowle Juniors and Merrywood Boys' School. Although *Wishing on a Star* propelled them into the top 10, the follow-up *Release Yourself* disappeared without trace, and so did Fresh Four. (See Bristol Beat).

Naked Truth

Dame Clara Butt
❝Bedminster Town Hall in Cannon Street (now demolished) was the venue for the first ever performance by Dame Clara Butt, Britain's greatest ever contralto, who studied in Bristol.❞

Five things...
Not to do in S Bristol

❶ Go shopping in Ashton in a Rovers shirt.

❷ Leave a car unlocked in Filwood Broadway.

❸ Try to make new friends in The Friendship in Knowle West.

❹ Go for a romantic evening in Bedminster.

❺ Ask for 20 Capstan Full Strength gaspers at the Tobacco Factory.

VICTORIA PARK

QUICK PINT?
Grab a pint of organic lager at **The Windmill** on Windmill Hill, Bedminster.

Victoria Park lies between Totterdown and Windmill Hill and boasts fine views over the city. The park may lack a central feature, such as a lake but, is being increasingly used by the local community for fun days, sponsored cycle rides and dog shows. There's an active Wildlife Group which has created a butterfly and wildlife garden near the bowling green and has initiated various conservation schemes. The park is home to St Mary Redcliffe Primary School and a water maze. The maze, on the Totterdown side of the park, is on the original course of the St Mary Redcliffe pipe, which supplied the citizens of Bristol with clean water in the 12th Century. Since 1984, the water has flowed from Knowle into the maze, which is built in brick as a replica of a medieval roof boss in St Mary Redcliffe Church.

■ **Watch the pigs at Windmill Hill City Farm.**

WINDMILL HILL

Like Totterdown, Windmill Hill was a semi-rural area until the railway line from Bristol to Weston-super-Mare and beyond was built in the mid 19th Century. Windmill Hill takes its name from the fact that there was a windmill there – another one faced it across the valley in Totterdown, probably on School Road. Historically, Windmill Hill housed railway and tobacco ★ *Turn to page 44*

THE OUTER CIRCUIT ROAD

BRISTOL'S ROAD 'REGENERATION' IN THE 1970S

Devastating town planning

Residents of many English cities claim that what the Luftwaffe didn't destroy in the 1940s, the town planners blitzed with far less imagination in the 1960s and 1970s. This is certainly the case with Totterdown.

It's difficult to imagine now that the famous Three Lamps signpost (one of the best examples of early 19th Century signs in Britain, pictured above) at the junction of the Bath and Wells Road once marked the gateway to a vibrant inner city community lining the Wells Road and the Bath Road.

The Three Lamps sign is still there, but that's all that remains of that part of Totterdown. It all went horribly wrong for the area in the 1960s when Britain was obsessed with bulldozing cities to make room for new roads. On 15 December 1966, the Ministry of Transport approved a Bristol City Council plan for a £30 million outer ring road, or urban motorway. The brainwave of the Planning Committee and its chairman Alderman Wally Jenkins (or 'Mr Traffic', as the *Western Daily Press* dubbed him), the plans were truly devastating. Essentially, the planners wanted to drive a dual carriageway-cum-motorway from what is now Junction 3 of the M32 through Easton and St Philip's, over the Feeder behind Temple Meads, across the

Three Lamps Junction, through Totterdown, across Victoria Park and through Bedminster.

Totterdown demolished

It got worse. The motorway would then head across the Floating Harbour, skirting the Cathedral and heading through Jacobs Wells to the Victoria Rooms. The precise route of this section is unclear: certainly there were proposals to turn Park Street into a dual carriageway and there were alternative plans for a flyover to Brandon Hill and a tunnel underneath the Cabot Tower.

From the Victoria Rooms this monster road would demolish Cotham on its way to Montpelier, where it would stop for breath before bulldozing St Paul's and rejoining the M32 (or Parkway as it was then called) at Junction 3. The plans also included surrounding St Mary Redcliffe Church with dual carriageways and driving a main road straight through the middle of Queen Square. In a word: it was madness.

But to the everlasting shame of the City Council, the area of Totterdown above the Three Lamps between the Bath and Wells Road was demolished in 1972 to make way for a four-level spaghetti-junction motorway on stilts. Between Three Lamps and Temple Meads, would be a giant interchange centre about the size of Broadmead where happy motorists would jump on fleets of buses to complete their journey into what was left of the city. Communities, shops and pubs were flattened to realise this nightmare. A total of 500 homes and 40 shops and pubs were demolished. Places like the Lahore Cafe and Club, the Three Lamps Canine and Feline Beauty Centre, the Maypole Dairy, the Bristol Co-operative Society, the Prince Rupert, the Totterdown Hotel and the Phoenix were lost.

Thankfully, the full awfulness of that road scheme was never realised; North Bristol was spared, Totterdown was destroyed but the road was never built. Easton suffered terribly. Ironically, new flats and houses were built on the Totterdown site in the 1990s, but the community has been lost for ever.

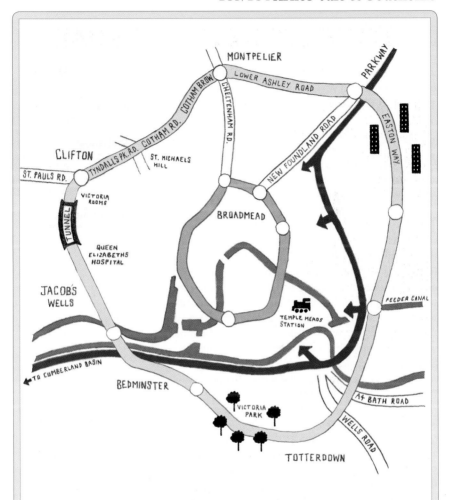

THE ROAD TO RUIN

This map of the proposed route of the outer circuit road is based on an illustration that appeared in the *Bristol Evening Post* on Friday 15 October 1971. The black line shows the route proposed by *Evening Post* reader Paul Chadd, which would have taken the traffic through the largely derelict area of St Philip's.

The grey line is the route preferred by the City Council which was to join the M32 at Junction 3. Much of Easton was demolished to build the first section of the outer circuit road and the lower part of Totterdown was bulldozed in 1972 to make way for it.

It is worth noting the tunnel which would appear to go either under Brandon Hill near the Cabot Tower or under the area of Clifton opposite QEH School on Jacobs Wells Road before emerging near the Victoria Rooms and ploughing straight through Cotham.

workers. The Hill is a curious area. It has got a trendy element, but it took the refit of The Windmill in 2006 to give it a decent pub with good food. In 2010 The Raymend was relaunched as The Victoria Park gastro pub. The only other reason to visit Windmill Hill is to go to an exhibition at the Off Centre Gallery in Cotswold Road.

■ **Zone A is a small area of land on Wells Road that has been designated as for community use.**

BITE TO EAT?

The **Magnet Fish Bar** on Dean Lane, opposite South Bristol Baths, once won an award for the best chippy in Bristol.

BEDMINSTER

Bedminster is older than Bristol and probably takes its name from a monastery or church founded by the monk Beda, or from the old English word 'bedydd', which means baptism. In the 15th Century, this is where the lepers came to live. Bedminster is separated from the rest of the city by the Cut. This was dug (probably by French prisoners from the Napoleonic War) between 1804 and 1809, when the Floating Harbour was built to carry the River Avon around the Harbour. It runs from Hotwells to Totterdown. When the Cut was built, Bedminster was part of Somerset; it was included in the Bristol boundaries in 1897, by which time it was an important industrial area with a coalfield, engineering works, tanneries, tobacco factories, paint and glue works. The population of Bedminster grew from 3,000 in 1801 to 78,000 in 1884.

Bedminster was an important area in the very early years of Bristol. The church of St John the Baptist (destroyed in World War Two, but not demolished until 1962) dated from 1003, and it was the mother church to St Mary Redcliffe, which was officially a chapel-of-ease to Bedminster until 1852.

Nowadays, Bedminster is a run-down, rough-and-

Poet's Corner, North Street

☀ If you look up at the wall of the house on the junction of Merrywood Road and North Street, you'll notice a weathered and crumbling bust and the words 'Poets Corner'. Thomas Chatterton is Bristol's most famous poet, but this memorial commemorates one of the city's worst: Alfred Daw Collard, the poet/butcher of Bedminster.

The Collards were a well known South Bristol family and provided four generations of butchers. There's still the front of a closed Collards' butchers farther up North Street. Collard was famous in the late 19th Century for his dreadful music hall-style poetry, copies of which he sold for a penny to raise money for Bristol General Hospital.

One of his works, *The Redcliffe and Bedminster Christmas Meat Show of 1885*, named the 26 butcher's shops between North Street and Redcliffe Hill. Collard's brother ran a butcher's shop on the site of Poets Corner and erected the memorial as a joke.

ready part of town with a lot of character (and characters) but not much else going for it. It has steadfastly resisted attempts to smarten it up and, despite forming a heartland of Labour support in the city, has been overlooked by the Labour Party when it has control of Bristol City Council and, like much of South Bristol, has seen significant inroads by the Lib Dems and Green Party. The housing development on the junction of Bedminster Parade and York Road has been heralded as opening 'the Gateway to South Bristol' and has certainly set the tone for rampant home building in Bedminster. But will such developments smooth the rough edges of East Street? History suggests not.

Naked Truth

Ashton Court Festival

66Ashton Court Festival (RIP) was masterminded from a small room above The Albert Inn in Bedminster for several years in the late 1980s. Landlord Ian Storrer gave the organisers the room for free.99

■ The old police station in Bedminster High Street is now an Italian restaurant.

QUICK PINT?

The Ropewalk in Bedminister Parade is your best bet for a pint in Bemmie.

Heading over Bedminster Bridge, Nelson Parade becomes Bedminster Parade, which turns into East Street, the main road through Bedminster, which supposedly follows the route of a Roman Road used to carry minerals from the Mendips to the Roman Port at Sea Mills. Just off Bedminster Parade in Stillhouse Lane is the old Bedminster Bridge School, a Grade II listed building designed by WV Gough and built in 1895. Equally impressive is the police and fire station on the right. This grand castle-like building was opened in 1882 by Mr ES Robinson of the paper-bag and printing company. The tower is there for practical rather than aesthetic reasons: it was a watch tower to spot fires. The original police and fire station that once stood here was one of the three built by an Act of Parliament in 1834; the other two were at Brandon Hill and St Philip's. In 1850, Bedminster had only one street light and one flushing toilet: both were at the police station. Shamefully, the building had been left in disrepair for more than 20 years. After the City Council sold the police station to property developers, the buildings around it have now been developed into (yep, you guessed it) flats and a library. Where villains once did time, diners can now do thyme in Bottelinos Italian restaurant which has moved into the police station.

■ This Grade II listed building was built in 1895 and used to be Bedminster Bridge School.

Area Guide

The Grant Bradley is a pleasant gallery space with a small cafe and on the left is Philip Street and Windmill Hill City Farm and one of Bristol's last real cider houses, the Apple Tree. Fiddler's club is in Willway Street off Philip Street. Opposite Philip Street is the Asda supermarket that was built on the site of the former Wills tobacco factory after that was demolished in 1986. In the 18th Century, the site of the current Asda car park was called the Paddock and was a meeting place for Bedminster's active Methodist community – John Wesley is known to have preached there at least four times. The shops next to Asda are in an original Wills building.

> **BITE TO EAT?**
>
> **Grounded** on Bedminster Parade is a large stylish cafe bar with a wide selection of food and a garden out the back.

■ The Apple Tree in Bedminster is a cider pub through and through.

Before the arrival of Asda, the lower part of East Street was home to several small greengrocers, a fishmongers and other high-street stores; these were unable to compete with the supermarket and closed down leaving the Bristol end of East Street in a somewhat shabby state. There's little of note as you walk through the pedestrianised part of East Street. The site of St John's Church is about half way up on the left in a small park off Church Road.

Emerging from East Street, Cameron Balloons was housed in the old red-brick Robinson paper bag factory which has been redeveloped as even more flats. The gabled London Inn, (which has a beer garden), is just to your right. Another famous Bedminster pub is The Albert

Billy Butlin of Bedminster

Billy Butlin launched his multi-million pound holiday camp empire with the takings from a hoop-la stall in Bedminster.

Having moved from South Africa to Bedminster and then Canada, after World War One, Billy Butlin worked his passage from Newfoundland to Liverpool. He arrived in England with £5 and headed for Bedminster to find his mother's fairground family. Butlin walked and hitch-hiked the entire way from Liverpool to Bristol. He was given the job of painting and re-fitting rides owned by the family and eventually his uncles set him up a small hoop-la stall at a cost of 30/- (£1.50), with prizes loaned to him by his kinsfolk. His first fair was at Axebridge, where business was very good: Billy made £10 clear profit, far more than the more experienced stall holders.

Butlin had a different outlook to the other stallholders, who made it difficult to win prizes by making the blocks too wide for the hoops to easily fit over. Bill made his blocks smaller so that the hoops went over more easily. He therefore got rid of all his prizes and made a very nice profit. He re-invested his profits and quickly moved from hoop-la stalls to amusement parks. By 1936, he had made enough money to open his first holiday camp in Skegness. His business philosophy goes all the way back to the success of his Bedminster hoop-la stall: give the punters a fair deal and they'll keep on coming back.

46

which closed in 2005. Its landlord Ian Storrer was one of the city's good guys, though you wouldn't necessarily guess it from his sometimes gruff disposition. The Albert was Bristol's best jazz venue. The lounge walls were covered with Reid Miles' superb artwork for the Old Blue Note covers, and the bar was plastered with covers from *Wire* magazine. Bristol's brilliant jazz saxophonist Andy Sheppard started out at The Albert and all of the city's jazz luminaries have played there. In the mid 1980s and early 1990s, Ian gave the Ashton Court Festival free use of a room for meetings. Bristol owes a lot to Ian Storrer. The Albert re-opened in 2007, sadly without Ian.

Naked Truth

Bristol firestarters
❝The first record of a bonfire night celebration in Britain is in Bristol on 5 November 1607. Two years after the Gunpowder Plot. Bristol Corporation paid for a giant bonfire at the High Cross in Broad Street.❞

■ Artwork from Bedminster Station in Fraser Street, Windmill Hill. Take a look, these guys are real good.

QUICK PINT?

The Coronation in Dean Lane, Southville has a good selection of beer and cider.

Past the London Inn is The Bay (although it's changed names so much in recent years it may now be called something else). It's a clean-cut bar with beer garden and pool tables at the back. The pub dates back to the 18th Century when it was called The Bull. Around 1900, it was changed to the Star, became a Florikan and Firkin in the 1990s and then the Aurora and after that was Bar Salt. In 1827, when it was The Bull, Mr Martin, the publican, bought a tiger and put it on show inside a cage in the pub. He paid a man, Joseph Kiddle, to get inside the cage with it. The tiger mauled Mr Kiddle to death.

Opposite Bristol South Swimming Baths, you'll find the Magnet Chip Shop. This was voted the best chippy in Bristol in the mid 1990s. The Argus in North Street is also famous for its fish and chips. Keep following Dean Lane past the bendy bit of road to The Coronation which can lay claim to being one of South Bristol's best pubs along with the Spotted Cow in Southville.

Just before Dean Lane joins Coronation Road, there's a Blue Plaque on the house which was home to the famous 1950s and 60s ivory tinkler Russ Conway (real name Trevor Herbert Stanford). Strangely, the house just a few doors down where Bear Hackenbush, Skate Muties, the Bugs 'n' Drugs crew and Chaos UK used to live has been afforded no such civic recognition.

■ The Coronation in Dean Lane is one of the most popular pubs south of the river.

SOUTHVILLE

Southville is the residential area between Bedminster and Ashton. It's the poshest part of South Bristol and estate agents periodically try to rename it Lower Clifton or Clifton View. Southville was largely built on tobacco money from the Wills family, who were teetotal. It is for this reason that there isn't a single pub in Southville, but there are many on the boundaries including the Hen & Chicken, which became Bristol's first theatre pub in 1989 when it was home to the Show of Strength theatre company.

BITE TO EAT?

Al's Tikka Grill in Ashton Road is a regular greasy spoon by day and a popular curry bistro by night.

■ The Tobacco Factory has helped make North Street one of the trendiest places in town.

North Street is the main shopping street in Southville. It has always been a busy high street but in recent years, it has helped Southville become Bristol's coolest neighbourhood. The impetus for Southville becoming so trendy is the Tobacco Factory project. The Tobacco Factory is housed in the last remaining part of the 1906 Old Wills Number 3 factory site on Raleigh Road. It contains a cafe bar, a theatre and various media-related enterprises. The building was saved from demolition by architect George Ferguson and is the centre of a movement for urban regeneration inspired by the Manchester Independents Campaign. The campaign philosophy is to encourage independent outlets and businesses and support local character and enterprise.

■ Gaol Ferry Bridge, Southville.

It certainly seems to be working in North Street: since the Tobacco Factory opened, the area has attracted many new bars, restaurants and shops while retaining its greengrocer, two butcher's shops, bakeries (including the fabulous Mark's Bread) and the mighty Lions hardware store. Sadly, there has been a significant loss in the midst of the über-trendiness. The Metro cafe, home to one of Bristol's best fried breakfasts, was replaced first by the Mediterranean-style Cafe Ceiturica and then by the excellent Souk Kitchen. Where students and builders once tucked into fried Saturday morning feasts, middle-class parents now scold their children for fiddling with their falafel. Please observe a few moments' respectful silence before you order.

If you follow North Street down towards Ashton Park,

where it becomes Ashton Road, you'll find Al's Tikka Grill. This is a cafe by day and BYO curry bistro and take-away by night, and is regarded as one of Bristol's best curry houses.

PAINTWORKS

The left side of Bath Road is the self-styled 'Creative Quarter', not exactly abuzz with life but it does house some serious players in Bristol's creative industries such as Wildfire media, and the BBC/Endemol studios which bear witness to the daily arrival of black-clad worshippers paying homage to his Holiness Noel of St Edmonds (it's where they film Deal or No Deal). The publishers of this book also work here, but don't let that put you off.

■ The Bocabar at Paintworks gives South Bristol the kind of bar it was crying out for.

On the other side of the river in St Philips is Bristol Fruit Market, the biggest wholesale outlet to the fruit, veg and flower trade in the South West. On Sundays, there's a 'cheap cuts, CDs and clothes market' on the site. You'll also find Charles Saunders, the city's main fresh and frozen fish wholesaler, down this way too. Underneath the bridge from Bath Road to St Philips behind the old Esso Garage site is a wall loved by the city's graffiti artists.

QUICK PINT?

The Tobacco Factory has led to a food and drink revolution in South Bristol.

WD & HO Wills, Bristol

There were already several other tobacco manufacturers in Bristol when Henry Overton Wills arrived in the city from Salisbury in 1786 and went into partnership with Samuel Watkins. Their first shop was in Castle Street but by 1791, the firm had moved to 112 Redcliffe Street.

The company quickly established a reputation for integrity and quality. The firm made steady progress and in 1871 entered the cigarette market with the original Bristol brand. This was followed in 1874 by Passing Clouds, in 1878 by Three Castles and in 1888 by one of the most famous cigarette brands in the UK, Woodbines, at a price of five for 1d.

In 1886, the firm moved to Bedminster and expanded its operation throughout South Bristol with sites in Southville, Ashton and Hartcliffe. In 1901, the Imperial Tobacco

Company was formed to resist an attempt by a powerful association of American tobacco manufacturers to capture the British market; WD & HO Wills took a leading part in its formation. The tobacco industry dominated South Bristol for much of the 20th Century.

In 1969, the Wills' Redcliffe Street premises were demolished and in 1974 production started at the new Hartcliffe Factory. Production was gradually phased out on the East Street and Southville sites and the whole operation was moved to Hartcliffe. In 1986, the original factory buildings at the bottom of East Street were demolished and an Asda supermarket was built on the site.

In 1989, the Hartcliffe head office building was vacated and in 1990 the Hartcliffe factory ceased production. All Imperial Tobacco cigarette production moved to Nottingham, though cigar production stayed in Bristol until the Hartcliffe factory was demolished in 1999.

ARNOS VALE CEMETERY

THIS 45-ACRE SANCTUARY HAS BEEN RESTORED WITH A £4.8M HERITAGE LOTTERY FUND GRANT

■ Morbid as it may seem, a visit to Bristol's most famous cemetery is an interesting and educational experience.

Save Arnos Vale campaign

Restoration work at Arnos Vale Cemetery was officially completed in April 2010, but before and army of volunteers and contractors had spent years repairing and restoring this fascinating site had been in a state of neglect for 25 years. In 2003 the cemetery was runner-up in the BBC's *Restoration* TV series. In 2005, Arnos Vale was handed a £4.8 million grant by the Heritage Lottery Fund. Work started immediately on clearing and renovating the cemetery, setting up a visitor centre and introducing educational, wildlife and conservation programmes.

The 45-acre cemetery was owned by Anthony Towner, head of the Bristol General Cemetery Company. In 1987, faced with falling revenue, Mr Towner announced that he wanted to sell a large part of the cemetery for residential development. A public meeting was arranged and the Campaign to Save Arnos Vale Cemetery was formed. Within weeks 20,000 people had signed a petition against the proposed development plans.

In 1998, the City Council refused Mr Towner a cremation licence because the crematorium failed to meet the regulations of the Environmental Protection Act 1990. So the crematorium ceased to operate and Mr Towner threatened to lock the gates. An angry crowd besieged Mr Towner in his office at the cemetery; the gates remained open and the Friends of Arnos Vale (led by Richard Smith MBE) took charge of the cemetery, unlocking and locking the gates every day and doing their best to maintain the site.

High Court appeal

Bristol City Council was granted a Compulsory Purchase Order for the cemetery in April 2001 and a public inquiry was held in May 2002 to hear the evidence in connection with Mr Towner's objections. The inquiry ended early when the company withdrew its objections. The Council bought the cemetery under the CPO and handed it over to The Friends of Arnos Vale Cemetery.

The cemetery was founded in 1837 when a private Act of Parliament established the Bristol General Cemetery Company. It was planned as a Greek-style Necropolis and was landscaped using trees and plants noted in classical legend. Its Grade II listed Arcadian Garden contains four buildings designed by the architect Charles Underwood: two neo-Greek Doric entrance lodges (both are Grade II listed buildings), an Anglican Mortuary Chapel and a Non-Conformist Chapel.

Arnos Vale is the final resting place of several Lord Mayors of Bristol, an American consul, members of the Wills and Robinson families, George Muller and possibly Mary 'Princess Caraboo' Baker, who managed to persuade the Squire of Almondsbury that she was an Eastern Princess. Further down the Victorian social scale, you'll find the unmarked mounds of the common graves of the poor and the flat markers of the guinea graves of those whose relations had managed to collect 21 shillings (£1.05) to avoid a pauper's burial.

Murdered in donkey dispute

The grave of Mary Carpenter, the Victorian pioneer of juvenile care, was lost in the undergrowth until it was discovered when part of the graveyard was being cleared of brambles. At least two survivors of the Charge of the Light Brigade are buried at Arnos Vale, as is a police officer who was murdered in Old Market whilst trying to intervene in a fight over the ill-treatment of a donkey.

Arnos Vale also contains a considerable number of individual war graves, a small military cemetery with a Cross of Sacrifice, and a World War One memorial classical stone arcade built into the hillside close to the main entrance. Approximately 250,000 burials have taken place in 50,000 graves and 750,000 cremations have also been carried out, with most of the cremated remains scattered in the Arnos Vale Gardens of Rest.

Raja Rammohun Roy

The most famous resident of Arnos Vale Cemetery is Raja Rammohun Roy, the great Bengali social reformer who died from meningitis on 27 September 1833 while he was staying with friends at Beech House in Stapleton (later to become Purdown Hospital and now a residential development).

Rammohun Roy was a scholar fluent in many languages including Greek, Hebrew and Latin. He wrote books on grammar,

■ Inkie painted the old caretaker's house in Arnos Vale as part of the 2010 Totterdown Art Trail.

geography and geometry and published newspapers and is especially remembered for his campaign to end the Hindu custom of 'sati', the burning of a widow on her husband's funeral pyre. As head of the Atmiya Sabha he spearheaded reform on all fronts: he was against polygamy and the caste system and was a supporter of education for women. The 19th-Century Indian social reformer Ranade called him the 'father of modern India' and Indian academic Professor Brajendraneth Shil described him as 'the pioneer internationalist'. There's now a statue of him outside the Central Library on College Green.

On his death, the Raja was buried in the garden of Beech House. Ten years later, in 1843, his body was moved to a permanent burial site at Arnos Vale so that the public might have access to it. The canopy over the tomb was styled by a Calcutta designer and there are plans for it to be restored to its original glory.

■ The Arnos Vale Cemetery Trust is continuing to raise money through its Guardian Angel scheme.
■ Arnos Vale Cemetery Trust, West Lodge, Bath Road
■ Tel: 971 9117
■ www.arnosvale.org.uk

■ The tomb of Raja Rammohun Roy – Arnos Vale Cemetery's most famous resident.

MAP
BS3 & BS4

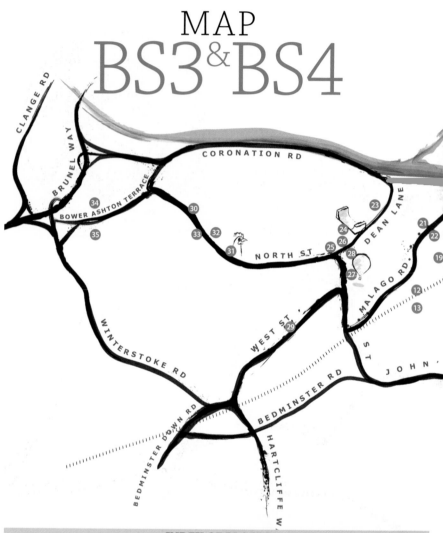

INDEX OF PLACES

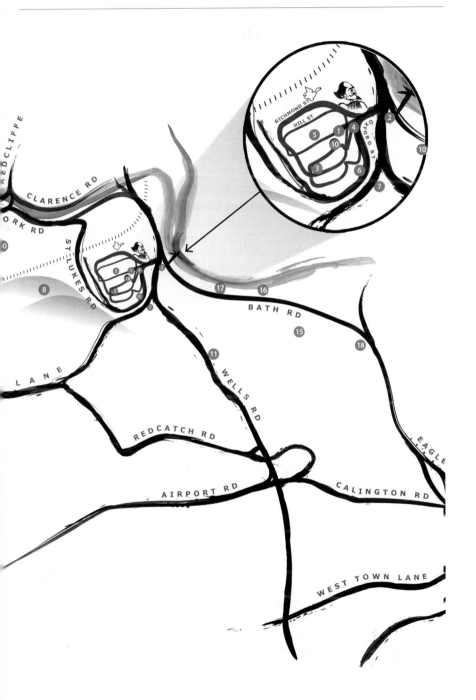

BS5 Easton to St George

Home to Bristol's radicals from Ben Tillett to Tony Benn and the Bristol anarchists...

At face value, there may seem little to recommend a visit to the East Bristol inner-city areas bordered by the M32 and the A420. But here you'll find one of Bristol's most pleasant walks (along the banks of the Frome at Snuff Mills), a fantastic shopping street (St Mark's Road), a dub reggae and techno paradise (the Black Swan), loads of good curry houses and some of the city's best street art. Easton is also home to Bristol's active radical element. But

■ It is unlikely that Tory party activists ask if they can count on Kebele's vote at election time.

be warned: crime is an issue in the area, particularly near the bridge across the M32 and around the underpass at Lawrence Hill.

Past Notes

▶ **1793** First Easton coal mine opens.

▶ **1881** Cricketing legend and ZZ Top beard originator WG Grace becomes Easton's local doctor.

▶ **1886** Eight die in the notorious Easton pit disaster.

▶ **1990** Easton Leisure Centre opens on Stapleton Road.

EASTON

There is little evidence of it now, but Easton was built on coal. The earliest mining area in Bristol was further east at Kingswood where coal was produced from the 17th Century to fuel the soap-making, glass, brewing and pottery industries. The first Easton mines were developed in the late 18th Century and the industry boomed in the 19th Century.

Today Easton is a buzzing, run-down inner-city area alongside Stapleton Road and home to the city's largest ethnic population. It has a history of political activism dating back to the Weavers' Riots in 1728; there were miners' strikes in the 18th and 19th Centuries and it was the birthplace of Ben Tillett, one of the founders of the Labour movement and the creator of the first unions for unskilled workers. It is currently a base for the Kebele

■ The Sugar Loaf on St Mark's Road has a great beer garden out the back.

Kulture Projekt anarchist centre in Robertson Road (see Underground and Radical Bristol). It's where the anti-car lobby park their bicycles and is the area of choice for a sizeable gay (particularly lesbian) community.

Every visitor to Bristol should take a stroll down St Mark's Road, where you'll find Moroccan cafes, a Bangladeshi restaurant, a Thali cafe, an African-Caribbean clothes store, a sari shop, the veggie cafe Maitreya and the mighty Bristol Sweet Mart. The Sugar Loaf on St Mark's Road is a well-known and busy pub that has merited an entry in the Good Beer Guide. It's a good spot to sit outside and watch the Easton world go by – there's regular live music in the evenings. The Chelsea on Chelsea Road is the venue of choice for Easton's radical community. The Black Swan near the junction of St Mark's Road and Stapleton Road was the headquarters of Bristol Rovers FC between 1897 and 1910. The original building is thought to date back to 1640, although it was rebuilt in the 19th Century. It's now one of the city's leading dub reggae and techno venues, regularly hosting leading sound systems – a must for bass addicts.

Naked Truth

Ben Tillett

❝One of the founders of the Labour Party and the Trade Union Movement, Ben Tillett, was born in 1860 in the now demolished John Street off Felix Road in Easton. He died in 1943.❞

QUICK PINT?

You can sit outside **The Sugarloaf** in St Mark's Road at the front or back.

EASTVILLE PARK

Eastville Park was created as a result of public pressure to tackle the problems of overcrowding and poor health in the parish of St Philip's. After much lobbying, 70 acres of land were purchased in 1889 for £30,000 on estate land owned by Heath House and Ridgeway House. At the time the land was on the outskirts of the growing city and many people were against the idea of a park at Eastville because they thought the area was too remote.

Some mature trees already growing there were kept, the existing boundary walls were repaired and paths were laid out with 100 seats and several small wooden shelters. Walks were created by planting an avenue of lime trees (now partly replaced by horse chestnuts) and London planes. The grass was managed with both sheep-grazing

Five things...
To buy on Stapleton Rd

1 Fresh red snapper and frozen frogs' legs, **Toveys fishmongers.**

2 Goat curry, rice and peas, **Caribbean take-away.**

3 Downbeat the Ruler, Killer Instrumentals, Best of Studio One, **Genesis Musik and Clothing.**

4 Bones for your dog, from **R Jenkins Butchers** (bones free, but make a donation to Cadbury Heath FC Under-13s).

5 Halal chicken and chips, **Lick 'n' Chicken.**

■ The Bristol Sweet Mart is a legend in Bristol and beyond.

and mowing. The outdoor swimming pool followed in 1905, the bowling greens in 1907, and finally the lake in 1908 to 1909.

The lake is one of the best public park lakes in England; it is designed in a serpentine shape so that wherever you stand you cannot see how big it is. It is bordered by lawns, specimen trees and a hanging wood.

■ Cafe Maitreya is St Mark's Road's award-winning cafe.

BITE TO EAT?

Cafe Maitreya in St Mark's Road has won national awards for its outstanding veggie food.

The park has now lost most of its original features; the bandstand and little kiosks had gone by 1950; only the plinth and footings of the octagonal drinking fountain by the Fishponds Road entrance still survive, with a stand pipe which no longer supplies water.

The Crimean War cannon which stood on a plinth near the bowling green was removed during World War Two to be melted down to make weapons. Almost all the grand entrances to the park have been lost to road-building. The widening of Fishponds Road in 1909 involved cutting back the Park for nearly the whole of its edge by the road. The M32 took away the lower entrance, with its walls, gates and drinking fountain, back in the 1960s. The best entrance is the original one up in the north-west corner, right under the remains of a clump of London plane trees. The pennant wall and gateway are both listed buildings.

You can join the 20km Frome Valley Walkway to Old Sodbury at Eastville Park.

■ Try Toveys on Stapleton Road for Bristol's freshest fish.

Easton Colliery, Felix Road

The Easton Colliery in Felix Road was opened in 1830 and closed in 1911 and was at its peak production in 1870. In common with mines everywhere, conditions were terrible. Children and women worked in the mines because they were able to squeeze through the narrow passageway. At the coalface, miners worked with pickaxes and spades in a choking atmosphere.

The underground workings spread for miles. The Easton Pit was linked to Whitehall pit by an underground railway two miles long.

In his memoirs, Ben Tillett recalls how he was persuaded not to become a miner:

'One of my relatives cured me of my plan to go down the pit. He took me down into the seemingly bottomless pit and terrified me. I saw awesome blackness: spluttering candles on greasy caps, dirt and mud, pools of filthy water, stifling heat, the rush and tempest of everyone pushing, bawling, shouting and cursing.'

On 19 February 1886, eight Easton colliers died in an explosion at the pit. A relief fund was set up and each widow received £5 towards the funeral and 5 shillings (25p) a week for herself and one child under 13, and a further 2/6d (12.5p) if there were other children. The inquest into the disaster was held at Lebeq's Tavern on Stapleton Road.

EASTVILLE

Eastville used to be home to Bristol Rovers Football Club (it is now IKEA) but now people only go to Eastville (or Eastgate as it's been renamed) to shop at Tesco and IKEA, which was built despite a vociferous campaign by locals who objected to the increase in traffic (among other things) that the store would bring. Their arguments were dismissed by the planners, but guess what? Yep, the M32 to IKEA is solid with cars every single weekend. Distressingly for Bristol Rovers fans, the IKEA store is almost exactly the dimensions of the old Eastville pitch. This is because the old Eastville site was developed piecemeal and the pitch was the last bit to go. Bizarrely, a floodlight from the Muller Road end of the old ground was left standing in the Tesco's car park as a memorial to Rovers' home. It stayed there until 2003 when it was removed because it was becoming unstable. As is the way with these things, the lights were auctioned to grateful supporters. Rovers, strangely, plunged into the darkness of the bottom division of the football league for the first time in their history just about the same time as the floodlight was taken down. Now, what does that tell you?

The arrival of IKEA meant the loss of a Bristol institution, Eastville Market, which used to be held in the old Rovers' car park. To be honest, other than shopping at IKEA, there's not a great deal going on in Eastville. The area sits between Easton and Fishponds and marks the transition from inner city to suburban Bristol. Recently, this residential area has seen a drift of prostitution and street crime from the inner city. The police have clamped down on sex workers in the soon-to-be-gentrified St Paul's area, so the women have been forced over the M32 into Easton and Eastville. Nadine Hill, a 25-year-old sex worker, was murdered in Eastville Park in October 2003, increasing calls to establish a regulated red light area in the city.

Naked Truth

Emma Jane Holden

66International opera star, Emma Jane Holden, was born at 7 Brooklyn Terrace in 1890. She died in 1938. The house was demolished in the mid 1960s to build Easton Way.99

QUICK PINT?

The Plough in Easton is home to the Easton Cowboys football radicals.

Five famous
Rovers games at Eastville

1 **Bristol Rovers 15 Weymouth 1**
17 November 1900, FA Cup (played at Stapleton Road). Rovers' record scoreline.

2 **Bristol Rovers 4 Manchester United 0**
7 January 1956, FA Cup. Busby Babes demolished.

3 **Bristol Rovers 3 Preston North End 3**
30 January 1960, FA Cup. Record attendance of 38,472.

4 **Bristol Rovers 4 Bristol City 0**
14 December 1963, Division 3. Biggest post-war win over City.

5 **Bristol Rovers 0 Sheffield United 0**
(Rovers won 7-6 on penalties). 5 Aug 1973, Watney Cup Final. Rovers' only Cup Final win.

STAPLETON

Stapleton has a village feel about it, despite being right next to the M32 and on the main road from Eastville to Frenchay. The peculiar impression of being time-warped from IKEA into rural England is strongest if you stroll down Colston Hill between Holy Trinity Church and Colston's School. The lane takes you down to the Frome Valley and Snuff Mills, a riverside walk that is one of the unspoilt gems of Bristol.

BITE TO EAT?
Why not stop off at **Bristol Sweet Mart** and sample one of their delicious samosas.

The impressive Stapleton parish church, Holy Trinity, is a particularly fine building. The first record of a church on this site goes back to 1438, but this one was built by Bristol architect John Norton in 1857 – the only other surviving example of Norton's religious architecture in the city is St Mary's in Stoke Bishop. Holy Trinity is built in the Victorian Gothic style with an elaborately carved door and a huge 170-foot tower. It is usually floodlit at night, so it is one of the first buildings you see when you enter Bristol via the M32 after dark. The square font, which now sits in the west porch, has been dated to about 1000AD. It was sold to a bishop's butler at one point in its history; the butler went on to become landlord of The Bell pub opposite the church and took the font with him to use as a geranium pot. It was later discovered and returned to the church sometime in the late 19th century. Colston's School, next to Holy Trinity, is for stripy-blazer posh kids. The nearby Masons Arms has a pleasant garden which offers fine views over the Frome Valley. And that, my friends, is Stapleton.

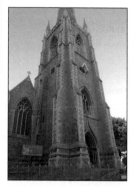

■ The Holy Trinity in Stapleton is built in the Victorian Gothic style.

■ The Bell opposite Holy Trinity once housed the church's old font. It was used as a flower pot.

Snuff Mills

One of the best things about living in Bristol is that you don't have to head out of town to find pleasant walks. The Downs and Arnos Vale are both fantastic, but if you want to discover a riverside walk near the centre of town, head down to Snuff Mills. Take a picnic, or, even better, a dog. You can also go fishing in the River Frome down there too.

Snuff Mills is the area between Blackberry Hill and Eastville Park and despite its name, as far as anyone has been able to ascertain, there has never actually been a mill there that ground snuff.

The mill that used to stand on the Frome here in the 19th Century was called Whitwood Mill but there's evidence of a mill on this site from 1297. It's thought that Snuff Mills got its name from a local character called Snuffy Jack who worked in a snuff mill further upstream and whose smock was always covered in snuff. He may also have worked in or lived near Whitwood Mill.

WHITEHALL TO ST GEORGE

Bob Hope (yes, that Bob Hope) lived at 326 Whitehall Road and at 14 Clouds Hill Avenue, St George when he was a nipper. Like most fortunate people, Bob (or Leslie as he was called then) passed through Whitehall and St George on his way to somewhere better. St George's Park, which has a lake and skateboard park, lies between Whitehall and St George, where Tony Benn used to have his Labour Party office on Church Road. The monument on the 'fountain' junction of Church Road, Clouds Hill Road and Summerhill Road is the Don John Cross, which is more than 400 years old and once marked the beginning of the Kingswood Forest. It's said to have taken its name from when the funeral bier bearing the body of a Spanish nobleman rested at the cross for a while before resuming its journey. It's probably not called after the grubby little boozer of the same name that used to be just down the road past the Fountain Cafe.

Naked Truth

Famous faces

66Frances Milton, the mother of writer Anthony Trollope was born in Stapleton back in 1780. Sarah Young, the mother of poet Thomas Chatterton was also born in Stapleton.99

QUICK PINT?

The Old Stillage in Church Road is where Arbor Ales brew their lovely beer.

■ The Blue Plaque on Bob Hope's childhood home in Clouds Hill Avenue, St George.

■ The Don John Cross is more than 400 years old.

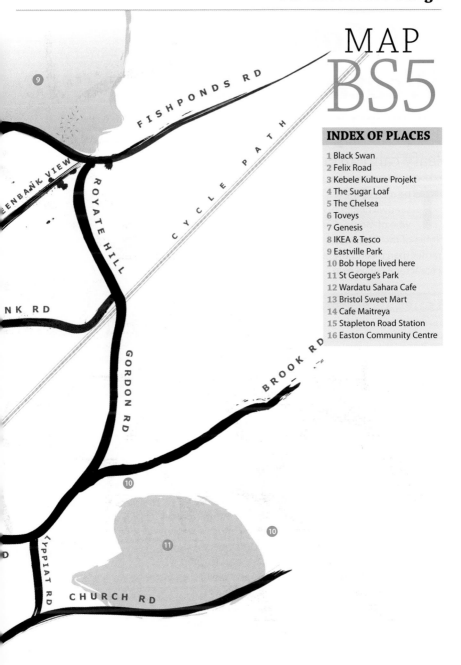

MAP
BS5

BS6 Cotham to Westbury Park

Despite being full of bedsits and students, there's a leafy calm around the Redland area

The area to the left as you go up Gloucester Road is sandwiched between the multi-cultural alternative vibe of Montpelier and St Paul's and the bright lights of the Whiteladies Road bars and restaurants. But rather than mixing these two distinct flavours, BS6 has a character all of its own…

■ Havana Cafe on Cotham Hill is the perfect spot from which to watch the world go by.

Past Notes

▶ **1230** Redland is namechecked in history books under the names 'Rubea Terra' or 'la Rede Londe' because of its ruddy soil.

▶ **1737** The Montague Tavern on Montague Hill in Kingsdown is built. Its turtle soup becomes famous in the gastronomic world.

▶ **1849** An outbreak of cholera kills 444 people.

▶ **1940** Redland Church is all but destroyed by that Hitler fellow.

COTHAM

Cotham can be confusing to the first-time visitor. It's a compact, bohemian kind of district and yet Cotham Brow has one of the longest zebra crossings you've ever seen. It's full of students, but a one-bedroom flat around here will set you back a tidy wedge. The first recorded resident of this area, then known as Codd Down, was a careless snuffmaker called William Hulme. Why careless? Well, he only decided to live in a windmill – not the most sensible thing to do with all that snuff lying around. Needless to say, his business was blown away and he was declared bankrupt soon afterwards.

Cotham is dominated by elegant old houses and occasional speciality shops, pubs and restaurants. Cotham Hill, the road that runs off Whiteladies Road at Clifton Down, is easily the most vibrant area. By day it buzzes with the coffee bar crowd who kill time and sip espresso in the very continental Havana Cafe, take coffee on the pavement

French style at Bohéme, or top up their vitamin intake at Bluejuice. There are also a few half-decent charity shops, an antiques shop and a shop devoted entirely to kites.

By night, Cotham picks up some of the spillage from the bars and restaurants on Whiteladies Road but has a very distinct neighbourhood quality of its own. It's packed with loads of restaurants from right across the global spectrum. The Deco Lounge is the Cotham branch of the Bristol bar group and has more of a wine bar or restaurant atmosphere than its more bar-ish cousins south of the river or on Gloucester Road. Diners with a traditional English palate should set their wallets on stun and head for Juniper on Cotham Road, one of the finest contemporary diners in the whole of the South West where you'll find the likes of slow braised shanks of lamb on the menu with rhubarb crumble with stem ginger custard for pudding.

Naked Truth

Slave Trader's Almshouses

❝Slave trader Edward Colston built the almshouses and chapel on St Michael's Hill in 1691. It's possible that the ships' timbers panelling in the chapel is from Colston's slave ships.❞

QUICK PINT?

The Hare on the Hill in Kingsdown is a cosy Bath Ales pub with great bar food.

KINGSDOWN

According to a Civic Society report published in the 1980s, of all the architectural crimes that were committed in Bristol in the 1960s, 'the destruction of Bristol's most important Georgian suburb' was the most despicable. If you want to see what they mean, take a look up at Kingsdown from the city centre. Interrupting the elegantly distressed original houses are the harsh, slab-like faces of some grim multi-storey council blocks. Equally irritating is the way Bristol City Council has effectively isolated Kingsdown by blocking off the handful of roads that gave vehicles access from Cheltenham Road.

Despite the best efforts of the town planners, Kingsdown has actually been getting more popular in recent years with drinkers looking to escape the nightmare of the naff pub experience. The Highbury Vaults at the top of St Michael's Hill is one of Bristol's best-known pubs thanks to its popularity with students. According to the *Observer Food Magazine* 2004 Awards, it's the Best Place to Drink in the South West, which certainly raised a few

Five things...
To buy on Cotham Hill

1 Full English breakfast and a mug of tea, **The Friary.**

2 Calypso 125GX stunt kite, **Kitestore.**

3 A Flu-Fighter from **bluejuice.**

4 Stifado with rice, salad and a bottle of Demestica, **Zorbas Taverna.**

5 A *Step-by-Step Guide to Yoga* at **Books at 58.**

■ **The Friary on Cotham Hill has been serving top quality breakfasts (and a lot else) since way back in 1979.**

eyebrows in the South West. The garden at the Vaults seems to get bigger every year and has a forest of outdoor heaters to keep the regulars warm as they tuck into their pints of Brains SA. They have been known to offer a nice pheasant roast dinner on a Sunday too. Over the road, The White Bear has had some interesting promotions over the years, including a gameshow-style happy-hour wheeze where you could hit a button to determine the price of your drinks from free to full price. More recently, the former coaching inn joined forces with the Rajpoot Express restaurant who have moved in upstairs, so curry is big on the menu alongside the more traditional pub grub.

■ Generations of Bristol students have passed through the doors of the Highbury Vaults.

BITE TO EAT?

The **Deco Lounge** on the popular Cotham Hill is a relaxed diner which boasts a great menu.

Cutting through the houses behind St Michael's Hill, you'll find The Green Man in Alfred Place and loitering just above the A-road traffic of Stokes Croft are three excellent pubs: the Hillgrove in Dove Street South, the nearby Hare on the Hill in Thomas Street North and The Bell in Hillgrove Street. The Bell is a local institution where you can find the likes of Dope on Plastic's John Stapleton and the Blow Pop DJs delving into their back catalogue in a low key kinda way. Because of The Bell's consistent popularity, people have been hiking up Nine Tree Hill to the Hillgrove, Bath Ales' Hare on the Hill and The Green Man lately. They are all relaxed, back-street boozers, perfect if you want to get away from the busy centre, but be careful of choosing the back table in the Hillgrove: the real fire gets real hot.

The Kingsdown story

☀ Wealthy merchants began moving to new homes in Kingsdown early in the 19th Century. Their aim was to escape the horrible grime of the city and the overwhelming stench of the foul-smelling Avon and Frome rivers.

Much of the Kingsdown area was owned by a man called Giles Greville. The open fields were known as the Montagues and Greville divided them into plots and then built the Montague Tavern. His plan was to attract Bristol's businessmen to set up home in Kingsdown. The tavern's turtle soup, said to be based on a recipe that had been created by a Lord Mayor of Bristol from the 13th Century, was once the talk of the turtle-supping world.

Civic banquets were held at the Montague Hotel – it has changed is name from Tavern at some point during the 18th Century – and boys from Colston School were taken there for their annual swig of grog. The fields around the Montague Hotel became the site for dawn duels and this continued well into the 19th Century. Even though the areas escaped any serious bomb damage in World War Two, sadly many of Kingsdown's finest houses and landmarks were lost in a wave of post-war redevelopment tantamount to civic vandalism.

REDLAND

If Clifton is Bristol's Chelsea and Montpelier its Notting Hill, then Redland is its Hampstead. There are probably more slightly distressed-looking bay window shutters here than anywhere else in the West Country. It has one of the highest levels of houses in multiple occupancy in the city. Yep, Redland is home to a vast army of students, former students, dope heads, media heads, musicians, teachers and some jaded beatniks who got in before the rents went mad and have managed to stay here ever since. However, not many of these folk can remember what happened last week, let alone when the district was called Rubea Terra in the 13th Century.

■ The Temple Meads to Severn Beach line was opened in 1885; Redland Station opened in 1897.

> ### Naked Truth
> **Portland Street Chapel**
> 66One of the most important buildings lost when the bulldozers moved into Kingsdown was Portland Street Chapel where Thomas Webb was buried. Webb introduced Methodism to America.99

Geographically, Redland stretches from Redland Green at the top of Redland Road to Cotham Park at the bottom. On either side, Chandos Road and Zetland Road are where its heart beats fastest. Chandos is a deeply cosmopolitan road that has the look and feel of a provincial European back street. The number of new restaurants that have opened here over recent years is bewildering. Culinaria and Moreish are just some of the names now sharing space with more established haunts, such as Ahmed's Curry Cafe. Sadly long-time resident Old Possums Wine Bar closed in 2006.

> **QUICK PINT?**
> **The Scotchman and his Pack** on St Michael's Hill has a roof terrace.

■ Ahmed's Curry Cafe offers top-quality curry and knock-down prices. And they have happy hour.

A short walk via the Kensington Arms will take you past Redland Station and onto Zetland Road. There you will find Casa Mexicana which brings a Central American flavour to Redland's varied eating out options. For those who prefer their food in liquid form, the area has three pubs, The Shakespeare, The Kensington and The Clyde. Of these, only the Kenny has ever been anything other than a quiet place to have a drink.

WESTBURY PARK

Westbury Park has always been culturally split down the middle. Half the residents have an affinity with Redland; the other half side with half-witted Henleaze. Tellingly, the most interesting thing to ever happen in Westbury Park is the famous episode of the White Tree on the Downs.

According to local legend, there are a number of suspects in the frame for painting the bottom half of the tree trunk with white emulsion. All the stories date from the 1850s. The warm-hearted version has it pinned on a bloke called George Ames who lived at the nearby Cote House and did it as an act of kindness in order to stop his children's German tutor from getting lost at night when he was on his way over to teach them. The funny version blames a Mr Woodward, who did it in a last-ditch attempt to help his regularly inebriated coachman find his way home after another night on the booze. Whoever it was and whatever they meant by it, the original was dug up in the 1950s to make way for a new roundabout. The current incarnation, number three, was planted in 1974.

BITE TO EAT?

The **Culinaria** bistro on Chandos Road, Redland is run by the highly-respected chef Stephen Markwick.

Westbury Park's main street, Coldharbour Road, is a little underwhelming to say the least. A restaurant, one pub, a fish and chip shop and a couple of pine furniture stores doesn't encourage many people to stop on the way through. North View is more compact and more lively. Once dominated by the cavernous AutoSpeed tyre fitting garage, the road is packed with little specialist shops such as the independent and slightly grumpy vacuum retailer called Homevac Electrics. Sadly a few places have now closed down, such as the weird shrunken Victoriana of the Gillian Richards' Dollshouse Shop. However, Cheung Kong Chinese Restaurant and La Terrazza, with its al fresco dining lend some glow after dark.

■ The Kensington was once the centre for Bristol's thriving Pinball League in the mid 1980s.

■ The house that smells – the most curious landmark in Redland is this sculpted nose on the side of resident Jane Tarr's house in Kensington Road.

Mother Pugsley's Well

Some historians say that Mother Pugsley's Well (aka The Virgin's Well) stood near the junction of Nugent Hill and Arley Hill. Others say that the site is in Hillgrove Street, near the current site of The Bell. It obviously makes more sense for a well with curative powers to be on the site of one of Bristol's finest boozers, so Hillgrove Street it is. The story goes that Pugsley was killed on the day of his marriage when Cromwell's troops stormed Prior's Hill (Kingsdown). Pugsley's wife vowed to remain faithful to his memory and visited the grave on the spot where Pugsley had fallen every day for the rest of her life. Two springs of water appeared next to the grave, one of which flowed into the well. When she died, Old Mother Pugsley was buried in her wedding dress, flowers were strewn in front of the cortege and St Nicholas Church played a joyful peal of wedding bells to celebrate her being reunited with her beloved husband.

MAP
BS6

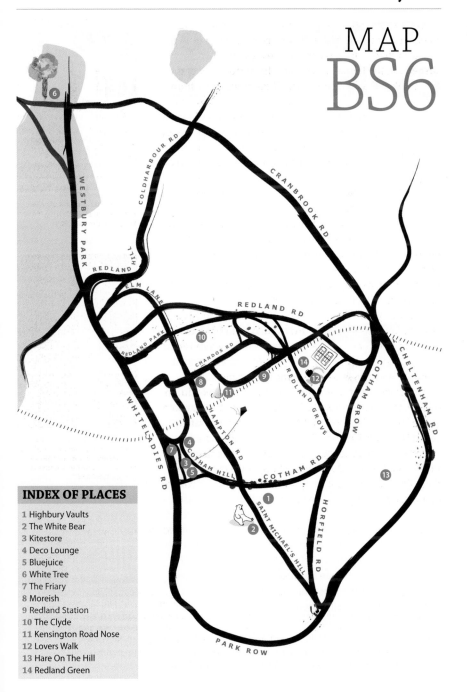

INDEX OF PLACES

BS7 Ashley Down to Cheltenham Road

Welcome to Gloucester Road. It may be a bit shabby, but it has got a certain chic quality as well

I f you're not rich enough to live in Clifton, and don't like the idea of being south of the river, BS7 is the place for you. The A38 Gloucester Road is the main artery that connects the more sedate parts of the area to the fleshpots of the town centre. It's an odd mixture of the chic and the shambolic; parts of it are in decay, other bits are bursting with energy. But beware of heading too far out of town on the A38, Patchway beckons…

■ The Arches on Gloucester Road are one of Bristol's best known landmarks. It is also useful for carrying trains over the road.

Past Notes

▶ **1750** Two mounds of earth used for archery practice are christened 'Horfield Butts'.

▶ **1880** Horfield Road is renamed Gloucester Road.

▶ **1921** Postmaster General FG Kellaway lends his name to the Kellaway bit of Kellaway Avenue.

▶ **1990** Despite 16,664 local objections, a Tesco store is built on Golden Hill.

ASHLEY DOWN

Set between Gloucester Road, St Paul's, St Andrew's and St Werburgh's, Ashley Down is one of those places you walk through on the way to somewhere else. It wasn't always this way. A couple of centuries ago, a spring in Ashley Down provided most of Bristol with its water supply. And the ludicrously steep allotments on Ashley Hill are a reminder of the days when the area was nothing but farmland. It wasn't until the 18th Century that houses began to be built here, when a number of well-heeled gentlemen chose the site because of its panoramic views over the city. But the most significant resident was a German immigrant called George Müller. Indeed Müller could be called the Patron Saint of Ashley Down. During his lifetime, he educated more than 120,000 children at his orphanage, which is now part of the City of Bristol College. At his funeral in 1898, thousands of people lined

■ After two makeovers, Robin Hood's Retreat is a right nice boozer with great food.

the streets in silent tribute. Today, Ashley Down hums with trainee electricians and beauticians from the College on a weekday, and Rovers and Bristol Rugby fans on alternate Saturdays and Sundays. The Foresters and the Ashley Arms are packed accordingly.

BISHOPSTON

The Nobel Prize winner of 1933, Paul Dirac, began unravelling the mysteries of quantum physics from 15 Monk Road, Bishopston, but even he'd struggle to calculate the rise in house prices around here in the last few years. According to a BBC property programme, Bishopston is one of the UK's 'golden miles': one of the county's hottest areas, where average prices have more than doubled since the previous century shot its bows. It's stupid, it benefits no-one except the banks, but it's easy to see why Bishopston has become so appealing.

Naked Truth

Massive Attack's schooling

66 Robert Del Naja (aka 3D or Delge) of Massive Attack was kicked out of the sixth form at Monks Park School, Horfield, for repeatedly turning up with his hair dyed different colours. The last time it was blue. 99

QUICK PINT?

The Robin Hood's Retreat has real ale and an impressive menu.

Close enough to the Gloucester Road to pop out for a drink at half past ten on a Tuesday night, but far enough away to ensure you don't step in any Miss Millie's Fried Chicken carcasses as you walk through your front door, Bishopston gives its residents the best of both worlds.

As well as all the shops, cafes and restaurants, it can also claim to be the home of Bristolian sport. Both the Memorial Stadium, where Bristol Rovers and Bristol Rugby Club play, and Gloucestershire County Cricket Ground are located within walking distance. The city's oldest public swimming pool, Bristol North Baths, had been right at its centre. The baths are now closed, but not without a fight from local protestors.

GLOUCESTER ROAD

One of Bristol's longest and most interesting streets, Gloucester Road is an extraordinary mish-mash of trendy bars, spit 'n' sawdust pubs, chic restaurants and cheap cafes. It also has more charity shops per square metre

Five things...
To buy near Gloucester Rd

1 A wooden giraffe and a brightly-coloured shirt from **La Maison du Zigou Dam, African shop**, 336 Gloucester Road.

2 A bag of 100 singles from **Plastic Wax Records**, 222 Cheltenham Road.

3 A Smeg fridge from **Nailsea Electrical**, 171 Gloucester Road.

4 An onion-coated salami and some Y Fenni Welsh cheese from **T & P A Murray** butchers and delicatessen, 153 Gloucester Road.

5 A nice fairtrade, organic cotton shirt from the **Bishopston Trading Company**, 193 Gloucester Road.

than anywhere else in the South West. Cancer Research, St Peter's Hospice, Sue Ryder, Tenovus… you name them, they're all selling terrible jumpers from the 1980s.

Daytime browsers should be prepared to lose hours and sacrifice the soles of their feet in order to fully explore Glossy Road's multitude of nook-and-cranny stores. The best place to begin is around the junction with Ashley Down Road where the Tinto Lounge shares pavement space with the Antiques Warehouse. As you tread southwards, you'll stumble across a vintage Sicilian delicatessen (Licata's), several 1950s-style Italian barbers, hundreds of unwanted Spandau Ballet LPs, thousands of dusty Penguin novels, enough vintage furniture to decorate a castle, an entire shop devoted to the footwear of a certain Dr Marten and an ever growing range of 'gert lush' Bristol dialect T-shirts from Beast.

BITE TO EAT?

Try the Bhel Puri at **Dil Se** 386 Gloucester Road, a vegetarian Indian take-away and delicatessen.

■ The Prince of Wales on Gloucester Road offers excellent food which is almost all organic.

If you get hungry along the way, the choices are just as varied; from deep-fried chicken in a bucket to award-winning curry, pavement-fried hot-dogs to authentic pizza houses. Gloucester Road is alive with a dizzy melody of aromas from all over the world, especially after dark. New flavours such as the Mediterranean-influenced Bistro La Barrique and the Turkish eaterie Ezo now sit alongside old favourites such as the Sheesh Mahal, the Ganges and the Taste of Morocco and an ever-increasing number of

Three strangest shops

Romantica
A peculiar cross between a Liberace museum and the bedroom of the person with the biggest collection of greetings cards in the world. Twee cuddly toys vie for your attention alongside posters of semi-naked girls near motorbikes.
■ 139 Gloucester Road ■ Tel: 949 3303

Help The Animals
Beware. You may find yourself drawn into this place, such is the bizarre nature of the frontage. With its original 1960s sign lettering, this is the charity shop that time forgot on a road that boasts some of Bristol's least

bijou charity dens. The window displays are notoriously bleak. The design team drape, say, a yellow cardigan next to a snakes-and-ladders game and lean a broken tennis racket against a naked, one-eyed doll.
■ 7 Gloucester Road ■ Tel: 942 7822

Brewer's Droop
Fermentation vessels, thermometers, hydrometers, yeasts, sterilisation equipment, dried hops, empty bottles and bizarre corking devices aplenty live in this musty and decidedly bearded cathedral of home brewing. If you've ever had the urge to make beer that tastes like old socks, this is the place to come for advice.
■ 36a Gloucester Road ■ Tel: 942 7923

take-aways for the inebriated to stumble into after closing time. Typically, these places are of the strip-lit, no-frills, get-it-down-yer-neck variety. The reason there are so many late-night temples of grease is the number of pubs on Gloucester Road these days. Some are mysterious, net-curtained affairs that haven't changed since the 1960s. But the stylish refurbishments of familiar haunts such as the New Prince of Wales and the Prom Wine Bar and the arrival of the 'shabby-chic' likes of the One30 bar (now The Social) and the Pipe & Slippers on Cheltenham Road suggest that the area is shaking off its reputation as a bit of a rough place to drink on a Saturday night.

Naked Truth

Jack Board

❝Jack Board, the Gloucestershire and England wicketkeeper in the early 1900s, lived at 22 Manor Road in Bishopston. He died in 1924 on board ship returning to Bristol from South Africa.❞

■ Second-hand clothes emporium RePsycho is also home to the Prime Cuts record store.

But what really gives Gloucester Road its 'there and back again' charm is the mixture of old-established businesses and curious newcomers attracted by the cosmopolitan vibe. Butchers Stutt & Son has been trading on Gloucester Road since 1919, Pawsons the greengrocers first opened its doors in 1958 while the Bizarre second-hand furniture shop and Bishop Antiques have been there since the 1970s. It may be long, mainly straight and often scruffy, but Gloucester Road has got deep roots.

QUICK PINT?

The Prince of Wales on Gloucester Rd has organic food and a beer garden.

Archibald Alec Leach better known as CARY GRANT was born in this house 18th January 1904

■ Cary Grant was born in Hughendon Road, Horfield, and went to Bishop Road School in Bishopston.

HORFIELD

When Buffalo Bill and his Wild West extravaganza came to town in September 1891, he headed for Horfield Common where a 15,000 seat stadium had been built for his twice-daily performances. It was the biggest show ever staged in Bristol: four trainloads of animals, performers and equipment arrived at Temple Meads; the parade up Gloucester Road to Horfield was a mile long. Buffalo Bill (real name Colonel William Cody) staged 12 performances over six days to a combined audience of more than 100,000 people who all paid a shilling each to attend this huge spectacle.

Horfield could attract the stars in those days, although, even 100 years ago, the residents of Horfield were so badly behaved that the area was considered a no-go zone for travellers. All manner of nasty vagrants and thieves liked to lurk in the large wood near the common and records show that one commentator believed the area was 'lawless… worse even than Filton'. Maybe it's appropriate that Bristol's main prison was dumped here.

By the 1930s, Horfield had grown into one of those solidly working-class communities where people left the doors open and no-one ever got burgled. These days the recycling bins of the two-up-two-down terraced streets are full of *Guardians* and *Observers*.

■ Tinto Lounge on Gloucester Road is just one of the locally-owned chain of bars to hit Bristol.

BITE TO EAT?

Pop in to **Oh! Calcutta** on Gloucester Road and sample their modern slant on traditional Indian cuisine.

Conversely, the shops remain cheap and not very cheerful. Just so you know, everything in the Pound Store is a quid, so don't make the mistake of asking the assistant how much something is, as someone not a million miles away from the keyboard that is typing these words once did.

The Tinto Lounge, one of a chain of Lounge bars around the city, has brought a touch of sophistication over the road from The Royal Oak (winner of Evening Post Pub of the Year 2010) it is a very good family pub and reflects

Bristol's last execution

Russell Pascoe, a 23-year-old Bristolian, was the last person to be executed in Bristol. He was hanged at Horfield Prison at 8am on Tuesday 17 December 1963 for his part in the murder of a Cornish farmer. Dennis Whitty, convicted with him, was hanged at the same time in Winchester.

The execution was one of the last to be carried out in Britain before the abolition of capital punishment in 1965. About 70 protesters held a silent vigil outside the prison gates. The Bishop of Bristol, the Rt Rev Oliver Tomkins, who had earlier protested at the death sentence, visited Pascoe in his cell shortly before the hanging. According to the newspaper reports of the time, he emerged pale-faced and weary at the prison gates.

The Bishop asked the 70 people keeping the silent vigil to pray for the condemned man. But when he asked for 'a kind thought for the men who hate having to carry out this unpleasant task', a man shouted: 'They don't have to do it!' The Bishop replied: 'They do.' The demonstrators had kept up a day-and-night protest vigil since the previous Saturday and were joined by Bristol South East MP Tony Benn the night before the execution. Pascoe and Whitty, who had been living with three women in a caravan near Truro, were sentenced to death at Cornwall Assizes for the murder of 64-year-old farmer William Rowe during a robbery. Their appeals were dismissed and on the Saturday before their execution the Home Office said that the Home Secretary had found no grounds for a reprieve. The demonstrators at Horfield included university students, lecturers and a contingent from Cornwall. The *Bristol Evening Post* reported that as the demonstrators dispersed shortly after 8am, one man shouted: 'Sickening! The people of Bristol should have torn the gates down instead of just standing around!' The Bishop of Bristol issued a statement in which he said Pascoe's execution: 'no more justifies hanging than the fact that war may evoke heroism is a justification of war'.
Horfield Prison, 17 December 1963

the growing trend for people with young kids to drag them to the pub and chuck them in the beer garden whilst supping red wine).

The top end of Gloucester Road is overcoming its reputation as the land that time forgot as the Golden Lion, The Chimp House bar and coffee house Lashings and new shops and small galleries bring new life to the area.

■ **St Andrew's Park is a large green haven just off the busy Gloucester Road.**

ST ANDREW'S

This area is clustered around the charming, softly rolling features of St Andrew's Park. Most people laugh when they drive along Effingham Road because it's as close to swearing as a street name can get without someone alerting the authorities. But it's possible that only a handful of people who live outside this most underrated of BS7 areas have ever laid eyes on the very unexpected Sefton Park Post Office and Shop on Surrey Road. This is retailing as a fish out of water; one lone money-making mirage right in the middle of a completely unspectacular residential street. It might be just around the corner from the County Ground but this shop belongs to a more gentle commercial age. Please try to visit. But, a word of advice: think of something to buy before you go in.

Apart from its undiscovered shop, St Andrew's is probably best known for its park.

> **Naked Truth**
>
> **The Memorial Stadium**
> 66 Bristol Rugby Club moved to the Filton Avenue Ground in 1921. It was dedicated as a memorial to local rugby players who died in World War One. Bristol defeated Cardiff 19-3 in the opening match. The Rugby Club now shares the ground with Bristol Rovers. 99

> **QUICK PINT?**
>
> **The Wellington** on Horfield Common is a Bath Ales boozer and handy for the football.

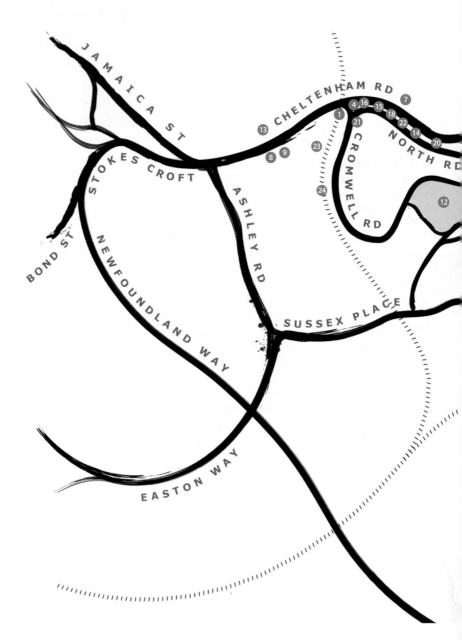

MAP
BS7

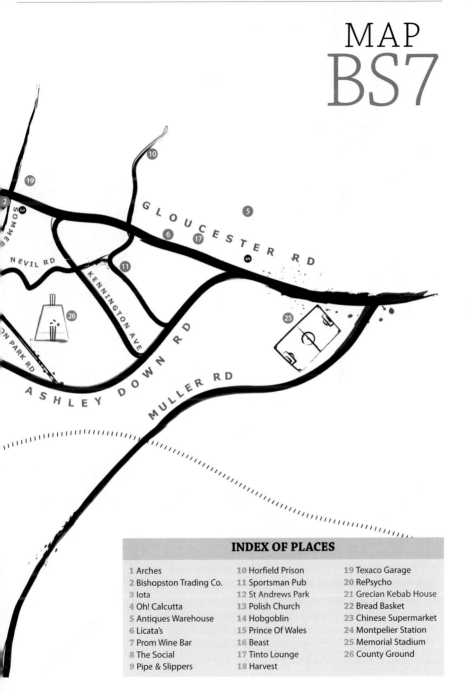

INDEX OF PLACES

BS8 Clifton to Blackboy Hill

The Merchant Venturers built much of Clifton, and quite a few of them still live there

I t wasn't that long ago that the only places to get a pint on Whiteladies Road were in the intimate surroundings of the Vittoria and the less hospitable environs of the Dug and Duck next to the ABC Whiteladies Cinema. Now Whiteladies Road is a bar-and-restaurant student playground awash with cafes and cocktails. Clifton hasn't changed that much though…

Past Notes

▶ **350BC** An Iron Age camp appears on Observatory Hill, just above the Suspension Bridge.

▶ **1080** Clifton is described in the Domesday Book as a settlement of around 30 agricultural folk.

▶ **1130** The area falls into the aristocratic hands of a certain William de Clifton.

▶ **1791** Building begins on Royal York Crescent. It takes almost 30 years to complete.

CLIFTON

Bristol's most affluent area sits high above the rest of the city on top of the Avon Gorge. Clifton has got it all: it has an observatory, a camera obscura, the second oldest zoo in Britain – even its very own 'designer' suspension bridge. There's more. Clifton is quiet without being boring, lively without being rowdy; it has more than its fair share of pubs and places to eat, but take-aways are few and far between. No matter where you are in Clifton, you're only a brisk stroll away from Park Street, Whiteladies Road and the City Centre. And then there's Durdham Down, Clifton's unofficial back garden; not to mention Ashton Court and Leigh Woods about a mile over the bridge. And it's not just geographically and aesthetically superior; Clifton has the edge historically too. The fact that it is mentioned in the Domesday Book means Clifton is older than Bristol itself.

There are remains of an iron-age camp near Clifton Suspension Bridge that date back to 350BC. But this

■ Clifton Arcade on Boyces Avenue is just the ticket for jeans, vinyl, pet portraits and urns.

■ The Albion is tucked away down the end of Boyces Avenue. The food is expensive pub grub but the cocktails are worth the visit.

being Clifton, it wasn't long before those primitive ways made way for a more refined design for living. From the late 18th Century onwards, the area became a magnet for artistic types and the wealthy. Cricketing legend WG Grace bought a house in Victoria Square, Charles Dickens and Oscar Wilde paid a visit and then the bizarre camera obscura was built.

Clifton stood for culture. And even as recently as the giddy days of post-punk, Clifton was a hotbed of creative activity. In the daytime, the long-gone Focus Cafe was full of dangerous-looking people with long coats and connections to

Naked Truth

Camera Obscura
66William West may have been one of the first ever conceptual photo-artists. Why else would he lease an old windmill on the Downs and turn it into an observatory, complete with a telescope and a camera obscura?99

The Pop Group. In the evening, in the back bar of The Lion in Cliftonwood, bands were formed and the record labels Heartbeat and Fried Egg were born. From this whirr of DIY energy came The Cortinas, Social Security, The Europeans, Maximum Joy, the Spics, Jimmy Galvin, Pigbag and more. In 1979, Clifton was the only place to be.

QUICK PINT?
The terrace of the **Avon Gorge Hotel** has fantastic views over the bridge and gorge.

But by the end of the 1980s, the Albion was full of tosspots and their cling-on girlfriends. They thought they were Ben from Curiosity Killed The Cat but they looked more like Huey Lewis from the News. These tragic Jeremys and Nigellas used to be known as 'sloanes'. And they're still hanging around the village now. Sure, they've swapped the rugger-shirts and Barbours for jeeps and beats but the accents and manners are unmistakable. 'An evening at Bar Ha! Ha! and then onto Po Na Nas.' Useless. Boring. Ignore them. But whatever you do, don't ignore Clifton. It might have lost most of its jagged bohemian edges but at least the activity in Christchurch Studios which is run by the Bristol Old Vic Theatre School and whose clients include Massive Attack and Andy Sheppard means it's not an entirely dry zone. And there's plenty of life too at the Amoeba cafe-bar and gallery, the Clifton Arcade, the Grapes, the Corrie Tap and The Lansdown. But who put that skanky supermarket right in the middle of Princess Victoria Street?

Five unusual...
BS8 landmarks

1 **Blackboy Hill Victorian urinal**: needs must and all that.

2 **Queens Court:** the art-deco flats on St Paul's Road.

3 **Toilets** near the water tower on the Downs: Victoria Hughes cared for sex workers when she worked here as a lavatory attendant from 1929 to 1962.

4 **The Trim Trail** on the Downs: bizarre pre-gym outdoor training option.

5 **BUPA hospital,** top of Blackboy Hill: once Tiffany's, Bristol's leading plastic-palm-tree disco.

CLIFTON SUSPENSION BRIDGE

One of the most famous landmarks in the world and the most obvious reminder of Isambard Kingdom Brunel's engineering genius, the Clifton Suspension Bridge story goes back to 1753. This was when Bristol wine merchant William Vick left a legacy to build a bridge over the Avon Gorge. In 1829, the Merchant Venturers appointed a bridge committee which announced a bridge design competition with a first prize of 100 guineas. Brunel was 23 and recuperating in Clifton from the injuries he had received when the Thames Tunnel (on which he was working with his father, Marc Brunel) had flooded. He submitted four plans for the competition. His favourite design involved a 91-metre tunnel which emerged from the side of the gorge and ran into another tunnel on the Leigh Woods side. In all, 22 plans were submitted. The elderly Thomas Telford, one of the best engineers of his day, dismissed all the designs, including Brunel's, and instead offered one of his own that involved two mammoth pillars being built from the foot of the gorge. The Venturers rejected this too and in 1831 Brunel's design was accepted. However, big business was reluctant to invest in Bristol following the Queen Square riots of 1831 and it was five years before work began.

In 1836, an iron bar 305 metres long was hauled across the gorge and a basket to transport men and materials slung from it. Brunel himself made the first crossing and the basket stuck at the lowest point 60 metres above the

■ The legendary Primrose Cafe is cafe by day and cosy restaurant by night.

■ Clifton Suspension Bridge was designed in 1831 for horsedrawn traffic, but now carries four million cars each year.

BITE TO EAT?

The York Cafe in York Place is famous for waving a greasy spoon at Clifton's more refined eateries.

Clifton Lido

One of the more unusual places in Bristol is the restored Clifton Pool tucked away in Oakfield Grove next to the Victoria pub behind the Victoria Rooms. Yet it took a monumental effort to prevent this genuine oddity from being demolished and turned into yet more drab flats. The Grade II listed pool – the first electrically-heated pool in the UK in the 1930s – was closed in 1990 after springing a leak. In 1997, Sovereign Homes told the City Council they wanted to demolish the 150 year-old Egyptian-themed heritage site and build some flats. 'No problem,' said the culture-blind suits at College Green. But then the Glass Boat Company (the people behind innovative eateries Glass Boat and Spyglass) bought the site and put forward ambitious plans to renovate the pool, introduce sauna, spa and massage rooms and create a restaurant and cafe. Despite the application getting gagged and bound in council red tape, the project was completed and the resulting Clifton Lido is a sophisticated urban misfit.

river. Brunel climbed out of the basket, up the rope and released the cable from the jammed pulley. By 1843, the two towers were completed but funds were exhausted. To save money, the committee reduced the height of the towers and scrapped the decorative sphinxes on them. Brunel died in 1859 aged 53, through overwork and 40 cigars a day, without seeing the completion of his bridge, which he referred to in his diary as: 'My first love, my darling.' The opening ceremony for the bridge was on 8 December 1864.

■ Royal York Crescent is one of the longest terraces of its type in Europe. There is no number 13.

Naked Truth

Flying under the bridge

❝The first plane to fly under Clifton Suspension Bridge was piloted by Frenchman M Tetard in 1911. The practice was banned but in 1957 a pilot from 501 Sqn, Filton flew a Vampire jet underneath the bridge at a speed of 450mph. He crashed into the side of the gorge and was killed instantly.❞

HOTWELLS

As part of the extensive research carried out on your behalf for the

QUICK PINT?

Enjoy the **Merchants Arms,** a peaceful Bath Ales pub on Merchants Road.

purpose of writing this book, the entire publishing team, plus one hitch-hiker on crutches, descended on Hotwells to see what, if anything, had changed. And the one single most significant thing we can report about the area is that it is really, really noisy. Standing on the pavement trying to cross four lanes of traffic on Hotwell Road, the peaceful drink or two we had planned down by the Harbourside felt as if it was in another dimension. Still, it's not as if there's a shortage of ale houses around here. From the Adam & Eve on Hope Chapel Hill to the Three Tuns in St George's Road, Hotwells has more great pubs than its status as Lower Clifton deserves.

■ The terrace of the White Lion at the Avon Gorge Hotel offers a great view of the Clifton Suspension Bridge.

Until 1934, there used to be an almost perpendicular railway at the foot of the gorge that could take passengers up to Clifton in 40 seconds. You can still see the facade of the Clifton Rocks funicular railway on Hotwell Road near the suspension bridge. The station at the top was next to the current Avon Gorge Hotel. There also used to be a spring that gushed out of St Vincent's Rock that drew tourists from miles around. But back to our walk around the pubs of Hotwell Road. What places like The Bear Inn (261 Hotwell Road) offer is something a little off the cultural beaten track. Every Friday night, for example, The Bear turns into the Bebop Club, a live jazz happening for purists. But for this gang of fume-choked investigators, it's the places that sit on the docks that beckon. Timbers well and truly shivered, we sail into the Nova Scotia (1 Nova Scotia Place), one of the city's last great 19th-Century maritime haunts. It's cosy inside; cold outside. We sit down by the water and freeze. After that we hit the Pump House (Merchants Road), just on the other side of the water. It's more of a restaurant than a bar, but a good place to sit outside in the summer. Next up there is the impossibly pink Rose of Denmark (6 Dowry Place) which offers a friendly welcome and excellent food downstairs in the old cellar. Then on to the Merchants Arms (5 Merchants Road), a Bath Ales pub with an excellent selection of fine beers and the snuggest of wood-panelled snug bars. Back on the main road, the Spring Gardens (118 Hotwell Road) has reverted back to a live music venue after several years as a gastro pub. The Mardyke (126 Hotwell Road) isn't best known for its food, (although there's the Mardyke Cafe next door), but rather as Bristol's premier bikers' pub. On the day of our visit it was biker-free – and very empty. The Plume of Feathers (135 Hotwell Road) on the opposite side of the four lanes of traffic used to be a lively, if cramped, music venue; now it seems to have reverted back to being a quiet local.

BITE TO EAT?

The **Clifton Sausage** on Portland Place offers classic English cuisine and tasty bangers.

The Hope and Anchor on Jacobs Wells Road has a lovely large Victorian walled garden, a good selection of real ale, a lively atmosphere and a wide range of excellent food. Just round the corner the Three Tuns (78 St George's Road) has been given a new haircut by Arbor Ales and adopted a woody and relaxed feel. It also has a dog that rings the pub bell to call Time. Sadly real ale favourite the Bag 'O Nails (141 St George's Road) was closed at the time of writing. It used to be called the American Eagle. Top beer and all that, but surely they could have come up with a better name – from a noble bird of prey to a something that your dad keeps in his shed. It would be a little unfair to say that described Hotwells.

■ The entrance to Clifton Rocks funicular railway can still be seen on the Portway. The railway closed in 1934.

■ The Merchants Arms in Hotwells is one of the growing number of Bath Ales pubs in the city.

HOTWELLS SPA

HOW BRISTOL BECAME A TOP BRITISH SPA TOWN

Hot hot hot

The Hotwells area of Bristol takes its name from the hot well or spring that once made Bristol one of the most important spa towns in Britain. The spring is still there, it runs into the Avon below Hotwell Road, just south of the Suspension Bridge. The gassy water emerges at 76 degrees Fahrenheit (23C). According to an analysis carried out in 1912, the water is 170 times more radioactive than the public water supply. Hardly surprising then, that those who have taken the water say it produces a similar sensation to being drunk. The spring was once at the centre of an impressive spa and leisure complex, but today very few Bristolians would even know where to find it. The problem was that the spring was beneath the water level of the River Avon for all but one and a half hours a day.

Bristol's worldwide fame

There is some evidence that the waters were being taken as far back as the 15th Century when sailors used it as a cure for scurvey and other skin conditions. Certainly, it was attracting enough publicity by 1676 for the Merchant Venturers to buy the land, along with most of Clifton. The water was held in a brick reservoir (or well) to prevent contamination from the river. By the end of the 17th Century, bottled Bristol spa water was being sent all over the world.

In 1695, the Venturers leased the spring to Charles Jones and Thomas Callow for £5 a year, on condition that they spent £500 on developing the area. By 1723, a pump room and assembly room had been built and high society flocked to Hotwells to take the waters, attend lavish balls and take river cruises on the Avon. The restorative powers of the water attracted the medical profession to Hotwells and by the mid 18th Century, Dowry Square had become Bristol's Harley Street. In 1729, a playhouse was built at Jacobs Wells then another spring was discovered in the Avon Gorge. Another pumphouse and more lodging houses were built as the Hotwells boom continued. But the second spa

had closed by the end of the 18th Century because access was difficult. The original hot well continued to draw worldwide visitors to take the waters and enjoy this lively resort.

Fallen from grace

A second assembly room was built and the Colonnade was constructed to house expensive shops; it's a private house now on the side of the Portway, but the distinctive columns are still standing. Then the boom economy went bust almost overnight. Samuel Powell, who took over the lease in 1790, more than doubled spa prices; at around the same time a Dr Beddoes in Dowry Square publicly questioned the healing powers of the water and the rumours began to spread that the spring was no longer effective. The boarding houses became known as Death Row with only those desperate for a cure coming to Hotwells. The Avon was highly polluted and the area rapidly fell into decay. It's not a pretty picture: incurable consumptives, run-down houses and a river full of turds. Unsurprisingly, polite society preferred the attractions of Bath or the Continental spa towns.

Various attempts were made to revive the spa and to pump the water up to Clifton to avoid the increasing stench from the Avon. The last serious effort to reestablish Bristol as a spa town was in 1890 when the Merchant Venturers granted permission to George Newnes to build the Clifton Rocks funicular railway on condition that he pumped water to Clifton and built a spa next to the station at the top of the Gorge. In 1894, Newnes opened the Grand Pump Room; four years later he completed work on the Grand Spa Hotel next to it (now the Avon Gorge Hotel). But the spa was closed on health grounds in 1913. By 1920, the Grand Pump Room had become a cinema and, in the 1950s, it became one of Bristol's premier rock 'n' roll dancehalls. It's difficult to imagine that the area around the Portway was once one of the most fashionable resorts in the country, or that the hot spring that brought that wealth to Bristol still pours into the Avon.

WHITELADIES ROAD

It's wrongly assumed by some newcomers to the city that the origin of the Whiteladies Road and Blackboy Hill names are a tasteless reminder of the city's shameful slave past. But it was never the case that white ladies would go up the hill to buy black boys. There was no significant domestic slave trade in Bristol, the slavers unloaded their human cargo in the Americas and brought back sugar, tobacco and cotton so there were relatively few black slaves in service in Bristol.

■ The Vittoria used to be one of the few places to get a pint on Whiteladies Road.

> **BITE TO EAT?**
>
> **Falafel King** on Cotham Hill offers a tasty and good-value range of middle eastern dishes. Good for vegetarians.

The name Blackboy is more likely to refer to the tar-painted faces of criminals who were hanged on the gallows on the Downs. Or it could be that the Blackboy Hill takes its name from the Blackboy Tavern, or Blackamoor's Head, a name popularised at the time of the Crusades when it was used as a description of North African Muslims – many inns were given this name complete with a suitably illustrated sign. It's also possible that the name is a reference to Charles II who was known as the Black Boy because of his swarthy complexion. Whiteladies Road is also probably called after an inn.

Up until a few years ago, the long, straight stretch of road that heads down from the top of Blackboy Hill and comes to an end when it reaches the Victoria Rooms was little more than somewhere you'd pass through on your way to Park Street. But as consensus politics got comfy at the end of the 1990s, so an invasion of super-bars arrived to suck up all the affluence. Suddenly, the street was packed full of swish new drinking dens with names, such as Boom, Bar Humbug, Henry J Beans and the Fine Line and the more established haunts, such as the Vittoria, looked like an oddity from a last orders that time forgot.

Someone, somewhere in marketing, nicknamed the whole thing 'The Strip' and it became Bristol's most sellable night-time leisure mile. Yes, it was bad as that. When the weekend came around, thousands of call centre operatives dressed up like *Blind Date* contestants so they could stand and shiver in queues. And what was it they craved so desperately? Five-deep scrums at every bar, gormless

■ Birdcage Walk in Clifton once led to the 12th-Century St Andrew's Church. The church was destroyed in a bombing raid in 1941.

Ministry of Sound re-mixes chugging away on maximum volume and a wall of bottled alcopops that taste like piss. Thankfully those days are behind us and almost as quickly as it became The Strip, Whiteladies Road has matured into something much more interesting. Along with Stokes Croft, it's the most-changed part of the city in recent years and it's once again possible to spend a great evening here without bumping into somebody who reads *Heat* magazine every week. Planet Pizza (83 Whiteladies Road) does easy eating; Picture House East (85 Whiteladies Road) offers tapas, a huge selection of beers and home-made breads; Entelia (50 Whiteladies Road) has brought its friendly Greek style over from Clifton while Asian eaterie Bangkok House (70 Whiteladies Road) and Italian restaurant Zio (96a Whiteladies Road) have been providing good quality food for as long as anyone can remember. Sasparilla (65 Whiteladies Road) is surely worth at least one visit and almost threatens to be cool. And if all else fails you can always prop up the bar in the old Blackboy Inn (171 Whiteladies Road). 'Pint of Mild is it?'

> ## Naked Truth
>
> **Pembroke Road**
>
> 66 Until the last century, Pembroke Road in Clifton was known as Gallows Acre Lane, a reference to the gallows that stood on the edge of the Downs. 99

> **QUICK PINT?**
>
> **The Quinton House** in Park Place has a good selection of real ales.

■ This doorway round the back of the Avon Gorge Hotel is one of the few remaining clues that the Pump Room used to be here.

MAP
BS8

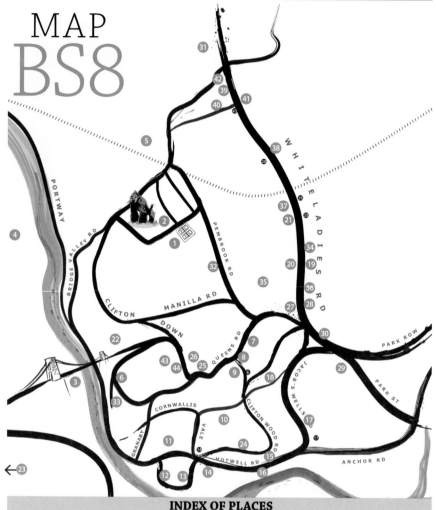

A brief history of Bristol

Everything you need to know about Bristol history from 978 to now...

Bristol was originally a Saxon settlement called Brigstow or Bricgstoc (the place of the bridge) which was formed where the River Frome met the River Avon near the present-day site of Bristol Bridge. The Frome was later diverted and now joins the Floating Harbour in the Centre. The original settlement was on the site of Castle Park (handy for Broadmead) while the Medieval city expanded into the area surrounding Corn Street and St Nicholas Market.

There is little evidence of major Roman influence in Bristol – they seem to have preferred Bath and (unusually) Keynsham, although a Roman Villa was discovered at Kings Weston during the construction of Lawrence Weston housing estate in 1947. Perhaps Bristol is jealous of Bath's Roman heritage, because since the Middle Ages various historians have fabricated a Roman past to help enhance the city's reputation. It's an equally dubious story with Bristol's founders Brennus and Belinus, whose statues are on St John's Gate (the last remaining section of the city wall) at the bottom of Broad Street.

According to *A History of Bristol* by John Corry, printed in 1810 and based on earlier works, Malmutius (c.483BC) – King of Cornwall, and later Monarch of Britain – and Queen Corwenna had two sons, called Brennus and Belinus. It is said that they reigned jointly as Kings of Britain following their father's death and founded a major settlement at Bristol. Many stories are heard about Brennus and Belinus, but there is no evidence that they actually existed, or even that Bristol was founded earlier than Saxon times. Saying that, some records report that the Romans referred to Bristol as *Caer Bren*, or City of Brennus. However, despite allegedly founding Bristol long before Christ was born,

■ Queen Elizabeth I entered through St John's Gate when she visited the city in 1584. It is not recorded whether she popped into Horts for a goblet of Youngs.

Thomas Clarkson
1760 – 1846

Stayed here in 1787 to research the condition of slaves being transported

■ The plaque at the Seven Stars pub in St Thomas which commemorates the site of Clarkson's investigations which led to the slave trade being abolished.

the statues of Brennus and Belinus on St John's Gate show them with crucifixes. Which is slightly odd.

In Welsh legend, Brennus and Belinus were the sons of Dyfnwal Moelmyd, who became King of Britain and built four great roads across the Kingdom, one of which ran alongside a wide gorge at a city known as *Caer Odor*, or The Castle at the Gap. The only remaining reference to Caer Odor appears in the name of the Bristol Welsh Society: *Cymdeithas Cymry Caerodor*.

Even further back in time, the Avon Gorge was said to have been hewn from the rock by two giants, the brothers Vincent and Goram. Goram, who was an idle giant, fell asleep and was tragically killed when Vincent threw a pickaxe to him and it accidentally split his skull in half. This left Vincent distraught and he subsequently left Bristol and headed to Somerset to build Stonehenge. Following this, Vincent swam across to Ireland so that he could construct the Giant's Causeway in what is now County Antrim. He then returned to Bristol and lived by the side of the Avon Gorge, which is why the area is known as Vincent Rocks.

■ Belinus sits alongside his brother Brennus on St John's Arch.

■ A sketch of Bristol believed to date from 1640. It is certainly before 1664 because that is when Cromwell ordered Bristol Castle to be destroyed. Note the shops and houses on Bristol Bridge and St Peter's Church which still stands on Castle Green.

THE BRISTOL HIGH CROSS

A BIT OF MEDIEVAL HISTORY IN BERKELEY SQUARE

One of the few remaining links with Medieval Bristol is tucked away in the corner of a small park in Berkeley Square, off Park Street. It's a replica of the Bristol High Cross, a fine piece of craftsmanship that stood at the centre of the Medieval town. If you imagine that the junction of Corn Street, Broad Street, Wine Street and High Street once formed a town square, that's where the new High Cross was erected to commemorate the granting of Bristol's Charter in 1373. It replaced the previous High Cross, of which there are no remaining records.

The High Cross had four niches containing the statues of King John, Henry III, Edward III and Edward IV, all of whom had contributed to Bristol's expansion by conferring important charters. The whole Cross was gilded and coloured. In 1633, the Cross was repaired and altered to include the figures of Henry VI, Elizabeth I, James I and Charles I, who had further endowed privileges on the city. The Cross was later painted vermilion, blue and gold. By the beginning of the 18th Century, the large Cross, surrounded by steps and an iron fence, was becoming an obstruction in the increasingly busy streets. In 1733, the deputy chamberlain, Mr Vaughan, who lived at the corner of High Street and Wine Street, claimed his life and house were in danger from it every time the wind blew. A petition for its removal described the Cross as 'a superstitious relick' and 'a public nuisance'. Magistrates ordered the Cross to be put away in the Guildhall.

After protests, the High Cross was re-erected on College Green. However, in 1763, the fashionable set, who walked eight or ten abreast on the Green, complained that it impeded their promenading. It was taken down again and stored in a corner of the Cathedral. In 1765, it was given away by the Dean of Bristol to his friend Henry Hoare of Stourhead to use as an estate ornament. The High Cross is still at Stourhead and, in 1973, the Lord Mayor of Bristol unveiled a plaque there as part of the celebrations for the 600th anniversary of the granting of the city's

■ **This hidden gem can be found in the corner of Berkeley Square, just off Park Street.**

charter. In 1848, a replica High Cross was built and erected on College Green. That, too, was demolished because of vandalism; it is the top part of this replica that survives in Berkeley Square. One of the missing statues from the replica is said to be in a private garden in Bedminster, South Bristol.

Occasionally there are campaigns to re-site the High Cross near the top of Corn Street, but they are usually greeted with remarkable indifference. However, the plans announced in 2006 to redevelop the St Mary le Port site opposite St Nick's Church by Bristol Bridge caused such public outrage, that the future of this area and perhaps of the High Cross could well come to the fore. There was another medieval High Cross on Gallows Hill (St Michael's Hill) that marked the city boundary, but there is no record of what happened to it.

A BLUFFER'S GUIDE TO BRISTOL HISTORY

55BC The Romans invade Britain. The Dobunni tribe who live in the Bristol area defend themselves at Blaise, Leigh Woods and Clifton Down. There is no Roman Bristol, though there is a fort and port at Sea Mills.

C10 th **978** Two silver coins minted in Bristol at the beginning of the reign of Ethelred II (978-1016) are the first evidence of Saxon Bristol as a centre of commerce and proof that it has its own mint. They carry the stamp of the coin maker 'Aelfward on Bric'.

C11 th **1066** Population of Bristol thought to be somewhere between 4,000 and 5,000.

1067 Bristol surrenders to William The Conqueror without a fight. Then King Harold's sons launch an unsuccessful attack on the town from Ireland in an attempt to unseat the Normans. They are beaten back from the city gates and pillage Somerset instead.

1086 The Domesday Book records that Bristol is part of the Manor of Barton. The name Barton survives in the Barton Hill (pronounced 'Bart Nil') area of Bristol, famous for its multi-coloured tower blocks and the Rhubarb public house. By now Bristol is an established port trading with Dublin. There is some evidence of a white slave trade between Bristol and Ireland.

1088 First record of the original Bristol Castle near Bristol Bridge.

C12 th **1115** First church built on the present site of St Mary Redcliffe.

1120 Robert, Earl of Gloucester, begins strengthening Bristol Castle. The Castle is built of Caen stone and has a large dungeon. The foundation walls of the keep are reputed to have been 25 foot thick.

1140 Robert Fitzhardinge, Bristol's richest citizen, begins work on St Augustine's Abbey, later to become Bristol Cathedral.

1155 Bristol is granted its first Royal Charter confirming certain rights of the townspeople. No record of this charter survives.

1171 After the English conquer Ireland, Henry II gives Dublin to the people of Bristol as a colony. Many Bristolians settle there.

1188 Date of the earliest surviving Royal Charter. King John's Charter reveals that Bristol is by now a thriving merchant town with a penchant for protectionism – a tradition carried on to this day by the Society of Merchant Venturers (see Underground & Radical Bristol, p98). According to the Royal Charter, non-Bristolians could not buy leather, corn or wool from 'foreigners', only from Bristol merchants.

C13 th **1203-41** Princess Eleanor of Brittany is imprisoned in Bristol Castle for all of her life in order to prevent her producing an heir to the throne to rival the Plantagenets: King John and his son Henry III.

1216 The first Mayor of Bristol is appointed.

1220 Foundation of Gaunt's Hospital, later to become the Lord Mayor's Chapel.

1239-47 River Frome is diverted, using just spades and wheelbarrows, to provide more quays to cater for the increase in trade at the port. The work costs £5,000 and the river now provides a soft muddy bottom for boats to rest on when the tide is out. The diverted Frome is 2,400 foot long, 18 foot deep and 120 foot wide. It is one of the most remarkable feats of civic engineering of its time. It was so remarkable that future town planners concrete over it years later.

1247 First record of a High Cross at the junction of High Street and Corn Street.

C14th

1312 The Bristol Tax Riots: the earliest recorded riots in Bristol and the beginning of a tradition of civil disobedience that saw its most recent expression in St Paul's in 1980. Bristolians rise up in anger when Edward II introduces another tax on shipping. The Mayor, William Randolph, takes over control of collecting the taxes and the ship money from Bristol. Rioting starts soon after; Edward II appoints the Constable of the Castle with powers to overrule the corporation. Thomas de Berkeley is appointed to stop the riots. Twenty men are killed and the King's officers are driven into the castle by the rioters. They remain under siege until the barons call in the army. After four days, the city surrenders. Edward II pardons the rioters but fines them.

1327 Edward II is imprisoned at Bristol Castle. He is then moved to Berkeley Castle in Gloucestershire where he is murdered by having a red-hot poker shoved up his bum.

1371 Bristol linen merchant Edward Blanket, the (ahem) inventor of the blanket, dies. His tomb is in St Stephen's Church, just off the Centre. Blanket lived in Tucker Street and was MP for Bristol in 1362.

1373 Edward III grants Bristol a charter on 8 April making the city the first provincial borough to be a county in its own right. Bristol pays 600 marks for the charter. Edward needs the money to fund the war against France. The first Sheriff of Bristol is appointed; a new High Cross is erected at the junction of Broad Street, Wine Street, Corn Street and High Street to commemorate the event.

1390 Work begins on Temple Church, Bristol's equivalent to the Leaning Tower of Pisa. Work on the church stops when the tower begins to lean and starts again in 1460. The sloping is partially corrected thanks to some heavy stone laying. But by the time it is hit in the Blitz, it has been tilting again for some years and isn't going to stand up straight for that Hitler fella.

C15th

1446 With rebuilding work almost complete at St Mary Redcliffe Church, the roof is struck by lightning during a violent electric storm and destroyed. The repair work is funded by merchant William Canynges who was Mayor of Bristol five times and the city's Member of Parliament twice.

1497 John Cabot sets sail from Bristol in The Matthew and discovers North America. Born Giovanni Caboto in Genoa around 1451, Cabot is thought to have arrived in Bristol in about 1480 with an ambition to look for Hy-Brasil, an island somewhere in the Atlantic, according to Celtic legend. Cabot leaves Bristol on 20 May 1497 on board The Matthew with a crew of 18. He lands on the East Coast of America on 24 June 1497. On his return to Bristol, Cabot is rewarded for his discovery with a pension of £20 a year. In 1498, he sets off for America again, this time with five ships, and is never heard of again. Cabot's new-found land is named America after the Bristol merchant Richard Amerike.

C16th

1532 Foundation of Bristol Grammar School by Robert and Nicholas Thorne.

1542 Diocese of Bristol created by Henry VIII.

1552 Society of Merchant Venturers formed.

1555–57 Several martyrs are burned at the stake on St Michael's Hill during the reign of Bloody Queen Mary. The prisoners were led to their deaths from the gaol up the muddy hill that is now Christmas Steps.

1574 Queen Elizabeth visits Bristol and describes St Mary Redcliffe Church as 'The goodliest, fairest and most famous parish church in England'. This is the most overused quote in the history of Bristol and will not appear in this book again.

1586 Foundation of Queen Elizabeth's Hospital School by John Carr. You may see QEH borders around Park Street; they wear traditional Bluecoat uniforms: dark cloaks with white neckbands, knee-length breeches and yellow stockings. Do not be alarmed.

C17th

1610 Bristol merchant John Guy becomes the first governor of Newfoundland.

1634 Foundation of Red Maids' School. John

Whitson, merchant, Mayor and Member of Parliament for Bristol, dies in 1629, bequeathing monies for a hospital for '40 poor women children' to be 'apparelled in red cloth'. The Red Maids School is originally in Denmark Street next to the present-day Hippodrome, but moved to Westbury-on-Trym in 1930. Girls from the school still celebrate Founder's Day.

1636 Slave trader Edward Colston is born in Bristol. Colston funds the development of much of modern Bristol with money from the slave trade and bequeaths a fortune to the city.

1642 Outbreak of the Civil War. Bristol joins the Parliament side.

1643 Bristol is captured by Royalist forces.

1645 Bristol surrenders to Cromwell's Parliament forces.

1654 The destruction of Bristol Castle by Oliver Cromwell.

1655 First Quaker meeting is held in Bristol at a private house in Frenchay.

1660 Bristol apprentices revolt, demanding a free Parliament and the restoration of the Monarchy. On 5 March 1660, the bellman of Bristol makes the usual Puritan proclamation banning cock-throwing and dog-tossing. The rowdy apprentices attack him and the next day (Shrove Tuesday) squail a goose and toss cats and dogs into the air outside the Mayor's Mansion House. To squail a goose is to throw sticks, weighted with lead at one end, at it. The object is to maim the bird without killing it. The authorities are able to quickly bring the apprentices under control and halt all tossing and squailing.

1674 Ralph Ollive becomes Mayor of Bristol on an anti-Quaker ticket. Major persecution of the Society of Friends continues.

1680 Edward Teach (aka Blackbeard the Pirate) is born in Bristol. Blackbeard is believed to be the inspiration for Robert Louis Stevenson's Long John Silver in *Treasure Island*.

1681 William Penn of Bristol establishes a Quaker community in Pennsylvania.

1694 Society of Merchant Venturers organises protests against the Royal African Company's London monopoly of the slave trade.

1695 William Bonny sets up Bristol's first printing press.

1698 The slave trade begins in Bristol when the London monopoly of the Royal African Company is broken.

C18th **1700** The population of Bristol is estimated to have risen to around 25,000.

1702 Work begins on building Queen Square to celebrate a visit to Bristol by Queen Anne.

1702 Bristol's first newspaper, the *Bristol Postboy*, is founded. The 91st issue, published in August 1704, is the earliest surviving copy of a provincial newspaper in the world and is now at the Central Reference Library. It was produced weekly as a single sheet.

1709 Food riots sweep the city. 200 coal miners from Kingswood, always a rowdy bunch, march into the city and riot against a big increase in the cost of food – a bushel of wheat had doubled in price to eight shillings. The miners disperse after being promised a reduction in the price of a bushel to five shillings and sixpence.

1710 Colston School is founded.

1714 Celebrations for the Coronation of George 1 turn into a riot and two people are killed in the violence.

1727-49 The introduction of tollgates on 26 June 1727 sparks off far more serious riots than those of 1709 or 1714. Two days after they are installed, the turnpikes are destroyed. Wherever they appear, the tollgates are wrecked. For a time in 1734, not a single tollgate is left standing between Bristol and Gloucester. This continues for 21 years, the length of time that the law that allows the tollgates is in force.

1728-33 Riots by Easton and Kingswood weavers, impoverished by the industrialisation of their industry, results in a ★ *Turn to page 95*

COLSTON & THE SLAVE TRADE

THE HISTORY OF THE SLAVE TRADE IN BRISTOL FROM 1698 TO ITS ABOLITION IN 1807

BUILT ON SLAVERY

It has been suggested that Bristol should perhaps be the site for a permanent national exhibition about the African slave trade. Perhaps it will take a gesture of that magnitude to make the city finally confront the demons of its past – there's no getting away from the fact that the wealth of modern Bristol is built on slavery.

At the height of the slave trade, in the mid 18th Century, the Bristol economy and the Society of Merchant Venturers thrived on slavery. For example, sugar was returned to the port from the plantations where the slaves were sold, so refineries were built in the city; the refineries needed power, which was provided by the coal mines of Kingswood. The rapid growth of the city and its growing prosperity in the 18th Century and beyond was significantly based on the brutality and immorality of slavery.

Many of the families and institutions that still prosper and hold considerable influence in the city made their money from slavery. The legacy of Edward Colston dominates Bristol. A statue of the MP and slave trader stands in the Centre near the Colston Hall, (opposite the Colston Tower), there are at least a dozen streets named after him and, of course, there's Colston's Schools. There's even a Colston Bun.

COLSTON'S SECRET

Edward Colston was born in Bristol in 1636, the son of a wealthy merchant. He made his money initially by trading with Spain and other Mediterranean countries. However, although he went to great lengths to keep it a secret, Colston became a member of the Royal African Company in 1680 and took an active part in the planning and financing of slaving ventures to Africa, his name appearing in the company records for 11 years.

The African slave trade began in Bristol in 1698 when the London-based Royal African Company lost its monopoly on English trade with West Africa. Between 1698 and the

■ Edward Colston donated much of his fortune from slavery to set up schools and other institutions in Bristol.

abolition of the slave trade in 1807, more than 2,000 ships set sail from Bristol in search of slaves on the West African coast. It's estimated that 500,000 slaves were carried on Bristol vessels out of a total trade of 2.8 million (*The Bristol Slave Traders: A Collective Portrait,* David Richardson), although other researchers put the figure as high as 8 million (*A Shocking History of Bristol*, Derek Robinson). As many as a quarter of the slaves died or were murdered at sea. So it's possible that around two million bodies of slaves were thrown overboard from slave ships.

Liverpool and London were the other two major slave ports, but it is estimated that half of the slave ships that left England for Africa in 1730 sailed from Bristol. The city's share of the slave trade had fallen to 25% by the 1750s as Liverpool became the dominant slave port and, by the time of abolition in 1807, Bristol had just a 2% market share.

WEST AFRICAN TRADERS

The slave trade worked on the triangular model, making a profit on each stage of the voyage. Ships left Bristol with a cargo of cotton, brass, copper, gin or muskets, which were bartered for slaves with the West African traders. The ships then embarked on the Middle Passage to the West Indies or America where the surviving slaves were sold at a profit, often to plantation owners originally from Bristol. The ships then returned home with a cargo of sugar or tobacco which was again sold for profit. During the 18th Century, 32 of the city's leading slave traders became members of the Society of Merchant Venturers and 16 went on to become Master.

Naturally, the Africans fought the traders sent to capture them and many committed suicide when they were captured; thousands more were killed in mutinies or died due to the dreadful conditions at sea. Perhaps most shocking of all, there is a body of evidence which suggests that Bristol captains drowned their entire cargo of diseased slaves so that the loss could be claimed on the owners' insurance as 'legal jettison'.

WOMEN AND CHILDREN

Slave ships were specially converted so they could carry the maximum number of bodies. Typically, a ship would have a hold about five foot high, so the owners built two six-foot wide platforms either side of the hold to create two decks. Slaves were driven into the hold and forced to lie on the bottom in rows until it was covered. Then another layer of people were forced onto the platforms.

On some of the larger ships a second platform was added, giving a headroom of about 20 inches for the three layers of people. The tallest slaves were put amidships; the smaller ones and children were wedged into the stern. The space per person was very restricted. A male slave was allowed a space six foot by 16 inches; a woman was allowed five foot by 16 inches; a boy five foot by 14 inches and a girl four foot by 12 inches. They lived, and died, in these conditions on the passage from Africa to the West Indies and America. They were often seasick and had no alternative but to foul themselves.

The Africans were supposed to be brought on deck every morning to be fed and cleaned, but some captains left them in the holds for the entire journey (between six weeks and three months). Bristol merchants, sea captains and crews were responsible for the most appalling and degrading treatment of human beings. This was a crime as great as the Holocaust.

In June 1787, the Rev Thomas Clarkson arrived in Bristol to begin his fact-finding tour of the slaving ports that was to lead to the abolition of the slave trade some 20 years later. However, it was not just the suffering of the Africans that began to change public opinion, but the poor treatment of the Bristol slave crews.

Naturally, the Society of Merchant Venturers did everything possible to halt Clarkson's investigations, but he persevered. He interviewed 20,000 sailors and collected equipment used on the slave ships, such as iron handcuffs, leg shackles, thumbscrews, instruments for forcing open slaves' jaws, and branding irons. Clarkson set himself up in the Seven Stars pub (which is still there, next to the Fleece and Firkin on Thomas Lane) whose owner was sympathetic to William Wilberforce's anti-slavery movement. Pub landlords played a key role in recruiting crews for the slaving ships, and the landlord of the Seven Stars explained to Clarkson the way the business worked and introduced him to the slaving underworld that inhabited Bristol's dockside taverns. He pieced together a picture of the reality of the business and discovered that crews were recruited in three ways:

Lying: men were lured from the drinking dens of Marsh Street with promises of high wages and an exotic life at sea.

Doping: pub landlords were bribed to spike sailors' drinks and they were abducted.

Blackmail: the landlords encouraged men to borrow money for drink and then threatened them with jail unless they joined a slaving crew.

Once on board, the crew was forced to sign ship's articles legalising their poor pay. Often the crew were paid in virtually worthless foreign currencies.

Clarkson managed to gain access to the Merchant Venturers' records. From their own Muster Rolls, he found that the mortality rates of Bristol slave ship crews were very heavy in comparison to those of other cities involved in the triangular trade. His interviews revealed that the crews were treated appallingly by slaving captains. Some men were murdered; sometimes a quarter of the crew died at sea from disease, ill treatment and torture. Obviously, their suffering was nothing compared to the African people, but Clarkson's revelations began to get the attentions of the Bristol public. Not surprisingly, these revelations started to disturb people.

PUBLIC OUTRAGE

Clarkson managed to take the murder of two seamen on board a slaver to trial, despite two slave traders sitting on the bench at the initial hearing. His witnesses all mysteriously disappeared by the time the case was due to be heard, but finally the word was out and the Bristol public were shocked by what they heard about the treatment of their local sailors. It seems they cared little for the suffering of the slaves, although there was an anti-slavery movement in the city led by Quakers and Methodists. In fact, Bristol was the first city outside London to set up a committee for the abolition of the slave trade; some 800 people volunteered to sign the first Bristol petition against the slave trade in 1788.

The Yorkshire MP William Wilberforce, the public face of the abolition campaign, came to Bristol in 1791 to encourage the local campaign. The poets Robert Southey, William Wordsworth, Hannah More, Anne Yearsley and Samuel Coleridge all wrote against the trade. John Wesley, who founded the Methodist Church, wrote against slavery and preached against the trade in the New Rooms in Broadmead. This was one of the first political campaigns in which women played

an active part and, in 1787, Hannah More was instrumental in organising a boycott of West Indian slave sugar in Bristol.

Parliament first debated a motion calling for the abolition of the slave trade in 1788. The Society of Merchant Venturers and other business interests in Bristol lobbied strongly against Wilberforce and the abolitionists, claiming it would be 'ruinous in the extreme to the petitioners engaged in the manufacture, but the mischief would extend most widely throwing hundreds of common labouring people wholly out of employment'. The slave business won the day and Parliament merely passed an Act aimed at improving conditions on slave ships by limiting the numbers carried. The Bristol Corporation ordered church bells across the city to be rung in celebration.

The Society of Merchant Venturers fought against abolition to the last, even though Bristol's share of the trade was fairly insignificant by comparison at the end of the 18th Century. The merchants could make handsome profits by trading directly with the plantation owners, many of whom were from the city, rather than undertaking the far more risky triangular voyages. The abolition movement suffered a setback in 1793 when Britain went to war with France. The slave trade was seen as the 'nursery of seamen' and abolition of the trade was postponed. Eventually, in 1807, the slave trade in the British colonies was abolished and it became illegal to carry slaves on British ships.

■ The Slave Trail leaflet is available from museums and tourist offices.

■ For further information, please contact the City Museum & Art Gallery, Queens Road, Bristol BS8 1RL. Tel: 922 3571

■ A diagram from the 18th Century showing how slaves were packed onto the lower deck of a Bristol vessel.

mill owner shooting dead eight protesters. Two of the Easton weavers' leaders are executed.

1737 Bristol Royal Infirmary opens.

1739 John Wesley invents Methodism. On 2 April, Wesley gives his first open-air sermon in St Philip's. The New Room in the Horsefair is established as the world's first Methodist chapel later in the year.

1743 The Exchange in Corn Street is built by John Wood The Elder.

1745 The original glass-roofed St Nicholas Market is built.

1749 John Wesley's brother Charles, the greatest ever hymn writer, moves to Bristol and lives in a house at 4 Charles Street, opposite the present site of the bus station.

1750 Population of Bristol about 50,000: the city has doubled in size in just 50 years.

1752 The poet Thomas Chatterton is born into an impoverished Bristol family in Redcliffe.

1753 Very bad harvests in 1752 are the cause of food riots in 1753. Despite shortages, Bristol merchants are still exporting grain for huge profits. On 21 May 1753, Kingswood miners lead a march into the city and ransack a ship, The Lamb, that was preparing to sail with 70 tons of wheat to Dublin. On 25 May, a crowd of 900, made up mostly of colliers and weavers, break into the Bridewell and release prisoners. Four rioters are killed, around 50 injured and 30 are captured.

1766 The Theatre Royal is opened.

1774 The future Poet Laureate Robert Southey is born the son of a linen draper at 9 Wine Street on 12 August.

1780 The development of Upper Clifton begins.

1786 Tobacco company WD & HO Wills is founded by Henry Overton Wills when he moves from Salisbury to Bristol and goes into partnership with Samuel Watkins. They start with their first shop in Castle Street but, by 1791, the firm has expanded and moved to 112 Redcliffe Street.

1799 Humphry Davy administers nitrous oxide to visitors to the Pneumatic Institute in Dowry Square, Hotwells. After watching the effects on people who inhale it, Davy coins the term 'laughing gas'.

C19th **1800** Humphry Davy works with Thomas Beddoes at his clinic in Dowry Square, Hotwells. Davy publishes the book *Researches, Chemical and Philosophical: Chiefly Concerning Nitrous Oxide* in which he describes inhaling nitrous oxide (laughing gas) and obtaining a degree of analgesia from a painful condition he was suffering. Davy's research into anaesthetic effect are not tested and utilised for another 45 years; instead, the primary use of nitrous oxide is for recreational enjoyment and public shows. So-called 'nitrous oxide capers' took place in travelling medicine shows and carnivals, where the public paid a small price to inhale a minute's worth of gas. Many dignitaries and famous individuals come to inhale Davy's purified nitrous oxide for recreational purposes, including the poets Coleridge and Southey, the potter Josiah (later Sir Josiah) Wedgwood, and Roget of Roget's Thesaurus. 'I am sure the air in heaven must be this wonder working gas of delight,' wrote Southey after a swift inhalation in Dowry Square.

1801 Population of Bristol is around 68,000.

1803 An Act of Parliament is passed to allow the construction of the Cut, a new course for the River Avon to enable the Floating Harbour to be created.

1806 Isambard Kingdom Brunel is born at Portsea, near Portsmouth, on 9 April. His mother is English; his father is the great French engineer Sir Marc Isambard Brunel.

1823 The Bristol Chamber of Commerce is established.

1823 A Bristol inventor takes his Charvolant, or Flying Car, to Ascot Races to demonstrate it to George IV. This magnificent contraption, which was tested on Durdham Downs, is the brainchild of Clifton schoolmaster George

Pocock, an eccentric boffin who had already built an automatic caning machine to deal with his wayward pupils. The Charvolant is made up of a carriage for four people that is powered by two giant kites. On a good day, it can reach speeds of 25mph. After displaying his machine to the public, Pocock begins using the Charvolant as a family vehicle, tearing through towns and villages outside Bristol at speeds that scared the living daylights out of the locals. While he might have seemed a complete maniac at the time, in hindsight he looks like an Eco travel pioneer. Albeit an eccentric one.

1831 Riots in Queen Square. The Mansion House, Customs House and other buildings in the Square are destroyed.

1831 Brunel begins work on the Clifton Suspension Bridge. Building stops in 1836 and the project is abandoned in 1853. Work restarts in 1862 and the bridge is eventually opened on 8 December 1864. The final cost of the project is £100,000, about £45,000 over budget. Brunel does not live to see the completion of this wonderful bridge, he died in 1859, aged just 53.

1831 Bones belonging to the Bristol Dinosaur (Thecodontosaurus Antiquus, to give it its proper name) are discovered in a quarry on Durdham Downs. The dinosaur is similar in size and table manners to the Diplodocus and is thought to be one of the oldest of all the giant plant-eating reptiles dating back some 210 million years. Now scientists have even been able to pinpoint the exact spot that the big beast called home. In 1881, local geologist Charles Moore identifies the dinosaur's stomping ground as being in the Belgrave Terrace area off Blackboy Hill, just a rock's throw from the Downs. The area has now been built on, so no more evidence can be found, not that any more fossils are needed. In 1975, five tonnes of Thecodontosaurus bones were found in a quarry near Bristol and the whole lot was taken to the University for further study. It took 25 years for the Bristol Dinosaur Project to secure the funding they needed to start work. In 1999, a team of palaeontologists began the laborious process of separating rock from bone. Needless to say, they're still at it.

1836 Bristol Zoological Gardens opens.

1837 Brunel's Great Western steamship is launched in Bristol.

1841 The opening of Brunel's Great Western Railway between Bristol and London.

1843 Prince Albert visits the Great Western Dockyard in Bristol and names Brunel's new ship the Great Britain.

1848 Hirsute cricket legend WG Grace is born on 18 July in Clematis House, North Street, Downend, though the family lived a few doors away in Downend House.

1861 The Durdham Downs in Clifton are secured as public open spaces.

1862 Clifton College opens. Its most famous old boys are Douglas Haig, the Commander in Chief of the British Army in France in World War One and John Cleese of *Monty Python* and *Fawlty Towers* fame.

1864 On 8 December, the ceremonial opening of Clifton Suspension Bridge takes place – five years after the death of Isambard Kingdom Brunel. A long procession sets off from the city centre, including soldiers, sailors and groups with banners representing various trades, plus organisations and friendly societies of the city. At least 16 bands take part, flags fly, field gun salutes are fired and church bells are rung. After the ceremony at midday there is a banquet for invited guests in the Victoria Rooms and at night the bridge is illuminated for the first time. In 1753, Bristol wine merchant William Vick left a legacy for a bridge to be built over the Avon Gorge. After 110 years of uncertainty, Vick's vision is finally realised.

1870 Gloucestershire Cricket Club is founded.

1876 University of Bristol is founded.

1881 Population of Bristol is 266,000.

1883 Bristol Rovers Football Club is founded as the Black Arabs FC at a meeting at Collins Restaurant on Stapleton Road.

1880s The tradition of a Jack-in-the-Green is resurrected in Victorian Bristol. Jack is nine foot tall, covered from head to toe in flowers and dances like a demented Morris dancer with a firework up his trousers. On the first Saturday in May, Bristol's Jack-in-the-Green still makes his way from the Arnolfini all the way to Horfield Common followed by a colourful procession of flute-blowing vegetation. Why does he do this? In order to release the spirit of summer, of course. Isn't it obvious! This bizarre Victorian tradition probably has its roots in ancient pagan rituals and has only recently been resurrected in Bristol. Crowds are encouraged to follow Jack through the streets and on to his final destination, where he eventually curls up and dies. This is one spectacle that's guaranteed to frighten the life out of any children unlucky enough to be watching.

1881 Robert Louis Stephenson writes *Treasure Island*. The Spyglass Inn in the book is based on the Llandoger Trow pub in King Street. It is still there to this day.

1888 Bristol Rugby Football Club is founded.

1894 Bristol City Football Club is founded as Bristol South End.

1896 On a cold and rainy night on 18 September 1896, a bankrupt grocer called Charles Brown took his two daughters, Ruby and Elsie, up to the Clifton Suspension Bridge and threw them into the muddy water below. Luckily, there was a high tide that night and as the girls plunged into the water, the crew of a passing pilot boat spotted them and dragged them away to safety. Ruby suffered injuries to her spine while Elsie had only minor leg injuries. Both girls had recovered within a couple of weeks. Charles Brown was subsequently arrested and brought to trial. 'Father caught hold of me and I began to scream,' said Ruby while giving evidence in court. 'He lifted me up on the side of the bridge and put me over.' Unsurprisingly, the judge concluded that the poor girls' old man was utterly insane and should spend a considerable amount of time in an asylum.

1897 Bristol Rovers' Eastville Stadium is officially opened on 5 April with the visit of League Champions and FA Cup holders Aston Villa. Rovers lose 5-0 to set the tone for the next 89 years at Eastville.

C20th

1901 Population of Bristol rises to an estimated 330,000.

1904 Hollywood actor Cary Grant is born at 15 Hughenden Road, Horfield on 18 January. He was christened Archibald Alexander Leach.

1908 Edward VII opens the Royal Edward Dock in Avonmouth.

1911 Bristol miners strike for three months over pay and loss of jobs.

1911 Bristol Aeroplane Works opens in Filton.

1914–18 About 55,000 men from the Bristol area enlist for World War One. More than 7,000 men from the Bristol area died.

1917 Avonmouth becomes the centre of the British chemical warfare manufacturing drive. The plant makes 20 tons of mustard gas a day. In December 1918, the plant Medical Officer reports that in the six months it has been operational, there are 1,400 illnesses reported by its 1,100 workers – all attributable to their work. There are 160 accidents and over 1,000 burns. Three people die in accidents and another four die as a result of their illnesses. There are 30 resident patients in the factory hospital tended by a doctor and eight nurses. The gas produced at the Avonmouth plant doesn't arrive in France until September 1918, two months before the Armistice.

1920 On Sunday 11 July 1920, Charlie Stephens, a barber from Bedminster, tries to shoot Niagara Falls in an oak barrel. Sadly, Charlie's barrel is way too heavy and he crashes straight onto the jagged rocks at the bottom. The following morning, an arm is rescued from the water bearing a tattoo that reads, 'Forget me not, Annie.' Charlie has previous: when he was five years old he was pronounced dead and laid in a coffin before springing back to life; at 16 he was almost run over by a coal wagon. Then he spent three years in the trenches of World War One and came home without a scratch. As well as running a busy barber's shop and bringing up 11 children with his wife Annie, Charlie fancied himself as a bit of a stuntman. First, he began performing daring tricks in a lions' den; then he parachuted from a balloon;

then he dived off the Forth Bridge head first. Niagara should have been Charlie's finest hour. Instead, Bedminster's answer to Houdini had tried his luck once too often.

1925 King George V and Queen Mary open the new University buildings.

1926 Opening of the Portway between Bristol and Avonmouth.

1930 Official opening in May of Bristol Airport at Whitchurch by Prince George. Whitchurch is only the third civil airport in the country.

1940 Hitler claims Bristol has been completely destroyed following a night of intensive bombing on 2 November in which 5,000 incendiary and 10,000 high explosive bombs are dropped on the centre of the old city. On 24 November, the entire area that is now Castle Park is destroyed in a bombing raid. During World War Two 1,299 people in Bristol are killed by German bombing. About 3,000 buildings are destroyed and 90,000 are damaged.

1941 The infamous Good Friday air raids on Bristol see more destruction in the centre of the city plus major damage to Knowle, Hotwells and Filton. The last air raid on Bristol is on 25 April 1941, when Brislington, Bedminster and Knowle are badly hit. Prime Minister Winston Churchill visits the devastated city on 12 April 1941 and is booed by crowds amid rumours that the city's air defences are not being properly managed.

1945 Prime Minister Winston Churchill, Chancellor of Bristol University, receives the freedom of the city.

1947 Some Bristolians begin to complain about an odd buzzing noise and the Bristol Hum is born. According to the 5% of people who can hear it, the hum sounds like the dull drone of a distant aircraft. It varies in intensity from a soft background noise to an overpowering onslaught and causes headaches, nausea, dizziness and even muscle spasms.

1949 The Bristol Brabazon, the world's largest passenger airliner, makes its maiden flight from Filton on 5 September.

1952 Following the failure of the Brabazon project, the Bristol Britannia makes its maiden flight from Filton. It goes on to become the first plane to carry 100 passengers non-stop across the Atlantic.

1956 Queen Elizabeth II opens the new Council House on College Green.

1957 The Duchess of Kent opens Bristol Airport at Lulsgate.

1958 On 5 December, Queen Elizabeth II makes the first trunk dialling call in Britain from Bristol Central Telephone Exchange. Trunk dialling is making a long-distance call without the aid of an operator. She calls the Lord Provost of Edinburgh. Her call lasts two minutes five seconds and costs 10d (4p).

1959 Bristol's first curry restaurant opens. The Taj Mahal in Stokes Croft is run by Mr Ahmed, a Bengali. It is the first Indian restaurant in the West Country. Writing in *Muktodhara, Bengalis In Bristol*, Mr Ahmed says: 'I put a poster in the window saying "Indian Restaurant Opening Shortly". People used to come in, push the door and say "When are you opening, I can't wait for a curry!" My second restaurant was in the Centre by the Hippodrome Theatre, called Koh-I-Noor. Every night there was a fight. We used to sell curry for 3/6d. They used to eat and then run without paying. And we used to catch up with them!'

1961 The Arnolfini is established by Jeremy and Annabel Rees above a bookshop on the Triangle, Clifton.

1963 Paul Stephenson leads anti-racist protests against Bristol Omnibus Company following the company's refusal to consider black people for jobs.

1965 The Race Discrimination Act is passed by Parliament after Bristol South East MP Tony Benn takes up the campaign started by Paul Stephenson.

1965 The Cumberland Basin road and bridge scheme opens.

BRISTOL RIOTS OF 1831

THREE DAYS OF RIOTING IN QUEEN SQUARE

The Queen Square riots began on 31 October 1831 and remain one of the most serious outbreaks of civil disobedience in the history of England. The disturbance is thought to be connected to uprisings across the country sparked by the rejection by the Lords of the Reform Act. However, there is evidence that the fighting was a local uprising in protest at a corrupt City Corporation: it was more of a revolution than a riot.

It all kicked off thanks to the arrival in town of the Recorder of Bristol, Sir Charles Wetherell, a committed opponent of reform Sir Charles pitched up on 29 October to preside over the Court of Assizes. Two days later, the centre of Bristol was in flames. The fires could be seen in Newport and Sir Charles was forced to escape from the Mansion House in disguise by clambering over rooftops.

The Bristol Riots lasted for three days and were centred on Queen Square. The Mansion House, Excise Office and Custom House were torched and the Toll House destroyed. Prisoners were released and the prisons set on fire at Bridewell, New Gaol and Gloucester County Gaol. Private houses on two sides of

Queen Square were destroyed. A watercolour of the riots by TLS Rowbotham (on show at the City Museum and Art Gallery in Queen's Road) shows the mob being attacked by soldiers from the 14th Light Dragoons, or the Bloody Blues, as they were known. The 3rd Dragoon Guards, who were based in the city, were thought to be sympathetic to the cause, which could explain why Bristol was controlled by the rioters for three days.

The arrival of Sir Charles Wetherell may have sparked the Queen Square riots, but it's likely he was the catalyst for the uprising against a 'rotten' Corporation. The Corporation had become secretive, out of touch with the city and, by 1831, was as unpopular with the Tories as it was with the masses.

In 1833, a Royal Commission on Municipal Corporations investigated the Bristol Corporation and reported that: 'The ruling principle of the Corporation appears to have been, at all times, the desire of power, the watchful jealousy that nothing should be undertaken within the limits of the city over which they cannot, at pleasure, exercise their control.'

■ TLS Rowbotham recorded the scenes at the Queen Square riots in this watercolour. It shows the protesters being attacked by solidiers from the 14th Light Dragoons, or the Bloody Blues, as they became known.

Up Close

1966 The Queen opens the £10 million Severn Bridge on 8 September.

1966 Frogmore Street leisure complex opens.. It's been an entertainment centre ever since. Academy is the latest arrival to move in.

1967 Steve Marriot writes the Small Faces hit *Itchycoo Park* while staying at the Grand Hotel.

1968 The first St Paul's Carnival is held with the procession trouping past the Lord Mayor of Bristol.

1969 In April, Brian Trubshaw pilots Concorde 002 on her British maiden flight from Filton to RAF Fairford in Gloucestershire. On emerging from the cockpit he says: 'It was wizard! A cool, calm and collected operation!'

1970 On 12 April, more than 100,000 people line the banks of the River Avon to watch the ss Great Britain being towed home on the last leg of her journey from the Falkland Islands.

1971 Christine Preece becomes Bristol's first woman bus driver.

1972 Theatre Royal and Coopers' Hall restored and re-opened.

1974 A bomb goes off in Park Street on 18 December. 15 people are injured but amazingly there are no fatalities.

1974 Royce Creasey organises the first Ashton Court Festival, a series of four Sunday events at Ashton Court. Fred Wedlock plays one of the days, as does a band called Pussy Spasm.

1975 The Arnolfini moves from the Triangle to its current site, Bush House, a former tea warehouse on Narrow Quay.

1977 Royal Portbury Dock opens.

1978 Bristol Industrial Museum opens.

1978 Louise Joy Brown, the world's first test-tube baby is born on 25 July to Lesley and John Brown of Hassell Drive, Easton.

1980 Rioting breaks out in St Paul's following a police raid on the Black and White cafe in Grosvenor Road. It is the first of the inner city riots of the early 1980s.

1982 The Watershed, Britain's first 'media centre', opens across the water from the Arnolfini. To this day, nobody in Bristol is quite sure what makes two cinemas, a bar and a gallery a 'media centre'.

1982 Bristol City FC goes bust and is reformed as Bristol City (1982). Eight of the club's highest earners from the Division One days agree to tear up their contracts so the club can survive. They become known as the Ashton Gate Eight.

1986 The Dug Out club closes following a campaign by police that culminates with police solicitor Richard Crowley telling the City Council's Public Protection Committee that the club is like a 'Fagin's kitchen'.

1986 On 26 April, Bristol Rovers play their last ever game at their spiritual home, Eastville. It's a 1-1 draw with Chesterfield.

1991 *Blue Lines*, the first Massive Attack album is released on 6 January.

1991 New shopping centre the Galleries opens in Broadmead. It's a 'totally enclosed mall with three levels of shopping and eateries and a 950-space car park' and replaces the old concrete monstrosity, Fairfax House with a new brick monstrosity. Hurrah!

1995 Portishead win the Mercury Music Prize with their debut album *Dummy*.

1996 The second Severn crossing opens. It cost about £300 million.

1997 Roni Size wins the Mercury Music Prize with his album *New Forms*.

1999 Pero's Bridge opens linking the Watershed with the Arnolfini. Designed by Irish artist Eilis O'Connell and named after a slave brought back to Bristol by John Pinney, the bridge is generally regarded as one of the better things built in Bristol in recent years.

1999 The new-look City Centre opens to the public on Millennium Eve.

C21st

2000 The £97 million At-Bristol project opens, comprising Explore, Wildwalk and the Imax cinema (see Children's Bristol. p182). The project is the first stage of a £450 million urban rejuvenation scheme, covering 11 acres of Bristol's Harbourside.

2001 Tony Blair is hit by a tomato during a protest against sanctions against Iraq when he opens City of Bristol College.

2001 PJ Harvey wins the Mercury Music Prize with her album *Stories From The City, Stories From The Sea*.

2002 In October, Bristol is short-listed as a candidate for European City of Culture 2008.

2002 Downing Street insists there was nothing wrong in Cherie Blair's purchase of two Bristol flats with the help of a convicted fraudster. She faced criticism in December after confirming Peter Foster had helped her, despite earlier denials from the Number 10 press office. The flats are in the Old AA building opposite the nice Victorian toilets on Park Row.

2003 The Labour Party is swept from power in the May local elections after the best part of 30 years running the city. No party has an overall majority and it takes the local politicians a couple of weeks to come to agreement about how to share power. Strangely, the city seems to run itself perfectly efficiently without anybody being in control.

2003 Liverpool is chosen ahead of Bristol as European City of Culture for 2008. According to the judging panel, Bristol was the most European of the nominated cities, but its road system counted against it. The judges felt that the districts were 'divided by motorways'.

2003 Massive Attack make a triumphant homecoming in August with a huge gig in Queen Square. 'Keep Bristol music progressive!' is Robert Del Naja's message to his hometown crowd. He dedicates *Teardrop* from the *Mezzanine* album to Bristol.

2003 Tens of thousands of people stare into the Bristol skies on 27 November as Concorde returns to the city for the last time. For many,

it's an emotional moment as the beak-nosed supersonic jet appears out of the clouds and zooms over the Clifton Suspension Bridge.

2005 Bristol is awarded Fairtrade City status in a ceremony at the ss Great Britain during Fairtrade Fortnight in March.

2005 On the same weekend in October that Aardman Animation celebrate *Curse of the Were-Rabbit* breaking box office records, a fire destroys the company's warehouse in St Philip's. The blaze destroys the entire collection of Wallace and Gromit props and models plus many other artefacts from the last 30 years.

2006 At the Oscar ceremony in March Aardman's *Curse of the Were-Rabbit* wins the gong for the Best Animated Feature. Aardman mainman Nick Park says: 'This is a great day for Aardman and most importantly recognition for the 200-plus dedicated crew that gave up over two years of their lives to work on the film.'

2006 Labour take a predicted battering in the May local elections. The Lib Dems don't have an overall majority but take control of Bristol City Council. Charlie Bolton becomes the city's first Green Party Councillor after winning Southville from Labour by seven votes.

2006 Work is halted on the Cabot Circus redevelopment and Bristol is gridlocked after a suspected Second World War bomb is discovered under the demolished Allied Carpets shop. It turns out not to be a bomb.

2006 In July, Louise Brown announces she is pregnant. Bristol girl Louise who lives in Knowle became the world's first test-tube baby in 1978.

2007 The 200th anniversary of the passing of the Abolition of Slavery Act is commemorated in a series of Abolition 200 events.

2008 Cabot Circus opens. Bristol becomes the UK's first Cycling City.

2010 A second Green Party councillor is elected to Bristol City Council.

2011 The £27m M Shed museum opens on the site of the old Industrial Museum.

SORELY MISSED

GIL GILLESPIE PAYS A PERSONAL TRIBUTE TO SOME OF BRISTOL'S ABSENT FRIENDS

1. The Dugout, Park Row
It didn't seem seminal at the time; you shuffled along the corridor, you shoved your quid under the glass, you wandered about for a few hours with your shoes sticking to the floor and then you went home. And yet the Dugout is a hugely significant landmark in the history of the city of Bristol. This is the place where all our musical boundaries were shifted. We saw our first multi-million pound pop videos here, upstairs on the giant screen. This is where we were when Live Aid happened, when the St Paul's riots kicked off, when trousers began to get really baggy. Almost always trouble-free, its closure was at the hands of a bunch of misguided Park Street shopkeepers worried about their windows.

2. The Kings Arms pub on Whiteladies Road
Another social landmark that was sent to an early grave. In its heyday, the Kings Arms (now Babushka) at the top of Whiteladies Road was one of the city's most popular meeting places. Its lighthouse location and sheer size made it impossible to miss. And with wheeler-dealer Crystal Palace fan Terry at the helm, the place was rocking every night of the week. We'd often spend all day and night there; you could never be too drunk to be in the Kings. 'Is it all right to cash another cheque, Tel?'

3. Wendy the Elephant, Clifton
Ask anyone who knows me and they'll tell you that I am the least animal-sentimental person they know. But something very strange happened to me on both occasions I have visited Bristol Zoo. When I laid eyes on Wendy the Elephant, I began to cry, yes cry, right in front of all the other 'human browsers'. When I returned in 2002, the same thing. Why? Maybe it was something to do with dignity and small cages not mixing. I might set up a charity called Complete Freedom for All Medium to Large Animals Except Lions and Tigers, in honour of my now-departed elephant friend.

4. Six Fox Launderette, Zetland Road
Back in the days before 'I can't believe it's not butter' branding became the language of choice for signs, almost anything could have a really good name. Zetland Road's Six Fox Launderette was one such place. But what in the name of half a dozen Basil Brushes did the name mean? As far as I know, foxes have absolutely no link with the business of washing clothes, whatsoever. Truly, the Six Fox was a legend in its own spin cycle.

5. Revolver Records, The Triangle
My mate Rick worked at Revolver in the days before I knew him. Rick is damn cool. He ran Planet Records. He was in Flying Saucer Attack. Anyway, one day I went into Revolver and asked if they had two Beck albums I'd heard about that were only available on import. 'You mean *One Foot In The Grave* and *Stereopathetic Soul Manure*?' sneered Rick with the cynicism of someone who had bought them ages ago. 'You were a right snotty twat,' I told him a year later and we both laughed at the notion that working in Revolver was a one-way ticket to taste fascism. The shop's motto could have been 'you're not really going to buy that are you?'

6. ABC Cinema, Whiteladies Road
In the early 1980s, me and my mate Kerry Turner wandered into the ABC Cinema in the middle of a weekday afternoon just for something to do. Kerry was the best punk in Bristol at the time, a Bambi-faced pretty boy with giant glue-sharpened spikes exploding from his head and the word 'discharge' painted across the back of his thousand-stud leather jacket. Anyway, we went to see *Arthur* – there was nothing else on. We were the only ones in the whole auditorium, so we put our feet up on the velvet seats in front of us and laughed our heads off. A couple of years later Kerry got a nasty type of schizophrenia and was carted off to a mental institution

somewhere in Wales. All he needed was a couple of hours with Dudley Moore in the ABC on Whiteladies Road.

7. The Cellar Bar, Stokes Croft

For a few decadent months at the end of the 1990s, Stokes Croft had an after-hours underground bar that felt like the centre of the universe to anyone who went there. Like all cool clubs, the hidden basement of this little cafe was always packed way beyond its capacity: a heaving, sweating, choking mass of beer-deprived early Herbie Hancock aficionados and a slow-motion barman. Yeah, it was great: the Stooges, Credence Clearwater, Chairmen Of The Board, DJ Shadow… hey, it was only rock 'n' roll and we liked it.

8. The Montpelier Hotel, Montpelier

The Mont was like the Cadbury with tattoos and a cocaine problem. It was not a place to take your parents. Whatever happened at the Mont did so upstairs in the pool room. It was a bit rough around the edges, a bit lairy, full of discreet hand-to-hand exchanges and shifty-eyed blokes looking well scary. You never heard anyone say, 'oh we met some lovely people in the Mont last night'.

9. The Redcliffe Flyover

As with most non-permanent things, the Redcliffe Flyer had more than an element of irresponsibility about it. It was an eyesore in an eyesore part of town but it gave bored drivers the opportunity to have the occasional Scalextric moment in a lifetime of gridlocked traffic. It is for this reason that we must salute it. Apparently, a bloke called Bill Spring was the first and last person to drive over it.

10. Paradise Garage

For the nervous 14-year-old looking to jump on the punk bandwagon, Paradise Garage was a terrifying but empowering shopping experience. Stashed away at the end of a concrete tunnel off the Broadmead Bearpit, it was the coolest shop in the universe, a hangout for Bristol's punk elite. They sold bondage trousers, Sid Vicious's cowboy T-shirts, and shock-coloured mohair jumpers. Some kids had to go there with their mum, which must still rank as the most humiliating experience of many people's lives. They sold me my four-inch-heeled electric blue Chelsea boots, a Clash T-shirt, a shiny two-tone suit and several silver-buttoned cowboy shirts. By the time it closed down, I got to know the shop's owner Rich and we would sneer and laugh at a whole new generation of terrified 14-year-old kids. According to Massive Attack legend, it was in Paradise Garage that Daddy G met Milo Johnson and they went on to form The Wild Bunch.

11. Western Star Domino Club, St Paul's

When a work colleague told my friend Simon that the Western Star had been pulled down to widen the junction of the M32 with Broadmead, he cried in front of the whole office. 'It was brilliant,' recalls Simon. By day, the place was an actual domino club, with its tables packed full of old West Indian guys who made the game look as exciting as ice hockey. And by night, it was a great music venue, attracting bands such The Cortinas and the Blue Aeroplanes. Occasionally, it would also attract trouble and one night someone was killed at a Crazy Trains gig. But despite this, the place oozed with first-generation West Indian street spirit and friendliness. Without it, the M32 is now only a long, straight road to nowhere in particular.

12. Dreadlocked Ex-Bank Manager Tramp

He looked like Santa Claus after 200 years of heavy drinking and for the best part of a decade he lumbered all over Bristol as the undisputed king of the down-and-outs. People used to say, 'he used to be a bank manager, you know', as if being a bank manager was better than being a tramp. Nobody knew the real story of his life and it was perhaps fitting that he left without saying goodbye. I wonder what happened to him? Let's hope he's all right and hasn't fallen back into banking.

13. The AA Building, Park Row

Okay, so it was a characterless concrete lump of a building with a few yellow signs. But the former home of the Automobile Association was preferable to what we have now. The Blairs bought a flat for their student son Ewan in the new building.

Underground & Radical Bristol

Ian Bone decries the inept political establishment in Bristol and applauds those who are undermining it

Bristol's going Green. Slowly. Probably. The city that has tons of lycra-clad cyclists battling the smog-hazed traffic every morning, that hosts more vegan, veggie and organic food fayres than any other, that's home to the Soil Association, Sustrans and more sustainable eco-friendly, self-build initiatives than you can shake a teepee at, might become the first city in Britain to go Green politically. But it'll take ten years. At least.

The Green Party won its breakthrough seat on the City Council in May 2006 with the election of Charlie Bolton with a majority of seven votes. Bolton wasn't re-elected in the 2010 local elections, but Tess Green took a Southville seat and she was joined in 2011 by Gus Hoyt who gained Ashley ward with a whopping 744 vote majority and 42.6% of the vote, taking it from the Liberal Democrats. The problem is that we have a ludicrous system where only one third of council seats are up for election every year so it may well take another decade before the Greens get the whiff of power in their nostrils. But political inertia and gradualism somehow matches the modern mood of the city. After the 20111 elections the Lib Dems were the single biggest party but didn't have an overall majority. The state of the parties was: Conservatives 14 (no change); Greens 2 (+1); Labour 21 (+4); Lib Dems 33 (-5).

So the Lib Dems and Labour muddle through at proving equally inept at managing the city. In truth, the City Council has had most of its powers passed on to unelected quangos such as the South West Regional Development Agency but, even so, the Council is enmeshed in a soggy, swampy mire of management speak and unfulfilled promises that fuels cynicism and undermines belief in the possibility of any real change.

■ Banksy's monkey stencils: you can still spot some if you look hard enough.

■ The Spark is a curious organ that has been going since 1993.

There are no discernible political differences between Labour and Lib Dems, no identifiable left or right wings of either party, no discernible ideas on anything except management by muddle and fudge. For election night fun, you have only the Filwood ward where the candidates' loathing of one another teeters on the possibility of outright and physical warfare!

Filwood is the heartland of former Paymaster General Dawn Primarolo's South Bristol constituency. 'Dimarolo' – as christened by *Private Eye* – has presided over fiasco upon fiasco from child tax credits to flogging off the Inland Revenue's offices to an offshore tax avoidance company. However, not only did she appear immune from the sack, but her loyalty to Gordon Brown had her even being touted as Deputy Prime Minister. The saints preserve us!

Her loyal constituents in Hartcliffe are rewarded with a burnt out shopping centre in Symes Avenue worthy of downtown Baghdad and a housing office fortress worthy

Top six...
Bristol riots

❶ Bristol Bridge Riot (1793): Second only to the Gordon Riots in terms of those killed and injured in the 17th Century.

❷ Queen Square Riot (1831): The Biggie: 20,000 rioters over three days, 500 killed, three executed. The most violent riot in British history.

❸ Poll Tax Riot (1990): A feisty little rucker – right outside the Council House. We won!

❹ St Paul's Riot (1980): People outside the city were shocked to realise there were black people living in Bristol. It set the tone for 1981's summer of countrywide rioting.

❺ Hartcliffe Riot (1992): Two local lads were killed in a police car chase, feelings erupted and the cops took a battering on Symes Avenue. Part of 1992's wave of council estate riots.

❻ Stokes Croft Riots (2011): Simmering resentment at the siting of a Tesco store in Stokes Croft boils over when police make a heavy-handed raid on a squat where petrol bombs are alleged to have been hidden. The new Tesco store is trashed.

■ You're left in no doubt what the Kebele Kulture Projekt thinks of America's 'peacekeeping' role.

BRISTOL'S FIGHTING HEROES

RADICAL PAST AND PRESENT

Past

1. Dorothy Hazzard
Early Baptist dissenter who, with 200 women, defended the Frome Gate from Prince Rupert in the Civil War. Commemorated in a painting in the city's registry office. A lotta bottle.

2. James Nayler
Model Army Leveller whose Quaker radicalism was disliked by the authorities who prosecuted him for blasphemy after he rode up Corn Street on a donkey in 1656 claiming he was Jesus Christ. His barbaric torture and humility suggest they may have been right!

3. Thomas Clarkson
Came to Bristol to expose the slave trade – a risky business given the balance of power in the city. From his base in the Seven Stars, Clarkson dug out the crucial eye witness reports. Bristolians turned against the trade because of the high mortality rates of the slave ship crews!

4. Kingswood Colliers
Lawless bunch who'd march on the city to wreak havoc and mayhem. Commemorated by a Wetherspoons on Kingswood High Street. Not to be confused with that equally lawless desperado crew the Cock Road Gang from Hanham. Just don't mention 'the Cainses' in Hanham High Street. Still crazy.

5. Blackbeard & Long John Silver
Blackbeard was born in Redcliffe and Long John Silver came to life in Bristol boozer, the Llandoger Trow in King Street. Shamefully there's no plaque to either but there are plans for a Long John statue. Radical? Long John was. Pirate crews were very democratic electing their leaders and sharing booty. Who stood against Blackbeard for Captain? Er, well, um… no secret ballot, so no one fancied it.

6. The Black Hand Gang
A gang of leftie Bemmy toughs from the 1920s – sworn enemies of The Monkey Town Mob from The Dings. Again no plaque. I can't think why not!

Present

1. Tony Benn
He is not strictly a Bristolian cos he don't live here no more, but this ex-MP was first elected to represent Bristol South East in 1950. He was eventually 'got rid of' with the help of the boundary changes in 1983. Benn was a hugely committed local MP who still has strong links with the city he served for almost 25 years and can still pack out the Colston Hall.

2. Julie Burchill
Well, yes, she don't live here neither and by the time you read this she may have reverted back to her 1980s Thatcher adoration. She is currently as acerbic a proletarian socialist columnist as there is and it all comes straight out of her years growing up in Fishponds and Barton Hill.

3. Jo Wilding
Feminist, human rights activist, smuggler of banned Iraqi dates, sanctions buster, tomato thrower at Mr Tony Blair. Wilding also travelled to Iraq to defy Bush's bombs. This lady certainly has guts!

4. Dr Margaret Jones
A veritable Bristol institution as the city's most arrested activist. Veteran of road and anti-war protests who regularly takes a toothbrush to Magistrates Court hearings. She once blocked Bristol University/UWE boat race with her own boat protesting for the Gandalf Three. No? You'd better ask her!

5. Massive Attack
They bottled it when their name changed to 'Massive' in the Bush production Gulf War One. However, for the Bush Jnr production Gulf War Two, Massive Attack were fully on the anti-war campaign. This local band have consistently refused to play at the city's Colston Hall because of the fact it is named after the notorious Bristol slave trader Edward Colston. Throughout the Gulf War, the official Massive Attack website automatically redirected thousands of its visitors through to the CND website.

of an American outpost in Falujah – well worth a tourist trip to check out the benefits of the city's regeneration initiatives. These have attracted an army of 'poverty chasers' who follow government money round the city from St Paul's to Barton Hill hoovering up millions in the process and leaving the locals unaware they have had their capacities built and been empowered and regenerated.

A similar cabal of culture wallahs and wonks hovers between the Arnolfini, At-Bristol and the ss Great Britain risibly touting Brunel as a great Bristolian – and ignoring fearsome Bristol-born natives like the mighty, terrible Blackbeard – and even explored an even more ludicrous Charles Darwin connection to keep their snouts in the trough for another three years!

But it's the slave trade question that has Bristol collectively on the psychiatrist's couch – which is lucky because Bristol has more counsellors per head than any other city in Europe. But even this army of dreamcatchers and rebirthers can't beat the class divide on this vexed issue. The guilt-ridden middle classes want to apologise for the slave trade whereas the feckless proletarians don't see why they should. The black community remains largely indifferent. There's probably a strong case to be made for the Society of Merchant Venturers to apologise since they initiated the trade and still dominate the economic life of the city. However, expecting an organisation that still worships arch slave trader Edward Colston's fingernail annually to apologise is not a likely winner. Tellingly, no

■ Street art stencil on a wall at the steps at the bottom of Park Street.

■ The Yellow Pages billboard by the Three Lamps junction is a subvertising hotspot.

vestiges of political activism from the 1960s and 1970s remain in the city's black community.

Indeed, very few signs of any radical political activism at all remain and those that do play only to an in-house ghetto of the usual suspects. Greenleaf, the city's long-running radical bookshop, closed in 2005 unable to withstand the pincer movement of Waterstone's and Borders. The muckraking scandal sheet *The Bristolian* ceased publishing shortly before being nominated for the Paul Foot Award for investigative journalism. The Centre hosts a Peace Vigil opposite the Hippodrome – staffed by heroic octogenarians, it is now the world's longest running peace vigil. But it is perhaps more of a threat to the Guinness Book of Records than the continuation of the Iraq and Afghanistan wars.

On the plus side, the Bristol Radical History Group has become increasingly active and produces an excellent series of pamphlets which you'll find at www.tangentbooks.co.uk or go to www.brh.org.uk. Bristol Anarchist Bookfair is now a focal point for the alternative Left in the South West.

You can't really begin to understand political Bristol without appreciating the role of the sinisterly-named Society of Merchant Venturers which is headed by 'the one they call the master'.

Historically, the SOMV has dominated the economic and commercial life of Bristol for 450 years, profiting greatly from the slave trade. Today, it has eased up on the Masonic secret password, roll-your-trouser-leg-up connections, and puts more emphasis on its charitable work. In reality, it still functions as a clique of powerful businessmen who dominate the commercial life of Bristol in a way not found, or tolerated, in any other city in Britain. Edward VI granted letters patent on 18 December 1552 to form a body to protect merchants from those 'not brought up in the merchants' art'. Only those admitted to the Society of Merchant Venturers were allowed to trade by sea from Bristol. In the 16th Century, the SOMV moved into property and still owns and controls the development of large swathes of Bristol.

■ *Ian Bone is one of the founders of the Class War anarchist group and produced the Bristolian scandal sheet.*

■ The famous Greenleaf radical bookshop was closed in 2005.

■ The Bristolian Party's attempt to sweep to power on a wave of popular disaffection didn't quite work out.

THOSE IN THE KNOW

A WHO'S WHO OF BRISTOL POLITICS

■ The Kebele Kulture Projekt is a cafe/shop and anarchist collective in Easton.

The Cube

The Cube building has a history of radical entertainment dating back to the 1950s when an am-dram group built the wooden theatre. In the 1970s, it was Bristol Arts Centre, home to the radical Avon Touring Company and where earnest young men read Orwell and Marx in the bar. Nowadays, The Cube screens local films before the main features and holds an astounding diverse set of gigs and events.
■ 4 Princess Row, Kingsdown
■ Tel: 907 4190 ■ www.cubecinema.com

The Spark

The now venerable *Spark* magazine underwent a stylish revamp in 2011 while maintaining its position as the fount of all wisdom on all things green with a comprehensive listing of the city's alternative therapy practicioners. Quarterly. Free.
■ 86 Colston Street ■ Tel: 914 3434
■ www.thespark.co.uk

Kebele Kulture Projekt

Easton-based cafe/shop and anarchist collective, Kebele came into being as a squat collective in the mid 1990s. It now runs a weekly (Sunday) vegan cafe and bike workshop. There is a radical library and internet access and it hosts film nights, exhibitions and more.
■ 14 Robertson Road, Easton ■ Tel: 939 9469
■ www.kebele.org (archive only)

Bristol Indymedia

Web-based volunteer run alternative news service linked to Indymedia worldwide and providing a vital source of news distinct from the local Northcliffe media monopoly. This hard-working and resilient collective has survived police seizures and endless whinging from the moaners of the Left and spamming by local nutters. A good first point of call for a what's on guide to local radicalism.
■ Box 7, Booty, 82 Colston Street
■ www.bristol.indymedia.org

Easton Cowboys

A whole social network of football, cricket and netball teams with a vivacious group of can-can dancers now added to their roster. Close links with the Zapatistas in Mexico through regular trips to Chiapas. They even played cricket in Compton, Los Angeles. Gigs, meetings, local campaigning – usually found in their spiritual home, The Plough in Easton.
■ www.eastoncowboys.org.uk

Subvertisers

At least two long established crews of subvertisers are out radically altering the messages of advertisements most weeks. Playful and funny with a hard edge – the best traditions of situationism. Offshoots have moved on to chopping down intrusive billboards altogether. Check out the excellent *Politics and Protest* book by Pete Maginnis.■
www.tangentbooks.co.uk

Bristol Radical History Group

Since 2006 BRHG has organised a bewildering range of history events; staging walks, talks, gigs, reconstructions, films, exhibitions, trips through the archives and fireside story telling. They also publish a range of pamphlets and host an archive on the website.
■ www.brh.org.uk

Who's Who of Bristol Celebrities

Nipper, Cary Grant, Bananarama, Julie Burchill, WG Grace, Jane Couch: all made in Bristol

For a long time, Bristol had a celebrity count as low as a rattlesnake's belly. In the 1970s and 1980s, even if famous people lived in Bristol, they didn't seem to want to admit to it. With no big sports teams and no music celebrities, Bristol didn't feature on the cool map of the world. Sure, it was an exciting place to live – particularly the late 1970s with the vibrant fusion of punk and rasta culture based around the Dugout club on Park Row. But Bristol simply didn't have the heritage that football and The Beatles brought to Liverpool, or Two-Tone gave to Coventry. Sheffield had Joe Cocker, the Human League and the Leadmill; Hull had the Housemartins; Oxford and Cambridge had their universities; and is there anyone in the world who hasn't heard of Manchester United? Even Shrewsbury was associated with T'Pau. And Basingstoke had John Arlott. But if you'd asked the Great British public to name a famous Bristolian, they would probably have said Brunel. And he was from Portsmouth.

■ OK, he's from Portsmouth, but nobody has done more to distinguish Bristol than Brunel.

But now, all that has changed. The BBC series *Casualty* did what *Shoestring* never quite achieved in terms of raising the city's profile, and then came Massive Attack (see Bristol Beat). Robert Del Naja, Grant Marshall, Mushroom and their collaborators propelled Bristol from its status as an inland port where people talk 'gert funny' to being the coolest place in the universe. And suddenly we discovered that Bristol is full of famous people and has a long tradition of producing major talents in the arts and sciences, from Thomas Chatterton and Humphry Davy to Paul Dirac and Cary Grant.

We bring you a comprehensive list of Bristol's finest talents from way back when, right up until the present day. Who knows, you may even be surprised!

■ Charlie off of the BBC's *Casualty*. See if you can spot the Bristol backgrounds on the old episodes. They've moved to Cardiff now.

Celebrities

A Sophie Anderton

Famously spoilt former Redland High School pupil who found fame and fortune by modelling underwear and dating, amongst others, Marc Bosnich. Sophie is originally a Henleaze girl. 'Her astonishing beauty only became apparent after she was hit by a car,' reckons one of her ex-school chums.

B Edward Hodges Bailey

Sculptor born in Bristol in 1788 who is best known for the statue of Nelson in Trafalgar Square. The frieze over the Freemasons' Hall in Park Street is one of the few examples of his work in his native city.

Bananarama

Two-thirds of Bananarama (the most successful British girl group ever) were born in Bristol and the other one married Dave Stewart. Keren Woodward and Sarah Dallin from Mangotsfield certainly had their moments, *It Ain't What You Do...*, *Really Saying Something*, and *Cruel Summer* being the most memorable.

■ David Neilson used to commute from Bristol to Coronation Street where he became Roy Cropper.

Cathy Barry

Living, silicone-enhanced proof that erotica and the Kingswood accent do not mix. Despite having tits the size of Jordan's and heels higher than her IQ, Cathy Barry remains Britain's most accidental and most unlikely porn star. But her video sales tell a completely different story. We can only assume that the nation's biggest wankers aren't put off by a girl who seems only mildly interested in shagging and sounds like a dinner lady. It's too good to be true, but yes, Cath does come from Cock Road in Kingswood.

Ernest Bevin

A founder member of the Transport and General Workers' Union, Bevin became the Union's first Secretary in 1921. He was born in Winford near Bristol and then lived at 39 Saxon Road, St Werburgh's, where there's a blue plaque in his honour. In World War Two, Churchill made Bevin Minister of Labour and National Service. He is best known for introducing a scheme for young conscripts to work in coal mines rather than join the forces – hence the term Bevin Boys. He was Foreign Secretary from 1945 to 1951.

■ Kurt (Navin Chowdry) from the tele programme Teachers, which is filmed at the old Merrywood School in Knowle West.

Elizabeth Blackwell

The first woman doctor, Elizabeth Blackwell was born in Countership, St Thomas in 1821 and also lived in Wilson Street St Paul's. She emigrated to America with her family where she qualified as a doctor. On eventually returning to England, she became the first woman to be enrolled on the British Medical Register and was an ardent campaigner for the reform of the medical profession.

Norman Bowler

Regular viewers of *Emmerdale*, after it lost the Farm bit of its title will remember this fella as the craggy-featured down-on-his-luck

BANKSY

AN INSIGHT INTO BRISTOL'S MAN OF MYSTERY

Time was that you could hardly cross the road in Bristol without spotting a Banksy stencil. Now there are only about 12 pieces left on the city's walls, many of them in a state of disrepair. Banksy started painting with the DryBreadz Crew (DBZ) from Kingswood around 1992 working with graffiti writers including Tes, Kato, Lokey and Inkie.

'I started off painting graffiti in the classic New York style... but I was never good at it,' he revealed in one of his rare interviews. Not long after, he cut his first stencil. 'The ruthlessness and efficiency of it is to start revolutions and to stop wars,' he says of his weapon of choice, 'they look political just through the style'.

Easton, Bedminster, Windmill Hill and St Paul's became his canvas as images such as *Mild Mild West* and Abi's Wall. Now he is an international man of mystery. London, New York, the Israeli/Palestine security wall. He also sabotaged The Turner Prize and designed the cover of Blur's *Think Tank* album.

In 2009 Banksy single-handedly saved the Bristol economy with his show Banksy vs Bristol Museum, staged at the City Museum and Art Gallery on Queen's Road. According to research carried out by the Museums Libraries and Archives Council the show (which ran from June to August) attracted 308,719 people; 106,744 visitors lived within 25 miles and 201,975 lived farther away. Visitors who stayed in Bristol generated additional income of £6,169,610 by staying visitors. Day visitors spent a total of £4,238,736. According to a leaked copy of the contract between the museum and Banksy, the artist was paid a fee of £1 to exhibit his work.

The Museum show was outstanding. Apart from taking over the the two main galleries and the central space, Bansy's work was scattered around the Museum, often hidden among existing exhibits. The Paintpot Angel remains on permanent display on the plinth to the left of the central staircase.

In 2010 Banksy released the Oscar-nominated 'documentary' film Exit Through The Gift Shop which continues to amuse and confuse Banksy watchers. Is the whole thing a front for Banksy's own work or is the story of Terry aka Mr Brainwash to be taken at face value? Also in 2010, Banksy created an intro scene for The Simpsons which is easily one of the most radical and subversive pieces of film to appear on prime time American TV. It shows workers and animals in a sweat shop making Simpsons merchandise. If you haven't checked it out already on YouTube (and more than 7.5million people have), go tohttp://www.youtube.com/watch?v=DX1iplQQJTo.

In May 2011, Banksy showed that his work continues to be as radical as ever when he released a limited edition print of a Tesco petrol bomb.The print went on sale exclusively at the Bristol Anarchist Bookfair just a few days after the Stokes Croft riots in which the controversial Tesco Metro store was controversially trashed after police were forced to retreat from Stokes Croft.

'It's all about retribution really,' Banksy once said about his work in a *Guardian* interview. 'If you don't own a train company then you go and paint on one instead. It comes from school when you had to have name tags in something – that makes it belong to you. You can own half the city by scribbling your name over it.'

For his relentless pursuit of the things he believes in the face of clear and present danger, we salute him.

More about Banksy and Bristol street art:
Banksy's Bristol:Home Sweet Home (Tangent Books, www.tangentbooks.co.uk)
The Banksy Q (Tangent and PRSC)
Children of the Can (Tangent Books)
www.weaponofchoicegallery.co.uk – New show info and a shop from WoC gallery.
www.woostercollective.com – worldwide street artists, many from Bristol.
www.ekosystem.org – an influential street art site, which features Bristol's best.
www.12ozprophet.com – graffiti magazine and forums.
www.upfest.co.uk – Gallery in North Street, Southville that hosts the Urban Paint Festival at Tobacco Factory in early June.

squire grizzler Frank Tate. Frank, y'see, had everything – beautiful wife, beautiful house, beautiful horses – but he ended up losing it all in a relentlessly soapy cyclone of heavy alcohol, double-crossing and sexually confused offspring. Frank had a heart attack and nearly died. Then his conniving, unfaithful wife Kim cheated on him, died in a car accident, came back to life and gave him the fright of his life. Or his death, to be more accurate. Bowler later revealed that he had based his alco-acting on the behaviour of his one time drinking partner Jeffery Bernard.

Derren Brown

Britain's answer to David Blaine is one of those people who came to Bristol to study and liked it so much he stayed. The genuinely spooky mind-controller has said he enjoys dining out in the city alone, so anyone who starts feeling queasy in a restaurant should take a look at the table behind them.

■ As well as surviving five days trapped on a boat, Tony Bullimore also used to co-own The Granary rock club and the Bamboo Club.

Isambard Kingdom Brunel

The great engineer's legacy to Bristol is Temple Meads railway station, the ss Great Britain and Clifton Suspension Bridge, plus various bridges and bits of railway. Strangely, there is only one monument to Brunel in Bristol: a fairly anonymous affair tucked out in the Temple Quay redevelopment.

Tony Bullimore

Sailor who famously capsized 1,500 miles south west of Australia and spent five days trapped in an air pocket in the upturned hull of his yacht. He was once the co-owner of The Granary rock club and ran the Bamboo Club in St Paul's.

Julie Burchill

The only original thinker in the British press had her rough edges sharpened by a childhood in Bristol. 'The dog whimpers in its sleep,' she once wrote. 'It's having a bad dream. So am I. It's called living in Bristol.'

■ The Death of Chatterton: the boy poet from Redcliffe was one of our greatest ever writers.

John Cabot

John Cabot set sail from Bristol in 1497 in a small ship, The Matthew, in search of the Far East. Instead, he discovered North America. Anyone who tells you that Columbus was the first European to land on the continent don't know Jack Shit. A replica of The Matthew is now moored alongside the ss Great Britain in Hotwells. The Cabot Tower on Brandon Hill (see Children's Bristol) is the best public monument in Bristol.

Princess Caraboo

Mary Willcocks, a cobbler's daughter, fooled Bristol for three months in 1817 as Caraboo, Princess of Javasu. She turned up at a cottage in Almondsbury speaking in a strange tongue. Many people tried to identify her language until a Portuguese sailor, claiming comprehension, announced that she was from an island in the East Indies. He said she was brought to Bristol against her will and was a person of rank. She maintained the ruse, never lapsing from her peculiar tongue and even managed enough consistency for a dictionary to be created. Her beautiful manners and peculiar habits captivated everyone, but she was eventually found out and a benefactress quietly shipped her to America.

Mary Carpenter

The 19th-Century social reformer was the daughter of the Minister of the Unitarian Church in Lewins Mead. Moved by the plight of homeless children in Bristol, she opened the Red Lodge reform school for girls in 1854 on a site which is now covered by the Colston Hall.

Glenn Catley

It may surprise you to hear that the WBC super middleweight world champion lives and trains right here in Bristol. The former electrician is a product of the Empire Club and a bit of a hero south of the river.

■ **Roger Greenaway:** half of one of the most successful songwriting partnerships ever.

Thomas Chatterton

He was either the Nick Drake of the 16th Century or the Dom Jolly of ecumenical prose. The story of Bristol's doomed boy poet is the stuff of rock and roll mythology. Born next door to St Mary Redcliffe Church in 1752, the teenage Chatterton was clearly one of life's more reflective souls. With time to ponder, he became obsessed with odd bits of Medieval manuscript that he found stored away in Redcliffe Church. Eventually, he began writing poetry in the name of an imaginary 15th Century monk called Thomas Rowley. Rowley's challenging 'work' was at first authenticated and then universally applauded and Chatterton set off for London to pursue his own literary career. Sadly, all his attempts were greeted with indifference. Apparently crushed by the criticism, Chatterton swallowed a bottle of arsenic and was found dead at his home on 24 August 1770. This gifted, rebellious youth later became a hero to the romantic and pre-Raphaelite poets, several of whom, notably Keats and Coleridge, wrote poems about him. He became regarded as the first Romantic poet. A statue of Chatterton used to stand outside St Mary Redcliffe Church, but fell into disrepair and was removed. The house that Chatterton grew up in is on the other side of the dual carriageway from St Mary Redcliffe. Sadly, it is not open to the public; it is occupied by one of the City Museum staff, but if you're lucky, he might let you look round.

■ **Roger Cook:** the other half of one of the most successful songwriting partnerships ever.

John Cleese

Although born in Weston-super-Mare, the *Monty Python's Flying Circus* founder member and one of Britain's favourite comedians was a pupil at Clifton College in Bristol. Rumour has it that it was at the College where he first developed a penchant for silly walks. Allegedly, Cleese practised his silly walks on the cricket pitch to annoy teachers and impress fellow pupils. A match report from the 1950s refers to 'many Cleesian glides'.

Stephanie Cole

Just as she did when she played Diana Trent in *Waiting For God*, Stephanie Cole isn't afraid to speak her mind. In an interview with the *Evening Post,* she once launched a savage attack accusing the toothless local media of going out of their way to damage arts in the area. Would it be so difficult for *HTV News* and *Points West* to include a five-minute arts feature occasionally, she asked. Unfortunately, Steph, they do like to devote themselves to mediocrity on a full-time basis.

Justin Lee Collins

You know the bloke. Scruffy, shoulder-length, strawberry ginger hair, shouts a lot and gets over-excited in a broad Bristolian accent about nothing in particular on pointless late night Channel 4 programmes commissioned by overpaid half-wits who clearly didn't understand *Nathan Barley*. Yeah, the irritating one. Well, he's a Southmead boy, so he reckons. And, apparently, when he's not fronting terrible telly such as *10 Things You Didn't Know About...* and the even more unnecessary *Strictly Come Dancing* BBC 3 update, he is a half-decent stand-up comedian. Don Ward from the *Comedy Store* even described Justin as 'the most original comic I've seen since Harry Hill'. Are you sure about that?

■ Cook and Greenway as David and Jonathan in their George Martin days.

Russ Conway

Born in Bedminster (there's a blue plaque on the wall of his home in Dean Lane), Trevor Stanford changed his name to Russ Conway and rose to stardom in the late 1950s. He went on to have more than 20 hit records. In fact, he spent a total of 168 weeks in the charts and remains the biggest selling pianist in UK pop history. Unless you count Elton John.

Cook and Greenaway

One of the most successful songwriting partnerships ever, Roger Cook and Roger Greenaway were born in Bristol in 1940 and 1938 respectively. Cook lived at 8 Forest Road, Fishponds; Greenaway was brought up at 98 Spring Hill, Kingswood. After knocking about with various Bristol bands (such as the Kestrels), they were discovered in 1965 by Beatles producer George Martin. Martin's wife, Judy, suggested they record under the name David and Jonathan and they reached number 11 in the charts with Lennon and McCartney's *Michelle* in 1966. A string of other singles followed, but it is as songwriters that Cook and Greenaway made a huge impact. They've written for artists including Gene Pitney (*Something's Gotten Hold Of My Heart*), Cilla Black, Cliff Richard, Kathy Kirby, Hank Marvin, Deep Purple and the Sweet, to name but a few. Cook joined Blue Mink in 1969 and recorded Cook and Greenaway's anti-racism classic *Melting Pot*. But it's as the writers of the 1970 Coca-Cola jingle *I'd Like To Buy The World A Coke*, that Cook and Greenaway reached an audience of millions around the globe. This was recorded as *I'd Like To Teach The World To Sing* by the New Seekers and released in December 1971. It brought Cook and Greenaway their first number one in January

■ Jane Couch: you try telling her boxing is just for blokes. Go on then!

Up Close

1972. In that month, three of the top four chart songs were Cook and Greenaway creations: at number two was *Softly Whispering I Love You* (The Congregation) and Cilla was at number four with *Something Tells Me Something's Gonna Happen Tonight*. They were only prevented from a straight top three run by the number two sound of Benny Hill with *Ernie: The Fastest Milkman In The West*. Cook and Greenaway have always been proud of their Bristol roots and have returned to the city regularly over the years. They rival Massive Attack as Bristol's most successful musical export.

■ Adam Hart-Davis relaxes in the garden of his Bishopston home.

Jane Couch

After years of hard living, Jane Couch has done more for women's boxing than anyone before her. Her motto, 'man or woman, if you take me on, you're history', has more than a ring of truth to it. She even left the British Boxing Board of Control on the canvas. That's feminism. The world welterweight champion trains with Tex Woodward at the Spaniorum Gym in Compton Greenfield. Couch burst onto the world boxing scene in May 1996 when she out-pointed French star Sandra Geiger in Copenhagen to win the WIBF welterweight title. The 10-round fight was watched by a European TV audience of 3.5 million. Couch said after this fight: 'My cheekbone was busted, my eye was out to here and I was a mess of bumps and bruises'.

Robin Cousins MBE

Ice skating's very own Alan Partridge won gold at the 1980 Winter Olympics and had a sports centre named after him in his home area of Shirehampton. Cousins is set to return in an 'ice extravaganza' up on the Downs'. No change there then.

David and Jonathan

See Cook and Greenaway.

D Sir Humphry Davy

Born in Penzance in 1778, Davy pursued his scientific career from a laboratory in Dowry Square, Hotwells. He discovered laughing gas and invented the miners' safety lamp.

■ Sapphire: has been a famous face of Bristol for as long as anyone can remember.

Adam Hart-Davis

The eccentric historian and TV boffin lives in Bishopston. Adam is, among other things, a companion of the Institution of Lighting Engineers, a Fellow of the Royal Society of Arts and a member of the British Toilet Association, a pressure group that campaigns for 'better public toilets for all'.

E Noel Edmonds

Noel hit the national headlines for driving his London cab in the taxi lane on the way to the BBC/Endemol studio in Paintworks, Bath Road for the filming of Deal or No Deal. Fair play to Noel, he didn't deny it was wrong, he simply put a mannequin on the back seat to fool the CCTV cameras that he was indeed a passenger carrying cabbie. Just be grateful it wasn't Mr Blobby.

LOCAL HEROES & ECCENTRICS

PEOPLE TO SPOT IN YOUR AREA

Cider Jim

'Cider' lurches around Redland/Clifton like some sort of Ziggy-fixated Quaker, frightening the life out of new students and anyone with a nervous disposition. The stories about his antics are legendary. He can usually be spotted swaying through Clifton Village shouting: 'In the 1960s I took cannabis, in the 1970s heroin, in the 1980s cocaine and in the '1990s… cider! cider! cider!'

Sapphire

If you've been handed a club flyer in Bristol in the last 20 years, chances are you already know this absurdly flamboyant transvestite firework on legs. Sapphire (pictured left) has been around for as long as anyone can remember. Who is he? He's Ru Paul from the street, Grace Jones with added self-belief, Sugar Plum Mary with God and the DHSS on her side. A BBC documentary broadcast to commemorate his 50th birthday did little to dent his outrageous public persona.

Leather Jockstrap Caveman

You know you're going to see him striding nowhere in particular at the Ashton Court Festival. But if you're lucky you might get to see him going about his daily business, at the top of Park Street, by the big post office on Queen Square, or heading off in the direction of the bus station. Whatever the day, whatever the weather, you can be sure he'll be wearing nothing except that old leather jockstrap he loves so much. A beautiful sight.

The Singing Lady on the Stoke Bishop bus

The Singing Lady looks just like any other pensioner. This is why nobody is afraid of sitting next to her. Old dear, what harm can she possibly do? But as soon as the bus pulls away, she bursts into song: a high-pitched, high-volume and completely unashamed medley of pre-Elvis chandelier-shakers leaving you in the most uncomfortable seat. Do you grit your teeth and stay on the bus, or bottle out at the next stop?

Andy Sloan and Matt Holyfield

In the spring of 2002, two Bristol students set off on the adventure of a lifetime with a 141lb table football as their luggage. Sloan and Holyfield spent £10,000 and played matches in 41 countries, crossing Europe, India, Thailand and the Middle East before reaching their final destination of South Korea in time for the start of the World Cup. Along the way, they played table football in the Olympic Stadiums of Rome and Munich and had a game with FIFA president Sepp Blatter at his offices in Zurich.

Clint

Unless you misspent a large part of your youth hanging around in Westbury-on-Trym village, chances are you won't know who Clint is. If you did, you'd swear Clint had based his daily performances on Groucho Marx. He'd throw funny one-liners at anyone who looked as though they were taking themselves too seriously. I once saw him standing in the chemists holding a glass of water. He looked around shiftily and whispered, 'I'm only here for the water,' out of the corner of his mouth. A living genius in Bristol BS9.

Bill Spring

As claims to fame go, Bill Spring's is one of the most pointless and most unusual to make the record books. Bill, you see, was the first and last person to cross the Redcliffe flyover, the now deceased temporary road bridge that once made driving in the Temple Meads area a bit like being in loop-the-loop Scalextric

Late Bus Woman

Described by one witness as being 'terrifying, absolutely bloody terrifying,' this elderly lady from Westbury-on-Trym has got a problem with buses being late. If the bus is so much as a minute behind schedule, Late Bus Woman attacks the driver with a painful torrent of expletive-riddled abuse and doesn't stop until she gets off half an hour later down the route. As a sideline, she also shouts at girls who wear Dr Martens boots.

Up Close

Lee Evans
You begin to understand just why Lee Evans is so nervously hyperactive when you discover that he was born in Avonmouth, the home of petro-chemical spillages. The supple-limbed comedian couldn't wait to live somewhere else and has now settled in Southend.

George Ferguson
The 'Red Trousered Philanthropist' is doing more to shape a creative vision of Bristol than any number of planners and developers with their mind-numbing plans for Cabot Circus or absurd justifications for building a concert arena with no car park. George, who is famed for wearing red trousers and being on Channel 4's *Demolition* programme, is one of the country's leading architects and is a passionate believer in building sustainable communities by reclaiming land and buildings. He has also been a Merchant Venturer, but we'll forgive him that. He has been in Bristol since his student days in the 1960s and has been the creative force behind many leading initiatives. George's vision is best realised in his Tobacco Factory and Bristol Beer Factory projects in Southville which paved the way for the boom of independent businesses migrating to North Street. The Tobacco Factory was originally part of a much grander scheme under which George would have created an 'urban village' on the sites of all the former tobacco industry buildings in Southville. His Canteen bar in Stokes Croft swiftly became the focal point for the alternative movement and he is trying to discourage big chains from clogging up Bordeaux Quay with Stage and Hen Parties by opening the Harbourside Bar by way of encouraging similar local businesses to reclaim the bit outside the Watershed. George was President of the Royal Institute of British Architects from 2003 to 2005 and has won numerous awards for his work.

■ Cary Grant: the most famous old boy of Bishop Road Primary school and Fairfield School.

■ Ian Holloway, who was born in Kingswood and played for Bristol Rovers, has a way with words.

Keith Floyd
Legendary snorter of claret and one of the first TV celebrity chefs, the bon viveur's bon viveur used to have his very own restaurant on Chandos Road, in Redland. He died in 9009, aged 65.

Josie Gibson
Winner of the last C4 series of Big Brother in 2010, Josie is credited with bringing classic Bristol wit to the masses with quips like: "I'm cool as a cucumber and you've just made me look like a complete turnip", "Times like this I wish I was an ostrich". After pocketing the £100,000 prize money she astonished many by immediately giving away £20,000 to her ex-employer children's cancer charity Clic Sargent.

WG Grace
Cricket's first ever superstar was an extremely bearded and notoriously fierce fella who annihilated bowlers and intimidated batsman for Gloucestershire and England. William Gilbert Grace was born in Downend in 1848; he played 22 times for England

between 1880 and 1899, scoring 1,038 runs. He was a GP in Bristol with a surgery in Stapleton Road, Easton from 1881 to 1895.

Cary Grant

Bristol's golden boy. (See profile, p126).

H Anthony Head

This Bristol-based actor was once known only as 'that prat off the Gold Blend ads' but a leading role in *Buffy The Vampire Slayer* changed all that. He claims his 19th-Century house in Bristol is haunted by the ghost of a young girl. 'She is not frightening at all,' added the demon destroyer.

Damien Hirst

Of all the 'enfant terribles' of the over-hyped late 20th-Century Brit Art uprising, this Bristol-born originator remains the most convincing. Sharks, cows and sheep have been preserved in formaldehyde, flies have been given life and promptly killed again and medicine bottles have been used as the theme for a restaurant. And yet, somehow, pretentiousness has never been an issue… Damien was born in the city in 1965, the son of a car salesman. His family moved to Leeds when he was a nipper, but those vital formative crayoning years were spent in Bristol.

Ian Holloway

Bristol Rovers player and manager who hails from Kingswood. Ollie gained national celebrity for the bizarre way in which he expressed himself at press conferences when he became manager at Queens Park Rangers. There's an excellent collection of his best quotes called *Let's Have Coffee: The Tao of Ian Holloway* (Toilet Books, £4.50, www.letshavecoffee.com) which contains such gems as 'Every dog has its day and today is woof day! I just want to bark!'

Bob Hope

Yes, that Bob Hope. The legendary Hollywood entertainer spent his early years at 326 Whitehall Road. Hope returned to Bristol in 1943 and met his former next-door neighbour Annie Pugh. Asked if he remembered her, Hope replied: 'Remember her? Oh sure: I was four at the time and we were going steady.'

Wayne Hussey

It's a little known fact that the goth superstar from the Sisters of Mercy and the Mission spent his formative years as a pupil at the Ridings High School in Winterbourne, just outside Bristol.

J David James

When ex-England goalkeeper was looking for a club after the relegation of Portsmouth FC, he claims he was called the morning after a stag do by in-coming Bristol City manager Steve Coppell. Still drunk from the night before, he took the call and was talked into playing between the sticks at Ashton Gate. Like all drunken tales, he has had plenty of time to regret his actions.

■ The house in Whitehall Road where entertainer Bob Hope spent his childhood.

■ Kwame Kwei-Armah (second left) not only stars in Casualty, he is also an ambassador for Christian Aid.

ON LOCATION

THE VERY BEST OF TV FILMED IN BRISTOL

■ The famous Batman and Robin scene from Only Fools and Horses was filmed in Knowle, South Bristol.

Casualty

The BBC's flagship hospital drama was filmed in Bristol for so long that most locals don't take any notice of speeding ambulances any more. 'Bloody *Casualty*,' drivers mutter, as another 'emergency' brings traffic to a halt. Now filmed in Cardiff.

Shoestring

For most TV viewers, Eddie Shoestring was a beige radio phone-in host/private eye who seemed to solve even the most complex of West Country crimes through a series of half-arsed shrugs. For Bristolians, however, it was a weekly opportunity to spot places you knew on the telly. 'Oh look darling, there's the post box at the end of Coldharbour Lane.'

The Young Ones

Once considered seminal, now thought of as pretty crap, the madcap student sitcom that launched a dozen comedy careers was filmed in and around Redland. The most memorable Bristol scene took place in Henleaze's bizarre circular drinking den, the Cock O' The North, which was renamed the Kebab & Calculator for the occasion.

Teachers

The former Merrywood school was turned into Summerdown Comprehensive for Channel 4's gutsy and eventually hilarious drama starring teachers who smoke, drink, use expletives and one who rides his bike

into school every morning giving the director an opportunity to show off some excellent panoramic views of the lovely Bristol.

Animal Magic

Johnny Morris was fortunate that none of the animals he got into conversations with at Bristol Zoo in *Animal Magic* were born and raised in Bristol. Can you imagine a camel with a Hartcliffe accent? *Animal Magic* ran for 21 years and more than 400 editions. Morris, who was from Newport, adopted the persona of a keeper at Bristol Zoo and created a range of voices for each of the zoo's animals. The show was dropped in 1984 when it was felt to be too old fashioned. Johnny Morris died in 1999.

House of Eliot

This very crap and very prim-and-proper period drama about needlework was shot on location in some poncy guest house in Clifton Village. According to Mrs Fotheringham-Herefordshire from the Keep-The-Unemployed-Out-Of-Clifton Society, you can still hear the sound of hems being stitched as you walk past the filming site.

Paper Mask

The presence of Paul McGann, the I from *Withnail & I*, doubled the local interest. A Bristol-based movie starring a Bristol-based actor. In a chilling precursor to the Bristol Royal Infirmary heart scandal, this half-decent medical thriller told the tale of a fake doctor administering pin-the-tail-on-the-donkey science to the city's ever-dwindling population. Much scarier than *Casualty*.

Only Fools and Horses

Not so much 'stick a pony in your pocket' as 'whack a dirty gurt twenny in thur me babs'. It's true! Nelson Mandela House was actually Whitemead House in Duckmore Road, Bristol. The BBC switched filming to Bristol from an estate in Acton, London. The Nag's Head was a Bristol boozer (among others) and the famous Batman and Robin scene was filmed in the Broadwalk shopping precinct in Knowle.

Nik Kershaw

Nicholas David Kershaw was born on 1 March 1958 in Bristol. His mother was an opera singer; his father a flautist. Nik is best remembered as one of the most forgettable singer/songwriters of the 1980s; the man responsible for the turgid *I Won't Let The Sun Go Down On Me* and the Cluedo-like *The Riddle*. He moved to Ipswich with his family when he was a nipper.

Kwame Kwei-Armah

Anyone who knows Kwame only as paramedic Finlay Newton in *Casualty* is only dipping their toe in the shallowest end of a reasonably deep ocean. As well as charging about the familiar *Holby City* area in an all-in-one green jumpsuit, the London- and Bristol-based father of three has written two plays, *Blues Brothers, Soul Sisters* and *A Bitter Herb*, plus a musical called *Hold On*. He showed off his vocal talents on BBC dirgefest *Fame Academy* and acquitted himself more than adequately as a cultural critic on *Late Review*. He's also an ambassador for Christian Aid and a keen supporter of fairtrade. 'I can honestly say that *Casualty* is the best,' he enthused once. No it isn't. ER is.

David 'Syd' Lawrence

Dangerously inconsistent Gloucestershire and England fast bowler turned high-profile restaurateur. The man who gave us Boom on Whiteladies Road is the most visible BMW owner around town.

The Mabbutts

The nearest thing that Bristol has to a football dynasty. Ray Mabbutt played almost 400 League games for Bristol Rovers between 1957 and 1969. Younger son Gary overcame diabetes to follow Ray into the Rovers first team and he played 122 League games between 1978 and 1982. He then moved to Spurs and went on to win 16 England caps. He was awarded an MBE for his services to football, but most fans will remember him as the bloke with the squeaky Bristol accent. The elder brother, Kevin, was regarded as having more potential than Gary and played for Bristol City between 1977 and 1981 before joining Crystal Palace where his career was cut short by injury. He moved to America where he owns an exclusive restaurant in Santa Fe, California.

Paul McGann

He will be forever remembered as the I from *Withnail & I*. McGann lives in Clifton and tries to avoid blokes in pubs who shout 'we've come on holiday by mistake' at him. He was special guest at the opening of the Katmandu restaurant in the Colston Tower after being a regular at the take-away in Easton for 16 years.

Precious McKenzie MBE

The little fella with the big dumbells was born in Durban, South Africa. He is the only Bristol celebrity whose father was killed while hunting crocodiles. McKenzie became a top weightlifter in South

■ World weightlifting champion Precious McKenzie with the world heavyweight champion Muhammad Ali.

■ Precious McKenzie: more than 30 British and world titles and four consecutive Commonwealth gold medals. What a guy!

Africa, but wasn't allowed to compete because he is black. He moved to England, made Bristol his base and went on to become British and World Champion and represent Britain in three Olympic Games between 1968 and 1976. McKenzie was a hugely popular local character who worked tirelessly to promote sport, especially with youngsters. He lived in Leighton Road, Southville, trained at the Empire Gym in St Paul's and worked at an Ashton tannery. Legend has it that the Queen was late for an official engagement because she was so determined to see Precious McKenzie win his third Commonwealth weightlifting gold medal. The 4ft 11in tall McKenzie was nicknamed the 'Pocket Rocket'. Although he now lives in New Zealand, Precious is fondly remembered as one of Bristol's finest adopted sons.

■ **Nipper: this statue of the most famous dog in the world is at the junction of Woodland Road and Park Row.**

Steve Merchant

Former *Venue* magazine work-experience hack turned award-winning comedy writer and Ricky Gervais' lanky other half added some unmistakable touches of Bristolian weirdness to the BBC 2 sitcom *The Office*.

Sean Moore

The Manic Street Preachers' drummer is rumoured to be living in deepest, darkest Emerson's Green, Mangotsfield, with his girlfriend. 'It's a good place… and it's far enough away that my mother doesn't visit me every day,' he says of his adopted home.

Nipper the HMV dog

The Bristol-born dog (part bull terrier with a trace of fox terrier) was bought as a pup in 1884 by flamboyant local artist Mark Barraud. Fame beckoned after Mark's death when his brother Francis painted an oil painting in 1895 of Nipper listening to an old phonograph which was chosen to be 'the loyal mutt' for the His Master's Voice advertising trademark.

■ **Wallace & Gromit were created by Aardman Animations main man Nick Park.**

David Neilson

Aka Roy Cropper from Coronation Street. As Mike Baldwin once put it: 'He's a bit of a nutter, but harmless enough.' The actor responsible for Corrie's nervy, transsexual-marrying anorak loves Bristol so much, he commutes to Weatherfield every week. Or he used to until the traffic got so bad that he moved to Spain and commuted from there instead.

Nick Park

The Oscar-collecting Aardman Animations main man with an ill-advised love of revolving bow ties. Park acknowledges the debt Wallace & Gromit owe to the city: 'I think a lot of the humour has come from being rooted in the Bristol area,' admits the patient Plasticine botherer.

Jonathan Pearce

Every nation gets the punditry its football deserves. In England, Bristol-born Jonathan Pearce is now the voice you hear more often than any other. Radio 5 Live, Channel 5, Saturday afternoon, every week night, he was even on *Robot Wars*… The shouty Pearce is a Bristol City fan who attended Queen Elizabeth's Hospital School at about the same time as Hugo Weaving (see p127).

Colin Pillinger

The son of a Bristol gas-fitter, the world's only inter-planetary Wurzel admits he was: 'rubbish at chemistry at school and dreamt only of playing for Bristol Rovers'. Despite getting Damien Hirst and Alex James from Blur to work on the art and sound, the Mars Express orbiter and its Beagle 2 probe still haven't sent so much as a postcard.

Samuel Plimsoll

Born at 9 Colston Parade, Redcliffe in 1824, Plimsoll came up with the idea of putting a line on a ship's hull which would fall beneath the waterline if the vessel was overloaded. This led to the Merchant Shipping Act of 1876, which made it law for all boats to carry a Plimsoll Line. He died in 1898.

Vicky Pollard

Matt Lucas and David Walliams based the character of Vicky Pollard in *Little Britain* on working-class Bristol teenagers when they were drama students at Bristol University in the mid 1990s. Stroll down Filwood Broadway in Knowle West and you will be surrounded by Vicky Pollards. It would be bold to claim that their presence is an ironic gesture, but it really is like that out West.

Dave Prowse

Originally a weightlifter, Prowse was not only the original Green Cross Code Man, but the body of Darth Vader. Why only the body? Can you imagine hearing: 'May the force be with you, me babber' in a deep Bristolian accent? He once worked as a bouncer at Romeo and Juliet's on Nelson Street.

R Sir Michael Redgrave CBE

Actor, author, director, producer, great grandfather of thespianism and one half of the couple that gave us Vanessa and Lynn Redgrave and Natasha and Joley Richardson. Born the son of a silent film actor in Bristol in 1908, this giant of stage and screen made his first professional appearance at the Liverpool Playhouse in 1934 and went on to star in movies such as Hitchcock's *The Lady Vanishes*, *Kipps*, *The Dam Busters* and *Mourning Becomes Electra*, which earned him an Oscar nomination. He is most fondly remembered for his towering Shakespearean performances and lived long enough to open Clifton College's very own theatre named in his honour.

Tony Robinson

Once upon a time, he was Baldrick in *Blackadder* and everybody loved him. Now he gets paid to spend two weeks digging up tiny fragments of iron-age flint in Channel 4's remarkably tedious *Time*

■ **Dave Prowse as Darth Vader: the most evil man in the universe used to be a bouncer down at Romeo and Juliet's in town.**

■ **And here is Dave Prowse again. This time he is the Green Cross Code Man.**

Up Close

Team. Live archaeology? Whatever next?

Isaac Rosenberg

Arguably the greatest of the First World War poets, Rosenberg was born in Bristol in November 1890 of Russian Jewish immigrant parents. The Peugeot garage diagonally opposite Temple Meads stands on the site of his birthplace.

JK Rowling

Joanne Kathleen Rowling was born in Chipping Sodbury near Bristol to an apprentice engineer and a French/Scottish mother. She also lived in Yate and then Winterbourne. If you'd bumped into a young JK, you would have found her (in her own words): 'A shy, snotty, swotty little kid and very insecure'. Hermione Granger is supposed to be based on her. While living in the Bristol area, she wrote her first book, *Rabbit*, at the age of six.

■ Tony Robinson inspects his change from the pie stand at Ashton Gate where he is a keen Bristol City fan.

Richard Scudamore

The flappy-eared Premier League chief executive is originally from Soundwell, Kingswood. He went to St Stephen's Primary school, where he no doubt shaped his views on supporting Bristol City, the offside rule and making football more inclusive for the community. If he still lived in Soundwell, you'd probably find him in the Jolly Cobbler reading the Green 'Un of a Saturday evening.

Paul Stephenson

Paul Stephenson came to prominence as one of the leaders of the Bristol Bus Boycott in 1963. The Bristol Omnibus Company, backed by the leadership of the Transport and General Workers Union and the Bishop of Bristol refused to employ black drivers and conductors. Black activists Stephenson, Guy Bailey, Owen Henry, Roy Hackett and others organised a boycott of Bristol buses which was championed by Tony Benn and Harold Wilson. Eventually the company gave in. Paul Stephenson went on to become one of Britain's leading civil rights campaigners. In 2007 he became the first black person to be awarded the freedom of the city of Bristol and in 2009 he was awarded an OBE for his services to equal opportunities and to community relations in Bristol.

■ JK Rowling, the author of Harry Potter, was born in Chipping Sodbury, just outside Bristol.

Adrian Stone

Former light-middleweight world boxing champion nicknamed The Predator. He was brought up in Horfield and went to Monks Park School. Stone is now based in America, but is still managed by Bristol promoter Chris Saniger.

Randolph Sutton

The music hall performer who popularised *On Mother Kelly's Doorstep* was born in Anglesea Place, Clifton in 1888. Sutton was able to pack in his job as an accounts clerk at Robinson's packaging in Bedminster when he won a talent contest while on holiday at Burnham-on-Sea. His trademark stage outfits were pink or mauve suits and he quickly became one of Britain's most

JOHNNY BALL

KIDS' PRESENTER SHARES HIS BRISTOL MEMORIES

■ **The nation's favourite children's presenter relives some stories from his early life in Kingswood**

I was born at the Royal Infirmary on 23 May 1938, the only child of Daniel and Martha Ann Ball. I was christened Graham Thalben Ball after the organist and religious composer, Dr G Thalben-Ball (my parents didn't know that the G stood for George).

The infirmary is only a few hundred yards from Johnny Ball Lane, but I wasn't called Johnny until about 1953. That was the year of the Matthews Cup Final when Blackpool beat Bolton Wanderers, 3-2. The right-back for Bolton was Johnny Ball and my Bolton schoolmates started calling me Johnny Ball and it stuck – I have not used Graham since.

My parents lived in a cottage on Warmley Hill, but we soon moved to 111 New Cheltenham Road – the fourth house up from the shops, on the right. I add that, because I remember the Kingswood Cubs was also the 111th Bristol so I wonder if my memory has tricked me here?

I went to Kingswood Primary School from five-years-old and took and passed my eleven plus there, before we moved to Bolton in 1949. The Head was Mr Benson and it may have been he who instilled in me a love of maths. However, my parents were also a help there, as we always played dominoes, cards or a complex bagatelle game in which I learnt to handle numbers well from an early age.

Dad worked at the Magnal in Warmley, moulding aluminium aircraft parts and worked nights almost all the way through the war. Mum worked at Pratt's Boot factory making Burma Boots for the Far East. On air raid nights, we used next door's (Mrs Church's) air-raid shelter once, sat under the stairs a couple of times, under the table a couple of times and then ignored the raids. Mum and I would just play 20 Questions.

My mother talked of being machine-gunned in Kingswood High Street, by returning German aircraft. She tried to get into Woolworths doorway but it was already crowded and they would not let her and myself in the pram, get in. I wonder if anyone else remembers this incident?

I never missed the Odeon Saturday morning show. There was also a cinema across the road, which I think was called the Regent. My parents loved to walk (miles) to pubs in the area. Mangotsfield and Syston Common were summer weekend destinations and especially Frenchay Common – Dad loved cricket. Their favourite pub was the Queens Head at Hanham – I popped in there last year and said I had been in before. 'When?' they asked. 'Oh around 1948!' I said.

There was a very tall man called Albert at the Queen's Head, who would charm warts. If you had warts, you went home, stripped off, counted them and wrote the total on a piece of paper. You brought it to Albert. He secretly looked at the number, threw the paper in the fire and a few day's later, your warts were gone. If it failed, he made you count your warts again, as the right number was essential. He had a large smooth bump on his forehead and everyone said that was where the warts ended up.

He once came from the garden into the Children's Room with a huge garden snail. As we kids watched mesmerised, he placed the snail on his tongue. It slowly crawled further and further down his throat until his mouth closed with a 'crunch' and that was that.

CARY GRANT

THE BEGINNINGS OF OUR MOST FAMOUS STAR

Unlikely as it may seem, Hollywood's smoothest ever leading man was born to Elias and Elsie Leach in Hughenden Road, Horfield. The small terraced house bears a blue plaque outside which reads, 'Archibald Alec Leach, better known as Cary Grant, was born here on 18 January 1904.'

After attending Bishop Road School in Bishopston, he won a scholarship to Fairfield Grammar School in Montpelier, where there is a plaque commemorating the school's most famous pupil. It doesn't mention that Grant was expelled. The exact reason for the expulsion is unclear, but on one occasion Grant said it was because he was found in the girls' lavatory.

Grant had a confused and unhappy childhood. His father was a womaniser who had a son by another relationship. When Cary Grant was 10, he left home to go to Boy Scouts one evening and on his return found his mother had disappeared. In fact, she had been placed in the Fishponds Country Home for Mental Defectives by his father. His father never told Grant what had happened to his mother, but in 1935, he learned that she was still alive in an institution.

By the time he found out his mother was still alive, Grant was already on his way to becoming one of Hollywood's greatest ever leading men. He was introduced to the theatre at the Bristol Hippodrome where he worked as a caller and, in 1920, he headed for the USA along with a troupe of acrobats from the Hippodrome.

Archie Leach became Cary Grant in 1932 when Paramount purchased his contract. Part of that contract stipulated that he change his name. Paramount gave him a list of Anglo-Saxon sounding surnames, and the man known as Archie Leach became Cary Grant.

Grant established himself in a series of screwball comedies such as *The Awful Truth* with Irene Dunne, *Bringing Up Baby* with Katharine Hepburn, *Girl Friday* with Rosalind Russell and *Arsenic and Old Lace* with Priscilla Lane. Alfred Hitchcock was a great admirer of Grant's smooth, charming, yet complex screen persona and once described him as: 'The only actor I ever loved in my whole life'. Grant appeared in such Hitchcock classics as *Suspicion, Notorious, To Catch a Thief* and *North by Northwest*.

Apart from being a great actor, it transpired that Grant was also a famous adventurer with LSD. During the filming of the movie *Operation Petticoat* with Tony Curtis, he told astonished reporters that his relaxed condition was due to the insights he had achieved using the then experimental mind drug on about 60 occasions. 'I have been born again,' Grant said. 'I have been through a psychiatric experience which has completely changed me.'

Grant was a proud Bristolian and returned to the city many times to visit his mother. Sometimes hundreds of fans would turn out to welcome him 'home' when they knew he was arriving in town. He continued to visit Bristol regularly, even after her death.

Cary Grant died just hours before he was due on stage for *A Conversation With Cary Grant* in Iowa on 29 November 1986. A bronze statue was unveiled in Millennium Square in December 2001. Perhaps the many dilemmas in his life are best summed up by Archibald Leach himself who said: 'Everyone wants to be Cary Grant. Even I want to be Cary Grant.'

Celebrities

popular comedians before the Second World War. He was offered *On Mother Kelly's Doorstep* by a London coalman called George Stevens who was inspired to write the song by the sight of two ragged children sitting on a doorstep. Stevens sold the song for five shillings on condition that it was performed by Sutton. A few years before he died in 1969, Sutton recorded a nostalgic trip around Bristol for television with his old friend Sir John Betjeman.

Dave Thompson

Stand-up comedian and a TV gag writer, Dave Thompson is best known for being sacked from the role of Tinky Winky out of the *Teletubbies*. 'I was never stoned in front of the camera,' he retaliated as the tabloids hurled accusations. 'The weirdest dude on the face of the earth,' concluded *Time Out* magazine.

Michelle Thorne

Local girl who made a name for herself as a singer, particularly by entertaining fans at Bristol City and Rovers games at half time. This encouraged Michelle to enter the *X-Factor* where she was knocked out in the third round. The classically-trained vocalist then opted for a career in the porn industry where she specialises in lesbian hardcore, sometimes working with Bristolian Cathy Barry.

Hugo Weaving

Better known as Elrond in *The Lord of the Rings* films, or Agent Smith in *The Matrix*, Hugo went to Queen Elizabeth's Hospital School on Jacobs Wells Road. The school was notable for not having a drama department and for making pupils wear moleskin britches and yellow stockings in public.

■ Hugo Weaving: the Queen Elizabeth's Hospital School old boy went on to become Agent Smith in The Matrix and Elrond in The Lord of the Rings.

Fred Wedlock

You might think that Wedlock was an irritating straw-haired yokel with one hit record, *The Oldest Swinger In Town*, who presented terrible HTV programmes about car boot sales. However, he was a major influence on the Bristol folk scene of the 1960s and beyond. The Wedlock stand at Ashton Gate is named after his grandfather, Billy Wedlock who played for City and England. Fred died in 2010.

Naomi Wilkinson

The face of *Milkshake!*, Channel Five's morning show for kids, Naomi no doubt perfected the Milkshake Shake in the playgrounds of Henleaze Infant and Junior School where she was a pupil. The North Bristol stunner went on to attend Colston's Girls' School where her celebrity credentials were confirmed by a virtuoso solo performance of the first verse of *Once In Royal David's City* at the school carol service at Bristol Cathedral. She was a regular competitor at the Bristol Dance Eisteddfod from the age of four and once played glockenspiel at a performance of Carmina Burana at the Colston Hall. With star credentials like that, a glittering television career clearly beckoned. Naomi is also a keen Fairtrade supporter.

History of the Bristol Beat

From the Pop Group to Massive Attack with a detour via the Moonflowers and Strangelove

I f there was any kind of music scene in Bristol before 1977, his name was Russ Conway and he liked to play the piano. It wasn't until the jagged edges of new wave began to cut the shock tactics out of the punk movement that the first serious local bands began to emerge from their Clifton and Redland hideaways. So we'll make 1977 our starting point for a tour of the Bristol music scene.

First out of the blocks were The Cortinas, four sneering teenagers in torn blazers not long out of grammar school sixth form. Fittingly, their feisty and dangerously energetic double-A-sided single *Fascist Dictator/Television Families* set the standard that others would have to follow. And sure enough, by the middle of 1979, hundreds of nervy young punk bands were popping up all over town. A fanzine called *Loaded* sprang up in support like a regional *Sniffin' Glue*. Suddenly, there were six or seven live venues. Then Heartbeat Records released the *Social Security* EP which featured four irreverent dum-dum bullets, including the immortal *I'm Addicted To Cider*.

Bristol was up and running as a music town. The fledgling label followed their debut release with another excellent single, *The Europeans*, by the Europeans. The Europeans became the first but certainly not the last Bristol band to be linked with a major record deal that never quite came off. The likes of the Pigs, the X-Certs, Joe Public and The Numbers all followed. Aggressive, confrontational upstarts all.

But from here on in, the sound of young Bristol splintered in several different directions. There was wheel-spinning R&B in the shape of 14-year-old rebel-rousers The Untouchables. There were experimental types, such as the Art Objects, Glaxo Babies and Essential Bop. Black Roots

■ Nick Cave called The Pop Group 'the best band in Britain'. This sleeve design is by Rich Beale who later joined ex-Pop Group conspirator Gareth Sager in Head.

■ The Cortinas appeared on the Bristol music scene in 1977 as 16-year-old grammar school boys.

introduced the dub influence while Shoes For Industry volunteered to be ringmaster for weird circus rock and confirmed their status by getting the lead singer to wear an inside-out brain on his head. And, most controversially of all, Melanie, the daughter of Bristol City manager 'Alan-Alan-Alan' Dicks did a pouty Wendy James type of thing for a band called Double Vision. Ashton Court Festival became a canvas for the city's eclectic range of characters. The Wurzels were not welcome.

But lording it over this newly-built sonic kingdom were the mightiest of all the pre-1990s Bristolian hollerers, The Pop Group. How good were The Pop Group? Well, when Nick Cave and his growling Birthday Party entourage first landed on these shores in 1980, they spent every night going to gigs all over the capital but were shocked and disappointed by the limp, bloodless bands they found. 'It was like being gang-banged by a pack of marshmallows,' commented Cave, savagely. Then one night he saw The Pop Group. The experience changed his life. As part of Channel 4's *Music of the Millennium* series, Cave chose *We Are All Prostitutes* as his favourite piece of music of all time. 'The beginning of the record is the greatest start of any record, ever,' claims the awesome Aussie. And you wouldn't want to disagree with him.

This is why it's The Pop Group who are cited as being one of the biggest influences on what became known as

Five great...
Bristol beat albums

1 Massive Attack, Blue Lines: As startling now as it was in 1991. One of the greatest albums ever made.

2 Portishead, Dummy: Monumental achievement: timeless, faultless and utterly unique.

3 Tricky, Maxinquaye: Brooding with sexuality and ghetto intent. Inspired and uncomfortable.

4 Roni Size and Reprazent, New Forms: Drum 'n' bass and urban noise engineering at its most precise.

5 Alpha, Come From Heaven: An LP of impossible beauty and poise that should have sold millions.

■ Bristol dub kings Black Roots were produced by the Mad Professor who remixed Massive Attack's Protection album.

the Bristol sound. Even if it's not all that easy to see why, or how, they laid the foundations for Massive Attack. The Pop Group, y'see, made a fearsome, chaotic noise that was always experimental and sometimes plain unlistenable. Their first single, *She Is Beyond Good And Evil*, might have been as infectious as it was deeply disturbing, but much of the *Y* album sounded like a load of out-of-time clanging and primeval hollering, interrupted by the occasional blast of raucous feedback. These elements burned on a fire already white hot with punk, funk and thunderous dub to make a protest music completely out on its own.

So what does all this have to do with the birth of The Wild Bunch and everything that followed them? Crucially, Mark Stewart's unholy Pop Group crew were the first to assimilate the city's black, or more accurately Rasta, counter-culture into their social life, their worldview, and ultimately their sound. Back then, music allowed you to define your enemies more clearly. 'With the roots worldview… the feeling of spiritual uplift was undeniable,' says singer Stewart of his dub days. As if this wasn't significant enough, the band also spent their youth going to clubs and listening to dance beats. 'We were like the Bristol funk army,' recalls Stewart. 'We'd go to clubs and dance to records by T-Connection, BT Express, Fatback Band, all this heavy bassline funk.'

And this is how The Pop Group invented the politics of dancing. Their dance was a warped, out-of-shape boogie, but a boogie none the less. 'They even used to dance in the most peculiar way,' remembers one fan. Sadly, by the time they'd made their third album, titled *For How Much Longer Do We Tolerate Mass Murder?*, all the incendiary radicalism had got a bit out of control. Maybe it's best to let the band explain their style of music. 'We were creating a wall of noise for the lyrics to fight against,' sighs drummer Dan Katsis. 'We were challenging the production process, disrespecting the machines.'

Something inevitably had to give, and the six members went their separate ways. Gareth Sager formed the distinctly patchy Rip Rig & Panic, bassist Simon Underwood sought relief in the happy honking of jazz-funkers Pigbag and had a top 20 hit, and Mark Stewart sank still deeper into the well of nihilistic creativity in which he had always prospered.

■ Social Security announced their arrival with a crashing guitar sound on their debut EP.

■ How good were Talisman? Good enough to support The Rolling Stones at Ashton Gate in 1982.

■ Barton Hill bass terrorist Gary Clail. A Clail and Tackhead Sound System gig at the Western Star Domino Club was so loud that the queue to get out was as long as the one to get in.

ALMOST FAMOUS

FIVE BRISTOL BANDS THAT DIDN'T QUITE MAKE IT

1. The Seers

Spider and his punky charges welded Beatles melodies onto Pistols energy a decade before those Gallagher brothers thought of the idea. Mouth-almighty manager David Darling whipped up controversy too. The single *Lightning Strikes*, about the Hungerford massacre, caused outrage in the tabloids and catapulted the band to a national level. The Seers were a formidable live act, but never found a producer capable of capturing their energy in the studio. Sadly, a European tour supporting Iggy Pop and a series of dates with their spiritual backing band, The Ramones, was as close as they got.

2. Monk & Canatella

Monk & Canatella started out as a feint Strangelove copy and went on to become one of the most incendiary hip-hop acts the UK has ever seen. Jim Johnston and Simon Russell would have made Limp Biskit and Co fill their shorts. A deal with Telstar, representation from Vision Management and a ferocious album should have put them straight on the cover of *Kerrang!* But the Jerry Lee Lewis-like Johnston chose to go to the pub instead.

3. Moorhaven

According to local industry gossip, Martin Barnard and Angelo Bruschini's acoustic rockers had a deal from a major label on the table but told them where they could shove it. They still failed to put pen to paper after playing in front of most of London's A&R army at The Fleece (see Nights Out Listings, p256). The momentum wilted and the arguments intensified and Moorhaven split. Martin Barnard went on to work with Alpha, Hazel Winter went solo and former Blue Aeroplane Angelo Bruschini got signed up by Massive Attack to work on their *Mezzanine* album.

4. High Coin

The premature demise of High Coin is one of the most distressing Bristol music tales of recent years. Everyone who knew them were convinced that they could and should have

■ The Seers are an excellent live band although they didn't quite make it to the big time.

gone further. Fusing elements of Jimmy Webb, Big Star and Gram Parsons, High Coin had the poise and grace of a band on the verge of greatness. 1997's *Raise A Smile* saw them really hit their stride but soon afterwards Geoff Cook and Jeff Green fell out big time. We were left with a couple of great singles and a case of what might have been.

5. The Cortinas

They burst onto the punk scene as disaffected 16-year-old grammar school boys in 1977 with the unstoppable and promising double-A-sided Step Forward single *Fascist Dictator/ Television Families*. Then they signed to CBS and completely lost their way. Guitarist Nick Sheppard later joined the last incarnation of The Clash to replace Mick Jones and resurfaced briefly to hook up with Gareth Sager, Rich Beale and Will Ng in Bristol sleaze-rockers Head.

Up Close

They were only around for two years or so but The Pop Group cast one hell of a long shadow. There were a lot of bands who found themselves permanently stuck in the shade. Performance art, free-festival politics, second-hand clothes, a vibrant live scene and copious amounts of cheap drugs all played their part in a shift towards an artier and more off-beat order. If you can track down copies of the compilation albums *Avon Calling, Fried Egg – Bristol 1979-1981, Wavelength/Bristol Recorder 1979-1980*, or *Western Stars Vol 1 – The Bands That Built Bristol* (now on Sugar Shack – www.sugarshackrecords.co.uk) you can hear for yourself. It's from this increasingly bohemian atmosphere that Gerard Langley's first band Art Objects sprang.

What we didn't know then is that Bristol was about to rewind to a second year zero. It began down among the funk jams and scratched beats of the St Paul's cafe sound system scene. With the fragments of post-punk scattered all over the place and pulsing electronic dub everywhere, something truly remarkable emerged. The Slits made an unlikely union with Dennis Bovell, The Clash raised swords with Mikey Dread, and The Specials united black and white to fight against anyone who wanted to make something of it. Bristol had reggae collectives Talisman, Black Roots and Restriction. At the Dugout on Park Row, DJs were lining up Chaka Khan against Superfly Soul as the first blasts of urban hip-hop began to filter across the Atlantic.

■ The Wild Bunch: from left 3D, Milo, Nellee, Mushroom. Smith & Mighty produced The Look of Love on the B-side of this ultra-rare Friends and Countrymen EP.

■ The Wild Bunch crew, circa 1985 outside Special K's (now gone) on Park Row. From left: Daddy G, 3D, Claude (aka Willie Wee), Nellee Hooper, Milo Johnson.

Meanwhile, somewhere around town, Robert Del Naja was getting arrested for decorating walls with a spraycan. Soon, he joined Nellee Hooper, Daddy G and Milo in a hip-hop collective called The Wild Bunch. That same year, St Paul's Carnival played host to a number of heavily-amped crews such as 3 Stripe Posse, 2Bad, City Rockas, UD4 and FBI Crew. But bigger and bolder than the rest were The Wild Bunch, who blocked off Campbell Street with their colossal, towering bass bins. The band's reputation spread by word of mouth and they were invited to play at London's Titanic Club. Then they set up residency on Wednesday nights at the Dugout, spinning 12-inches, rapping over the top, heads nodding eerily in time. 1986 saw Smith and Mighty produce The Wild Bunch's cover of Hal David's and Burt Bacharach's *The Look of Love*.

Hindsight has given The Wild Bunch a legendary status in modern music folklore. But Milo's retrospective album, *Story of a Soundsystem*, suggested this is as much myth as reality. It's party music, full of sax burps, cheesy disco jangles and it's very much of its time. Robert Del Naja puts his own perspective on it. 'People always ask us about The Wild Bunch,' he says. 'But the truth, is it's just history to us now. I don't know why people go on about it so much.'

No, the first truly staggering thing The Wild Bunch ever did was to become Massive Attack. And the first thing Massive Attack ever did was to take a giant leap ahead of anything that had come before. *Daydreaming* is one of the most original and self-assured debut singles ever made. Even now it sounds as fresh and as relevant as it did back in the early 1990s. And there was so much more to come.

From its majestic opening line – *'Midnight rockers, city slickers, gun men and maniacs'* – it was obvious the *Blue Lines* album was going to be a classic. Three hit singles – *Daydreaming, Safe From Harm* and *Unfinished Sympathy* – propelled the band right across the globe. At the same time, they redefined what dance music could be. As 3D put it at the time: 'We're not just interested in making something for people to throw their arms and legs about to on a dancefloor.'

Everything had changed. Suddenly, Bristol was being talked about as the 'coolest city on the planet'. Then someone, somewhere in the media, labelled the sound 'trip-hop' – a supposedly softer, near-ambient version of

Five more...
Bristol beat albums

1 **Bass is Maternal, Smith & Mighty:** The original beat gangsters' album is a monument of the Bristol scene.

2 **Coded Language, Krust:** This concrete-edged, crash-bang-wallop of a record is merely a warning of darker territory to come.

3 **Emotional Hooligan, Gary Clail:** Dub-heavy polemics in an On-U-Sound stylee.

4 **The Call is Strong, Carlton:** Falsetto, sparse, beautiful. Produced by Daddy G and very rare.

5 **Dub Plate Selection Vol 1, More Rockers:** A modern drum 'n' bass-cum-reggae classic rooted in the finest traditions of dub rockmillions.

LOCAL MUSIC MAVERICKS

A WHO'S WHO OF THE BRISTOL SOUND HEROES

1. Mike Crawford

Who is he? One of the longest enduring survivors of the Bristol music scene and easily its most handsome face. Back in 1979, Crawford formed nine-piece soft-soul groovers the Spics before heading across the Atlantic to work with the legendary Booker T. On his return, he started writing songs with ex-Head singer Rich Beale for Apache Dropout. In recent times he has been a guest for acts as diverse as Patrick Duff and drum 'n' bass soldier Krust.

Legend has it… In the 1980s mighty-mouth promoter David Darling secured Crawford a US tour supporting soul icon Geno Washington. But Mike missed his kids and caught a plane straight back home again.

Last seen… Crossing the road on his way to The Bell down by Stokes Croft.

2. The Insects

Who are they? From Massive Attack's *Karma Coma* and *Eurochild* to Alison Moyet's comeback album *Hometime*, from Strangelove's *All Because Of You* to a whole raft of film and television scores, Bob Locke and Tim Norfolk are two of the most respected behind-the-scenes writers and producers in Bristol. And they've got an Emmy award to prove it. They used to be called the Startled Insects and produced soundtracks to wildlife documentaries. Now they are working on their own album, featuring a who's who of a guestlist. It could be another huge moment in the history of the Bristol thing.

Legend has it… The Insects are among Bristol's most hard working musicians. They arrive at Christchurch Studios in Clifton not long after 9am and are usually still there around midnight.

Last seen… Late at night in Christchurch Studios working on a few soundtracks and that long-awaited Insects album.

3. Jimmy Galvin

Who is he? Jimmy Galvin's floppy fringe has been around since floppy fringes were fashionable. Describing himself as 'the missing link between Stravinsky and the Teletubbies', Galvin attaches bits of hip-hop, jazz, soul, punk and folk onto his piano-driven songs. He enlisted the help of Adrian Utley and Roxy Music's Andy Mackay on his 2002 album *Surburbia Kills*.

Legend has it… Galvin is an accomplished fine artist and one of the city's most professional coffee drinkers.

Last seen… Finally getting the recognition he deserves under the banner System Vertigo.

4. Davey Woodward

Who is he? Bristol's very own Edwyn Collins. Woodward is the man behind the Experimental Pop Band whose history goes back as far as the 1980s when he fronted jangly hooligan popsters the Brilliant Corners. His purist's charter may have shifted towards a more post-modern vision over the years, but the generously-lipped veteran of the Bristol scene has never strayed too far from his self-laid path of artistic obscurity. Despite this, you can't help feeling that one day you'll see him on a music show on tele.

Legend has it… Davey's uber-cool persona suggests a childhood spent in BS8, but he actually grew up in the wastelands of Lawrence Weston.

Last seen… Striding purposefully down the Wells Road.

5. Jesse Morning Star

Who is he? One of the founding members of The Moonflowers along with Sonik Ray, Jesse is fondly thought of as one of the Bristol music scene's flakiest flakes. But behind the whacked-out public persona there is a supremely talented multi-instrumentalist and songwriter who has devoted every hour of his adult life to the pursuit of his art. Jesse still has a twinkle in his eye that suggests that his finest hour may be yet to come…

Legend has it… Nobody in Bristol has as many rock 'n' rumours about them

Last seen… Fronting the excellent Morning Star and playing guitar with the soon-to-be-huge Jukes.

hip-hop, unique to the South West. Apparently. And within minutes, the city was overrun by gangs of A&R clowns frantically searching for the next Bristol sound sure-things. Not only was the local music mafia not talking, they were also trying to get as far away from the term as possible. 'Who in here likes trip-hop?' asked Tricky at an early live show. When the audience all raised their hands he retorted, 'Well fuck off home, then!'

Surprisingly, no staggeringly, the next giant wave in the West Country sound surf came not from the inner city but from dozy seaside nowhere resort Portishead. Geoff Barrow had been a tape operator for Massive Attack and Neneh Cherry and, with the help of an Enterprise Allowance grant, he recruited jazz head Adrian Utley, drummer/programmer Dave MacDonald and Janis Joplin cover singer Beth Gibbons to form a band named after his home town. Portishead's slow-burning cinematic scores were slow to make an impact but then a press campaign involving hundreds of mannequins placed in various locations around London grabbed the attention of the public and fired the band's third single *Glory Box* straight into the UK charts at number 13. By the end of 1994, Portishead's album *Dummy* had sold more than 1.5 million copies, won the Mercury Music Prize and been voted Album of the Year by *Melody Maker, Mixmag, ID* and the *Face*. Sales in the US topped 150,000. It was no more than Portishead deserved. *Dummy* is one of the best albums of the 1990s: a faultless and seemingly effortless record to rank alongside *Blue Lines*. And, with *Blue Lines*, it is still the chosen soundtrack for any television programme dealing with crime.

For Massive Attack, meanwhile, making a follow-up to the internationally lauded *Blue Lines* was proving to be a long and difficult affair. 'If a thing's worth doing, it's worth doing slowly,' deadpanned Del Naja. But while 1994's Nellee Hooper-produced *Protection* had its moments, most notably *Karma Coma* and *Eurochild*, it was, in truth, a bit of a disappointment. The choice of Tracey Thorn from Everything But The Girl as vocalist pushed the sound closer to the coffee table and away from the barrier-breaking low temperature hip-hop of *Blue Lines*.

By now the friction between the band members was well documented. Daddy G revealed just how bad it was. 'It's a nightmare, really... we hate each other,' said the mild-

■ Carlton McCarthy's *Cool With Nature* single. Daddy G produced this release before Massive Attack kicked in.

■ Rob Smith and Ray Mighty's Three Stripes label was based above a Blues Club in St Paul's. The duo were credited with inventing drum 'n' bass.

■ *Blue Lines*: one of the greatest albums ever made.

mannered bass boomer. Tricky was the first to exit stage left. The only 'kiddie' from Knowle West to ever go out in public wearing a wedding dress, Tricky had always been the unhinged little hooligan of the band. He was the voice of naivety who didn't understand the impact of Thatcher's economic policy. 'Maggie this, Maggie that, Maggie means inflation,' he had observed, incorrectly, on *Daydreaming*. Nobody really expected Massive's equivalent of Sid Vicious to release an album as stunning as *Maxinquaye*. It was a deep, dark and dangerous masterpiece and the third truly great record to come out of Bristol in four years. It seemed Bristol was the coolest city on the planet after all.

Predictably, the city's beat-dependent music scene was given fuel by the successes of the 'big three'. Some attempted mimicry and failed; some folk were barking up the wrong tree entirely; others drew a line in the sand and set about pushing back the boundaries even further. And a few brave souls continued to pick up their guitars and play the old-fashioned way. It was an odd time for Strangelove to come along, but on a cold February night at The Underworld in Camden Town, they arrived with the proverbial thump. Containing two Blue Aeroplanes escapees and a singer with charisma to burn, Strangelove instantly broke the city's 'guitar jinx'. The Camden gig got them a life-long fan in *Select* magazine's Dave Cavanagh and a deal with Food Records. Within a year they had become the biggest and best 'indie' band to ever come out of Bristol. Even Radiohead later described themselves as a 'post-Strangelove band'.

But if Bristol was famous for anything in the mid 1990s, it was its love affair with slow, slacker beats. All that was about to change: Smith & Mighty's More Rockers project had already signalled the start of some serious bpm multiplication, but it was Roni Size's 1997 album *New Forms* that really whacked the turntable into overdrive and span off the scale. Drum 'n' bass was thrust into the mainstream and the innovation spotlight shone on Bristol yet again. DJ Krust, DJ Die, DJ Suv and their miniature dreadlocked leader found themselves in the news, in the charts and on stage picking up the Mercury Music Prize. Yet again, journalists wanted to know about the Bristol sound. 'I am from Bristol, and I do make music from Bristol, so I am it and it is me,' said Krust to stun one American reporter

The Corners started out as psychobillies from Lawrence Weston and ended up as the darlings of Bristol's indie scene.

Despite boasting a Bristol superstar line-up, Head never really captured the popular imagination. A cruelly under-rated act.

Andy Sheppard lived in Southville, played at The Albert in Bedminster and became one of the world's most inventive jazz musicians.

into silence. Roni Size meanwhile, prophesised to anyone who'd listen: 'I'm a junglist and jungle is the future.' Utter nonsense, of course, but at least he said it with conviction.

The activity levels at Full Cycle records might be as frantic as ever, but drum 'n' bass has faded back into the underground again of late. Krust understands this too well: 'Forget drum 'n' bass,' he says. 'This is about endless possibilities, endless configurations, endless structures and restructures – it's infinite.' He is quite right, it is infinite. As are the possibilities. We've barely scraped the surface of electronica and Bristol is sure to be at the forefront of whatever comes next.

Massive Attack may be coming to their natural end, you are far more likely to bump into Tricky in New York than Knowle West and Portishead is again just an estuary town in Somerset, but the Bristol beat made the city the coolest place on the planet for a decade or more. It has left a legacy that a new generation of Bristol soundscapers will surely emulate. 'Some people say that Bristol is the graveyard of ambition,' Robert Del Naja once said. But ambition has now learned to dance to Bristol's tune.

Five great...
Bristol indie LPs

1 **Psych Out, The Seers:** The Ramones meet The Monkees and discover cider and P-funk.

2 **Everything I Ever Wanted, Brilliant Corners:** Lovely stuff. Davey Woodward's lyrical tour de force.

3 **The D Is For Drum, Automatic Dlamini:** Art rock with rhythms.

4 **Siamese Boyfriends, Gerard Langley and Ian Kearey:** Poems and tunes for the missing-a-beat generation from Blue Aeroplanes and Oyster Band frontmen.

5 **Love and Other Demons, Strangelove:** The last great Bristol indie album?

■ The Blue Aeroplanes with Gerard Langley in the foreground.

BRISTOL
STREET ART

> **Bristol's graffiti tradition stretches back to the 1980s when it was heavily influenced by** the New York hip-hop and street art crews. Street artists from the Big Apple who visited St Paul's and Barton Hill left a legacy that has been passed on from 3D, Nick Walker, FIX and Inkie in the 1980s to Banksy in the 1990s and on to the likes of Cheba, Sickboy, Paris and Xenz. Here we trace Bristol street art from that first 3D image of two policemen (the first example of graffiti in Britain?) through to the latest offerings from Bristol's dedicated army of taggers, stencillers and sprayers...

A WHO'S WHO OF BRISTOL MUSIC

■ Babyhead offer an energetic live set with their version of punk, ska and hip-hop.

The Bristol Beat doesn't exist,' said Daddy G in 1990. Well, if there was no discernible shared sound then, there sure as hell isn't one now. Here's our tribute to the people who have influenced the diverse sounds of Bristol in recent years and those who are shaping its promising future…

🅐 Joe Allen
Flexibly-jointed ex-Coltranes, Aeroplanes and Strangelove bassist, last seen zooming up and down his fretboard for Breakbeat Era. Trivia fans may like to know that he used to eat nothing except cold toast. And that he once drunkenly formed a pretend band called Fulham with the author of this book.

Aspects
Influential hip-hop crew with a West Country edge who went their separate ways in 2004. DJ Specify, MCs El-Eye, Bubbaloui and ProbeMantis along with scratch DJ Nu-Balance and engineer 7-Stu-7 were the earliest acts to sign for Bristol's Hombre Records.

The Autos
Ignore the disappointing name and the band's apparent unwillingness to spend a significant amount of time in the spotlight, these drainpipe 'n' daps upstarts are one of the most exciting new-wave bands in the land right now. Mercifully, The Autos influences are The Cars, The Saints, Telephone and the Only Ones – they sound nothing like the bloody Jam.

🅑 Queen B
One of the very few women to have been at the forefront of the Bristol DJ movement since the early days in the 80s. Queen B doesn't play out as much as she used to, but when she does you remember why she was in such demand on the European festival circuit for her very cool mix of Afro beat, hip hop and reggae.

■ Geoff Barrow and Beth Gibbons put a Somerset commuter town on the international music map.

Babel
It's difficult to think of any Bristol bands, past or present, who have been as original, as inventive or as shoe-stompingly self-assured as Babel. They are heads and shoulders and violins and tambourines above just about anyone. A swaggering chariot driven by their heroic leader Danny Coughlan.

Babyhead
Full-on fusion of punk, ska and hip-hop with horns. The band has a

justifiably impressive live reputation and are capable of delivering a truly stunning stage performance.

Geoff Barrow

A music industry insider once revealed that they had never met anyone as devoted to music as Portishead founder Geoff Barrow. 'His refusal to use backing tapes when playing live keeps him awake at night,' apparently. A bright light in an age full of dim stars.

Beak>

The > sign means 'greater than'. Beak> is a collaborative project between Portishead's Geoff Barrow and bass about town Billy Fuller (Robert Plant, Fuzz Against Junk).

Rich Beale

There is a rumour going around that Rich Beale has been on the dole since 1975. For this alone, he deserves an award. Add a CV that includes Head, Pregnant and Apache Dropout and you get a true renaissance man of the Bristol underground.

Blackout

Hard-hitting, live drum 'n' bass outfit formed in 2003, Blackout teamed up with ex-Breakbeat Era vocalist Leonie Laws in 2005. Their first single, *Massaka*, was released on Random Audio Records in the summer of 2006. Played a famous house party in Picton Street in July 2006. The windows were still rattling in August.

Beki Bondage

Self-styled Queen of Punk (for a few weeks in 1980 at least), Beki (real name Rebecca Louise Bond) joined Bristol punk outfit Vice Squad at the tender age of 15. The band was never fully accepted in Bristol, but enjoyed success in the States where Beki is still touring as Vice Squad, although she's the only original member.

Five great...
Bristol dub tracks

1 **Dole Age, Talisman:** Anti-Thatcher dub from the eclectic Talisman.

2 **No Protection, Mad Professor:** Dub-heavy remix of Massive Attack's highly-rated Protection album.

3 **Juvenile Delinquent, Black Roots:** Traditional Jah reggae from the St Paul's frontline.

4 **Tenth Dub, Henry and Louis:** From the excellent Rudiments LP on Smith & Mighty's More Rockers label.

5 **Jerusalem, Mark Stewart and The Mafia:** Peculiar goings on from Pop Group founder. Find it on On-U-Sound's compilation Pay it all Back album which also features Gary Clail's False Leader track.

■ **Chikinki's Experiments with Mother album took them to a new level in the Bristol scene.**

Matt Booth

Dynamic promoter turned manager, Matt Booth arrived on the scene like a whirlwind sometime in the late 1990s, totally transforming the local live arena with his finger-on-the-pulse booking policy. He then turned his attentions to the Ashton Court Festival and he played a pivotal role in shaping the local shindig that we knew and loved until it ended in 2007.

Dave Brailey

When promoter Dave Brailey came to town in the middle of the 1990s, he gave the local music scene a much-needed kick up the arse. It wasn't long before he graduated to The Fleece. Few people have done more for Bristol's live music culture.

Breakbeat Era

Defunct offshoot of the Full Cycle project featuring Roni Size, DJ Die and singer/songwriter Leonie Laws. The *Ultra-Obscene* album mixed drum 'n' bass with rock influences.

Emily Breeze

Irish refugee Emily Breeze has become the first lady of the new Bristol underground scene. "Somewhere between a punch in the guts and a tender tragic caress," is how she describes her muse and the 2010 breathtaking statement of intent 'The Penny Arcade' does both beautifully. A 21st Century post-feminist icon waiting for the world to catch up.

Bronnt Industries Kapital

You can tell by their name that they are in the business of making art noise. Their debut limited-edition EP contained a statistical information sheet, a map and a noose made of electrical flex. With gestures like this, they could well find themselves at the forefront of the UK avant-garde music scene.

Thomas Brooman

Former Spics drummer and founder of *The Bristol Recorder* magazine, the much travelled Brooman met a certain Peter Gabriel in 1981 and together they founded the WOMAD festival. He continued as its Artistic Director until 2008, the same year he was given a CBE by you-know-who for his services to charity and music.

Angelo Bruschini

When the former Numbers, Aeroplanes and Moorhaven guitarist got the call from Massive Attack, he can have had little idea just how vital he would become. Proof positive that Ange himself was wrong when he once uttered the immortal line: 'A leopard never changes its stripes.'

■ Call the Doctor

They might have taken it from a Sleater-Kinney album but it's still a terrible name. Call The Doctor's jerky, post-punk has a growing fan base that includes the world's oldest indie kid, Steve Lamacq.

■ Massive Attack's Daddy G.

■ Bristol photographer Beezer's classic shot of Robert '3D' Del Naja in his early days as a graff artist.

Kid Carpet

Whacked-out lank who hammers the living crap out of plastic toy instruments to create a squashed and fried hip-hop that he sometimes likes to call 'Kiddie disco punk'. He does gigs at carpet shops and car boot sales too. Brilliant and berserk.

Neneh Cherry

Miles Johnson, founder member of The Wild Bunch, went to Cotham Grammar School with Pop Group drummer Bruce Smith, who married Neneh Cherry, who sang for boho-funk surrealists Rip Rig and Panic, some of whom used to be in The Pop Group, who were fronted by Mark Stewart, who shared his squat with Tricky and worked with Smith and Mighty, who produced a Wild Bunch track. Much of Massive Attack's *Blue Lines* album (featuring Tricky) was originally recorded at Neneh Cherry's London home. Cherry also worked with Mark Stewart and Ari Up of the Slits as the New Age Steppers who recorded on Adrian Sherwood's On-U Sounds label, which later became home to Gary Clail…

■ **DJ Die: discovered hip-hop at an early age and preferred it to his mum's Big Country albums.**

Chikinki

This is what happens when you throw together a mix of krautrock, squelchbeat, blipfunk and unholy rock and give it a damn good shake. It could also be the future. Ever since the release of their *Experiments With Mother* album, these deeply unhinged art noise upsetters have been the lunatics that seem most likely to take over the asylum. Nobody who has seen them perform live was surprised when they signed to Island Records.

Gary Clail

Former car salesman turned sound system impresario turned 'emotional hooligan', Clail is usually remembered for his chart-troubling single *Human Nature*, but don't hold that against him.

■ **Neneh Cherry: Massive Attack created their debut Blue Lines album at her hoime studio.**

Sean Cooke

Spiritualised escapee turned Lupine Howl frontman who eats, sleeps and breathes rock 'n' roll with a conviction that goes way beyond the call of duty. Apparently, he never gets up before 4pm as a matter of principle. Respect.

Mike Crawford

Although he has won the Unofficial Best Looking Bloke in Bristol Award for the last 17 consecutive years, Mike Crawford shows no sign of hanging up his cheekbones. He was last seen working with Krust on the *Coded Language* album.

Ⓓ Daddy G

After taking time out from the recording of Massive Attack's *100th Window* album released in 2004, Grant has gone back to his roots on the local and national DJ and festival circuit. Grant has towered over the Bristol music scene for as long as anyone can remember. 'Oh yeah, that was cool shit,' he said, commenting on Massive Attack's back catalogue.

THE MOONFLOWERS

THIS LEGENDARY BAND HAVE A SPECIAL PLACE IN THE HEARTS OF BRISTOL'S MUSIC COMMUNITY...

■ The 1998 EP which includes the songs Rock and Roll, My Baby, All or Nothing and Johnny.

1. Accidental party people

In December 1987, Jesse Vernon got a sort of band thing together with the intention of playing a few parties. At the time, there was no wigged-out psychedelic funk scene in Bristol, so The Moonflowers created their own. Daubed in war paint and almost always naked from the waist up, the band began playing impromptu gigs wherever they could and soon had a fanatical following. Their audiences were encouraged to hold hands in an attempt to achieve world peace as the band cavorted wildly around the stage. You could say that they were the first hippies with a sense of humour.

2. The DIY approach to becoming pop gods

Never ones to create too much unnecessary hassle, The Moonflowers' first EP *We Dig Your Earth* had a pressing just large enough to cater for family and close friends. Amazingly, some copies found their way to London and the band's reputation went nationwide. They set up their own label, Pop God Records. And

with backing from hip indie label Heavenly released the magnificent *Get Higher* on 12-inch. It is chosen as *NME* single of the week. The superbly shrugged chorus chant *'Can't get what you want from life, might as well get higher,'* perfectly captures the E-swallowing mood of the day and propels The Moonflowers into the top 40. Trouble is, the 'single' is so long it actually qualifies for the album chart.

3. Exit Planet Earth

The success of their debut album *Hash Smits* left our heroes feeling a little empty. Desperate to throw off the shackles of their new commercial existence, they decided to release a statement declaring that they have left that world and now resided in a creative and spiritual utopia of their own making called Rainbowhemia. To the rest of us, it looked like an old yellow tour bus. It sounds like The Moonflowers had been taking a few hallucinogens.

4. Revolutionaries do the hoovering

1992 saw The Moonflowers really finding their comedy touch. After recording a bizarre, farmyard-animal-noise-assisted version of *Get Higher* for a John Peel Session, they release another EP with the truly inspired title *Tighten Up On The Housework Brothers and Sisters*. The EP's main track was the anthemic *Brothers and Sisters* but also included a well-chosen cover version of the Damned's *I've Just Got To Be A Discoman Today*.

5. Making an impression on A&R

Sooner or later, all this activity attracted the attention of the A&R departments of several major record labels. And, sure enough, The Moonflowers were invited to play a set in front of a collection of top industry spotters at the Marquee Club in London. They set off for the big smoke in an agreeable enough mood but something, quite possibly involving the consumption of illegal substances, altered their attitude along the way. By the time they hit the North Circular, they had decided that the whole thing was a load of rubbish and was not what they were about as a band in any way. Our heroes arrived, plugged in and proceeded to embark on an impenetrable and unbroken 30-minute jamming session. Needless to say, the sensitive A&R folk walked out half-way through and funnily enough vowed never to go near The Moonflowers ever again.

6. Big in Japan

Naoki and Miwako were running a record shop called Zero and a fanzine called *Grassroots* in their home town of Tokyo when they first heard The Moonflowers and decided to run an interview with the Bristol bohemians. The band saw the interview and duly invited the pair to Gloucester to watch them play live. The enthusiastic Japanese fans took them up on their offer. 'They

■ The Moonflowers were known for their outrageous and outstanding live performances.

welcomed us as friends,' recalls Naoki. 'We really wanted to invite them to Tokyo to play and we managed to get someone to pay for them to come and visit.' And so, with all the wonkiness of a seriously wasted Godzilla, the Moonflowers landed in the Far East. Against all the odds, the tour was a resounding success. In fact, the 'love' vibe was so strong, Naoki and Miwako decided to get married. The happy couple then chose to spend their honeymoon in the lovely St Werburghs.

7. Nous sommes des rock stars

In 1993, The Moonflowers released their second album, the cosmically-entitled *From Wales To Jupiter And Beyond The Stars To Rainbowhemia*. The album captured a jazzier, more relaxed sound, with tracks such as *Smile In The Face Of Evil And Dance* and *There We Will Find The Sun* even hinting at their most commercial edge to date. But anyone anticipating seeing some naked buffoonery on *Top of the Pops* was about to be disappointed. As soon as the album was released, the band upped sticks and moved to a remote farmhouse somewhere out in the sticks in Normandy in France. For the next couple of years, The Moonflowers all lived communally and continued to do their groove thing, but without the audience. When they next surfaced, they did so with a double album, *Colours And Sounds*. Unfortunately, it would be their last.

8. Toby Pascoe: 1970-2002

This is the story of a life less ordinary. When multi-instrumentalist Toby Pascoe joined The Moonflowers in 1990, his skills transformed them from a shambolic party band into the irresistibly funky boogie merchants that we all remember. Toby seemed to have the same effect on everyone he met. He was always out there, unafraid to put himself on the line in the name of art. Bizarre experiments involving a steam-powered drum machine programmed by a roll of paper followed. Then at the end of the 1990s, he joined the breakbeat era and really began pushing his remarkable percussive brilliance to the edge of its limits. When he died, Toby left a daughter Seren and a motto that will live forever in the hearts and minds of all those who heard it: 'Tread lightly,' he could be heard to say, 'and you'll never spill a drop.'

Up Close

Robert Del Naja
3D might be the hippest of hip-hop priests and one of the most underrated vocalists of the last 20 years but Massive's mainman has never forgotten his Bristol roots and has the Bristol City season ticket to prove it.

Mike Derby
Founder of Sugar Shack Records and the force behind the staggeringly complete Bristol Archive Records (www.bristolarchiverecords.com). BAR has re-released a number of classic Bristol albums in recent years and has enjoyed huge success with its highly recommended Bristol reggae collections.

DJ Derek
DJ Derek used to be the old bloke in the cardigan in the corner of The Star and Garter playing a cool set of obscure ska. He went on to become a leading figure in the world of dub, reggae and ska. His trojan collection *DJ Derek Presents Sweet Memory Sounds* was released in the summer of 2006. He used to be an accountant at Fry's but gave it all up to play ska and reggae. Good man!

DJ Die
Brought up in Totterdown, DJ Die discovered the hip-hop, graffiti and skateboarding craze that swept Bristol at a tender age in the mid 1980s. Those roots remain core to his work with Full Cycle and with Krust as I Kamanche. 'We make dark music, but it's still party music,' he says. Die is still an avid skateboarder and one of the biggest musical talents in town.

Conal Dodds
Promoter of some of the biggest acts to play Bristol in recent years, Conal Dodds once took a punt on a band called Oasis – whatever happened to them eh?

Dubrovnik
With origins in the heavy dub depths of Zion Train and Dubmerge, Dubrovnik know how to handle their bass levels. Add some warped beats, brass, and a troupe of exotic dancers and you've got a full-on carnival of dub with lashings of electronica. Dubrovnik's debut album was released in the summer of 2006.

Ben Dubuisson (100 Strong)
Hundred Strong is the musical project of producer Ben Dubuisson, a leading light on the club scene . There's usually a big slice of soul in his productions. The single *Dream On Delay* (from the 2005 album *Basement Blues*) featuring NYC soul singer Alison Crockett was nominated as a Gilles Peterson's worldwide track of the year. The classic soul production *Stylin Free* was released in 2011.

Patrick Duff
Ex-Strangelove heartthrob, often mistaken for a tortured soul drowning in self-pity. Not true. Yes, Pad is analytical to the point of

■ After the demise of Strangelove, singer Patrick Duff sat down for a bit before starting his solo work.

■ MC Dynamite: Reprazent's dynamic frontman has gone solo.

destruction. But he laughs just as intensely. Songwriter, storyteller, philosopher, comedian and Mervyn Davies fan.

MC Dynamite

Sensational frontman for the live Reprazent experience, MC Dynamite's musical background is in Motown and reggae. Like several of his conspirators in Full Cycle and Reprazent, he was drawn to fledgling hip-hop and house clubs. By the time rave and drum 'n' bass broke, he was already deeply absorbed by the party scene. As an MC, he has the ability to slip into the mix like a third turntable, hyping the crowds with his lyrics and rhymes but never dominating the experience.

E Matt Elliot

He might have a reputation for making soundtracks for a collapsing world but the former Third Eye Foundation bloke has clearly got a well-developed sense of humour. How else would he have come up with wonderfully self-mocking titles like *You Guys Kill Me* and *Borderline Schizophrenic*?

Rob Ellis

As the multi-instrumentalist and producer of PJ Harvey's *Dry* and *Stories From The City, Stories From The Sea* albums, Rob Ellis has gained a reputation as being Bristol's equivalent to Nick Cave's right-hand man Mick Harvey.

F The Fauns

As if to prove the ever-widening diversity of local music, along come The Fauns with a single-minded mission to resurrect shoegazing, the unfairly maligned 90s soft wall-of-guitar sound that gave us the likes of My Bloody Valentine and Chapterhouse. Appropriately enough, they spend a lot of time touring snowy Scandinavia. Beautifully out of step.

Duncan Fleming

Innovative boy wonder behind War Against Sleep. Fleming's welding of piano, Mini-disc and four-track continues to unsettle and amaze in equal measures with albums, soundtracks and live installations all part of his single-minded vision.

The Flies

Some bands are born with a buzz around them. 'It's about the occasional corruption of men by women and the ease with which men are susceptible to corruption,' says vocalist and former Spiritualised and Lupine Howl frontman Sean Cook of The Flies stunning debut album. With its dark hypnotic jazz beats and brooding, whispered vocals, Cook – and heavyweight Insects cohorts Bob Locke and Tim Norfolk – have sculpted a shadowy soundtrack to a freak-strewn post-midnight netherworld. Think Max Steiner doing electronica, the sharp shuffling feet narrative of a James Ellroy crime scene or William S Burroughs rattling down a sidewalk with a hatful of narcs in his head.

New beat...
How to speak the language of sound

1 Crunk: High energy, club-orientated hip hop. Not something you find between your toes after wearing dirty flip-flops.

2 Emo: Abbr. emotional. Form of punk often with angst-laden lyrics and big riffs. Not a character from Sesame Street.

3 Glitch: Electronic music utilising cut up beats and processed sounds. Not an uncomfortable irritation caused by the wearing of thongs.

4 Grindcore: Heavy metal characterised by intense drumming, grinding guitars and vocals like a frog's fart. Not a building aggregate.

5 Scrumpy & Western: Particular brand of comic folk music from the West Country. Not a pint of cloudy and a crap local paper.

ALCOHOL AND OTHER DEMONS

A STORY OF STRANGELOVE ON TOUR

1. Wannabe starting something?

Strangelove's complete lack of muscle didn't stop them from getting in a number fights with other bands on the road. One night at the Colombia Hotel, singer Patrick Duff 'went outside' with the Buzzcocks after calling them 'a load of has-beens'. Shelley and Co. bottled out. Terrorvision, however, were less willing to turn the other cheek when a paralytic Patrick waltzed into their dressing room after a particularly heavy binge and announced to them : 'Remember, you are Wombles'.

2. Premature Glastonbury experience

It seemed like a good idea at the time. You know, getting to Glastonbury early, avoiding the rush. Strangelove decided to head off on Tuesday night and arrived at around 2.30am. For the next three days most of the band continued in full-on party mode and unsurprisingly were in no fit state to do anything by the time the festival began on Friday. Somehow they took to the stage on Sunday and were one of that year's highlights.

3. I will walk a thousand miles…

Singer Patrick Duff went through a stage of going on walks so long they put Ian Botham

to shame. Following a heated 2.30am argument with the author of this book at Rodney Allen's house in Pilton, Pad stormed off in protest and began what was to be a very long stroll back to Stokes Croft. It took him and his co-sufferer Dodge eight terrible hours before they reached Bristol. A few weeks later the pair went even further. Nottingham, to be exact, most of it up the hard shoulder of the motorway armed only with a giant bottle of vodka. They eventually reached Nottingham and went straight down the pub for a rest.

4. Pushing the boat out with Pusherman

If the path of excess does indeed lead to the palace of enlightenment, then Strangelove's tour support Pusherman were some seriously enlightened gentlemen. Armed with a carrier bag full of E and a shoebox of assorted 'extras', the band set out to prove that they, and not lightweights Primal Scream, were the number one rock 'n' roll lifestyle band in Brighton. Strangelove hitched a ride and shared the prescriptions. "I saw Pusherman soundcheck pissed out of their heads one night," recalls Patrick Duff. "It was the most dangerous thing I've ever seen." Every day, for four long weeks, the party raged. Pusherman split afterwards and a few of them died soon after that.

5. Hear the drummer get wasted

It's 1996 and Strangelove are in London to play at the Clapham Grand. It's an important gig for the band with representatives from Food, Parlophone, EMI, Blur and the national music press on the guest list. Strangelove are due on stage at 9.30pm, which would be fine except that it's 6.30pm and drummer John Langley is paralytic. He's so drunk that he walks the length of Kentish Town Road saying, 'I'm John,' to each person who walks past. 'Pleased to meet you.' He's no better by 7.30pm. At 8pm, deep panic sets in. At 9.30pm, against all medical possibilities, Langers sits at his drum kit and plays a blinder. 'He's the best drummer in the world,' says someone afterwards. They're not wrong.

Dave Francolini

The legendary sticksman who leapt into the rock 'n' roll hall of
fame by running over a Bristol Grammar School security guard
who wouldn't let him into an exam. His drumming was once
accurately described as being 'like the first 20 minutes of *Saving
Private Ryan*'.

Four Track

Any band with a drummer who is as high profile as Purple Penguin
boss Ben Dubuisson has definitely started out on the right foot.
Four Track are the latest turntablists to look back to the days before
young people started gathering in fields and taking E.

Fuzz Against Junk

At first, they were just rumours. Ian Green, the most enthusiastic
and dedicated music collector in all of Bristol, had got a band
together. 'No. You're joking?' whispered the sceptical masses.
Then it was news. 'Green's band are brilliant,' we said, amazed.
FAJ are not just Green but they are as intricately layered and as
challenging as expected. But who'd have thought the ultimate fan
could pull off a transfer like this. Respect Sir.

■ **Alison Goldfrapp: sour-faced,
art house sex kitten.**

Freakeasy

Well-respected hip-hop crew with depth and intelligent lyrics.
Freakeasy are great live and played a legendary set at the Ashton
Court Festival way back in 2003.

Fuck Buttons

Born out of the need to worship noise, Andrew Hung and
Benjamin John Power soon discovered that if you hear a drone
for long enough it carves out its own rhythm. Two breathtaking
albums of relentless, almost transcendental, percussion and
atmospherics have seen them establish themselves at the
forefront of the nu electronica movement, if we can call it that.

Ⓖ Gonga

Hairy, heavy, headbanging. Although the chords may hark back to
the days when Black Sabbath were being introduced to the rock
world as 'a promising young group from England', the band's sheer
unrelenting ferocity takes them way beyond retro. Gonga's debut
album *Stratofortress* was released on Geoff Barrow and Fat Paul's
Invada label.

Gravenhurst

What's the best way to describe Gravenhurst? There have been the
inevitable Nick Drake comparisons but this doesn't even begin to
tell the story. Nick Talbot is a fast-fingered virtuoso of the strings
and it is this, more than anything else, that separates him from
what's come before. A prince of scattered nostalgia.

Ian Green

Mind-bogglingly enthusiastic 13th Floor Elevators fan around

town and DJ who once harangued a clearly frightened Hank
Marvin for half an hour with an in-depth discussion of the
Shadows twanger's Marshall amp.

Will Gregory

When a classically trained multi-instrumentalist decided to move
into the arena of experimental electro pop the results were
utterly startling. Will Gregory is the synth-collecting genius who
gives the often underrated Goldfrapp their warped, future world
soundscape.

Alison Goldfrapp

Notoriously sour-faced art house sex kitten who has purred
studied perfection all over Goldfrapp's admirably oblique
nu-disco flavoured rise up the charts. Has been known to wear a
tail. Think Marilyn Monroe meeting Shirley Temple in outer space.
Or something like that. Your move Roisin Murphy.

■ The most inspirational female
rock artist of her generation, Polly
used to live in Totterdown.

🅗 PJ Harvey

OK, she's from Dorset, but Bristol (Totterdown) was the base
from which Polly worked with Automatic Dlamini, John Parish's
experimental percussive music project which Polly joined as a slide
guitarist, saxophonist and backing singer. She toured extensively
with the band before going solo.

The Heads

These legendary Bristol psychedelic purists have been churning
out superb sneaker-to-the-floor sonic mis-shapes for more than
twenty years now and show no sign of veering anywhere near
the mainstream. However, as their nine-page interview in *Optical
Sounds* magazine proves, they are treated like Gods in the scuzz
underground.

■ Simon John played on Roni
Size's Mercury Music Prize-
winning album New Forms.

Nellee Hooper

A gang of us called round Nellee Hooper's house once when we
were mods but his mum said he was out. A few years later, there
he was on *Top of the Pops* with Jazzy B. Nellee, Mushroom, 3D and
Milo were The Wild Bunch line up for the *Friends And Countrymen*
EP in 1988 and became one of the most sought-after producers in
the biz.

Graeme Howell

He might look like a friendly plumber but this is the fella who
bought together the London Philarmonia and I Am The Mighty
Jungulator. The affable Colston Hall business director is one of
the city's prime movers when it comes to experimental music and
he somehow finds time outside his day job to act as the director
of the Bristol Music Foundation and the chair of the Bristol Music
Industry Forum. Sainthood surely waits.

Steve Hunt

Steve, or Stem to his friends and about a thousand local bands who have wanted to be his friend over the years. For longer than can possibly be good for the health, Stem has been co-ordinator of the Ashton Court Festival. He is a hero and he deserves your thanks. And your money. Now organising St Paul's Carnival.

🄸 The Insects (Bob Locke and Tim Norfolk)

Aka the Startled Insects. These two Emmy-award winning behind-the-scenes maestros have been responsible for a vast library of film and TV scores, as well as tracks for the likes of Massive Attack, Goldfrapp and Alison Moyet.

I Am The Mighty Jungulator

Ever since Bristol's very own genre-stomping, ultra-sensory, avant-garde virtuoso electronic supergroup picked up the best new electronic act at the Diesel New Music Awards 2004, they've exuded an air of anything's possible. Not content with a sonic canvas that takes in krautrock, drum 'n' bass, speed garage, dream-core and ambient, they invented 'a sonic philosophers stone' in the form of an audio engine. Whatever next?

🄹 Andy Jenks

One half of Alpha and the only person in Europe to have decorated his living room with a 12-foot billboard of Roy Castle. Jenks' thirst for the perfect sound is unparalleled.

Joe 90

DJ and musical connoisseur of the highest order, Joe 90 is responsible for pushing the freshest jazz, funk, soul and hip-hop sounds to lift Bristol's clubbing scene out of the 1990s. Joe 90 is the promoter of Bristol's highly- acclaimed club night Seen. Described by those who know him as: 'a master of the low-slung bling'.

Simon John

Talented and thoroughly likeable Federation main man and former Roni Size bassist whose free-flowing finger noises were the scaffolding of the Mercury Music Prize-winning *New Forms* album.

Jim Johnson

Somehow the craziest half of the recklessly insane Monk & Canatella has managed to come out alive and, indeed, kicking. The fully-reformed Mr Johnson also has a hugely promising new band behind him. We await the results with interest.

Jukes

According to reports, this lot are something very, very special indeed. The sound is a high and happy country soul that resonates with all the melancholic grace of Nielsson or Jimmy Webb. When they finally announce their arrival, they will probably do so in front of a wall of expectant A&R people.

🄺 Kosheen

The trio who make up drum 'n' bass adventurers Kosheen are

Five Great...
Experimental albums

❶ Mirror, Flying Saucer Attack: From their lofty position at the top of the steps in Revolver Records, Dave Pearce and company spent 15 years or so as darlings of the alt. fanzine Underground. Bristol's most challenging band.

❷ You Guys Kill Me, Third Eye Foundation: 'I got a bigger, fatter sampler, the biggest and fattest you can buy. You Guys Kill Me is the result of that,' says soundscaper Matt Elliot.

❸ For How Much Longer Do We Tolerate Mass Murder?, The Pop Group: Nihilistic, tribalistic white boy funk and one of the sit-up-and-listen albums of the post-punk era. An anti-Fascist groove thing.

❹ Teenagers In Trouble vs Fat Paul: Eponymous mini-album of beats and breaks featuring Rick from Planet Records, Fat Paul, Andy and Corin from Alpha and Receiver.

❺ Weep Hippies Weep, Pregnant: Second album from the queasy Beefheartian slouch funksters with Gareth Sager as unsettling and off-the-wall as ever.

Markee Substance, Darren Decoder and Sian Evans. The band's grounding is in the Bristol Roughneck Ting drum 'n' bass raves and the Breakbeat Culture shop and record label. Their *Hide U* single was voted best single at the 2003 UK Drum 'n' Bass Awards.

Knowledge of Bugs

Live electronica outfit responsible for Bristol label Clean Cut Records. *Venue* magazine said of the *Woodwork* EP: 'a kind of autumnal melancholy that will have you gazing out of the window to watch and see if the leaves are turning brown.'

Krust

Krust (real name Keith Thompson) had a wide-ranging beat education that included acid house, hip-hop, drum 'n' bass and rave. He progressed through Fresh Four and Smith & Mighty to co-found the Full Cycle collective with Roni Size. The solo *Coded Language* album followed along with the *I Kamanche* collaboration with DJ Die and the 2006 *Hidden Knowledge* project.

■ **Keith Thompson, aka Krust, has worked with Bristol's finest.**

🅛 Laid Blak

Fronted by MC Joe Peng and kilt-wearing vocalist Flex, Laid Blak may have a name that makes them sound like a cabaret act but in fact they are the leading local exponents of urban reggae and ska.

Gerard Langley (Blue Aeroplanes)

One of the most original voices in British art rock of the last 20 years. The Blue Aeroplanes founder and wordsmith hasn't wavered from his poetic mission in all that time and still has the fan base to prove it. The Aeroplanes signed to EMI in 2006.

John Langley

A genuine Bristol rock 'n' roll legend with a thousand stories to tell, most of them involving heavy drinking and broken spectacles. Langers is a drummer and a human being of unparalleled genius. He's also Gerard Langley's brother and used to play drums for Gerard's band the Blue Aeroplanes.

Alex Lee

Ex-Coltranes, Aeroplanes and Strangelove, Lee became Suede's multi-instrumentalist who Brett Anderson calls 'my little virtuoso'. Lee was born with a plectrum in his fingers and everything he has done since has been blessed with easy, unaffected cool.

Rita Lynch

A truly astonishing performer, Rita first came to public attention with her 80s punk outfit Rita and The Piss Artists. There followed a long solo career which saw her re-emerge as a guitarist with the Blue Aeroplanes. Her most recent project has seen Rita team up with Aeroplanes drummer John Langley to deliver a stripped down, raw set of extraordinary power and emotion.

BRISTOL'S BEST-EVER GIGS

Roxy Music: Colston Hall, 1973
Unlike those dismal comedy copycats The Darkness, this bunch of intergalactic space lizards did not seek permission to land. But land they did. In 1973, they brought art rock to the West. Eno and all.

The Clash:
Exhibition Centre, 1977
It's bonfire night 1977 and Strummer and co. roll up in their subversive drainpipes and chop out every ferocious gem from their incendiary debut album. Excited Bristol almost has a riot.

The Pop Group:
Hope Chapel, 1979
Troublesome funk meets terrible noise in front of every member of the Clifton Experimental Post-Punk Disco Society. After much howling and hollering, the assembled hipsters go home and plan to start their own bands.

The Specials: Locarno, 1980
'This one's for the Barton Hill mods,' said Terry Hall and over a thousand two-tone-clad ace faces nodded in respect. The Specials bounced, shuffled and moonstomped with an unbelievable energy. Completely exhausting.

Rolling Stones:
Ashton Gate, 1982
From the opening bars of *Under My Thumb*, Mick strutted and snarled for the full 90 minutes. A 'relaxed' Keef produced the noisiest set of guitar feedback ever heard in Bristol.

Blue Aeroplanes:
Victoria Rooms, 1990
The moshpit faithful went so beserk, they went through the floor. Aeroplanes management duo Simon Esplen and Cerne Canning had to form a protective barrier around the hole to prevent anyone from falling in.

Nirvana Bierkeller, 1991
The start of the UK Nevermind tour and the night Kurt met Courtney. Those who went left knowing Nirvana played the most super-charged garage punk since The Stooges. Nothing would be the same again.

PJ Harvey: The Fleece, 1996
Two hot, steamy nights in the company of the coolest chick to ever slouch in a pair of stilettos while strumming a battered guitar. Those lucky enough to get in saw Polly Harvey confirm her place as the most outstanding alt. rock female on the planet.

Portishead: Ashton Court, 1997
A staggering end-of-tour homecoming where the band's fragile, ultra-precise soundscaping seemed to hang like dust in the misty evening air. A truly spellbinding end-of-the-day, end-of-the-tour set; one of the most memorable homecoming gigs of all time.

White Stripes: Louisiana, 2001
The Louis is the best place in town to see up-and-coming Yank schmindie bands plus get yourself a sauna in the bargain. In more recent times, the likes of Interpol, Outhud and Wolf Parade have played blinders but this White Stripes' show is still the yardstick by which all Louis gigs must now be measured. Sweaty, loud and a genuine sense of seeing something very special gaining momentum before your very eyes, this was good enough to make the cover of the next week's *NME*.

Massive Attack:
Queen Square, 2003
Great choice of venue, fantastic support bands, menacing triumph of a mega set, awful catering. But after more than a decade of trying, Bristol's biggest band finally got the homecoming they deserved.

Stephen Malkmus & The Jicks:
Anson Rooms, 2005
'He never does Pavement songs…' So why's he singing *Grounded* then? Yet another example of this city bringing out the best in passing musical trade. In his Pavement guise, Malkmus has played Bristol a fair few times (even playing the Anson Rooms a decade earlier) but rather than the brainy slacker lo-fi of old, here was a relaxed (read sozzled) Brit folk troubadour so happy with his West Coast audience that he decided *Eye of the Tiger* would make a perfect encore. And he was right, it did.

Up Close

Ⓜ Dave McDonald

Started out as frontman for wannabe Goths Fear of Darkness many years ago and promoted in various venues before taking over the Turnpike on Bath Road with wife Sophie. Dave and Sophie transformed it into The Thunderbolt, a pub music venue that punches hugely above its weight thanks to Dave and Sophie's energy, imagination and the respect with which they are held in the biz. An essential venue for new acts, The Thunderbolt has also attracted the likes of The Stranglers, The Christians, John Cooper Clark, Jerry Dammers, Wilko Johnson and Will Self.

Moonshot

Hugely entertaining ska band who formed in the skinhead/ska revival the end of the 1980s and still resurface now and again.

Jim Moray

From his makeshift studio in a Bedminster bedroom, Jim Moray has become a genuine phenomenon. Bono's journo pal Neil McCormack called the 24-year-old 'the biggest leap forward in folk for 30 years'. Other writers are saying that he could do for folk music what James Blunt has done for whimpering like a girl. In February 2004, he was presented with the BBC Radio 2 Album Of The Year Award for *Sweet England* as well as the BBC Radio 2 Horizon Award 2004 for best newcomer.

Ⓞ Onslaught

Five lads from the Banjo Island badlands of Cadbury Heath moved from punk to death/thrash/speed metal. Onslaught became big news on the European circuit, signed to London Records and released their heavy metal monster *In Search Of Sanity*. Management fall-outs, sackings and acrimony followed and Onslaught split up in 1991 but reformed in 2005.

Julian Owen

It takes either a brave or desperate man to set himself up as the target of a thousand crap local band demo tapes every month, but hey, someone's gotta do it. The hugely approachable *Venue* music editor can be pestered at venues around town most nights.

Ⓟ John Parish

AKA Scott Tracey. John is the founder of Automatic Dlamini who featured Polly Harvey on slide guitar and vocals. Parish went on to be a mainstay of Polly's success. He is now one of the most highly-rated producers in the business and a hugely versatile musician. He produced the 2003 Eels album and has shared studios with loads of local bands, including the Experimental Pop Band and many of Fat Paul's Swarf Finger artists.

Fat Paul

Paul Horlick is the Swarf Finger and Espionage labels main man and money-where-his-mouth-is champion of experimental

■ **John Parish is one of the most highly-rated musicians in the Bristol scene and beyond.**

noiseniks everywhere. Horlick has spread his wings Down Under and is now one half of the UK arm of Aussie label Invada.

Dave Pearce

Bristol's professor of feedback has been a bit quiet of late but he's still the closest thing Bristol has got to its very own Kevin Shields. He juggled his Flying Saucer Attack duties with a job at Revolver.

Phantom Limb

Fronted by Yolanda Quarty who toured with Massive Attack in 2008, Phantom Limb combine soul, country and jazz in an effortless, dreamy soundscape in which less is most definitely more. Tipped as the next big thing from Bristol, Phantom Limb have been threatening to make the national breakthrough for a few years. Surely their time will come.

R Jim Reynolds

Hugely respected guitarist and songwriter whose distinctive style is influenced by blues, ragtime, folk and most tellingly music hall.

Beth Rowley

Her 2008 album Little Dreamer went straight into the UK album charts at Number Six and in 2009 she was nominated f or a Brit Award in the category for Best British Female Solo Artist. Despite her global success, the former St Mary Redliffe pupil still found time to play a fundraiser at Windmill Hill City Farm in 2011.

S Gareth Sager

The legendary Pop Group loon came snaking out of Redland over 20 years ago and can now be thought of as Bristol's uncle avant-garde. Rip Rig and Panic, Head, Pregnant and now the excellent Nectarine No. 9 have kept him busy.

Saturation Point

Like gob smacking Canadian instrumentalists Holy Fuck, Saturation Point are just so damn near perfect they make the

■ Yolanda Quarty worked with the Blowpop DJs before fronting Phantom Limb.

■ Automatic Dlamini's photoshoot for The D Is For Drum album was at the old Bristol gaol on Cumberland Road. See Parish, John and Harvey, PJ.

Up Close

whole business of dispensing with a vocalist seem like the easiest idea in the world. The ex-Strangelove three piece melt calm and precise Krautrock into frayed feedback and like to release albums in batches. Mysterious. Hypnotic. Brilliant.

Mike Scott
A legend on the Bristol acoustic music scene, Scott employs a distinctive style of dark humour and story-telling that many try to imitate but none have bettered.

Michele Schillaci
Remember Toto Schillaci, the brilliant bug-eyed Sicilian goal-poacher from the Italia 1990 World Cup? He's Michele's uncle. Michele himself is a veteran of several commercially attractive indie bands. His dad owns the Louisiana.

Andy Sheppard
South Bristol jazz genius always experimenting with new forms. Andy is of the few artists in any genre to constantly set new musical challenges.

Nick Sheppard
Original punk and guitarist in Strokes-esque dot-dash new wavers The Cortinas. Sheppard famously went on to replace Mick Jones in The Clash shortly before they took the final curtain. Very much part of the where-are-they-now brigade since moving to Australia.

Roni Size
Drum 'n' bass adventurer, Mercury Music Prize winner and sometime shopper at Waitrose in Henleaze, Roni seems to be permanently tuned into some pioneering noise frequency. His impact and influence on the local scene is immense.

Mark Slater
'I like to look at musicians as unique characters', is not the normal spiel you get from music promoters but Mark Slater is no ordinary promoter. Passionate, innovative, open-minded, openly kneeling at the alter of greatness and perfection. Slater claims to be just one of an army of volunteers who put everything into the organisational side of the Bristol's independent recording and live scene in order and take something out.

Smerin's Anti-Social Club
Already assured of cult status thanks to their huge underground and festival following, Smerin's Anti-Social Club are a real oddity. A 10-piece band including a brass section who mix funk, reggae, ska and drum 'n' bass to astounding effect. Their 2011 dub version of the Dr Who theme featuring Tenor Fly is mighty good.

Smith & Mighty
Generally regarded as Bristol's seminal dance music duo, Rob Smith and Ray Mighty were there when the storm broke and

■ John Stapleton is known for his huge vision.

■ Bristol's Smith & Mighty produced Carlton's (above) Call is Strong album.

are still hugely influential today. They were joined by reggae man Peter D Rose in 1998 and have been the inspiration behind numerous collaborations, including 3 Stripe, Henry and Louis and More Rockers. Rob Smith released his solo album, the excellent *Up On The Downs*, in 2003.

Spider
At well over six foot tall with legs like fireworks, the lead singer of the Seers, Bonesaw and Zoomer must rank as one of the most dangerous stage performers since Arthur 'My Head Is On Fire' Brown. Not many Crowded House fans are as reckless.

John Stapleton
There aren't too many DJs anywhere on the planet who have a vision as wide as John Stapleton's. Dope on Plastic's vinyl flicker supremo can trace the line that links Pere Ubu to Aphex Twin and will survive the club crash because of it.

Mark Stewart
Towering ex-Pop Group lamppost and all-round awkward sod, the consistently difficult Mr Stewart has been wearing the same nihilistic boots that inspired him to make crazy noises in the first place. An English icon.

Stoloff & Hopkinson
Montpelier's Mr Stoloff and Mr Hopkinson are a mysterious pair of electronica gents known for their prankish sense of humour and huge production talents. Their *Trademark* EP was described by one reviewer as: 'a genre-dodging journey through the record collections and video libraries of the eccentric duo'.

🆃 Nick Talbot
Drawn to Bristol in the late 1990s by a love of Third Eye Foundation and Flying Saucer Attack, Talbot's solo project *Gravenhurst* signed to Warp they released the albums *Black Holes in the Sand* and *Fires in Distant Buildings* to universal acclaim.

Team Brick
Its easy to get typecast when you're messing about at the edges of sonic sanity. 'I am not dark noise!' bellows the fantastically whacked-out Team Brick. 'I am not Nazi army jacket! I am happy noise fun!' Improvisation rules his chaotic one-man live shows while clarinet, cheapo keyboards, loops, carrier bags, wood and shouting are his tools. From free jazz to slamming metal, weird opera to manic psychedelia, the Brick boy makes the most appropriate modern noise possible.

Steve Tilston
Tilston was one of the most talented performers on the Bristol acoustic scene in the 70s and 80s and has an international reputation for his blend of folk and blues without ever breaking into the mainstream. He now lives in Yorkshire where he continues

■ **Mercury Music Prize winner Roni Size is hugely influential in the local music scene.**

to release highly influential music. In 2011, he published an excellent historical novel set in Bristol called *All For Poor Jack*.

Martina Topley-Bird

This Bristol schoolgirl was discovered by Tricky when she was having a crafty fag between lessons in Clifton. The voice of Tricky's *Maxinquaye* album, she released her outstanding solo album *Quixotic* in 2003.

Tricky

You've got to admire the single-mindedness of Adrian Thaws Knowle West's most famous son: instead of building on the critical and commercial success of his dysfunctional masterpiece *Maxinquaye*, he moved to New York and headed down a one-way street called Experimental and Obscure Avenue.

■ Tricky aka Adrian Thaws was born in the lovely Knowle West.

U Adrian Utley

The supremely talented Portishead bass boss is one of the hardest working men in alternative showbiz. Sparklehorse, Goldfrapp, Patrick Duff, Jimmy Galvin and Beth Gibbons are just a few who have benefited.

Unforscene

You've probably heard their cinematic soundscapes on TV documentaries, however, Unforscene also perform as a kicking live act with guest vocalists. Very much a behind the scenes outfit, with a heavyweight list of collaborations.

V John E Vistic

Coming from the same dark Australian hellhole that Nick Cave sprang from, this rebel rousing dark star is a Bristol resident now and the most exciting talent to come out of the city in a decade. Swaggering, blade-carrying re-invented rock 'n' roll from a visceral superstar in waiting.

■ Hazel Winter: the former Blue Aeroplanes and Moorhaven guitarist who went solo.

Joe Volk

There is, it seems, nowt so cool as folk. As the introspective acoustic movement grows another foot or two of stubble, its participants are beginning to show signs of being less boring than knitwear spods Damian Rice and Jack Johnson. The solo voyage of Gonga roar-maker Joe 'It's German for people' Volk demonstrates this more than most. And it's the reference points that lift it out of the ordinary. In keeping with English songwriting law, Nick Drake has been mentioned by all reviewers. But no one really sounds like Drakey do they? No, Volk is closer in style and spirit to someone like Elliot Smith.

W War Against Sleep

Another great name, another classy shimmy towards the leftfield. War Against Sleep is actually little more than Duncan Fleming and a keyboard. The resultant noise is startling: it's lip-curling, lovesick and loungey, a darkly comic voyage into an as yet unwritten chapter of rock 'n' roll. Fire Records, home of Pulp, won the signing war, offering the boy wonder a nice three-album deal. The 2011 *Vs Time* was released on Silent Age Records.

Ben Westbeech

With a list of influences that range from Roy Ayers to Dr Alimontado, Nirvana and DJ Shadow, you won't be surprised that it's not easy to categorise Ben Westbeech. The classically-trained singer, producer and musician was on the fringes of the Full Cycle crew before signing to Gilles Peterson's Brownswood label in 2006.

Hazel Winter

Former Blue Aeroplanes and Moorhaven guitarist whose critically acclaimed John Parish-produced solo album *Put The Sharp Knives Away* drew comparisons with PJ Harvey and Kristin Hersh. If you have heard but not seen Hazel, you could be forgiven for expecting her to look like a cross between a kewpie doll and the girl with the machine gun from the Bader Meinhoff Gang.

■ Davey Woodward formed the Brilliant Corners and the Experimental Pop Band.

Davey Woodward

The perennially groovesome ex-Brilliant Corner and Experimental Pop Band frontman has slowly grown into one of our most warped art pop visionaries over the years. It's a long way from the cheeky chappy sound of the Corners' *Brian Rix* to the EPB's *Tracksuit Triolgy* but it's been worth it.

ⓨ You & The Atom Bomb

This lot ooze cool bubblegum punk aesthetics. There's the name, for a start. Then there's the fact that they've got two vocalists, one called Suzi Gage and the other Jean-Marc De Verteuil. And on top of this, they manage to mix crazy lyrical gymnastics with a breezy 1960s pop sensibility that could well propel them into the charts. Their mini-LP *Shake Shake Hello!?* was in a new wave all of its own.

ⓩ Zen Hussies

Some call it goodtime swingska others label it boogaloo, but whatever the term the Bristol and Bath-based Zen Hussies deliver it with good-humoured, old-time panache.

Up Close

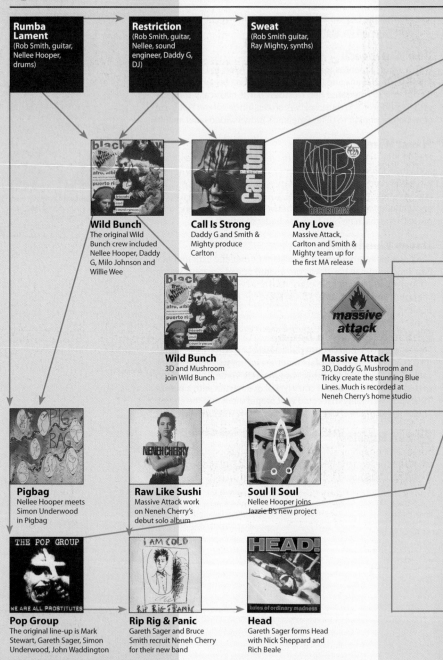

Rumba Lament
(Rob Smith, guitar, Nellee Hooper, drums)

Restriction
(Rob Smith, guitar, Nellee, sound engineer, Daddy G, DJ)

Sweat
(Rob Smith guitar, Ray Mighty, synths)

Wild Bunch
The original Wild Bunch crew included Nellee Hooper, Daddy G, Milo Johnson and Willie Wee

Call Is Strong
Daddy G and Smith & Mighty produce Carlton

Any Love
Massive Attack, Carlton and Smith & Mighty team up for the first MA release

Wild Bunch
3D and Mushroom join Wild Bunch

Massive Attack
3D, Daddy G, Mushroom and Tricky create the stunning Blue Lines. Much is recorded at Neneh Cherry's home studio

Pigbag
Nellee Hooper meets Simon Underwood in Pigbag

Raw Like Sushi
Massive Attack work on Neneh Cherry's debut solo album

Soul II Soul
Nellee Hooper joins Jazzie B's new project

Pop Group
The original line-up is Mark Stewart, Gareth Sager, Simon Underwood, John Waddington

Rip Rig & Panic
Gareth Sager and Bruce Smith recruit Neneh Cherry for their new band

Head
Gareth Sager forms Head with Nick Sheppard and Rich Beale

1977-1983   1984-1990   199

The Bristol Beat

THE MUSIC TIMELINE: 1977-2003

Smith and Mighty
Rob Smith and Ray Mighty form S&M and are later joined by Peter D Rose

Mark Stewart
Stewart releases Stronger The Love with Smith & Mighty

Fresh Four
S&M work with Suv, Krust, Flynn, Judge and Lizz E.

More Rockers
Heavy dub offshoot of Smith & Mighty

Mad Professor
Ex Black Roots producer remixes Massive Attack's Protection

Tricky
Stewart's lodger meets Martina Topley-Bird

Full Cycle
Roni Size forms Full Cycle from the Basement Project in St Paul's. He is joined by , Krust, Suv, Die, MC Dynamite, Onalee and others

Reprazent
Wins the Mercury prize for Roni Size

Sinead O'Connor
Nellee Hooper produces the Nothing Compares 2 U monster hit. He also works with Madonna, Bjork, Smashing Pumpkins, All Saints, U2 Janet Jackson and others

Gary Clail
Mark Stewart works with Gary Clail at Adrian Sherwood's On-U-Sounds

Tru Funk
Talented youngsters Jody and Sam and their mate Dan (DJ Die) persuade S&M to produce their 4am single

Portishead
Formed by Geoff Barrow, engineer on Blue lines

Massive Attack
100th Window released in 2003. Massive Attack (3D and Grant) play Queen Square

.995   1996-2000   2000+

Unusual Bristol buildings

John Hudson checks out some of the more interesting brickwork dotted around the city

Bristol may lack the architectural impact of its neighbouring city of Bath, but there are still a number of buildings of merit, particularly around Corn Street and up in Clifton. Sadly, many historic sites were destroyed in World War Two, but aside from the obvious architectural big names, such as St Mary Redcliffe and the Victoria Rooms, there are some unusual buildings tucked away among the modern buildings. Here we take you on our tour of some of Bristol's less obvious buildings of merit…

ART DECO

You can look long and hard for decent art deco in Bristol. It is not exactly one of our strong points. There's a pretty good Odeon building in Union Street in Broadmead, opened in 1938, not long before World War Two, but its curved corner tower has not been the same since it lost its canopy and top. Weston-super-Mare is the place to go for a classic Odeon, cinema-organ and all. But at least Bristol's has a ghost: a long-ago projectionist murdered in some steamy sex scandal. Not many people have seen him but there's always something about the layout of these old buildings, with their lonely back corridors and stairs, that makes you expect the unexpected. Not a place to go at night if you get spooked!

The hotspot for 1930s 'modern movement' buildings is in and around the Centre. At the Broadmead end of this huge traffic roundabout that replaced redundant docks is Electricity House, opened in 1938 and designed by Giles Gilbert Scott to look like an ocean liner. You can see its stepped upper decks best from the side angle in Broad Street. It was given a welcome facelift in 1990, but with so

■ Next time you're hurrying towards the Galleries, take a good look at the Odeon. It's art deco, don't you know.

■ The Evening World used to hit the streets from this art deco office on the Centre.

much destroyed by the War, and then the planners, it is still hard to imagine the first shock of its contrast with the medieval city around it.

After the War, a group of architects called for the whole of the Centre to be rebuilt in the same style. Some hope… But at least the ship theme was picked up on by Percy Thomas and Son when they designed the showpiece store for Broadmead in the mid 1950s, on the corner of Haymarket and the Horsefair. It helped pioneer the new shopping centre, and there was much grumbling about it at first – until critics saw that it was a Rolls Royce of a building compared with most of what followed. It's currently occupied by Primark, though a number of chains have come and gone over the years. The cold, commercial fact is that it's not all that big, with that wedge shape hemming it in. But it was refurbished lavishly in the 1990s by the Home Counties group Bentalls, who got their fingers burned mightily for their pains, leaving the way open for Primark to move over the road from its former shop.

NAKED FACT

The leaning tower of **Temple Church** in St Thomas is approximately 1.5m out of true.

Back around the Centre, swish apartments now occupy the symmetrical, angular offices from which the long-lost *Evening World* once hit the streets. There's something austere and Eastern European-looking about the place, but that's the way inter-war media moguls seemed to like their buildings. Around the corner, the redevelopment of the Colston Hall has meant the loss of the old Bristol Gas Company showrooms of

Five facts...
About Bristol buildings

1 The **Spike Island Arts Centre** was originally the Brooke Bond tea-packing warehouse. It was converted in 1998.

2 The distinctive **electric cranes** outside the Industrial Museum were to be scrapped until public outrage decreed otherwise in 1975.

3 The tower of the **Wills Memorial Building** on Queen's Road is 65.5 metres tall.

4 The **Paty family** were Bristol's leading architects, builders and craftsmen in the 18th Century.

5 **Bristol Bridge** was built by Thomas Paty in 1764-67 on the site of the previous 13th-Century bridge.

■ The former Lewis's department store (now Primark) dominates the Haymarket side of Broadmead with its ocean-going lines.

BRISTOL LOOS

☀ Bearing in mind all the usual health and safety warnings, you can have an interesting afternoon touring the vintage public loos of Bristol.

Three of them are classic iron pissoirs straight out of the seedier quarters of Paris, and you'll find them on Horfield Common, in Mina Road, St Werburghs and at the top of Blackboy Hill. The first two are listed buildings and the Blackboy one is also protected, being in a conservation area.

A tad more discreet is the ancient convenience on Park Row, which is not officially listed but everyone thinks it should be. Connoisseurs also speak glowingly of the facilities in Prince Street and Cheltenham Road, and the gents' beside the Suspension Bridge on the Clifton side. Sex discrimination is rife in this list, but not all is lost. "The ladies in Stoke Road are a joy to behold," says one who knows.

THE WORST TOILETS IN BRISTOL

1. Situation Vacant
We've 'retired the Number One shirt'. Nothing could compare to the toilets at Snuff Mills, but they've been replaced. The other Public Conveniences listed here are merely highly unpleasant. The Snuff Mills facilities were rank beyond description. They were named by the BBC's *Watchdog* programme in March 2003 as the worst public toilets in Britain. When *The Naked Guide to Bristol* last visited the toilets our photographer was almost overcome by the stench of stale urine, but still managed to take these snaps.

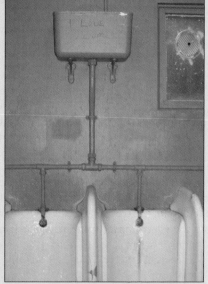

It's now a bright stainless steel affair with automatic hand-washing facilities. There's plenty of light to skin up in.

2. Next to Mary Le Port Church on the Centre
Deep, dark and concrete cavern of a convenience. You'd imagine that Siberian toilets at the height of the Cold War were just like this.

3. Temple Meads
They put in that funny low lighting for a while to discourage drug use. No self-respecting junkie would go anywhere near the place.

4. Blackboy Hill bogs
The funny little Victorian pissoir stranded on the traffic island is supposed to have some architectural merit. Sadly it stinks of piss.

5. Centre on a Saturday night
It must be those fountains that make everybody want to go.

1935 which, it has to be said, were sniffed at by purists as a deco cliché, but had an unusual air of seaside pavilion tattiness about them. Just up the road, Friary House, opened in 1938, is seen by those who know as a more worthy survivor of the modern movement.

Finally, if you're out in the suburbs at posh Sneyd Park, you'll find a clutch of cubist houses from the 1930s, all following Le Corbusier's lead. And in the Ridgeway at Westbury-on-Trym, not too far away, you can see through the trees an art deco classic of a house, with its style once more hinting at the ocean liners that never did come in to Bristol. It was built in 1934, and while it looks as if it should be basking in the sunshine of Miami Beach or St Tropez, its name is a reminder that it is pretty much one of a kind down in this part of the world. It's known simply as Concrete House.

BRISTOL GUILD

The Bristol Guild shop in Park Street really can trace its history back to the 'guilds' of the arts and crafts movement. Today it's simply a shop specialising in glass and ceramics, furniture and furnishings, kitchenware and toys, but it's still more willing than most to showcase up-and-coming talent. The William Morris Arts and Crafts Society was founded in 1883. There was a big stir when the London-based Guild of Handicrafts moved to Chipping Campden in 1902, and though the Cockneys in Arcadia experiment was short-lived, the idea of craftspeople banding together for support and marketing opportunities was not.

The Bristol Guild of Handicrafts was opened in Park Street in 1907, the forerunner of the city's Guild of Applied Arts which started in the following year. There had been earlier arts and crafts groups in the area but none with a chance to sell in posh Park Street, 'the Bond Street of the West'. The stained-glass artist Arnold Robinson became its sole owner in 1929 and moved across the road to the present premises four years later, and from then on machine-made goods were accepted, as long as they were 'original, functional and made to the highest standards'. Ceramics by Susie Cooper, Ruskin and Royal Lancastrian were among Robinson's early favourites, as well as Elton

NAKED FACT

lans to create **Park Street** started in 740. It was laid out in 1758 and work began in 1761.

Five tallest...
Offices in Bristol

1 Castlemead, Old Market **262ft (80m).**

2 Froomsgate House, Rupert Street, Broadmead **205ft (62m).**

3 Colston Centre, Colston Avenue **205ft (62m).**

4 One Redcliffe Street, Redcliffe **198ft (60m).**

5 Grey Friars, Lewins Mead **195ft (59m).**

Courtesy of www.skyscrapernews.com

■ The Bristol Guild on Park Street can trace its roots back to 1907.

Ware, made just along the road at Clevedon. Today the shop is owned by Bristolian Ken Stradling, who joined the company when he was demobbed from the Royal Corps of Signals in 1948.

PERCIVAL HARTLAND THOMAS

Percival Hartland Thomas was the most off-beat of Bristol's 20th Century architects. He started his career designing arts and crafts houses and ended it with gothic churches, but in the middle years, he hit on a weird style of simplified gothic, redbrick Norman and bauhaus white, which could have added up to something big if he'd been a more influential name and had given it a bit longer. His three key churches are St Oswald's, Bedminster Down (1927), St Mary's, Shirehampton (1929), which is probably his masterpiece and St Cuthbert's, Brislington (1933). Pevsner says Shirehampton Church is neo-gothic, 'but handled with so much freedom and personality and with so much of the spirit of the 20th Century that the compromise remains convincing'. Others say uncompromising is more the word, with its huge square windows and macho-looking rubble walls. He was never as adventurous again, but when it comes to ease on the eye, a lot of his fans like Brislington best. Outside, the Norman-arched brick doorways of St Cuthbert's are undeniably great works of art, while inside Thomas created a huge light space of white illuminated by windows which are gothic in shape if not in fussiness. Hartland Thomas lived on until 1960, but sadly, he was never on this kind of form again.

■ The shell of St Peter's Church is the centrepiece of Castle Park.

■ The carvers who created the choir stalls in Bristol Cathedral had a little fun with their designs.

CATHEDRAL CHARACTERS

The misericords on the choir stalls at Bristol Cathedral date mainly from around 1520 and, being half-hidden, gave their carvers plenty of scope for fun. They include images of Adam and Eve, Samson and the Lion, a mermaid, Reynard the Fox, the bear caught in the oak tree, dancing bears, a pig being killed, the spinster leading apes in hell, a woman taking corn to a windmill and a husband and wife doing battle with broomsticks.

Fast-forward more than 400 years and on the north windows on your left, just after you've entered the cathedral, you will see a memorial to all the Home Front services who helped guard the city and the cathedral in the World War Two. It shows a policeman, firemen, WVS member, air raid warden, nurses, and so on. The windows were unveiled in 1951, replacing earlier ones blown out by bombs, and at a 50th anniversary service in 2001, there were still plenty of old-timers around who'd served in those organisations. One of them even claimed to be the original model for one of the portraits. They're not exactly great art, but there's a nice human touch to them.

OLD MARKET AND CASTLE PARK

You need a huge leap of imagination to take on board the fact that the shopping heart of Bristol once stretched from Old Market up along the river to Bristol Bridge. The inner ring road of Temple Way and Bond Street – did you ever see a less likely looking Bond Street? – now cuts the wide Old Market off from the heart of town, while Castle Park has greened over a network of teeming little streets that had survived from the Middle Ages until the day the Luftwaffe called.

In the middle of them there were always the last traces of the Castle, a scene of Civil War derring-do when it fell to the Roundheads in 1645 but demolished a dozen years later. In fact, at the end of the park near the Marriott Hotel there are still some much-modified remains, but the most striking sight in the park today is the bomb-ruined shell of the 14th-Century St Peter's Church. Its paved areas and terraces have become quite a popular meeting place but, while it's great in a sunny lunch hour, it can be seen as a little seedy at other times. It cost £50,000 to restore it in the 1970s, which was widely derided as a scandalous waste of money then, but wouldn't buy you a garage in Clifton now.

It's more cheerful to imagine Old Market in its heyday, especially on a busy Friday evening, which was the main shopping time for many Bristolians. Most of them would take home 'tea fish' as a special treat – dried and salted and the local answer to the Manx kipper or the Arbroath smokie. You only had to leave it to soak in a pan for two days and it was just the job for Sunday tea.

NAKED FACT

Gardiner Haskins in Broad Plain was originally the Thomas Soap Works.

Five ugliest
Buildings in Bristol
(and the people who designed them)

1 **Student's Union, Queens Road** – Alec French and Partners, 1965. *'Perhaps Clifton's most bruising post-war intrusion.'*

2 **New Bristol Centre, Frogmore Street** – Gillinson, Barnet & Partners, 1963-1966. *'Brutalises everything around it by scale and texture.'*

3 **Froomsgate House, Rupert Street, Broadmead** – Alec French & Partners, 1971. *'The most offensive of the area's gargantuan monliths.'*

4 **Former Norwich Union Building, Castle Park** – Wakeford, Jerram & Harris, 1962. *'Deflates one of the city's prime sites.'*

5 **Trenchard Street Car Park, Trenchard Street** – Architect unknown, 1967. *'A multi-storey monster.'*

Descriptions from Pevsner Architectural Guide to Bristol. Buildings chosen by Naked Guide to Bristol

STATUESQUE

GIL GILLESPIE'S BRIEF GUIDE TO SOME OF BRISTOL'S INTERESTING MONUMENTAL FIGURES

■ **Neptune moved to make way for the fountains on the Centre. He is now opposite the Hippodrome.**

1. Neptune
Location: He keeps moving around Bristol, but he is currently in the pedestrianised area on the Centre.
Who's he when he's at home? Well that's just it, he hasn't had a familiar place to hang his ragged cape lately, moving all over town in the name of Harbourside regeneration. The Mer King was first erected in the Temple area, near Bristol Bridge. He then moved to Temple Street and was left on some glebe land until 1872. The statue was then moved to the junction of Temple Street and Victoria Street and was later re-erected at the Quay Head in 1949. He moved to his present site back in 2000.
Was it worth breaking the mould for?
The big man of the ocean has been clutching his fork of defiance for longer than he cares to remember. He's always been gnarly, shrivelled

and as stubborn as a limpet and there is no more heroic ocean figure around.

2. Equestrian bronze of William III
Location: Queen Square.
Who's he when he's at home? An unusually heroic-looking member of the aristocracy.
Was it worth breaking the mould for?
Dating back to the 1700s, this impressive looking, er, lump, of bronze man-and-his-mount was once so valued it was hidden away during World War Two and only put back again in 1948. 'Has he gone yet?' whispered his caretakers. 'Who?' came the reply. 'That horrible little German fella with the funny moustache.'

3. Edmund Burke
Location: St Augustine's Parade (the Centre).
Who's he when he's at home? MP for Bristol 1774-1780 but sadly no relation to either Solomon or the newsreader turned emergency service expert Michael.
Was it worth breaking the mould for?
Two moulds, actually. There is a marble replica in St Stephen's Hall, Westminster. Bristol gets the much cheaper version. "I wish to be a member of parliament, to have my share of doing good and resisting evil," reads the inscription. Looks like he is another berk who underestimated the persuasiveness of Tony Blair then.

4. Rajah Rammohun Roy
Location: Outside the Central Library on College Green.
Who's he when he's at home? Celebrated Indian social reformer whose standing, even after his death, did much to stop the bulldozers threatening to flatten Arnos Vale Cemetery where he is buried inside a mighty impressive tomb.
Was it worth breaking the mould for?
Absolutely. When it was unveiled in 1997, this public monument was a long overdue acknowledgement of the closest thing Bristol

has to Ghandi – even though he was only visiting the city when he died.

5. Sabrina, Goddess of the Severn
Location: Courtyard of Broad Quay House.
Who's she when she's at home? Naked, watery nymph types in hot lesbo action. Teenagers? Yes. Witches? More like suggestive fairies really.
Was it worth breaking the mould for? Well, artist Gerald Laing calls her: "A metaphor for the triumph of life over death." We think she is nothing of the sort.

6. William Penn
Location: New Millennium Square.
Who's he when he's at home? Quaker son of Bristolian Admiral Sir William Penn and the founder of Pennsylvania. His scroll reads 'Death is but crossing the World as Friends do the seas, they live in one another still'.
Was it worth breaking the mould for? Aren't a million boxes of Quaker oats memorial enough?

7. Small Worlds, a tribute to Bristol-born physicist Paul Dirac
Location: On Anchor Road outside the At-Bristol complex.

■ Bristol's most famous statue is the 1730s equestrian bronze of William III by Rysbrack in Queen Square.

■ There is a marble replica of the Burke statue in St Stephens's Hall in Westminster.

Who's he when he's at home?
Stephen Hawking reckons: 'Dirac has done more than anyone, with the exception of Einstein, to advance physics and change our picture of the universe.' He won the Nobel Prize for Quantum Mechanics in 1933.
Was it worth breaking the mould for?
Apparently, the concentric cones of the sculpture represent the theoretical movements of the physicist.

8. Charles Wesley
Location: The courtyard on the Horsefair side of Wesley's chapel in Broadmead.
Who's he when he's at home?
The lesser-known brother of that Methodist preacher bloke, John. Charles was a prolific hymn writer and regarded by some as the hymn writing equivalent of Lennon and McCartney. His biggest 'hit' is *Hark! The Herald Angels Sing*. He lived in Stokes Croft.
Was it worth breaking the mould for?
The most striking thing about this impressive 1939 tribute to one of the founders of Methodism is his extraordinary, and very ill-advised, Yeoman-about-town mullet. In bronze. Could Charles Wesley be sporting the heaviest hairstyle in history?

The best bits of children's Bristol

The top attractions for families in town and beyond researched by our enthusiastic team of adventurers

Bristol is an excellent place for kids: there's probably not another city in Britain with so much to do in a relatively small area, and it's got countryside and seaside within easy striking distance as well. In addition to the obvious attractions, such as Bristol Zoo and At-Bristol, there are also plenty of open spaces and hidden treasures to discover. The *Naked Guide to Bristol* asked 13-year-old Caitlin Telfer, her sister Mena (7) and Caitlin's best-friend Leonie Campbell-King (14) to choose their favourite places in Bristol and to pick the best destinations for a day trip away from the city.

AT-BRISTOL

- **Harbourside, BS1 5DB**
- **Tel: 0845 345 1235** ■ **www.at-bristol.org.uk**

The £97 million At-Bristol development is essentially the entire area to the north of the Floating Harbour and includes The Aquarium (formerly Wildwalk), At-Bristol (formerly Explore), the Imax Cinema and Millennium Square. It was *The Good Britain Guide*'s Family Attraction of the Year in 2001 and has won several other tourism and design awards, even one for its car park which was named as one of the best in the UK by the AA in 2005. It was Visitor Attraction of the Year at the Bristol Tourism and Hospitality Industry Awards 2011 (which seems a bit 'jobs for the boys'), and both the Guardian and Independent newspapers featured it in their best family attractions.

At-Bristol hit financial problems and, in August 2003, it had to ask Bristol City Council for a £500,000 loan to cover running costs. Although it is undoubtedly a major family attraction, there are two things that got it off to a bad start - it's expensive and it was sponsored by Nestlé. Eventually

■ Mena, Caitlin and Leonie (left to right) set out to explore the best children's attractions in Bristol and beyond.

■ The waterpools at Millennium Square are a favourite with kids in the summer.

Wildwalk closed down and was replaced by the Blue Reef Aquarium (which is nowhere near as good as Wildwalk was) which now incorporates the Imax cinema.

Explore: Science and natural forces are the themes of the two storeys of displays and exhibitions, many of them interactive. Highlights on the ground floor include putting the kids on a treadmill to lift water from one tank to another, several displays involving magnets and magnetic fields and a particularly visual film about the journey of a sperm. It's all a bit like *Tomorrow's World*, but without the lure of Maggie Philbin or the avuncular presence of Raymond Baxter. Upstairs, visitors get to enjoy a harp that uses lasers instead of strings and a gyroscopic briefcase with a 'mind of it's own'. The virtual beach volleyball court is a hoot once you get the hang of it and visitors can create their own music or play slap pipes. The TV studio is popular as the kids play weather forecasters and newsreaders in front of computer-generated backgrounds. The large silver ball you can see from outside is the planetarium where you can watch the universe go by.

Bristol Blue Reef Aquarium: A visit to the aquarium (which utilises 250,000 litres of water) is a pricey affair; a family ticket will cost you more than £40, though you can come and go as you please for the rest of the day. Built on the site of what was At-Bristol's Wildwalk, it's not the biggest aquarium in the world by any stretch of the imagination, but there are some pleasant features,

■ The At-Bristol project is the showpiece for the Harbourside regeneration project.

Five best...
Kids playgrounds

❶ Hengrove Park, Hengrove Way.

❷ Blaise Castle, Lawrence Weston.

❸ Easton Play Park, Chelsea Road.

❹ Oldbury Court, Fishponds

❺ Castle Park, Broadmead.

including an exotic coral reef tank and the allegedly "world famous" giant octopus Velcro (who didn't do much on our visit). The whole thing leads up to an IMAX theatre visit at the end, which promises a "wondrous adventure" in 3D. Expect a film about sharks or prehistoric dinosaur-fish… it's a bit cheesy, but the kids will love it. The cafe is remarkably poor (oddly enough, it doesn't sell fish and chips… thought you'd seen that gag coming, eh?) but the gift shop is rife with sea-related merchandise ranging from pencils to calendars. If you're not convinced, pay a visit and make your own judgement. It's all a bit fishy, if you ask me.

■ Ashton Court is a huge area for kids to run around in. Perfect for bikes, kites and picnics.

Imax Theatre: A seriously big cinema screen with surround sound, Imax shows 3D movies which are often about dinosaurs.
Open: daily except Christmas Day. Call for details.

ASHTON COURT ESTATE

■ **Two miles from Bristol City Centre. Main entrances are off the A369 Portishead Road at Kennel Lodge Road and at Clifton Lodge**
No gimmicks, no play area; just loads of grass, woods and a deer park. Fly a kite, ride a bike, take a picnic, play cricket. Use your imagination. Check out the sunken garden and pet cemetery behind the mansion house.
Open: 8am to dusk. Cost: free (excluding some events).

BLAISE CASTLE HOUSE AND ESTATE

■ **Blaise Castle Estate, Henbury Road, Henbury, BS10 7QS** ■ **Tel: 903 9818 for play area events**
There are three distinct attractions in the grounds of this estate to the north of Bristol: the large children's play area is one of the best in Bristol (but still not as good as Victoria Park in Bath); the house has exhibitions of Victorian domestic furnishings, toys and costumes and there's also a display about Edward Jenner, who discovered vaccination; the grounds surrounding the gothic-style folly castle are a mixture of open grass and woodland.

■ As well as exploring the castle and house, kids can also enjoy the play area at Blaise Castle.

You can walk by the side of the Hazel stream (quite marshy and spooky, even on a bright day) as far as the rocky outcrop where you'll find the 'castle' on the site of an iron age fort. The castle was built in 1766 by Thomas Farr, who in 1771 became Master of the Society of

Merchant Venturers and in 1775 became Mayor of Bristol. Farr was declared bankrupt after the American War of independence in 1778.

Open: Daily from 7.30am. Cost: Free.

BRANDON HILL AND THE CABOT TOWER

■ Off Park Street

One of the best things to do as a visitor to Bristol is climb the Cabot Tower: the views from the top are fantastic. You can see virtually the whole city and it's the only place where you'll get such a dramatic impression of Bristol past and present. Kids love huffing and puffing up the narrow spiral stairway and are usually fascinated by the distance finder at the top, which tells you how many miles it is to many of the major cities of the world and various places of local interest.

Brandon Hill Park is Bristol's oldest public space: it was given to the city corporation in 1174. It's an ideal place to take children for a picnic if you've been shopping on Park Street or wandering round the docks. The play area on the Hotwells side of Brandon Hill has equipment for toddlers as well as more adventurous climbing frames for older children. Brandon Hill is full of greedy tame squirrels, so take a bag of nuts along with you.

Open: Brandon Hill Park is open 365 days of the year. Cabot Tower is open from 8am until just before dusk.

BRISTOL HAWKS GYMNASIUM

■ Roman Road, BS5 6DH ■ Tel: 935 5363

www.bristolhawksgymnastics.org

One of the more civilised ways to spend an hour or so on a Saturday morning is to drop the kids off at Bristol Hawks and head to nearby St Mark's Road for a coffee and a mooch around Bristol Sweet Mart (see Shopping Listings). Bristol Hawks is a proper gym with vaulting and bars; it's cheap (about £3, depending on age) and fun. Parents aren't allowed into the classes, but you can watch the kids tumble and vault from a room above the gym. Interesting venue for children's parties.

Open: Phone or check website for details of opening hours and prices.

Five best...

Places to skateboard

1 Dean Lane Skate Park, Bedminster.

2 St George's Park Skate Park, St George.

3 Sk8 & Ride, St Philip's.

4 Hengrove Park.

5 Steps at Lloyds, Harbourside.

■ Brandon Hill and Cabot Tower are popular places to take the kids. Make sure the greedy squirels don't steal your lunch.

BRISTOL ICE RINK
■ **Frogmore Street, BS1 5NA** ■ **Tel: 929 2148**
■ **www.jnll.co.uk**

Going 'down the rink' is a Bristol rite of passage. Almost every teenager who has lived in Bristol in the last 30 years has slipped and stumbled their way round the ice while trying to look cool and attract members of the opposite sex. The ability to skate backwards helps in the rink courtship ritual, but only if you can do so without flailing your arms about like a windmill in a hurricane. Ice skating is fun, even if the skates can hurt your shins a bit and you might suffer the occasional tumble. There are various family offers and promotions available, or you can push the kids gently onto the ice and proudly watch them glide helplessly across the rink as you retire to the bar.

Open: Check the website or phone for timetable details.
Cost: Check with ice rink for details of special offers.

■ The Bristol Old Vic is kid-friendly. As well as its under-5 shows on Friday mornings, it also offers workshops and festivals.

BRISTOL OLD VIC
■ **King Street, BS1 4ED**
■ **Tel: 987 7877** ■ **www.bristol-old-vic.co.uk**

There are regular children's workshops and festivals at Bristol's main theatre. The programme is challenging and varied. You'll need to call to confirm the details or check the website. There are also shows for under-5s on Friday mornings. Best to book in advance.

BRISTOL ZOO GARDENS
■ **Clifton, BS8 3HA**
■ **Tel: 974 7399** ■ **www.bristolzoo.org.uk**

■ Wendy The Elephant was the star of Bristol Zoo. The whole city mourned when she died in September 2002.

The zoo's riposte to caged-animal criticism is that it's at the forefront of conservation campaigns. It's a world leader in breeding programmes for endangered species and is active in the campaign to halt the trade in gorilla and chimpanzee bush meat in Cameroon. They might also point out that the Pelican Restaurant doesn't sell cod.

If you visited the zoo in the mid 1960s and returned in the mid 1990s, you'd be hard pressed to notice any real change. The polar bear was still pacing up and down and had actually worn a furrow in its concrete enclosure. This sad, demented animal summed up everything that is wrong about zoos. But in recent years, there has been a radical change. Many of the larger animals (bears, giraffes, the grumpy kangaroo and the much-loved Wendy the Elephant) have gone and have been replaced by the excellent Penguin and Seal Coast, Twilight World, Zona Brazil and the Monkey Jungle. The giant tortoise enclosure is a popular attraction for the young 'uns. The gorillas sometimes look a bit forlorn on their island, although Romina, the female Western Lowland gorilla has perked up since it was discovered that she was virtually blind and had her sight restored by a cataract operation.

The zoo has a children's play area for toddlers and Zooropia – a ropewalk around the centre of the zoo will give the nippers a hi-wire thrill. The magnificent 12-acre gardens provide a safe and stimulating environment for kids. The progress made by the zoo was recognised in 2000 when it won the Zoo of the Year award. It won the award again in 2004. The zoo is particularly worth visiting out of season; it gets extremely busy in summer when most of the population of South Wales descends upon it. If you're visiting during the summer, try to get there early to avoid the rush. You can easily spend an entire day at the zoo and need a minimum of two hours to take in the highlights.

Open: Daily, 9am-5.30pm in Summer, 5pm in Winter. Last entrance is an hour before closing. Closed Christmas Day.
Cost: Check the Zoo website or phone for latest price details, under 3s free.

Five best...
Things to do at the zoo

1 Go underwater at the Seal and Penguin Coast.

2 Visit Biggie Smalls, the Giant Galapagos tortoise who was reunited with his mate in August 2003 after a separation of 25 years. Biggie is aged between 75 and 100.

3 Make sure the kids are clipped on to the safety harness when you send them on the Zooropia rope walk.

4 Visit the Animal Encounters sessions and let the kids get up close to something furry or scaley.

5 Buy a season ticket: you'll start saving money after three family visits.

■ Geoffrey's Marmosets are just one of the many fantastic attractions at Bristol Zoo Gardens.

CINEWORLD KIDS CLUB

■ **Cineworld, Hengrove Leisure Park, Hengrove
BS14 0LH** ■ **Tel: 0871 2208000**
■ **www.cineworld.co.uk**

Kids pay a quid to go to the flicks on a Saturday morning.
There's usually some entertainment, then a choice of three
films. Under-5s must be supervised.

Open: Sat, 10am. Cost: £1, under 11-year-olds.

CITY MUSEUM AND ART GALLERY

■ **Queen's Road, BS8 1RL**
■ **Tel: 922 3571** ■ **www.bristol-city.gov.uk/museums**

The City Museum combines all the old-fashioned qualities
of a civic collection (stuffed animals and bits of flint
from Severn Beach) with some excellent contemporary
exhibitions and regular events for children. The stuffed
animals seem to fascinate kids – especially the dodo and
Alfred, the gorilla from Bristol Zoo. As for the wolverine
and the tiger, they are just plain scary.

The museum has presence: it's as imposing and
impressive inside as its magnificent Venetian Gothic facade
would suggest. Hanging in the foyer is a reproduction
Bristol Boxkite aeroplane, which featured in the 1963 film
Those Magnificent Men In Their Flying Machines. It lends
the entrance a surreal quality. The Egyptology gallery
contains real mummies. The Family Fundays on the first
Sunday of every month are popular with kids. Check
with the museum for details of these and other children's
events. The cafe at the back of the Museum does a special
Munchkin Box and children's menu.

Open: Daily, 10am-5pm. Cost: Free.

CITY SIGHTSEEING OPEN TOP BUS TOUR

■ **Tel: 0870 4440654** ■ **www.bristolvisitor.co.uk**

Buy a 24-hour tour ticket and you can hop on and off the
red bus as it wends its way past Bristol's attractions. This is
an excellent way to see the city and makes an adventure of
your trip through town.

*Open: All days Apr-Sep. Cost: Check website for prices and
details of Family Deals , Bus/Boat deals and three-day tickets.*

■ **The City Museum offers Family Fundays on the first Sunday of each month.**

■ **The stuffed animals at the City Museum: Alfred, the gorilla from Bristol Zoo, will fasinate children of any age.**

CYCLING

Despite being the UK's first Cycling City, Bristol isn't the best city for cycling: the combination of steep hills and heavy traffic makes it hard work cycling around the city, particularly for kids. But there are several pleasant off-road rides. The Bristol to Bath Cycle Path is 15 miles of flat cycling along the route of an old railway line. The path was built between 1979 and 1985 by Bristol-based sustainable transport group Sustrans and features a sculpture trail by artist Katy Hallett.

You can join the path at a number of clearly-marked points at Temple Meads, Broadmead, Whitehall, Easton and Mangotsfield. Among the best stopping-off points are the Willsbridge Mill nature reserve, Bitton Station which is home to Avon Valley Railway Company which runs steam trains along a short length of track, and the Bird in Hand or Jolly Sailor at Saltford.

The Ashton to Pill Cycle Route heads out of the city under the Suspension Bridge alongside the River Avon. It's a fairly easy five-mile ride to Pill, although the path can get a bit muddy in places after rain. Eventually, the path is supposed to link Bristol to the old Severn Bridge. For off-roaders, there's an excellent Timberland Trail through the Forest of Avon at Ashton Court. It's an 11km twisty, loopy sort of ride through the Ashton Court estate and the adjoining 50 Acre Wood. There's also a pleasant ride along the banks of the Avon which you can join at the Conham River Park. For further details of cycling in Bristol and to get hold of maps, try the addresses below

- **BETTER BY BIKE**
  www.betterbybike.info
- **LIFE CYCLE UK**
  Tel: 929 0440 www.lifecycleuk.org.uk
- **SUSTRANS**
  Tel: 926 8893 www.sustrans.org.uk
- **TIMBERLAND TRAIL**
  Tel: 953 2141 www.forestofavon.org.uk
- **BRISTOL TRAILS GROUP**
  www.bristoltrailsgroup.com

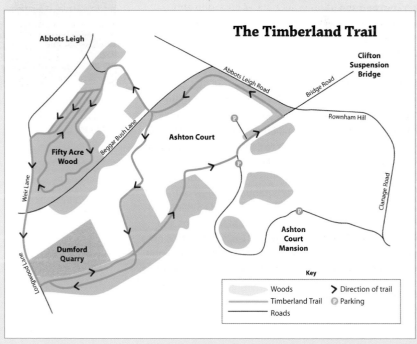

The Timberland Trail

Abbots Leigh

Abbots Leigh Road

Clifton Suspension Bridge

Bridge Road

Rownham Hill

Ashton Court

Beggar Bush Lane

Fifty Acre Wood

Weir Lane

Clanage Road

Dumford Quarry

Longwood Lane

Ashton Court Mansion

Key

Woods	Direction of trail
Timberland Trail	Parking
Roads	

CLIFTON SUSPENSION BRIDGE

- **Leigh Woods, BS8 3PA (visitor centre)**
- **Tel: 974 4664**
- **www.clifton-suspension-bridge.org.uk**

The two things that everyone should do on a visit to Bristol are climb the Cabot Tower and walk across Clifton Suspension Bridge. Both expeditions are healthy, educational and free. And you'll work up an appetite so you can gorge yourself on burgers and chips at The Mall afterwards. When you cross the bridge, call into the nearby Visitor Centre where you'll find a variety of interesting displays, models and Lego for the nippers.

Visitor Centre: Open daily, 10am-5pm. Admission free, donations welcome. Free 45-minute guided tours at 3pm on Sat, Sun and bank holidays from May to Sep. Please call to arrange group tours.

■ Spy on the unsuspecting Bristol public with the camera obscura at the Observatory.

DURDHAM DOWNS, THE OBSERVATORY AND CAVE

- **Litfield Place, Clifton Down**
- **Tel: 924 1379**

Spend an afternoon playing football on the Downs and then take a look at one of Bristol's more curious attractions, the camera obscura and observatory near the Suspension Bridge. Originally a snuff mill, the building was partially destroyed during a gale in 1777. Apparently the sails went round so fast in the storm that the machinery caught fire. The old mill was rented to the artist William West in 1828 for use as his studio. He installed the camera obscura and cut the underground passage to St Vincent's Cave. The cave's visiting platform can be seen clearly from the Clifton Suspension Bridge, set within the sheer 250-foot cliff face. The camera obscura projects a panoramic view of the surrounding area onto a white surface inside a darkened room. A box on top of the building contains a lens and sloping mirror. Light is reflected vertically downward onto the table, giving a true (not mirror) image. The technique, which originated in the 16th Century, gives best results on bright days. Odd but fascinating.

■ Hengrove Park offers a range of playground equipment.

FERRY TRIPS

■ **Tel: 927 3416** ■ **www.bristolferryboat.co.uk**

It may be an inland port, thus rendering it useless for shipping, but all that water in the middle of Bristol supports a thriving ferry boat service. The Bristol Ferry Boat Company has been going for more than 25 years now and provides a daily commuter service from Temple Meads to Hotwells and the city centre. A boat trip is an adventure for the kids in its own right and is a great way to see the city from a different angle and get across town.

There are occasional services along the Avon to the Avon Wildlife Park at Saltford at Easter and bank holidays and trips to Beeses Tea Gardens at Crews Hole, plus Booze Cruises and other events. A family multi-stop ticket for two adults and two children costs £17 for a day and means you can hop on and off the boats as often as you like.

HENGROVE PARK

■ **Hengrove Way, next to Cineworld**
■ **www.hengrovepark.com**

Skateboard and BMX ramps, a huge octagonal climbing frame plus loads more playground equipment and a separate under-5s area. There's also a good BMX and skate park at Dean Lane in Bedminster.

Open: All year. Cost: Free.

HORSEWORLD

■ **Staunton Manor Farm, Staunton Lane, Whitchurch, BS14 0QJ** ■ **Tel: 01275 540173**
■ **www.horseworld.org.uk**

A visit to this charity for rescued horses and donkeys is a must for the equine-obsessed or anybody who fancies a slightly different day out. Situated in listed Mendip Stone Farm buildings off the Wells Road on the outskirts of Bristol, there are (obviously) loads of horses and donkeys plus a video theatre, nature trail, play area, bouncy castle, shop and cafe. Available for children's parties.

Open: Visitor Centre open all year apart from Dec 24-Jan1. Check website for other opening times, Cost: Check website for prices and details of membership schemes..

Five best...
Surprise activities

1 Learn to climb at the Undercover Rock centre in St Werburghs.

2 Go ten pin bowling at the Bowlplex, Longwell Green; Hollywood Bowl, St Philips or The Lanes, Nelson Street.

3 Go karting at Castle Combe or West County Karting, Winterbourne.

4 Take a dog for a walk from Bristol Dogs' Home, St Philip's.

5 Go horse riding at Kingsweston Stables, Lawrence Weston or Leechpool Riding Stables, Yate.

M SHED

■ **Wapping Road, Princes Wharf, Bristol BS1 4RN** ■
Tel: 0117 352 6600

■ **www.mshed.org**

Opened in June 2011 to replace the old Industrial Museum, the £27 million M Shed may have been a couple of years behind schedule and the odd £10 million over budget, but it's a pretty impressive project. Somehow, the curators have managed to recreate the sense of clutter that was one of the most comforting aspects of the old Industrial Museum. There are some hi-tech, interactive gizmos, but not too many. Why would you need them when you can amuse yourself trying to find your house on the giant map of Bristol on the gallery floor? M Shed is a 'people's museum'. It attempts (and succeeds in) defining Bristol through the stories and achievements of its ordinary and extraordinary citizens. So here we will find the famous such as Cary Grant and Massive Attack alongside everyday Bristolians such as Princess Campbell (the first black ward sister) and George Pine who fought in the First World War and worked on Bristol trams and buses and told his story in 44,000 words of hand-written notes. There are three galleries (People, Places, Life) fantastic views across Bristol and most impressive of all, it's all free.
Open: Closed Mondays except Bank Holidays. **Cost:** *Free.*

■ M Shed and the distinctive cranes on the Floating Harbour.

SNUFF MILLS/OLDBURY COURT ESTATE

A lovely wooded riverside walk along the River Frome which you can start from Eastville Park or Oldbury Court in Fishponds. There's a good play area at Oldbury Court.
Open: Daily. **Cost:** *Free.*

SS GREAT BRITAIN

■ **Great Western Dock, Gas Ferry Road, BS1 6TY**
■ **Tel: 929 1843** ■ **www.ssgreatbritain.org**

Built in Bristol by Brunel, the ss Great Britain was the world's first iron-hulled, screw propeller-driven, steam-powered passenger liner, and the only surviving 19th-Century example of its type. It has now been restored and converted into a museum and visitor centre and is also available for hire as a banquet, wedding reception and

■ Walk along the Harbourside and take a tour of Brunel's ss Great Britain steamship.

conference centre. The ticket price includes entrance to the Maritime Heritage Centre (an exhibition on the history of shipbuilding in Bristol) and to The Matthew (a replica of the ship in which John Cabot sailed from Bristol to discover Newfoundland in 1497). The ss Great Britain won the Gulbenkian Prize for Museum of the Year 2006.
Open: Daily except December 24 and 25. Cost: Check website for lkatest prices, concessions, family tickets and group discounts, under-4s free.

ST WERBURGH'S CITY FARM

■ **Watercress Road, St Werburgh's, BS2 9YJ**
■ **Tel: 942 8241** ■ **www.stwerburghs.org**
Same proposition as Windmill Hill City Farm (see below), but on the other side of town. Apart from the allotments and animals, there's a wildlife pond, adventure playground for the under-8s and a cafe (closed Mon and Tues). St Werburgh's has the added attraction being near the highly-recommended Farm pub (see Pubs & Bars Listings).
Open: Daily 9am-5.30. Cost: Free (donations welcome).

WILLSBRIDGE MILL

■ **Avon Wildlife Trust, Willsbridge Hill, South Gloucestershire, BS30 6EX** ■ **Tel: 932 6885**
■ **www.wildlifetrust.org.uk/avon**
Delightful wooded valley on the eastern fringe of Bristol. The 18th-Century mill has been restored and contains a visitor centre with hands-on wildlife and conservation displays. The woodlands are at their best in spring when

Five best...
Places to go for a walk

❶ Ashton Court Estate: woods, deer park, gardens, cafe and visitor centre.

❷ Blaise Castle Estate: follow the stream through the woods. Can be muddy.

❸ Frome Valley Walkway: join the path at Eastville Park and walk to Snuff Mills.

❹ Leigh Woods: variety of walks, some on hard surfaces. Lovely display of bluebells in April/May.

❺ Kings Weston Wood, Shirehampton: walk through the woods leads to the mansion house and grotto.

■ St Werburghs City Farm has all you need for a kids day out with the benefit of a pub nearby.

they are full of flowers and birds. The ponds are important homes for frogs, toads, dragonflies and dippers. If you're lucky, you might even spot a kingfisher near the stream.

WINDMILL HILL CITY FARM

■ **Philip Street, Bedminster, BS3 4EA**
■ **Tel: 963 3252** ■ **www.windmillhillcityfarm.org.uk**

■ **Blossom the Gloucester Old Spot Pig is one of Windmill Hill City Farm's most senior residents.**

Windmill Hill City Farm is free, it's relaxed and it has a cafe. Admittedly, there's not much else to do in the immediate area – this is, after all, Bedminster – unless your idea of a good time is a trip to Asda. But you're only a few minutes away by car from the docks and it's a pleasant 20-minute stroll from Bedminster through Redcliffe to Queen Square and the dockside.

The farm was established in 1976 – the first city farm outside London – on a derelict World War Two bombsite. It's a working farm with ducks and some fairly formidable geese wandering around the farmyard, and pens for calves, goats, pigs and sheep. Behind the farmyard there are larger pastures for more goats, sheep and pigs and a small nature reserve with a pond full of newts and frogs.

The rest of the farm is given over to allotments, meeting rooms, computer rooms, conference and community rooms, a nursery, adventure playground and a children's activity centre. There is also a five-a-side football pitch for the kids to play on.

The cafe serves enormous meat and veggie breakfasts as well as a full lunch menu, cakes and snacks. Sunday morning breakfast at the Farm is something of a South Bristol institution. It can get quite busy at the weekends, especially when the weather isn't good enough to make the most of the outside seating area. The cafe is occasionally open in the evenings, check for details. The farm shop was given a makeover in 2006 and the opening hours became less erratic. It sells freshly-laid hen, duck, goose and bantam eggs, frozen and fresh meat, Ecover refills, bread, a small selection of fresh veg, tinned food, dairy products and some kids' toys and trinkets.

Open: Tues-Sun, 10am-4pm. Closed Monday. Entry free, donations encouraged.

TOP 10 DAYS OUT FROM BRISTOL

I f you fancy a break from city life, Bristol is perfectly placed to simply hop in the car or on the train and travel to any number of other great places which will help keep the children entertained. Whether you want animals, caves, beaches or countryside walks, we provide all the information you need for a great day out.

1. WESTON-SUPER-MARE

40 MINS

■ Just a quick snack before getting stuck into the candyfloss at Weston-super-Mare.

In the height of summer or on bank holidays, Weston can be too busy to enjoy. But out of season, it's a great place to spend a few hours. It offers loads of beach, the Grand Pier, donkey rides, pleasant sea-front walks and plenty of cafes. Weston is proper seaside; the only traditional seaside element it lacks is, er, sea – the water beyond the mud is actually the Bristol Channel.

The Weston experience comes wrapped in an atmosphere of faded elegance and seaside tackiness. OK, Weston is an acquired taste, and if you'd rather not experience the full-on kiss-me-quickness of the resort, try the long, sandy – and far quieter – beach at Brean to the south. Other attractions at Weston include the Aquarium on the Marine Parade seafront (01934 641603, www.sealife. co.uk), the Helicopter Museum on Locking Moor Road (01934 635227, www.helicoptermuseum.co.uk) or the Kidscove indoor adventure centre (01934 417411, www. kidscove.co.uk). The Tourist Information Centre is at Beach Lawns (01934 888800, www.n-somerset.gov.uk/tourism).

■ Amazing what you can do with a tree and a penknife at Westonbirt.

2. WESTONBIRT ARBORETUM

45 MINS

■ **Near Tetbury, off A46, Gloucestershire**
■ **Tel: 01666 880220**
■ **www.forestry.gov.uk/westonbirt**
More than 18,000 trees and shrubs from all over the world in 600 acres of beautifully landscaped countryside. There's a visitor centre, plant sales, a restaurant that does good Sunday lunches, and loads of fresh air. Westonbirt is invigorating in winter, inspiring in spring, beautiful in summer and stunning in autumn. It's also a great place to

take the kids to see Father Christmas. They make a special effort with the grotto and children are given a Christmas Tree seedling and a present. And the adults get to enjoy their lovely mulled wine while waiting.

Open: Daily, 9am-8pm (or dusk) April 1 to Nov 30. 9am-5pm Dec 1 to March 31. **Cost***: Check website.*

3. SLIMBRIDGE

45 MINS

- **The Wildfowl and Wetlands Centre, Slimbridge, Gloucestershire. Off the M5 at Junction 13 or 14**
- **Tel: 01453 890333**
- **www.wwt.org.uk/visit/slimbridge**

■ **Slimbridge Wildfowl and Wetlands Centre is a haven for birds and kids alike.**

Formed in 1946 by artist and naturalist Sir Peter Scott (son of Polar explorer Captain Robert Falcon Scott), Slimbridge is a haven for rare waterbirds. You can view them from hides or from high up in the Sloane Observation Tower which provides fantastic views over the River Severn. There's a cinema, a wildlife art gallery and a tropical house where the hummingbirds hum.

Open: Daily except Christmas Day, 9.30am-5.30pm (5pm in winter). **Cost***: Check website.*

4. CHEDDAR CAVES AND GORGE

40 MINS

- **Cheddar, Somerset, between A38 and A37**
- **Tel: 01934 742343** ■ **www.visitcheddar.co.uk**

Some of the caves can be tricky to navigate for the very young or the elderly (Gough's Cave has 70 steps), but it's worth making the effort to explore this ancient underground world in the limestone gorge. Above ground, the Gorge offers some fine walks and rather too many scrumpy and cream tea emporiums. Jacob's Ladder is a good climb while Britain's oldest skeleton is on display at the Cheddar Man Museum.

Open: Daily except Dec 24 and 25. July and Aug 10am-5.30pm. Rest of year 10.30am-5pm **Cost***: Check website for latest prices and online discounts.*

5. LONGLEAT

1 HR

- **Near Warminster off the A36 between Bath and Salisbury** ■ **Tel: 01985 844400** ■ **www.longleat.co.uk**

Watching the monkeys remove loose bits of car trim and wonky aerials in the Safari Park is great fun. Until it happens to you. Longleat is a big day out. In fact, you need more than a day to see everything. The Passport ticket allows you to come back and see anything you didn't see at a later date during the same season. Apart from the Safari Park with the giraffes, zebras, elephants, lions and tigers, there's also a safari boat trip where you can see hippos and sea lions. Other attractions include the Postman Pat Village, butterfly garden, maze, adventure playground, pets' corner and miniature steam railway. *Open: Safari Park is open from mid Feb to early November. Opening times vary so check the website for latest information. Cost: Check website for latest prices, discounts and offers. There is usually a discount of up to 15 per cent on day tickets if you book online.*

■ Feeding the deer at Longleat is a great fun for all the family. Be warned, your car will need a good clean afterwards!

6. AVON VALLEY PARK

15 MINS

■ Pixash Lane, Bath Road, Keynsham, off the A4
■ Tel: 986 4929 ■ www.avonvalleycountrypark.co.uk

Adventure playground with death slide and 32-acre farm with pleasant walks along the banks of the Avon. Animals include Shire horses, Shetland ponies, deer, donkeys, llamas, wallabies and many breeds of goat, sheep and cattle. Other attractions are an undercover soft-play area, mini steam train rides, mini quad bikes, boat trips and falconry displays.
Open: Apr-Oct, 10am to 6pm. Cost: Check website for latest prices and for details of season ticket deals.

■ Cerne Abbas is best know for its Rude Man. Take a walk up the hill with the kids before checking out the village pubs for lunch.

7. LYME REGIS OR THE GOWER PENINSULA

2 HRS

Though 'proper' seaside is difficult to find near Bristol, these are the two of the best bits of coast within two hours of the city. Lyme Regis is a charming Dorset seaside town. A higgledy-piggledy, steep-sloped town with a small fishing harbour, good beach and the Cobb wall made famous by that Meryl Streep scene in *The French Lieutenant's Woman*. The Gower Peninsula is an Area of Outstanding Natural Beauty and boasts many fine bays and coastal walks. The high-sided Three Cliffs Bay is worth the walk down through the dunes, while the long sands of Llangollen with the Worms Head and Rhosilli at the far end provide one of the most invigorating lengths of coastline in Britain. Don't forget your camera!

8. CERNE ABBAS

■ Dorset, A352 near Sherborne

There are many splendid villages and country walks around Bristol, but there's something compelling about the simplicity of a day trip to Cerne Abbas. This is the site of the Cerne fertility giant, or rude man – the 180-foot-high man wielding a large club and erection cut into the chalk hill above the village. There's an excellent walk up to the giant while the village provides a pleasant stroll. The New Inn, Red Lion and Royal Oak all welcome kids and do good food. The Red Lion is a particularly relaxing place to read the Sunday papers and sample the Palmer's beer. The church is fascinating and there's a walk through the ruins of the Benedictine Abbey to the well and up to the giant.

2 HRS

■ The Roman Baths are well worth a trip to Bath for. You might just learn something.

9. A DAY OUT IN BATH

30 MINS

■ Victoria Park, Roman Baths, American Museum

There's so much to do in Bristol that there's really no need to travel the 13 miles down the road to Aquae Sulis. But if you do, you'll find that Bath is a very different proposition, with three attractions that can't be found in Bristol. 1) The American Museum with displays of American decorative art from the 17th to 19th Centuries plus authentic furnished rooms and lovely terraced gardens. 2) Victoria Park – a fantastic kids' adventure play area with big skateboard ramp. 3) The Roman Baths and Pump Room: one of the most remarkable ancient sites in Europe. A living history lesson that's fascinating for adults and kids. *For more information, see The Naked Guide to Bath.*

■ Take it easy at Bowood House. There is more than enough to keep the kids busy.

10. BOWOOD HOUSE

1 HR

■ A4 between Chippenham and Marlborough
■ Tel: 01249 812102 ■ www.bowood-house.co.uk

Country house and gardens that boasts the best adventure playground in the West for children under 12. Bring a picnic and chill out while the young 'uns wear themselves out. Most of the items, including a superb pirate ship, have been designed by former boat builder Alistair Guy. Among the recent additions are the space dive and curving tubular metal slides entered from a wooden tower.

Open: *House and gardens daily, Apr-Oct, 11am-5.30pm.*
Cost: *Check website for latest prices and season ticket offers.*

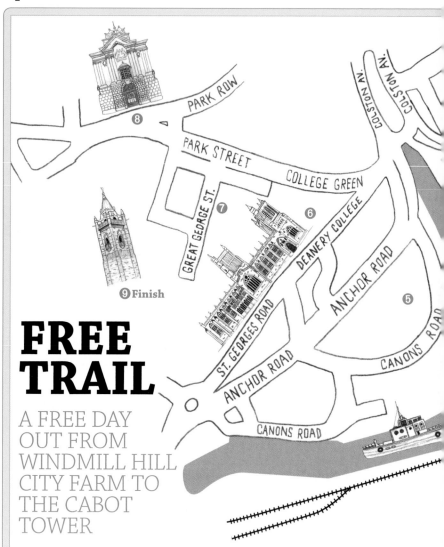

FREE TRAIL

A FREE DAY OUT FROM WINDMILL HILL CITY FARM TO THE CABOT TOWER

❶ **Windmill Hill City Farm**
Start the day with a hearty farm breakfast and a mug of tea.

❷ **St Mary Redcliffe Church**
See if the kids can find the Church Cat's grave and the tramline embedded in the grass from a World War Two air raid.

❸ **M Shed**
Loads to see inside and you can take a ride on a train or ferry or see some of the restored dockside cranes in action. Fab views over the city.

❹ **The Arnolfini**
Take the kids to the bookshop, cafe/bar or round the gallery or just join Cabot outside for a quiet sit overlooking the Harbourside.

❺ **The Millennium Square Fountains**
On a warm day, the fountains are full of children splashing around. Remember to bring a towel.

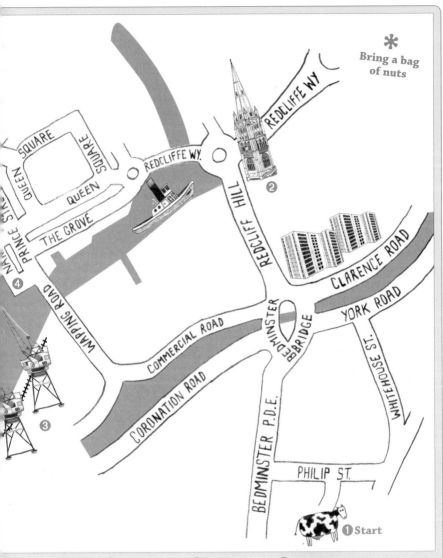

Bring a bag of nuts

⑥ **Cathedral**
Time for a snack in the refectory or a sandwich on College Green?

⑦ **Georgian House**
Call into this 18th-Century house which has been kept just as it was when merchant and slave trader John Pinney lived here.

⑧ **Museum**
If you follow this trail on the first Sunday of the month, you should find special children's activities laid on.

⑨ **Brandon Hill and Cabot Tower**
Climb the tower, visit the play area and dig out the bag of nuts you've carried with you all day. It's time to feed the squirrels!

Listings Pubs & Bars

Bristol, like every major British city from Aberdeen to Brighton, has undergone something of a drinking evolution in the last few years. An endless array of bars have been springing up all over the place while the number of independently-owned pubs has gradually been shrinking away.

Unless you like your ale stodgy and your seat splintered, this continental drift does have its upside as well as its downside. The best of the new Bristol bars have added a whole new dimension to the drinking experience. Places such as Big Chill, Start The Bus, Bocabar and the Lounge bars are chic, cosmopolitan alternatives to the tired

old oak-and-brass Victoriana of the pub. And they've got sofas. Unfortunately, the majority of new bars are more like a cross between the cattle-market and the super-club. Okay, so it's nowhere near as easy to find a scruffy little boozer with a decent jukebox as it used to be. But if you negotiate your way around the backstreets of Clifton or Kingsdown or Montpelier, you'll find that the old-school drinking hole is still very much alive and selling peanuts out of clapped-out machines. Ancient haunts like the Cadbury, the Highbury, the Corrie Tap, The Bell, The Lion and the Hare on the Hill remain popular places for those who don't want to drink in the city centre.

Harbourside, Centre BS1

THE APPLE
Welsh Back BS1 4SB
Tel: 925 3500 • www.applecider.co.uk
You might be forgiven for thinking that deep water and strong cider is an alarming combination, but not at The Apple, Bristol's floating cider house moored at Welsh Back. Bristol is enjoying a craft cider renaissance and Apple is particularly popular with student admirers of the juice of the fermented apple. Excellent for al fresco drinking and for building your own Ploughman's Lunches.

ARNOLFINI
16 Narrow Quay, Harbourside
Tel: 917 2300 • www.arnolfini.org.uk
The Arnolfini bar is no stranger to controversy. The original bar had terrible disabled access and was designed by artist Bruce McLean who once said: 'The only reason to be an artist is to be stupid.' Incredibly, the bar was handed over

to a multi-national catering company in 2005 after the major Arnolfini redevelopment and boasted some of the most expensive prices in Bristol combined with some of the worst service. Since the arrival of Connie Haughton, the introduction of an excellent Italian-inspired menu and the replacement of the bland corporate identity with a focus on celebrating local producers, the Arnolfini is back to its former glory. Sitting outside on warm summer evenings is one of the joys of Bristol bar life.

BIG CHILL BAR
15 Small Street
Tel: 930 4217 • www.bigchill.net
The first Big Chill outside London features very cool DJs, good-value food, regular drinks offers, a chill-out garden and a relaxed atmosphere with friendly staff.

BORDEAUX QUAY BAR
V-Shed, Bordeaux Quay BS1 5UH
Tel: 943 1200 • www.bordeaux-quay.co.uk
Spacious, modern bar with an interesting range of beers, ciders, wines and cocktails.

BRIDGE INN
16 Passage Street, St Thomas
Tel: 949 9967
This is a small pub with a big reputation for the excellent quality of its Bath Ales and guest beers and ciders.

BUNCH OF GRAPES
8 Denmark Street
Tel: 987 0500 • thebunchofgrapes.co.uk
One of the contributors to *Naked Bristol* was a regular in the Bunch of Grapes in 1975 and still pops in for an occasional pint today. He reckons the pub has hardly changed, maintaining its slightly boho, music and theatre credibility. The Grapes is renowned for its good beer and dodgy cover bands, and is opposite the Hippodrome stage door, so there is generally a whiff of greasepaint in the air.

CORNUBIA
142 Temple Street, St Thomas
Tel: 925 4415
Legendary Bristol real ale pub, a beacon in a metropolis of ugly office buildings. Has been through various landlords in recent years, some more successful than others.

GOLDEN GUINEAU
19 Guineau Street, Redcliffe, BS1 6SX
Tel: 987 2034 • thegoldenguinea.co.uk
Fantastic boozer tucked away in Redcliffe next to the General Hospital. Much-loved by street artists and DJs, there's a decent outside area on two levels that sometimes hosts live painting events. Look out for the timber-shivering Blackbeard Cider (8.4% abv) made exclusively for the pub.

THE GRYPHON
41 Colston Street
www.gryphonbristol.co.uk
Formerly The Griffin, a gay/gay friendly pub for many years, The Gryphon is now a real ale and heavy metal establishment. Regular student discounts. Check out the MetAle festivals.

H BAR
Colston Hall Foyer, 13 Colston St BS1 5AR
Tel: 352 1151• www.thehbar.co.uk
Large airy space in the Colston Hall Foyer with a wide selection of drinks, snacks and a full bistro menu.

5 ESSENTIAL BARS

1. CANTEEN
Where is it? Hamilton House, a former office building in the heart of Stokes Croft.
What's it like? Large utilitarian room, long bar, big terrace.
Upside: captures the energy, imagination and anarchy of Stokes Croft.
Downside: Noisy, busy.
Crowd: Bohemian Stokes Croft types – artists, anarchists, piss heads. People who say they don't shop at Tesco.

2. TOBACCO FACTORY
Where is it? On the corner of Raleigh Road and North Street, Southville.
What's it like? Unlike anywhere else in town. Relaxed, spacious, hip.
Upside: It has energised the whole area.
Downside: It's not exactly central.
Crowd: New Southvillians, boho Bemmies.

3. WATERSHED
Where is it? Harbourside.
What's it like? The coolest bar in town. It simply doesn't have to try too hard.
Upside: Location, location, location.
Downside: Stepping out into the middle of Harbourside stag/hen party.
Crowd: Hip people on their way in or out of the cinema, gay men, students.

4. SEVERNSHED
Where is it? The Grove – the more select bit of the Harbourside near the Thekla.
What's it like? Cavernous but lively. One of Bristol's slicker drinking holes.
Upside: Balcony overlooking the water.
Downside: Unisex loos confuse some folk.
Crowd: Lively mix of cocktailers, office workers and foodies.

5. MR WOLF'S
Where is it? Right in the middle of townie territory in St Stephen's Street.
What's it like? Small bar, DJs and live music. Lots of street art and photography.
Upside: Cool clientele attracted by Mr Wolf's attitude rather than its dress code.
Downside: If the music is crap, you'll suffer. At its best as an early or late venue.
Crowd: Skaters, artists, musos.

Listings

MR WOLF'S
133 St Stephen's Street
Tel: 927 32215 • www.mrwolfs.com
Offering noodles, live music and a late night bar, this is a hip and vibrant hangout bang in the centre of things. Try out the 'Gas Chamber', a drink which basically involves inhaling hot absinthe fumes and a lot of coughing.

NUMBER ONE HARBOURSIDE
1 Canons Road
Tel: 929 1100 • www.no1harbourside.co.uk
George Ferguson (Tobacco Factory, Bristol Beer Factory) and the team behind Canteen on Stokes Croft refurbished the old River bar with the express view to encourage independents to move to the area to replace the ailing chain bars. Like Canteen, you get free soup and bread with main courses. Also the booking office for the Bristol Ferry Co.

OLD FISH MARKET
59-63 Baldwin Street, BS1 1QZ
Tel: 921 1515
Big city centre pub with TV screens and a surprising amount of character. Lovely building, one of only two Fullers pubs in the city (The Cambridge in Redland is the other). Serves Thai food.

THE ORCHARD
12 Hanover Place, Harbourside
Tel: 926 2678
Reading the list of guest ciders on offer on the blackboard in this one-room bar tucked round the back of Spike Island, you could be forgiven for thinking that you'd died and gone to cider heaven. Landlord Stuart Marshall collects

the cider and perry direct from the craft producers and the emphasis here is on proper dry cider so expect to find the finest offerings from Somerset, Herefordshire the Wye Valley and sometimes further afield. There's also a selection of real ales and a menu that ranges from cheese and onion rolls and pork pies to full-on lunches and weekend breakfasts.

THE OSTRICH
1 Lower Guinea Street
Tel: 927 3774
Thought to date back to 1775, The Ostrich is now one of the largest waterside eating and drinking spots in Bristol. Great for a sunny day. Offers a fine view of Banksy's Grim Reaper piece on the side of The Thekla.

THE RUMMER
All Saints Lane, St Nicholas Market
Tel: 0845 004 3206 • therummer.co.uk
This famous old pub is remembered fondly by Bristolians of a certain age for its cellar bar crew and live music. There are records of an inn on this site going back to a joint called the Greene Lattis in 1241 so it could be that Bristol's first pub stood where the Rummer now is. Despite its history and prominent position on the approach to St Nick's Market, the pub fell into shameful disrepair and was closed for years before being reopened in 2006 as an elegant bar and cocktail lounge. It's tastefully decorated and boasts a huge array of spirits including about 40 rums and 20 brands of gin and vodka. Cellar bar is now a cocktail joint called Cellars.

Five worst bar names

1. BAR HA! HA!
What's so bloody funny? Bar Ha! Ha! has to be the most irritating name ever given to anything in the history of the world. Ever.

2. BAR EXCELLENCE
It's the name your parents would suggest if you told them you were thinking about opening a bar.

3. BAR HUMBUG
The owners must have been blind drunk

when they agreed to use this cringeworthy Dickensian cliche. Unbelievable.

4. TANTRIC JAZZ CAFE
No longer with us, but memorable for managing to combine the twin horrors of twiddly melodic meddling and Sting's favourite sexual technique in one moniker.

5. BAR ROOM BAR
Say that again please? Bar Room Bar, that's what we thought you said. Are those the only words you know or did you get stuck half way?

SEAMUS O'DONNELL'S
3 St Nicholas Street
Tel: 925 1283
Cool little Irish bar just opposite St Nicholas Market. Probably survived the Irish theme bar nonsense because it's the real deal. Try a shot of the Poteen (70% vol triple-distilled Irish potato juice) and you've as good as kissed the Blarney Stone.

SEVERNSHED
The Grove
Tel: 925 1212 • www.severnshed.co.uk
Its cocktails are top notch and there's a lovely waterfront balcony. The building was originally a Brunel-built boathouse. Now a sophisticated and chic bar with a good range of European food and grills. (See Eating Out).

SEVEN STARS
Thomas Lane, St Thomas
www.7stars.co.uk
There's been a pub here since at least 1760 and some claim the building dates back to the late 1600s. The Seven Stars is an important historical landmark as the base for the anti-slavery campaigner Thomas Clarkson who stayed there in 1787. As historians discover more about Clarkson, the more remarkable a character he appears to be. The clientele is traditionally a transient mixture of office workers and pre-Fleece and Firkin gig goers, but it has also built an enthusiastic following of real ale-seeking regulars. A plaque commemorating the pub's importance in the abolitionist movement was unveiled in 2009. CAMRA Bristol Pub of the Year in 2011.

START THE BUS
7-9 Baldwin Street
Tel: 930 4370 • startthebus.tv
Arty hipsters hang out with live music and DJs. A breath of fresh air in an area otherwise dominated by bog-standard city centre chain pubs. Menu includes hearty staples like pies, and sausage and mash, plus a full English or 'Hippy' (Veggie) breakfast which is sensibly available until 3pm.

URBAN WOOD
90 Colston Street, BS1 5BB
Tel: 929 3627 • www.theurbanwood.com
Relaxed atmosphere in two-room bar with big tables for groups and more intimate space for couples. Good food from brunch onwards.

UNDER THE STARS
Narrow Quay, Harbourside
Tel: 929 8392
Floating bar and cafe that combines regular live music acts with an arty agenda. Food is a mix of light bites and daily specials. Local art on the walls and locally produced craft for sale in a small shop.

WATERSHED
The Watershed, Canons Road
Tel: 925 3845 • www.watershed.co.uk
The relentlessly popular bar of the Watershed media and arts centre is one of the most difficult places to get a table anywhere in Europe. It's no longer the cutting edge radical place it was a decade ago, but is still a cool, lively place on the water serving good food and a wide range of drinks. There are computers with free internet access in the bar too.

WHITE LION HOTEL
Quay Head, Colston Avenue
Tel: 925 4819
Once the waters of the Frome would have run in front of this quayside pub. Now the White Lion is an oddity – a proper pub in the middle of stiletto and theme-bar land. You can sit and watch the Centre go by. A small, one-bar Wickwar Brewery boozer, the White Lion's spiral staircase provides the most challenging journey to a pub toilet in Bristol.

ZERODEGREES
53 Colston Street
Tel: 925 2706 • www.zerodegrees.co.uk
The concept is fine: giant glass-floored bar built around microwbrewery which is spread over two floors, and serves good food and is dedicated to the local and organic ethos. The reality is a little less interesting. If it's quiet, the stark interior seems impersonal and when it gets busy with pre-clubbers, Zerodegrees becomes beer city.

Clifton BS8

ALBION
Boyces Avenue
Tel: 973 3522 • thealbionclifton.co.uk
Stashed away down a short but sweet cobbled cul-de-sac in Clifton, the Albion is certainly a great find. With two open kitchens, the focus

here is on quality, but quite pricey, food. The jugs of classic cocktails go down far too well on a warm summer afternoon.

ALMA TAVERN
18 Alma Vale Road
Tel: 973 5171
The Alma has never been a cool pub, but it has always been a busy one. Attracting the more rugby-shirted end of the student market, this huge pub off the beaten track in Clifton boasts three large seating areas and a small garden and yet still manages to look like a scrum, especially at weekends. Theatre upstairs.

AMOEBA
10 Kings Road
Tel: 946 6461
Not so much a bar-cafe as a little explosion of ideas down a street in Clifton Village. This little corner of bohemia is stuffed with off-beat art, crazy kitsch and unsettling seating. Friday and Saturday evenings offer DJs spinning funk, classic soul and beatsy jazz. With 25 continental lagers and work from different local artists.

THE CLIFTON
6 Regent Street
Tel: 974 6321
No longer a dingy dive, this is now all cosy sofas, retro flocked wallpaper and one of the finest Sunday roasts in all of Bristol. They have a whole host of rotating guest ales, such as Bath Ales and Butcombe.

CLIFTON WINE BAR
Richmond Terrace, Queens Road
Tel: 973 2069
A large, cave-like wine bar that oozes cellar appeal. Giant oak vats and loads of nook-and-cranny seating areas add to the authentic atmosphere. Sadly, it has been known to fill up with tosspots at the weekend.

CORONATION TAP
8 Sion Place
Tel: 973 9617 • thecoronationtap.com
Bristol's longest-serving and best-known cider pub. For well over 100 years, committed disciples of the Church of the Fermented Apple Beverage have come here to worship, or to get 'Corried'. With a range of ciders wide enough to keep several generations of Wurzels happy, this one-room 19th-Century

pub is famous all over the world. That'll be the cider talking probably. Their celebrity drinkers include 3D out of Massive Attack.

GRAPES TAVERN
2 Sion Place
Tel: 9149109 • www.grapesbar.co.uk
Cool music and art bar that reverberates with passionately intelligent counter-cultural noise. Musician Sean Cook (Spiritualized, Lupine Howl and the much-underrated The Flies) and film maker Bill Butt (Echo & The Bunnymen, The KLF) took over the running of the pub in December 2009 and promptly sent out an invitation to the movers, shakers and watchers of the Bristol music community to come and 'be part of the solution'. And what a solution it has been. The Grapes has gone from strength to strength, despite persistent objections from culturally misguided local Round Table types, and become one of the coolest and most inspired music hang out in the city. The key here is authenticity. Where others aspire to hipness, this little corner of the sometimes overlooked village oozes it without even breaking into a sweat. And much of this is down to the vision and relentless hard work put it by the previously defiantly work-shy Cook and his partner in crime.

GREYHOUND
32 Princess Victoria Street
Tel: 973 4187
Anyone who wandered down the corridor into the back room of the Greyhound in the mid 1980s could expect to be greeted by an art-rock army of Edwyn Collins look-a-likes. Sadly, the days when this place was the only place to discuss Belgium import Josef K singles are long gone.

JOE PUBLIC'S
3 Queens Avenue
Tel: 973 1249 • www.joepublics.com
This extravagently-decorated live music bar and popular student hangout is literally underground (below Habitat).

LANSDOWN
8 Clifton Road
Tel: 973 4949
The rough-round-the-edges boozer that once lorded it over every other pub in Clifton has seen its reputation fade over the last few years but at least the close proximity

of the student halls of residence ensures continuing popularity. Had a bizarre interlude as a classical music bar. Celebrity fact: Buster Bloodvessel used to play pool upstairs when Bad Manners were in town.

LION
19 Church Lane, Cliftonwood
Tel: 926 8492 • www.thelion.biz
The Lion has a mythical status – in the 1970s and 1980s, this place was as trendy as it is hard to find. More Bristol bands were formed here than in any other boozer in Bristol. Now it's a perfectly agreeable local pub. You'd be more than happy to have it at the end of your street, but you wouldn't cross the city to visit it.

MALL
66 The Mall
Tel: 974 5318
Briefly, stupidly, re-named the Footbridge & Firkin, this sizeable corner pub is now defined by soft furnishings both upstairs in the smaller bar and downstairs the sprawling cellar bar. This is a popular meeting place pub for people of all ages and has good food options.

PORTCULLIS
3 Wellington Terrace
Tel: 970 6886
Built into a historic crescent, this is a rarity among Clifton pubs: a pub full of people from Clifton. Upstairs has the feel of a wine bar, downstairs is more like a traditional alehouse. Perfect for escaping all those weekend tourists.

RICHMOND PUB AND KITCHEN
33-37 Gordon Road
Tel: 923 7542 • therichmondclifton.co.uk
This used to be the Richmond Spring and was famous with generations of students who spent their grant cheques or increased their student loans on the premises. Lost its way when it rebranded as a sports bar but now back in the old Richmond groove.

QUADRANT
2 Princess Victoria Street
Tel: 973 6414
Despite its prime position in the middle of Clifton Village, only those in the gang used to dare enter. But now it has been transformed it into a light, bright affair upstairs, with good local beer and cider, and a great wine cellar in the basement. Beware the big screens.

QUINTON HOUSE
2 Park Place
Tel: 907 7858
A boozer's boozer. At lunchtime, it fills up with suits grabbing a sandwich and a pint but in the evening this tiny side-street hideaway is packed with local drinkers. A fraternal yet almost cultish experience.

RACKS WINE BAR
St Paul's Road
Tel: 974 1626 • www.racks-bristol.co.uk
Pleasant terrace and large cellar bar that's been around since the days when students got grants. Well regarded by many, but others accuse Racks of being determinedly nondescript .

SOMERSET HOUSE
11 Princess Victoria Street
Tel: 923 7214
When we visited this refurbished Princess Victoria Street pub, we were surprised to see a clientele made up almost entirely of the over-60s. A freak occurrence? An OAP coach party refuelling session? We're not entirely sure. Why not send your nan along to find out.

VICTORIA
2 Southleigh Road
Tel: 974 5675
This used to be a tremendously cramped and dowdy boozer chock-full of 1950s rock 'n' roll memorabilia when it was run by promoter Johnny Midwinter and wife Sue. Now a decent backstreet boozer with a staggering selection of Belgian beers. Fact fans, pay attention: Johnny Midwinter bought John Lennon's portable jukebox at auction in 1989 for £2,500. Johnny kept the jukebox in the upstairs room at the Victoria and spent years researching the discs that Lennon took on tour with him from scribbled notes that came with the jukebox. In 2004, The South Bank Show broadcast a documentary based on Lennon's jukebox. The show was commissioned just a few days after Johnny Midwinter died.

WHITE LION CAFE BAR
Avon Gorge Hotel, Sion Hill
Tel: 973 8955
This isn't just any old hotel bar, for it is blessed with a sprawling Monte Carlo-esque drinks terrace complete with a spectacular view of the gorge and Suspension Bridge. It offers a

better than the average bar menu and a small but well-chosen wine list. Is there a better way to spend a sunny afternoon than enjoying a whole oven-baked Le Pont l'Eveque cheese, freshly baked bread, a lovely bottle of wine and such a spectacular view?

Whiteladies Road, Blackboy Hill BS8

BAR HUMBUG
89 Whiteladies Road
Tel: 904 0061 • www.barhumbug.co.uk
Bar Humbug sits right at the heart of the old Whiteladies Strip and offers hip-hop, nachos and all manner of bottled bliss to a mostly under-25 audience. Prepare to queue to get in on Fridays and Saturdays.

BEAUFORT ARMS
23 High Street, Clifton
Tel: 973 5906
You'd never know it these days, but for a brief period in the 1980s, this was the hippest, mostly underage drinking hangout in town. Sadly, the smell of Country Born setting-gel has faded and the Beaufort is now just another quiet backstreet pub again.

BLACKBOY INN
171 Whiteladies Road
Tel: 940 6130
Old school pensioner chic dominates, from the age-sympathetic seating to the air of suspicion that greets anyone under the age of 65. 'I said, would you like a biscuit?'

CHANNINGS HOTEL
20 Pembroke Road
Tel: 973 3970
Come summer, anyone who is anyone in the teenage public school snogging association plays tonsil-tennis here. An absolute must for every Tim, Rick and Harry on the Clifton sixth form social scene.

COACH & HORSES
2 Highland Square
Tel: 974 5176
The largest of the just-off-Blackboy Hill pubs looks out on what optimists would call a square and realists would call a car park. Maybe this is why it used to be a popular

biker pub. Traditionalists will love the decor – hundreds of paintings featuring coaches and their all-too-familiar friends, horses.

HAUSBAR
52 Upper Belgrave Road, BS8 2XP
Tel: 946 6081 • www.hausbar.co.uk
Exclusive cocktail bar situated beneath the Rajpoot restaurant facing the Downs. Owner Aurelius Braunbarth says his mission is to bring an injection of Berlin class and style to the Bristol bar scene. Booking essential for groups of five or more at weekends.

JERSEY LILY
193 Whiteladies Road
The Jersey Lily was once a cosy, but fiercely local, pub from which it seemed far too easy to get ejected, so quickly was the landlord offended by youthful high spirits. It has now been reinvented as a bright bar-cum-pub with a couple of decent real ales, comfy sofas and benches and a big screen for sport. It's not quite in the gastro pub premier league but generous portions of organic meat dishes, a selection of fish, lite bites and a pudding club certainly keep it in the first division.

KINGS ARMS
168 Whiteladies Road
Tel: 973 9522 • www.kingsarmsbristol.com
More than any other pub or bar, The Kings Arms is an example of the transformation of Whiteladies Road from a posh shopping street into the superbar fuelled Strip and now back into something far more cool and grown up. Years ago the Kings Arms was the roughest biker boozer in town. It became Babushka and then Stark and now it's the Kings Arms again a multi-floored eating and drinking experience with a roof terrace aimed at the after work and student crowd.

PENNY FARTHING
115 Whiteladies Road
Tel: 973 3539
Like the advert says, 'it used to be a bank, now it's a trendy wine bar'. Or in this case an abstractly arranged, neither-here-or-anywhere-else pretend pub. The ultimate irony is that it used to be a NatWest bank.

PORT OF CALL
3 York Street
Tel: 973 3600
Traditional pub and the regular meeting place for the Bristol Book Publishers group, the Port of Call is a stranger to the paintbrush and the post-modern ornament. Traditionalists will love the wobbly table legs and the below-zero temperature in the toilets.

RED LION
26 Worrall Road
Tel: 903 0773
After spending decades undiscovered, Clifton's scabbiest cider house has been made over and was included in the *2006 CAMRA Good Beer Guide*. Expect to find new-fangled comforts such as seats, light-shades and cigarette extinguishing facilities. A revelation.

ROO BAR
Clifton Down Station, Whiteladies Road
Tel: 923 7204
Large Australian theme pub and sports bar. Big screen, cheap eats, too much bunting outside.

SASPARILLA
65 Whiteladies Road
973 0574 • www.sasparillabristol.co.uk
One of the last reminders of Whiteladies Road in its 'Strip' days when giant bars, alcopops and pissed up youth dominated the landscape. Sasparilla is more grown up than the old Strip bars offering a cocktail lounge and a degree of sophistication previously lacking.

SLOANES
66 Whiteladies Road
Tel: 946 6366
Not the ultra-posh place you might expect from the name. Sloanes is a regular kinda bar which often features appealing drinks promotions and has a 1am licence.

VITTORIA
57 Whiteladies Road
Tel: 330 9414
Compact and traditional one-bar local that suffers from an overspill of overspilt builder's bellies come summer. But this is a lovely olde worlde pub from back in the day when brass wall hangings were the only art you could ever possibly need.

Park Street, Triangle
BS1/BS8

ANTIX
44 Park Street
Tel: 925 1139
Bar, cafe and club. In the evening, there is a dance floor area and comfy sofas

THE BERKELEY
15 Queens Road
Tel: 927 9550
This Wetherspoon pub used to be a shopping arcade and still has a window display element for passing Park Street pedestrians. It's an ideal place to meet before or after shopping but pretty ordinary after dark.

THE BOTANIST
20a Berkeley Square
Tel: 927 7333 • thebotanistbristol.co.uk
Former Ha! Ha! Bar The Botanist promises something more sophisticated than the previous hang-out of posh students, posh chaps and loads of other posh tosh. A pleasant setting, stylish with an impressive range of drink and English dining with a dash of Mediterranean flavours

BRISTOL RAM
32 Park Street
Tel: 926 8654
What used to be the overcrowded and deeply uncool Château Wine Bar has been turned in to a relaxed Youngs-owned wood and mirrors pre-club zone. The stench of over-powering Blue Stratos and Impulse have gone. The whiff of Waggledance bitter has taken their place.

ELBOW ROOM
64 Park Street
Tel: 930 0242 • www.theelbowroom.co.uk
A feast of double kissing, plants and canons, the Elbow Room is a popular, posh pool joint with a cocktail bar, DJS and nice burgers.

GOLDBRICK HOUSE
69 Park Street
Tel: 945 1950 • www.goldbrickhouse.co.uk
Right in the middle of Park Street, finally we find something totally different from all the other bars and restaurants in Bristol. A collaboration between a number of local

restaurateurs, the elegantly decorated Goldbrick House is a huge space, offering a cafe-bar downstairs, a Champagne and cocktail bar upstairs and restaurant with a beautifully airy terrace on the third floor. If you want to know about the history, take a look at the blog on the website which has followed the growth of Goldbrick House from its original conception all the way to completion.

ILLUSIONS
2 Byron Place, Clifton
Tel: 909 3405 • illusionsmagicbar.co.uk
The country's first Magic Bar – just in case you need help making your pints disappear. There are shows or live music every night (closed Mondays) and a disclaimer for those nervous about men with rabbits in their hats that 'the magicians will not approach your table.' The images on the outside walls of Illusions are by renowned Bristol street artist Jody.

MBARGO
38 Triangle West
Tel: 925 3256
Another silly name for a bar. But at least the leather sofas, marble tables, classic cocktails and loads of imported bottled beers make up for it. Students can go in what used to be The Phoenix and be certain of not getting their heads kicked in.

THE PARK
38 Triangle West
Tel: 940 6101
Theme Magazine, the catering industry's answer to *Wallpaper*, once gave The Park a best-new-bar-in-the-West-and-Wales award and it's not hard to see why. This is everything a modern, city bar should be – you know, distressed wood, deep leather benches, funk, jazz and hip-hop DJs and Polish vodka. Big windows for summer drinking.

SQUARE BAR
15 Berkeley Square
Tel: 925 4000
Members-only 'celebrity' hangout where actors and media whores can earn some credibility by rubbing up against a few less-than-impressed local musicians. It's still a fantastic bar mind you. You can have drinks brought to your table all night long – truly a life-changing experience.

THE WOODS
1 Park Street Avenue
Tel: 925 0890
After suffering an avalanche of truly terrible Bristol bar names, at last the place behind the Elbow Room comes up with a funny and original one. Add press adverts showing a collection of threatening trees in silhouette and you have the concept of the year. A courtyard, a 6am weekend licence and a imaginatively-stocked bar should keep the wildlife happy.

Hotwells BS8

ADAM & EVE
9 Hope Chapel Hill
Tel: 929 1508
Upper Hotwells or Lower Clifton? It's neither here nor there. Location hasn't stopped the Adam & Eve from being hugely popular. The perfect place for a quiet sit and a read of their many books on a Saturday afternoon but gets busy later on. Get there early if you want one of their Sunday roasts.

ELDON HOUSE
6 Lower Clifton Hill
Tel: 925 7592 • www.bathales.com
After a brief flirtation with the pre-club gay scene when it changed its name to Bar Icon, the Eldon is still popular with the gay crowd but has reverted to being a neighbourhood pub with good food and beer. A Bath Ales pub.

GRAIN BARGE
Mardyke Wharf, Hotwell Road, BS8 4RU
Tel: 929 9347 • www.grainbarge.co.uk
Another George Ferguson and Bristol Beer Factory triumph. Grain Barge came 23rd in the Independent newspaper's Top 50 UK Bars feature and it's easy to see why when you're sitting atop this converted barge enjoying fantastic views across the Harbour with a pint of No. 7 on the go.

HOPE & ANCHOR
38 Jacobs Wells Road
Tel: 929 2987
Half-way down that hill that goes to Hotwells, you'll find the lazily hip Hope & Anchor. This is a real pub with its own identity, where the landlord chooses the sounds from his stack of classic vinyl under the bar. You might get

Dexys, you might get Credence Clearwater Revival. Relaxed alternative to the more 'bubbly' Clifton pubs. The steep garden adds another dimension to the place in summer.

MARDYKE
126 Hotwell Road
Tel: 907 7499
If you'd wandered in here a few years ago, you'd have found yourself surrounded by serious bikers including some from Bristol's chapter of Hells Angels. The bikers have mainly gone now, replaced by a pool table, a giant-screen telly and *Blackbird I'll 'Ave 'E* on the jukebox. The beer is a bargain here.

MERCHANTS ARMS
5 Merchants Road
Tel: 907 0037
Mer'chant n: A Bristolian male behaving in an inappropriately lairy manner while dressed in substandard clothing. Examples: scaffolder, XR3-i racer, middle-aged slob who wants a fight. Thankfully, you won't find too many merchants in this Bath Ales pub. There's too much wood panelling and quiet real ale appreciation for yer lads.

NOVA SCOTIA
1 Nova Scotia Place
Tel: 929 7994
Traditional waterside pub that's salty enough to have a Captain's Room and old enough to remember pirates. If you sit around long enough you might get to hear some tales of life on an ocean wave. If you sit around too long, you'll be the one telling them.

PUMP HOUSE
Merchants Road
Tel: 927 9557
Surprisingly enough, this used to be an old pump house. A large, riverside pub that benefits from a south-facing patio area that gets very busy in summer. The food is good.

ROSE OF DENMARK
6 Dowry Place
Tel: 940 5866 • theroseofdenmark.com
This wonderfully restored boozer is hidden away under the charmless Cumberland flyover, but is well worth seeking out. Big, bright wooden surfaces, loads of happy locals and friendly bar staff brighten the atmosphere. Upstairs, take a pew at the big tables or settle into an armchair by the massive fireplace. The airy restaurant does hearty, proper pub food and inventive Sunday roasts. For what is basically a roundabout with houses on, Hotwells doesn't half do well for drinking holes, and this is one of its finest.

THREE TUNS
78 St George's Road
Tel: 907 0689 • www.arborales.co.uk
Used too be a quirky dockside pub with a menu that boasted Fish Fingers and Chips in a Basket (£2.70) and Spaghetti on Toast (£2). Now one of only two Arbor Ales pubs in Bristol (the other is the Old Stillage in Redfield where the beer is brewed). Wooden floors, wooden tables and lots of wood on the bijou, decked and covered terrace out the back. The pub dog, Daisy the Jack Russell, calls Time by ringing the bell.

Gloucester Road BS7

ANCHOR
323 Gloucester Road
Tel: 924 1769
There must have been a huge number of Australians in the Horfield area because for the last few years this place was known as Bar Oz. Following a paint job but absolutely no injection of soul, it's now the Anchor – big, busy and beered-up at weekends.

BRISTOL FLYER
96 Gloucester Road
Tel: 944 1658
This was formerly the Horfield Inn, then the Bristol Flyer and then the Goose and is now back to the Bristol Flyer again. This huge identity crisis of a pub has always had about as much appeal as one of its fruit machines: full of flashing lights, promising much, but delivering nothing.

CAT & WHEEL
207 Cheltenham Road
Tel: 942 7862
You'd be forgiven for thinking you need a tattoo in order to be allowed entry here. It's the sort of pub Daisy Duke would shoot pool in. If it were made of cloth, it would be denim. Underneath the A38 Arches it may be, but the Cat & Wheel is half-way to Alabama.

Listings

GOLDEN LION

244 Gloucester Road
924 6449• www.goldenlionbristol.co.uk
Now that its former incarnation as Finnegan's Wake has been buried, this pub can get back to being a sizeable space for students, locals and, as you might expect from the painted exterior, street artists. A simple, decent boozer with live music, DJs or spoken word events most nights of the week. Nearest boozer to the prison – traditionally the first port of call for the newly-released.

HALO

141 Gloucester Road
Tel: 9442504
www.halobristol.co.uk
An essential part of the Gloucester Road mindset. It's a continental-style bar where you can get brunch, lunch or a pre-club drink on your way 'down town'. A good selection of cocktails a nice garden and regular live acoustic and spoken word acts.

HOBGOBLIN

69 Gloucester Road
Tel: 940 1611
Full of students on weekdays, known to attract gangs of shirts at weekends, the Hobgoblin is a long-time favourite on the Gloucester Road.

INN ON THE GREEN

2 Filton Road, Horfield
952 1391 • www.theinnonthegreen.org
A bit of a trek out the top of Gloucester Road but worth the visit. Pub food of real quality and a great guest range of real ale and ciders are just two reasons to visit this former CAMRA Bristol pub of the year. The beer garden, BBQs and quizzes all add to the essence of the place. There's an annual beer festival over May Day weekend.

LAZY DOG

112 Ashley Down Road
Tel: 924 4809 • www.barwarsltd.com
The most recent venture from Joby Andrews and Mike Cranney who are also behind The Pipe & Slippers and The Windmill. As with the other boozers the emphasis is on inventive, good value food, pleasant contemporary surroundings and a good range of nice drinks.

PRINCE OF WALES

5 Gloucester Road
Tel: 924 5552 • www.powbristol.co.uk
Arguably the best pub on the Gloucester Road, the PoW has a lovely wooden bar and interior, a fine selection of ales and ciders and top-notch food. A bustling pub, with a terrace out the back and a relaxed atmosphere.

PROM MUSIC BAR

26 The Promenade, Gloucester Road
Tel: 942 7319
www.theprom.co.uk
The transformation of the cramped old wine bar into a Mediterranean-flavoured cafe and blues bar has hit the lower end of the Gloucester Road like a ray of sunshine. Probably the best pub/bar refurbishment in Bristol in recent years, the Prom's capacity is bigger, its menu is bolder and its colour scheme is most definitely brighter. Friendly, relaxed, untouched by the fickle hand of fashion and home to one of the longest-running pop quiz nights on Planet Earth. Easy Mediterranean pavement cafe by day, beatific beat bar by night. Mo' better blues.

RISING SUN

86 Gloucester Road
Tel: 989 2471
Converted from what used to be one of the largest greasy chicken 'n' chip emporiums this side of Albuquerque, the name might suggest it's the city's first oriental boozer but sadly there isn't a pint of chow mein in sight. Now a Scream chain bar, this is home to gangs of teenage revellers hell bent on snogging anything that moves come kicking out time.

ROBIN HOOD'S RETREAT

197 Gloucester Road
Tel: 924 7880
The transformation of the Sherwood Forest hangout is complete. Not so long ago the only food you could find in here was the odd discarded crisp. Two smart and expensive looking make-overs later and Gloucester Road has a light and bright pub with a good reputation for its menu and beer selection.

ROYAL OAK

385 Gloucester Road
989 2522 • wwwtheroyaloakbristol.co.uk
When it was The John Cabot, this was where young men in Bristol Rovers shirts would

occasionally meet of a Saturday afternoon to fight young men in different coloured shirts. Now transformed into a spacious, contemporary neighbourhood boozer with a large garden and a strong emphasis on attracting families.

SPORTSMAN
Neville Road
Tel: 942 7525 • www.the-sportsman.co.uk
With 12 full-size eight-ball pool tables and four big-screen televisions, the Sportsman can make some sort of claim to live up to its name. Well at a push. For a backstreet neighbourhood pub it's very substantial and much livelier than you'd expect. And it's got another pub, the Annexe, and a restaurant attached to it.

TINTO LOUNGE
344 Gloucester Road
Tel: 942 0526
From the people who brought you the decidedly chilled Lounge cafe bar on North Street, Southville. Just like its south-of-the-river sister, the Tinto Lounge is a bar that buzzes with the low-decibel hum of the neighbourhood drop-in centre.

THE WELLINGTON
538 Gloucester Road, Horfield
Tel: 951 3022
Many people will know this as the pub in which to meet before a football or rugby match at the nearby Memorial Stadium. And it's an ideal pre-match venue with its excellent Bath Ales, spacious interior and beer garden. But there's so much more to the Wellington and a return trip on a non-sporting day is recommended when you can enjoy the Horfield Common surroundings, the food and lovely ale at a more sedate pace.

Stokes Croft BS2

THE BANK OF STOKES CROFT
84 Stokes Croft
Tel: 9232565
www.thebankofstokescroft.wordpress.com
Housed in the old Allied Irish Bank building, this is the brainchild of James Savage and Dave Smeaton, the people behind The Spotted Cow in South Bristol. The Bank is a warehouse-style bar-cum-club with a 4am licence at

weekends. There's a strong emphasis on food here with an extensive menu that runs from Brunch onwards. The any-time pizzas come highly recommended at just £5.50 and were described by Evening Post food critic Mark Taylor as 'the best value-quality deal in town.'

THE BELL
Hillgrove Street
Tel: 909 6612
The only pub in Bristol that celebrated DJs John Stapleton and Ian Green would have even considered giving up a few hundred Tuesday nights for. The Bell is one of those pubs that doesn't have to try too hard. Possibly the best pub in Bristol.

CANTEEN
Hamilton House, Stokes Croft
Tel: 923 2017 • coexist.hamiltonhouse.org
Busy, large bar with lots of seating outside. Captures the bohemian spirit of Stokes Croft. Live music most nights from 9.30, free entry. Good value food and drink.

THE CROFT
117-119 Stokes Croft
Tel: 987 4144 • www.the-croft.com
The Croft has assumed the mantle of 'Bristol's most chilled club-bar', and it certainly provides Bristol club culture with a left-sided kick up the arse. It's the bar of choice for the movers and shakers who look like setting the city's next music agenda. The clientele of leftfield musos and muses expect DJs and live acts playing everything from funk dub to alt. guitar and metal breakbeat disco. The fact that it used to have a club night called Twats' Disco suggests that it doesn't take itself over-seriously.

FULL MOON & ATTIC
1 Stokes Croft
www.fmbristol.co.uk
Attic stands for Alternative Technological Tourist Information Centre and is an ambitious scheme to turn what used to be the goth hangouts the Full Moon and Eclipse into an 'eco-hostel' with 70 beds and organic and free range food.

NO. 51
51 Stokes Croft
Tel: 9148048
This used to be the Beaufort Arms, a bleak, single-lightbulb dive favoured by hardcore

tramps. Then some bright spark noticed that it was just across the road from the Lakota club and turned it into the pre-club venue The Junction. And then the people behind Mr Wolf's took it over brightened it up and gave the entertainment a spring clean.

PIPE AND SLIPPERS
118 Cheltenham Road
Tel: 942 7711 • www.barwarsltd.com
When the Pipe and Slippers replaced rough old Irish joint the Berkely Castle in 2004, it was the first sign that Stokes Croft was changing. Plush seating and nice wooden tables set the tone. With quality DJs, occasional live music and yummy pies to chomp on. The music in the toilet is REALLY loud like there's another party going on in there, then you step back into the real world and it's back to being background music again. Odd. Sister pub of The Windmill and The Lazy Dog.

Redland BS6

CAMBRIDGE ARMS
Coldharbour Road, Redland
Tel: 973 9786
Large pub with a big beer garden. One of only two Fullers pubs in Bristol (Old Fish Market is the other). Good food and beer.

CLYDE ARMS
129 Hampton Road
Tel: 923 7936
Depending on your viewpoint, the Clyde is either a lovely quiet street corner local or one of the most consistently boring pubs in Bristol. Conversation usually revolves around the pub's unique stained-glass windows.

KENSINGTON ARMS
35 Stanley Road
Tel: 942 4394
Easily the best pub in Redland, the Kenny is now using its original name after a brief spell as the Rat & Carrot. It's worth hiking all the way to Redland for, and you don't hear that said too often.

SHAKESPEARE
Lower Redland Road
Tel: 973 3909
A regular sort of pub with a regular sort of clientele using regulation pub tables and regulation pub seating. It's the kind of place to go to on a damp Tuesday evening in February. You know, regular.

Cotham, Kingsdown BS6

COTHAM PORTER STORES
15 Cotham Road South, Kingsdown
Tel: 903 0689
www.cothamporterstores.co.uk
At last, a cider pub within stumbling distance of a hospital! The seating, the flooring, the wallpaper and the toilet facilities count for nothing. If you come in here, it's cider you're interested in and nothing but cider (although they do serve beer now). You should have had at least two of each before going to Casualty.

DECO LOUNGE
50 Cotham Hill, Cotham
Tel: 373 2688
The successful Lounge formula is to tweak the basic concept of a continental cafe-bar to suit the particular needs of an area. So Cotham's Lounge is more restaurant than bar. It's a pleasant, split-level affair where you're spoilt for choice whether you want a three-course meal, a quick after work snifter or elevenses and smoothies with the young 'uns.

GREEN MAN
21 Alfred Place, Kingsdown
Tel: 930 4824 • dawkins-taverns.co.uk
Committed to serving organic food and drink, the Green Man always has a selection of Dawkins ales and ciders on tap plus regular guest beers. There are plans for a regular organic beer festival. Formerly The Bell.

HARE ON THE HILL
41 Thomas Street North, Kingsdown
Tel: 924 6746
Another excellent no-nonsense Bath Ales pub in the lower Kingsdown/Upper Cheltenham Road area. When the Hillgrove is too crowded, a few steps to the right is all that's needed. You'll find another proper pub which is pretension and prat-free and has a great selection of bar snacks.

HIGHBURY VAULTS
164 St Michael's Hill, Kingsdown
Tel: 973 3203
One of Bristol's most celebrated drinking dens.

Complete with its stark wooden flooring and stark wooden seats, the Highbury is always busy and usually full of students. But don't let that put you off. Great beer, great staff, great big garden (now with great big heaters).

THE HILL
33 Cotham Hill, Cotham
Tel: 973 3793
Once upon a time, this used to be Crockers, a top live music venue and one of the most essential pubs of the 1970s. Then it became an 'Irish' pub, a real good craic, fiddles-R-us. Now it's a Bar Room Bar pizzeria pub, whatever the hell that is. Don't expect authenticity.

HILLGROVE PORTER STORES
53 Hillgrove Street North, Kingsdown
Tel: 907 7267
Laid back and modestly hip boozer that attracts a genuinely varied crowd. From real ale fans to frazzled freaks, ageing hippies to youngsters who want to avoid Stokes Croft at its busiest, the Hillgrove is more popular than ever but it somehow remains one of Kingsdown's best kept secrets.

KINGSDOWN VAULTS
31 Kingsdown Parade, Kingsdown
Tel: 924 9134 • www.kingsdownvaults.com
Lovely local pub, that welcomes families. Entertainment most evenings ranging from poker and quiz nights to wine club and Irish music sessions.

MICAWBER ALE HOUSE
24 St Michael's Hill, Kingsdown
Tel: 926 4500
Okay, hands up, who among you has been in here or knows somebody who has been in here? Not one of you? That's because this bizarre ornamental box of a pub only exists in Dickensian times, sometimes appearing as a hallucination to drunks on St Michael's Hill.

SCOTCHMAN AND HIS PACK
20 St Michael's Hill, Kingsdown
Tel: 929 1327
The Scotchman and his pack of what? Fags? Condoms? Geese? Who cares, all you need to know is that this is a popular and friendly real ale pub that gets busy without being rammed. It has a roof terrace for summer drinking.

WHITE BEAR
133 St Michael's Hill, Kingsdown
Tel: 904 9054 • whitebear-bristol.co.uk
One of Bristol's oldest pubs (dating back to 1650) the White Bear has always been something of a curiosity. Multi-roomed and multi-functional, it's a pleasant, unusual place.

Montpelier BS2/BS6

BEAUFORT
21 York Road
Tel: 955 5216
A great place to go if the Cadbury House is heaving and you don't fancy the fight to get to the bar. No landlord on earth was as unflappable as long-time host Garth and since his passing, the Beaufort has continued as a pleasing unpretentious boozer. Fab jukebox.

BRISTOL CIDER HOUSE
8-9 Surrey Street, St Paul's
Tel: 942 8196 • bristolciderhouse.co.uk
Characterful cider house where the Surrey Wine Vaults used to be. Always a decent range of cider on offer with 20 or more to chose from at the regular Saturday Cider Festivals..

CADBURY HOUSE
68 Richmond Road
Tel: 924 7874
The place most regularly chosen as the winner of any best pub in Bristol awards and probably quite rightly so. Always rammed to breaking point and driven by a pretty decent jukebox, it's the one thing that stops Montpelier from turning into a giant recycling centre. The Cadbury is a bit of a legend in Bristol.

COSIES
34 Portland Square, St Paul's
Tel: 942 4110 • www.cosies.co.uk
Bar of choice for reggae enthusiasts and dubstep devotees, Cosies' weekend club all-nighters are the stuff of legend. Yes in the daytime, this is a bistro/wine bar serving good-value grub to local office workers.

OLD ENGLAND
43 Bath Buildings
Tel: 924 7870
Has the Old E finally rid itself of its reputation as the pub where the crusties used to go? The answer is Yes. Once the centre of Montpelier

pub life, the Old E has a lot of catching up to do before it can rival the Cadbury in popularity, but it's on the way back. The only pub in Bristol with its own cricket nets.

STAR AND GARTER
33 Brook Road
Tel: 940 5552
The number of lock-ins that Dutty Ken has hosted at the Star and Garter defy calculation. It seemed his penchant for a late 'un would be his undoing when he was hauled before the beak in 2005, but such was the local support for Ken that, instead of being closed down, he got a legit late licence. Now you can play pool at the Star and Garter until sunrise. A Bristol institution and a strong community pub.

St Werburgh's BS2

DUKE OF YORK
2 Jubilee Road
Tel: 941 3677
This real community boozer can be spotted by the graffiti covering the outside. It has a skittle alley, games room, regular dub sessions and a nifty selection of guest ciders.

THE FARM
Hopetoun Road
Tel: 944 2384
Unsurprisingly, given it is a neighbour to the city farm, this feels like a country pub in the city. Catering for the hippies and young families of St Werburgh's, events are their passion, from fireworks night to New Years Eve.

MINERS' ARMS
136 Mina Road
Tel: 955 6718
Not a miner in sight but St Werburghs' biggest and most central pub isn't ready for forced redundancy just yet. The variety of local residents who drink here choose from a menu that includes cask ales, malt whiskies and decent wines. Good pub, now part of the independent Dawkins group.

Old Market BS2

BARLEY MOW
39 Barton Road, St Philips
Tel: 930 4709 • barleymowbristol.com
Technically this area is The Dings, the old working-class heartland of Bristol that was bulldozed years ago and the residents sent to Hartcliffe and Knowle West. There's now a small community of modern homes and the Barley Mow, which dates back to 1828. It's always been a decent, if isolated, pub and was saved from redevelopment in 2008 by The Bristol Beer Factory. There's a small garden, real ale and a good-value menu that includes Pieminister pies and curries.

OLD CASTLE GREEN
46 Gloucester Lane
Tel: 300 9140 • www.oldcastlegreen.com
Years ago, this used to be a cosy sort of place with a grumpy landlord who kept a nice pint of beer and (bizarrely) cooked the best pub curry you're ever likely to encounter with a choice of rice and/or Dauphinoise Potato.. It's been through loads of guises since then and is most recently a popular lesbian and gay venue with wall-to-wall music videos and a 4am licence on Fridays and Saturdays. (See Gay Bristol)

OLD MARKET TAVERN
29-30 Old Market Street
Tel: 922 6123 • oldmarkettavern.co.uk
Good homemade food, excellent 6X and a lovely beer garden make this old-fashioned boozer a popular lunchtime and early evening destination for Old Market office workers and journalists from the *Bristol Evening Post* building. The OMT is also one of the city's leading gay pubs. (See Gay Bristol).

PUNCH BOWL
23 Old Market Street
Tel: 929 4756
There used to be lots of Victorian pubs like the Punch Bowl in Old Market, but many, including the mighty Gin Palace, have fallen by the wayside. The Punch Bowl has a particularly nice tiled front. Inside it's a busy lunchtime pub and cosy in the evenings. There's a large beer garden out back.

STAG AND HOUNDS
74 Old Market Street
Tel: 929 7048
The 'Slag' as it has been so wittily nicknamed by nearby office dwellers, stands on the site of the 12th-Century Pie Poudre open air courts which were set up to deal with petty crims on market days when Old Market was the site for the market that served Bristol Castle. The Court still existed technically until 1973 because an annual proclamation had been made at the Stag every year inviting all who had business before the court to appear. But after the 1973 proclamation, some killjoy adjourned the court and 500 or more years of tradition was dropped in favour of an underpass.

Easton/St George BS5

BLACK SWAN
438 Stapleton Road
Tel: 939 3334
A very happening cultural centre in the heart of Easton, the Black Swan is a large pub with a huge room at the back hosting techno and dance all-nighters, national dub sound systems, local bands and DJs. An important alternative venue, Bristol would be the poorer without the Black Swan.

GREENBANK
57 Bellevue Road, Easton
www.thegreenbank.co.uk
Cosy but contemporary corner pub in the shabby-chic style much loved of Bristol boozers. There's table football and table tennis on offer, a range of real ales, the Greenbank's own-branded cider and perry and regular music and DJs.

OLD STILLAGE
147 Church Road
Tel: 939 4079 • www.arborales.co.uk
Easily the best choice if you're wondering where to go for a decent pint in relaxed, friendly surroundings in the St George/Redfield area. Arbor Ales brew their award-winning beer out the back.

SUGARLOAF
51 St Mark's Road
Tel: 939 4498
A busy pub on the bustling St Mark's Road. Several pool tables and a good range of real ale and cider. The Sugarloaf can be a bit gloomy indoors, but has an unexpectedly pleasant beer garden out the back where the geraniums are a sight to behold – no, really! There is also regular live music.

South of the river BS3/4

APPLE TREE
27 Philip Street, Bedminster
Tel: 966 7097
One of Bristol's few remaining working-class cider houses. Dark interior, lino on the floors. Don't spill anyone's cider. A curiosity.

AVON PACKET
185-187 Coronation Road, Southville
Tel: 987 2431 • www.avonpacket.com
Named after a passenger steamer from the 1860s, the Packet retains the offbeat character that it shares with many of Bristol's traditional waterside boozers. This is a friendly local with a wide range of beers, good-value home-cooked meals and a bar billiards table. The garden is surprisingly large and has a play area for nippers.

BANCO LOUNGE
107 Wells Road, Totterdown
Tel: 908 6010
The people behind the Lounge success story identified Totterdown as an area that was desperate for their 'community bar' format in 2001, but it took them more than four years to find the right building. They moved into the old Lloyds Bank in July 2006 alongside the Power Station gym. Lots of stripped wood, art deco lights, a big menu and a huge range of drinks from smoothies to Champagne set the scene. Could Banco Lounge be the catalyst for the regeneration of the Wells Road? It's a tall order, but you never know…

BAY
4-6 North Street, Bedminster
Tel: 953 1446
In the late 19th Century, the landlord of The Star, as it was then called, kept a tiger in a cage in the bar to drum up trade. Sadly, a pissed regular entered the cage and got eaten. That's the most interesting thing about a pub which went through a series of 're-blandings' from the mid 1990s before adopting the Bay persona. Bay is worth investigating in

summer for its courtyard garden. The pool tables are housed in old stables out the back. There's a tidy roster of DJs and live music most evenings.

BOCABAR
Paintworks, Bath Road
Tel: 971 3377
www.paintworksbristol.co.uk
Based in the valiantly well-intentioned Paintworks 'creative quarter', whatever that means, Bocabar is a massive, airy space with random sofas, wicker chairs and garden furniture dotted about. Extensive drinks menu, unobtrusive music and some fancy lager on draught make this a mecca for media types. Excellent lunch menu and pizzas in the evening. The trendification of Brislington starts (and ends) here…

CORONATION
18 Dean Lane, Southville
Tel: 940 9044
Delightful boozer serving a thriving local crowd, but also attracts beer and cider purists from far and wide

HEN & CHICKEN
210 North Street, Southville
Tel: 966 3143 • www.henandchicken.com
Long-time home to the Comedy Box, Bristol's leading purveyors of mirth who stage shows upstairs. The Hen and Chicken was always a split personality pub with large-screens and lager downstairs and comedy up above. Under new owners, the bar has been refurbished and offers a wide range of ales and food from breakfast till evening pizza time.

LOUNGE
227 North Street, Southville
Tel: 963 7340
The first of the Lounge chain spreading around Bristol and the south west. A good range of beers and wines, nice atmosphere. (See Eating Out Listings).

THE OXFORD
120 Oxford Street, Totterdown
Tel: 0871 951 100
Resurgent boozer, strong on community links with regular live music and other events. Popular early doors on Friday when there's a real ale promotion.

SPOTTED COW
139 North Street, Bedminster
Tel: 953 1483 • thespottedcowbristol.com
When the Spotted Cow first rebranded as 139 North, it didn't quite work. Bringing trendy North Bristol gastro pub ideas into darkest Bedminster was too much for the locals. But a change of name back to the original and a few years down the line things have changed. Great food and drink, nice garden and one of the pubs of choice for Bristol's thriving street art community.

THE SHAKESPEARE
1 Henry Street, Totterdown
Tel: 907 8818 • www.theshakey.co.uk
Once the home of Mad Ern and his less chaotic partner Sane Joan, the Shakespeare used to be the most peculiar pub in Bristol. Ern is long gone, yet The Shakey has retained some of his character and the DJ den he built in the middle of the pub. It's a busy pub with good beer, organic Sunday lunches and is the centre of a vibrant local scene. You'll either love it, or wonder what the fuss is about.

STAR & DOVE
75-78 St Luke's Road, Totterdown
Tel: 933 2892
When the regulars at The Cumberland threw a closing-down party, the new owners allegedly turned up a few days layer to find the walls painted with slogans suggesting they were yuppies and should remove themselves to Clifton forthwith. Was it a fair point well made? Depends on your perspective… The Star and Dove has changed hands several times since then and is now firmly established as a south Bristol gastro pub with an interesting, good-value menu and a wide choice of ales, ciders, lagers and wines.

THE THUNDERBOLT
124 Bath Road, Totterdown
Tel: 373 8947 • www.thethunderbolt.net
This used to be the Turnpike, arguably the roughest pub in the Western Hemisphere. Since being taken over by Dave and Sophie McDonald it's now one of Bristol's coolest music venues. The building marks the site of the toll house at the entrance to Bristol which was regularly trashed by revolting Kingswood miners and others. It was here that the troops entered Bristol to murderously quell the 1831 Queen Square riots. The 150-capacity venue

punches hugely above its weight having attracted artists including The Stranglers, Wayne Hussey, The Christians, Jerry Dammers, Dr Feelgood, Blue Aeroplanes and many more. Regular barbecues in the large garden, strong community ethos.

TOBACCO FACTORY
Raleigh Road, Southville
Tel: 902 0060 • www.tobaccofactory.com
The bar that' is responsible for changing the face of South Bristol. (See Eating Out and BS3).

VICTORIA PARK
66 Raymend Road, Windmill Hill
Tel: 330 6043 • www.thevictoriapark.co.uk
Used to be The Raymend, a large mid-terrace place with a big beer garden. Now it's one of the city's leading gastopubs. Previously you may have been asked: 'Did you spill my pint?' Now conversation is more likely to be focussed on the quality of the gazpacho salad dressing.

THE WINDMILL
14 Windmill Hill, Bedminster
Tel: 963 5440 • thewindmillbristol.com
The trendy young types of South Bristol have been crying out for a spot like this for ages. Run by the Pipe and Slippers and Lazy Dog crowd, they have worked out exactly what their fashionably-tousled crowd want: pies, tapas, groovy music, organic lagers, good wines and a courtyard 'garden'.

CIDER I UP LANDLORD

No other British city can rival Bristol for its cider consumption. This is the merry battleground where Thatchers and Gaymers vie for the hearts and tastebuds of thousands, as the city's highly trained bar staff respond to the cry of 'Cider I up Landlord!' ('I'd like a pint of cider please.') with the eternal question, 'Fatch or Forn?'. ('Would you prefer a pint of Thatchers or Dry Blackthorn?')

We might have a laid-back reputation, but where else would the population get so riled up by a cider maker's efforts to keep up with the times by changing the flavour of Dry Blackthorn that drinkers launch a campaign of Facebook protest and billboard vandalism? Black is back. No, it really is.

We're lucky enough to have several of the country's best cider pubs, only two of which are dangerously close to the docks. But you can walk into any number of Bristol pubs and find cider made by some of the world's best producers, and we're talking authentic old boozers, not outposts of some monotonous chain. Cider never really went away in Bristol, but the city is to the fore in the craft cider revival. So here's a highly subjective list of our favourites cider things:

1. PUBS
The Apple, The Apple Tree, Bristol Cider House, Coronation Tap, Cotham Porter Stores, Nova Scotia, The Orchard (see listings).

2. BRISTOL CIDER SHOP
The Bristol Cider Shop on Christmas Steps is *the* place to go if you're serious about cider. It stocks more than 80 varieties of draught and bottled cider and occasionally much sought-after offerings from small-scale Bristol producers such as Totterdown Press and Bristol Cider Works. The Cider Shop also organises festivals, talks and events. Check it out at www.bristolcidershop.co.uk.

2. NAKED GUIDE TO CIDER
The definitive guide to cider regions, orchards, cider history, making cider and more – www.tangentbooks.co.uk

Listings **Eating Out**

Many years back, *Sunday Times* food critic AA Gill described Bristol as 'a place where a tin of Heinz tomato soup passes for sophisticated grub'. Does he have a point? No, of course he doesn't. Some of you might say that AA Gill was a pompous, selectively educated tosser who wouldn't recognise a perceptive piece of cultural analysis if it came up to him and pissed in his gaspacho.

Bristol might not have the range of celebrity-endorsed eateries that London now boasts, but who wants to book a table six months in advance just so they can sit within chewing distance of Neil Morrisey anyway? Bristol's eating out

scene has undergone a similar explosion to the one that lifted London out of its pie-and-mash past but on a much smaller scale. We've seen the arrival of the aloof post-modern dining experience with restaurants such as Riverstation and Severnshed but nothing with a pretentiousness rating of, say, The Ivy.

What the city has now that it didn't have before is more choice. It's easy to find not only French, Indian and Italian cuisine but North African, Portuguese and Japanese these days. And if AA Gill thinks this amounts to the culinary equivalent of a tin of Heinz tomato soup, then he's clearly not familiar with the concept of a whole wide world of food.

Harbourside, Centre BS1

4500 MILES FROM DEHLI
8-10 Colston Avenue
200-seater Indian restaurant with a large menu and all-you-can-eat buffet.

BORDEAUX QUAY
V Shed, Canons Way
Tel: 906 5550 • www.bordeaux-quay.co.uk
This ambitious project, which incorporates a restaurant, brasserie, bar, deli, bakery and cookery school, applies the philosophy of using locally-sourced produce to a fine dining menu. BQ also aspires to zero waste objectives and responsible energy consumption. The food in the restaurant upstairs is exceptional while the bistro downstairs is great for informal (and cheaper) dining. Despite being on the Harbourside alongside a host of dreadful bars, BQ manages to offer both class and relaxation.

BYZANTIUM
2 Portwall Lane
Tel: 922 1883 • www.byzantium.co.uk
Byzantium conjures up an exotic cocktail of North African and Middle Eastern cuisine in a warehouse-sized entertainment palace where magicians and belly dancers float between the tables. The 'food lanterns', consisting of six starters, are particularly popular with the regular punters.

CITY CAFE
Temple Way
Tel: 910 2700 • www.minthotel.com
This wonderful restaurant inside the Mint Hotel has a great reputation in Bristol. It offers a menu that changes with the seasons as well as a wide range of vegetarian and healthy-eating options. Their wine list is huge too. A great spot. Not your average hotel restaurant.

DYNASTY
16a Thomas Street
Tel: 925 0888
When Wendy Ho decided to open a restaurant in Bristol, she didn't do anything by half

measures. She housed Dynasty in a glittering oriental ballroom, flew her head chef in from Hong Kong and laid on an authentic menu so vast it takes at least 15 minutes to read. In 2006, *The Observer* voted Dynasty as one of the top five Chinese restaurants in the UK. And very well-deserved too.

EL PUERTO
57 Prince Street
Tel: 925 6014 • www.el-puerto.co.uk
Boasting the biggest and most authentic tapas selection in town, El Puerto also has regular Flamenco nights.

FIREHOUSE ROTISSERIE
Anchor Square
Tel: 915 7323 • firehouserotisserie.co.uk
The Bristol version of the Bath eatery does the best spit-roasted chicken in the city. The menu is California/Pacific Rim influenced with a selection of gourmet brick-fired pizzas.

GLASS BOAT
Welsh Back
Tel: 929 0704 • www.glassboat.co.uk
Floating restaurant whose novelty value wore off about 100 years ago but whose menu continues to attract high praise from most quarters. If you come here, remember that people on glass boats shouldn't spit olive pips.

GOLDBRICK HOUSE
69 Park Street
Tel: 945 1950 • www.goldbrickhouse.co.uk
Cafe, Champagne and cocktail bar and restaurant. (See Pubs and Bars).

GRAZE BAR & CHOPHOUSE
63 Queen Square
Tel: 927 6706 • www.bathales.com
Most of the growing number of Bath Ales pubs in Bristol are cosy, traditional boozers, the Graze Bar is quite a departure from that formula. Inspired by the London and New York Chophouse themes, its decor is contemporary and the meat-laden menu includes light bites and full-on four-course blow-outs.

LA GROTTA
7 Union Street
Tel: 929 0466
Forget about deep pan, stuffed crust, ham and pineapple and all those other abominations, if you want real pizza, say 'buon giorno' to

5 LEGENDARY LATE-NIGHT TAKE-AWAYS

1. RITA'S
94 Stokes Croft
Tel: 924 9119
You haven't lived until you've stumbled into Rita's at 2am and ordered a huge portion of chips which you spill on the floor all the way home, just like Hansel and Gretel out on the piss.

2. FALAFEL KING
The Blue Van, St Augustine's Parade
You should be able to find him somewhere near the Neptune statue at the Centre. This is tasty, filling and, most remarkably of all, pretty healthy stuff. The Falafel King is the forward-thinking stomach's alternative to grim burgers and fries. So you won't feel quite as bad in the morning.

3. SLIX FAST FOODS
89-91 Stokes Croft
Tel: 924 8743
This place used to be the coolest burger bar in town. It was somewhere to hang out and look tough and put tomato ketchup on your burger in an aggressive manner after Lakota. How sad is that?

4. TRIANGLE KEBAB HOUSE
3-4 Triangle South
Tel: 927 3097
Perfectly situated on the Triangle, this kebab house is an old favourite if you're in the city centre a little worse for wear and the only thing that will hit the spot is a kebab. If you like your supper to drip down your chin and all over your shirt, this could be just the place for you.

5. JASON DONERVAN
Queen's Road
The name alone makes it worthy of mention, but Jason (real name Mustapha) was shortlisted in the Good Kebab Guide's search for the best kebab in the UK in 2010. The doners at this mobile stall are excellent as are the chicken or lamb in pitta and the service is quick and friendly. Don't overlook the cheesy chips.

Listings

Alfonso and Anita. This place is as Italian as a Franco Baresi tackle. But much friendlier.

HOTEL DU VIN
The Sugar House, Narrow Lewins Mead
Tel: 925 5577 • www.hotelduvin.com
Well-established as one of Bristol's leading restaurants, Hotel du Vin offers a Bistro-style menu of classic, but simple, European cuisine.

KATHMANDU
Colston Tower, Colston Street
Tel: 929 4455
When Paul McGann heard that his favourite Indian and Nepalese take-away was to become a restaurant, he was only too happy to be the guest of honour on the opening night. Importing their own spices from Nepal, this is authentic and truly enlightening.

MATAZI
13 Small Street
Tel: 927 7937
Quality Lebanese and North African restaurant in a vaulted cellar. Good selection of Lebanese wine, prices are reasonable and the lunchtime buffet is of belly-busting proportions.

MUD DOCK CYCLEWORKS & CAFE
The Grove
Tel: 934 9734 • www.mud-dock.co.uk
When the Mud Dock first opened, the owners admitted that 'the details of setting up the cafe were minor in comparison to issues such as which pumps and inner tubes to order'. Many awards later, this easy Mediterranean oddball is a testament to the value of not trying too hard. Look out for excellent-value lunch deals from the specials board.

MYSTRICA
51 Welsh Back
Tel: 927 2277 • www.myristica.co.uk
Slightly more upmarket than most Indian restaurants, Mystrica is now a hobble across the cobbles from its previous home on King Street. Serving dishes from all over India, the chef's aim is to be as authentic as possible rather than just offering up the usual Anglicized fare.

NAMASTE NEPAL
Unite House, Frogmore Street
Tel: 930 0779 • www.n-nepal.co.uk
Half Indian, half Nepalese menu. If you are new to Nepalese food, the Dhal Bat (a sort of Nepalese thali) is a good introduction. Loads of veggie options, generous portions, reasonable prices, friendly service. What more could you want ?

OBENTO
60 Baldwin Street
Tel: 929 7392
Japanese restaurant that specialises in Bento boxes (a sort of Japanese lunch box) as well as sushi, noodles and more. It also offers a lunchtime express menu which has proved popular with the locals.

OLD INDIA
34 St Nicholas Street
Tel: 922 1136 • www.oldindia.co.uk
Set in the Victorian splendour of Bristol's former stock exchange, Old India is worth a visit simply for the surroundings. But this place isn't just about location, it has one of the most innovative selections of contemporary and traditional Indian fare in town.

Vegetarian and vegan Bristol

Although there are very few completely vegetarian (and even fewer vegan) restaurants, cafes and takeaways in Bristol, most places do have decent options for the vegetarian and there is, nowadays, plenty on offer for vegans too. The city's dedicated veggie places include Cafe Maitreya in Easton, the various One Stop Thali Cafes, Tiffins on St Michael's Hill, Riverside Garden Centre Cafe in Ashton, Kebele Cafe (vegan) in Easton, St Stephen's Church Cafe off the Centre, Cafe Kino (vegan) in Stokes Croft and Falafel King in Cotham. The wonderful Royce Rolls in St Nick's Market doesn't sell meat but does use fish in its lovely rolls and bagels. We've highlighted in the listings text other places which particularly cater for the veggie palate. Bristol is home to the UK's largest vegetarian festival (Vegfest, held in May) and also has an active vegan community who tend to be admirably broadminded in their outlook and recommendations. For more info visit: www.bristol.vegangroup.co.uk and www.yaoh.co.uk.

OLIVE SHED
Princes Wharf
Tel: 929 1960 • therealolivecompany.co.uk
This instantly popular place typifies the bold new spirit of Bristol's restaurant renaissance. Offering fine views of the harbourside, the Olive Shed sighs with the aroma of the deepest Mediterranean flavours.

RISTORANTE DA RENATO
19 King Street
Tel: 929 8291
The sister restaurant of the much-loved La Taverna (see below) opposite, this is an altogether quieter affair offering genuine Italian fare in a warm, cosy atmosphere right in the heart of buzzing King Street.

RIVERSTATION
The Grove
Tel: 914 4434 • www.riverstation.co.uk
When Riverstation arrived in December 1997, Bristol had never had a diner quite this sophisticated before. And while the sleek glacial edges may be a little blunter these days, it's still the most modern European diner anywhere in Bristol. If you don't want to eat, you can just go for a waterside drink.

SAN CARLO
44 Corn Street
Tel: 922 6586 • www.sancarlo.co.uk
This is a huge and at times hectic modern eatery complete with vast and very impressive menu and authentic sneering Italian waiters. It is best to avoid Friday and Saturday nights if you like to be able to hear yourself chew.

SEVERNSHED
The Grove
Tel: 925 1212 • www.severnshed.co.uk
Housed in one of Isambard Kingdom Brunel's boathouses, this is home to Europe's only floating bar, a 360-degree rotating miracle on hydraulics. Its cocktails are top notch, and the three-hour weeknight 'happy hour' is a stroke of beautiful benevolence. The balcony overlooks the harbour, and you can get excellent modern European food.

SHANGHAI NIGHTS
Nelson House, Nelson Street
Tel: 945 0505
www.shanghainightsbristol.co.uk
Staggering selection of freshly-prepared Chinese dishes available a la carte or from the all-you-can-eat buffet menu. Kobe Karaoke lounge upstairs.

SPIKE ISLAND CAFE
133 Cumberland Road
Tel: 929 2266 • www.spikeisland.org.uk
This is a lovely bright space designed by swanky London architects Caruso St John in collaboration with artists. The menu is fairly basic but it's a nice place to grab a bite, take in an exhibition or sit outside. It's also on the way to The Orchard.

SPYGLASS
Welsh Back
Tel: 927 2800 • www.spyglassbristol.co.uk
With one half on the water and the other on dry land, Spyglass is a big hit in the summer. This is al fresco eating at its most appealing, with the simple barbecue and grill menu given added spice by the dream location.

ST STEPHEN'S CHURCH CAFE
21 St. Stephen's Street
Tel: 927 7977 • www.saint-stephens.com
Yemeni chef Edna Yeffet Summerell has turned this hidden Bristol cafe into one of the must-visit eateries in town. Not only is it just off the centre, but it also has a lawned garden. The menu is Middle Eastern/Mediterranean and includes a mezze platter, falafel, fritatta, shakushka as well as a full breakfast, baked potatoes, salads and cakes. Everything is veggie and much of the food is vegan. All the dishes are under a fiver .

SOURCE
1-3 Exchange Avenue, St Nicholas Market
Tel: 927 2998 • www.source-food.co.uk
Contemporary dining in the heart of Bristol's 'old quarter'. Source is a food hall/deli and bistro with an imaginative breakfast and lunch menu. There's usually a good selection of fish, but veggie options are limited.

RENATO'S LA TAVERNA DELL'ARTISTA
33 King Street
Tel: 929 7712
This pizzeria and bar is the more lively alternative to its sister restaurant Renato's (see above) across the road. Being next door to the Old Vic, it is no surprise that the walls are hung with autographed pictures of actors.

Listings

RENDEZVOUS CAFE
9 Denmark Street
Tel: 929 8683
The back room of this cafe/chip shop is plastered with posters from the Hippodrome opposite. One of the best caffs in town with that added theatrical twist.

Clifton, Hotwells BS8

BAUHINIA
5a Boyces Avenue, Clifton
Tel: 973 3138 • www.bauhinia-bar.co.uk
Pan-Asian menu featuring dishes from China, Japan, Malaysia and Thailand. The food is good and the prices offer exceptional value. Check out the early evening set meal offers.

BRIDGE CAFE
Avon Gorge Hotel, Sion Hill, Clifton
Tel: 973 8955 • www.thebridgecafe.co.uk
With spectacular view of Clifton Suspension Bridge, you can enjoy a classy meal chosen from an interesting menu.

BRUNEL WINE BAR
38 The Mall, Clifton
Tel: 973 4443
A friendly local wine bar that's worth checking out for the interesting range of tapas. Ideal starting point for a night out in the Village.

CHI CHINESE CUISINE
21 Regent Street, Clifton
Tel: 907 7840 • www.chi-chinese.co.uk
Specialising in Pekinese and Cantonese cuisine, Chi offers an extensive selection of dishes, including such favourites as aromatic Peking duck or stir-fried squid with ginger and spring onions. Be prepared for a very friendly welcome from the proprietors, the Lau family.

CLIFTON SAUSAGE
7-9 Portland Street, Clifton
Tel: 973 1192 • www.cliftonsausage.co.uk
This used to be the much-loved family-run Greek restaurant Bouboulinas, now it's a popular eatery specialising in English regional dishes and loads of sausages served with mash or as toad in the hole.

CLIFTON LIDO
Oakfield Place, Clifton
Tel: 973 4499 • www.lidobristol.com
Observer restaurant review supremo Matthew Fort described the Lido Restaurant as: "One of the more unusual restaurant locations, not just in Bristol, but also maybe in the whole country." He's not wrong. The restaurant overlooks a renovated Victorian swimming pool. The ambience is fantastic – surreal. And the food is first class.

CREATE CAFE
Smeaton Road, Cumberland Basin
Tel: 903 1201
Off the beaten track, but usually busy with workers and visitors to the Create Centre, the food here is far better than you would imagine. It was curry specials day last time the Naked Guide dined at Create and the Thai shrimp soup was exceptional. Tea and coffee and many ingredients are fairtrade. Good veggie options.

FISHERS RESTAURANT
35 Princess Victoria Street, Clifton
Tel: 974 7044 • fishers-restaurant.com
There is no sign of diminishing European fish stocks here. The appropriately-named Fishers has been so busy, they were forced to create additional seating upstairs. Sink your harpoon into shark, barracuda or skate.

HERMANOS
55 Queens Road, Clifton
Tel: 929 4323
Just when you thought Bristol was saying no more to tapas, along comes a southern European bar offering light Greek, Spanish and Italian finger-foods. Sound familiar? Fear not, it's authentically executed and offers soups, salads and pies too.

KRISHNA'S INN
4 Byron Place, Triangle South, Clifton
Tel: 927 6864 • www.mcdosa.com
Top-quality south Indian restaurant with a particularly good veggie and vegan selection.

LOCKSIDE
1 Brunel Lock Road, Cumberland Basin
Tel: 925 5800 • www.lockside.net
The peculiar pre-fab building on stilts tucked underneath a flyover used to be a famous greasy spoon and was the location for Sid's

Cafe in *Only Fools and Horses*. But since 2004, it has become one of Bristol's most pleasant family eateries. Perhaps in recognition of its transport caff roots, Lockside is open from 7am on weekdays (8am Sat, 9am Sunday) so it's ideal as a dockside breakfast location and equally appealing for candlelit dinners. Informal, relaxed and friendly.

MEME CHOCOLAT
19 The Mall, Clifton
Tel: 974 7000 • wwwmemechocolat.co.uk
Probably the best hot chocolate in town plus loads of other chocolatey treats including fab milkshakes. Soups, sandwiches also available in this bijou cafe. But why the distracting TV on the wall with annoying sub-titles?

NEW EMPEROR COURT
Portland Street, Clifton
Tel: 973 1522
They've been serving up high-quality Peking, Szechuan and Cantonese food in Clifton Village for longer than we care to remember. A simple, authentic Chinese restaurant.

PIZZA EXPRESS
31 Berkeley Square, Clifton. Tel: 926 0300
35 Corn Street. Tel: 930 0239
2 Regent Street, Clifton. Tel: 974 4259
www.pizzaexpress.co.uk
Long-established pizza chain that hit the headlines a while back when they reduced the size of their pizzas after floating on the stock exchange. Size issues apart, they are still streets ahead of the other big non-Italian pizza houses. Numerous local musicians have earned a crust in the Berkeley Square branch.

PIZZA PROVENÇALE
29 Regent Street, Clifton
Tel: 974 1175 • www.pizzaprovencale.co.uk
Not exactly authentic Italian but still an excellent pizza house. Decked out with wooden seating and wooden tables, the place has the feel of one of those farmhouse restaurants you accidentally wander into on holiday. Pizzas, pastas and pancakes.

PRIMROSE CAFE
1 Boyces Avenue, Clifton
Tel: 946 6577 • www.primrosecafe.co.uk
Hidden away in a quiet corner of Clifton, the Primrose is a cafe by day and in the evening it transforms into an intimate candlelit diner.

TOP 5 GREASY SPOONS

1. GALLERY CAFE
141 Wells Road
Tel: 977 6639
This used to be Greg's Cafe, a more than decent, long-established eaterie. Since being taken over and letting hooded youth with spray cans decorate the walls, it's become a much more modern affair. The meat breakfasts here are top notch (best in Bristol?) with free-range bacon, sausage and eggs, and Heinz beans. Veggie option is OK, but not up to the same standard.

2. THE FRIARY
2 Cotham Hill
Tel: 973 3664
One of Bristol's longest-established cafes that thrives on its uniquely friendly atmosphere. The long benches mean you inevitably have to eat one of their famous breakfasts with someone you've never met before. An interesting start to the day.

3. BRUNEL BUTTERY
Wapping Wharf, Harbourside
Tel: 929 1696
This dockside snackbar is home to the best bacon butty in Bristol. Sit outside and enjoy one on a Sunday morning. Mind the gulls!

4. HARRY'S CAFE
Fowler's 2-12 Bath Road, Totterdown
On the mezzanine overlooking a sea of chrome and high-revving horsepower, Harry's is sited in Fowler's motorcycle shop. The big biker breakfast includes at least two of every known fried breakfast ingredient. The curry sauce and chips is in fact a chip curry with sultanas like you got in those Vesta packs in the 70s, but (obviously) far better. Free table football. Genius!

5. TASTY STOP
202 North Street, Bedminster
Tel: 329 7276
This place used to be bonkers. Grumpy-but-shouty owners, fantastic portions, old blokes cussing and blinding, quick service, good value, big fish tank set in the wall. Rumours that it's all gone a bit normal now are probably just that. Rumours.

Eating out

Listings

PUMP HOUSE
Merchants Road, Hotwells
Tel: 927 2229
The downstairs bar menu is pretty impressive, but for the full-on fine dining experience head up to the mezzanine where you'll find an a la carte and chef's tasting menu awaiting you.

RACKS
St Paul's Road, Clifton
Tel: 974 1626 • www.racks-bristol.co.uk
Long-established Bristol favourite with a large terrace. A popular student choice for a spot of tucker before a night out.

SANDS
95 Queens Road, Clifton
Tel: 973 9734 • sandsrestaurant.co.uk
Sands is one of Bristol's most remarkable restaurants that aims to provide the complete Lebanese eating experience. As you walk in, you feel as if you've swapped continents; dim smoky lighting reveals a cavernous restaurant with stone floor and rounded sandy walls. Arabian Night on the last Thursday of the month features a set menu and belly dancing. The food is spicy and often unfamiliar; the post-meal bongs do not have dope in them.

SIAM HARBOURSIDE THAI RESTAURANT
129 Hotwell Road
Tel: 330 6476 • siam-harbourside.co.uk
Big on choice and bigger on service with a good range of veggie options. Lovely views over the harbourside if you can get a table at the back – wave to the Matthew as it sails past why don't you?

SS GREAT BRITAIN CAFE
Great Western Dockyard, Gasferry Road
Tel: 926 0680 • www.ssgreatbritain.org
Snacks, paninis and baked potatoes may not be at the cutting edge of Bristol's gastro scene, but the pleasant Harbourside location is the main attraction here.

Blackboy Hill, Whiteladies Road BS8

BANGKOK HOUSE
70 Whiteladies Road
Tel: 973 0409
For 30 years, this was the House of Wong but, in 2005, it shifted the emphasis from Chinese to Thai food. Good vegetarian selection.

CAFE COSMOPOLITAN
147 Whiteladies Road
Coffee, juice and paninis aplenty. Outside seating adds the European dimension.

CAFE DU JOUR
72 Whiteladies Road
Tel: 973 1563 • www.cafe-dujour.co.uk
Roomy French-style cafe with a light bite menu plus specials. Worth heading for the decked, sun-trap garden out the back.

COWSHED
46 Whiteladies Road
Tel: 973 3550 • thecowshedbristol.com
Not the place to take vegetarians. Meat, game, fish, meat and more meat are the themes here. But they do the meat thing well (or medium or rare) and some our carnivorous dining chums reckon this is one of the best places in town.

ENTELIA
50 Whiteladies Road
Tel: 946 6793 • www.entelia.co.uk
Well established Greek place made the move from Princess Victoria Street and plonked itself down into contemporary new premises on Whiteladies Road. The food is just as good and the hospitality is as warm as ever.

KOHI NOOR
211 Whiteladies Road
Tel: 973 1313 • kohinoorofbristol.co.uk
Formerly the Clifton Tandori, this is one popular Indian restaurant and take-away. One of the closest eateries to the halls of residence across the Downs, it caters for a regular student clientele.

PLANET PIZZA
83 Whiteladies Road
Tel: 907 7112 • www.planetpizza.co.uk
Small, brightly-coloured pizza joint where

Eating out

the front-of-house terrace makes it an ideal people-watching place in summer. And yes, the pizzas are named after the planets. They have a sister restaurant in Gloucester Road.

RAJPOOT

52 Upper Belgrave Road, Clifton
Tel: 973 3515 • rajpootrestaurant.co.uk
Elegant Indian restaurant with courtyard set over two levels in the basement of a Georgian townhouse facing the Downs. The Rajpoot is rated by many as being among the finest Indian restaurants in town and is in a fabulous location. Prices are reasonable, there's a good choice of fish, vegetarian and vegan dishes.

RENATO'S NUMERO UNO

203 Whiteladies Road
Tel: 974 4484
Like the Italian football team numero uno, Gigi Buffon, Renato's is an easily loveable keeper of the faith. Owner Renato Fucci has spent years at the top of Whiteladies Road and his commitment to authentic Italian food at reasonable prices has been unwavering.

PICTURE HOUSE

44 Whiteladies Road
Tel: 973 9302
www.whiteladiespicturehouse.com
Nothing typifies the changes on Whiteladies Road more than the Picture House. It was once called the Dog & Duck and was the anonymous sort of place you drifted into by mistake. Since 2004, it's been the ultra swish Picture House where you can enjoy first-rate food in tapas-sized portions. There's a strong local flavour to the menu and the Barrow Gurney Aberdeen Angus with all the trimmings is among the city's most famous Sunday lunches. Picture House East now occupies the former Quartier Vert site opposite.

ZIO'S

96a Whiteladies Road
Tel: 923 8105
Distancing themselves from the legions of American-owned fake Italian pizzerias, Zio's attempts to bring the spirit of the old country onto the high street. This means authentic pizza, pasta and seafood, and waiters who sound like Roberto Benigni.

Park St, Triangle BS1/8

BOSTON TEA PARTY

75 Park Street
Tel: 929 8601
This is a great space. Two floors (one with sofas) and a garden out back. A bit on the pricey side for a toastie even though they are good 'uns and often packed with posh students at lunchtime. Have a coffee and read a book out of peak hours when the students should be in class.

BROWNS

38 Queens Road
Tel: 930 4777• browns-restaurants.com
It's easy to feel lost in this cavernous former student refectory. In most respects, Browns typifies the multi-national chain restaurant experience. It's either cold, empty and hollow, or hot, packed and shallow. The hot chocolate is nice though. And the cocktails.

FOLK HOUSE CAFE BAR

40a Park Street
Tel: 908 5035 • bristolfolkhouse.co.uk
The Folk House cafe has always held a special place in the affections of many Bristolians. The lovely walled garden offers rare inner city calm just off Park Street and was recommended in a *Guardian* 'Urban Oases' feature. The cafe, though pleasant, was limited in its range, but then the Liz Haughton Cooking Company arrived in 2006. Liz is part of Bristol's Haughton Food Dynasty along with brothers Phil and Barney. Liz has introduced an organic and fairtrade menu at a reasonable price. Good veggie options.

GOLDBRICK HOUSE

67-69 Park Street
Tel: 945 1950 • www.goldbrickhouse.co.uk
Three floors of stylish dining, from the cafe bar with its English Tapas to the first-floor Champagne and cocktail bar through to the roof terrace. Check out the regular offers from the lunch menu and for early-evening diners. According to Venue magazine: "The presentation is immaculate, the flavours superb, and every detail is just right."

Listings

GOURMET BURGER KITCHEN
74 Park Street
Tel: 316 9162 •www.gbk.co.uk
Many Bristol eateries aspire to the shabby/chic style of decor, GBK does the shabby bit, but it stops there.

JAMIE'S
87-89 Park Street
Tel: 370 0265 • www.jamieoliver.com
The corporate Italian dining experience that is Jamie marched into Bristol to take over the sprawling Blackwell bookshop, which moved into something akin to a telephone box next door. There are many excellent small Italian restaurants in Bristol which offer better value and a more pleasurable (less noisy) dining experience than Jamie can. Strangely for an Italian restaurant, the vegetarian options are very poor. And what point is Jamie trying to make by not doing pizza?

WOODES CAFE
18 Park Street
Tel: 926 4041
Freshly-made homemade sandwiches for a couple of quid and good bacon butties before 11am. Proper choices – none of this 'skinny lattecino' rubbish – like a cup or a mug? Milk or cream? Red or brown sauce? White or brown bread? How refreshing.

Gloucester Road, Stokes Croft, St Paul's BS7

AMICI
239 Cheltenham Road
Tel: 924 5879
It may be vast and have a sign that looks like it's been taken from the set of *Blake's 7*, but Amici likes to go beyond the typical Italian restaurant experience. Legend has it that Milan-born owner Carlo Dall'Occo once ran a cabaret in Moscow.

ARTS HOUSE
108a Stokes Croft
www.theartshouse.org
Gallery, cafe, bar, cinema, live music and performance venue The Arts House serves a basic, but tasty selection of tapas, sandwiches, baked spuds, salads and quiche.

BIBLOS
62 Stokes Croft
Lebanese mezze bar. Cheap, incredibly tasty, often packed out. Go.

BISTRO LA BARRIQUE
225 Gloucester Road
Tel: 944 5500
Formerly called Picasso's, this substantial and airy bar-restaurant really comes to life in the summer when the large terrace lends Gloucester Road the air of a Parisian boulevard. The food is fantastic and there are millions of wines by the glass. Make sure you ask for a terrace table in the summer months as it gets mighty hot inside.

BLUE LAGOON
20 Gloucester Road
Tel: 942 7471
Sounding more like a shampoo from the mid 1980s than a coffee bar, Blue Lagoon is more sussed than its name suggests. Instead of becoming the latest volunteer to jump on the growing pile of sofa-strewn Gloucester Road bars, it offers a stripped down sandwich and coffee alternative in a more frivolous setting.

BUBALU
79 Gloucester Road
www.bubalu.co.uk
Fitness, Food, Fun is the theme at Bubalu's, a large comfortable cafe with a fitness studio out the back. As you would expect, the menu is for healthy eaters – no gutbuster breakfasts here. The fruit smoothies are nice and Bubalu serves good coffee

CAFE KINO
108 Stokes Croft
Tel: 924 9200 • www.cafe-kino.com
In many ways Cafe Kino represents all that is inspiring about Stokes Croft – it's fiercely independent, radical, creative and friendly. This vegan cafe started life on Ninetree Hill but moved to bigger premises such was its immediate success. Menu offers a wide selection including, soups, wraps, curries. Everything, including drinks, is ethically sourced and there are regular live music and other events.

DELMONICO
217 Gloucester Road
Tel: 944 5673 • www.delmonico.co.uk
If you are prepared to ignore the possibility that Delmonico is too upmarket for Gloucester Road, you will discover one of the most stylish restaurants in the city, serving a 'fusion' menu of meat, fish and veggie dishes.

ELEGANCE COFFEE SHOP
88 Stokes Croft
Tel: 942 6777
A non-pretentious European-style cafe which just focuses on quality coffee and some of the finest cakes this side of Patisserie Valerie.

EZO
6 The Promenade, Gloucester Road
Tel: 944 2005
Ezo offers a wide but unremarkable selection of mezze, kebabs and fish. There's a particularly good choice for vegetarians, both from the mezze and the main menu.

FUNG'S
330 Gloucester Road
Tel: 923 2020
No-nonsense Chinese eat in and take-away. Boasts a huge menu and friendly cafe atmosphere. Everything is freshly cooked and there's a wide (if tofu-heavy) selection of veggie dishes. Does a nice cuppa green tea.

THE GANGES
368 Gloucester Road
Tel: 924 5234
With the identity of Indian food being diluted more every day, it's reassuring to know that there are a few places that remain faithful to the glorious cuisine of the sub-continent.

HALO
141 Gloucester Road
Tel: 944 2504 • www.halobristol.co.uk
Another welcome addition to the increasingly cosmopolitan Glossy Road, Halo mixes easy English and Mediterranean food into a laid-back drinking atmosphere and manages to make you feel like you've got all the time in the world. A picture postcard garden makes Halo even more irresistible in summer.

TOP 5 FISH'N'CHIPS

1. ARGUS FISH BAR
114 West Street, Bedminster
Tel: 966 4850
An outstanding corner chippy that serves up consistently excellent chips and fresh fish cooked in a secret batter recipe that has been in the family for generations. It's one of only four fish 'n' chip shops in Bristol to have a Seafish Friers Quality Award. The others are the Clocktower, Farrows and the Frying Machine in Bradley Stoke. The Argus is a hidden gem in the not-so-lovely Bemster High Street.

2. FARROWS
146 Wells Road, Totterdown
Winner of an *Evening Post* Best Chippie in Bristol award, everything about Farrows (including the portions) is just as it should be. Home-made fishcake and pea fritters are among the highlights. There's another Farrows on the Kingsway in Kingswood.

3. KELLAWAY FISH BAR
4 Kellaway Avenue
Tel: 944 5220
Nominated in a *Guardian* online poll to find the best chip shop in Britain. Famed for its haddock and its light, crispy batter. Many North Bristolians rate this the best chippy in town. Those in South Bristol would beg to differ...

4. MAGNET FISH BAR
55 Dean Lane, Bedminster
Tel: 963 6444
Jim Singarda's famous chippy is a one-time winner of the *Evening Post*'s Best Bristol Chippy award. The secret of the Magnet's success is apparently the beef dripping that everything is fried in. Not really recommended for vegetarians.

5. RENDEZVOUS
9 Denmark Street
Tel: 929 8683
Conveniently placed next to the Bunch of Grapes, Rendezvous is renowned for both its cod and its curry sauce. Some adventurous diners have been known to combine the two.

Listings

HOOPER HOUSE
113 Stokes Croft
Tel: 924 7180 • www.hooperhouse.co.uk

Comfortable , relaxed coffee house with a nice selection of breakfasts, baguettes, salads and paninis. Takes its name from a fish and poultry market that used to be held here.

OH! CALCUTTA
216 Cheltenham Road
Tel: 924 0458 • www.ohcalcutta.co.uk
There are no booths or flock wallpaper at Oh! Calcutta. This popular, contemporary Indian diner is bright, open plan and has an equally modern take on the food. The old favourites are there, but you'll also find a good selection of fish curries and vegetarian dishes.

PIEMINISTER
24 Stokes Croft
Tel: 942 9500 • www.pieminister.co.uk
Jon Simon and Tristan Hogg started Bristol-based Pieminister back in 2002. They have gone national, with their delicious pies appearing in delis and pubs all over the country. They do a heap of veggie pies too.

PEAR CAFE
2 Upper York Street, St Paul's
Tel: 942 8392 • www.thepearcafe.com
Bijou take-away with table outside. Nice range of sandwiches and salads, but the soup is what makes this place special.

PLANTATION
221-223 Cheltenham Road
Tel: 907 7932 • plantationrestaurant.biz
Founded by Beverley Forbes in 2003, Plantation is a Caribbean restaurant with a menu that particularly respects Beverley's Jamaican family roots. Good for vegetarians and vegans. Excellent party venue with live music and much dancing most Friday and Saturday nights.

RICE AND THINGS
120 Cheltenham Road
Tel: 924 4832 • www.riceandthings.co.uk
Jamaican restaurant with an extensive menu of meat and fish dishes and a good vegetarian and vegan selection.

LA RUCA
89 Gloucester Road
Tel: 944 6810

La Ruca may sound like something that large French men do when they play Le Rugby, but in fact, it's a light and pleasant first-floor cafe over the wholefood shop of the same name. There's a Latin American twist to many of the dishes and a big emphasis on fairtrade ingredients. They offer a good vegetarian and vegan selection.

RUNCIBLE SPOON
3 Ninetree Hill
Tel: 329 7645 • the-runcible-spoon.com
Runcible Spoon is a co-operative venture including chefs and a gardener producing a menu of seasonal, locally sourced food. Suppliers include the Simms Hill Shared Harvest project in Frenchay and the Peasant Evolution Producers Co-op from West Dorset, South Somerset and East Devon.

SHEESH MAHAL
13a Gloucester Road
Tel: 942 2942
When you walk through the doors of the Sheesh, you enter a time warp that takes you back to Bradford in 1975. East is most definitely East in this place. Booths, net curtains and the colours purple and green figure strongly.

TAKE 5
72 Stokes Croft
Tel: 907 7502 • www.take5cafe.co.uk
One of the nicest places to eat in Bristol if you like your food accompanied by an atmosphere of calm. Many years ago Take 5 was set up by a Malaysian immigrant nicknamed Jake who is from an Indian Sikh background. The food is still prepared by 'Cosmic' Jake and very good it is to. There are always five curries on offer (veggie or vegan apart from Jake's special chicken tikka masala) and they all cost a fiver. At weekends there's a choice of a meat, veggie or vegan fry-up and roasts on Sunday. The veggie breakfast is excellent.

ZAZU'S KITCHEN
45 Jamaica Street, Stokes Croft
Tel: 923 2233
Everybody seems to be doing the locally sourced/seasonal/organic thing, but few do it better than Zazu's Kitchen. There's a cafe

menu by day and a Mediterranean-influenced selection in the evening with more than a hint of fine dining.

Redland, Cotham, Kingsdown BS6

AHMED'S CURRY CAFE
1e Chandos Road, Redland
Tel: 946 6466
A new concept in Indian food, Ahmed's is a curry cafe that offers a full range of top-quality curries at knockdown prices – they even have a happy hour where you can pick up a curry with rice and a naan bread for a bargain price.

ANTHEM
27 St Michael's Hill
Tel: 929 2834
The colourful Anthem sign is stapled onto a wonky looking 17th-Century building on the steepest bit of St Michael's Hill. Its menu is equally eccentric. One moment it's Cajun, the next it's Thai. A much-loved oddity.

BLUE JUICE
39 Cotham Hill
Tel: 973 4800
Funky, oasis-like juice bar at the heart of Cotham Hill with a great sunken terrace out front. Its exotic juices and smoothies (South American Acai berry anyone?) are sure to boost your vitamin levels, as are its vegan wraps and salads.

LA CAMPAGNOLA
9 Zetland Road, Redland
Tel: 924 8372
The only restaurant in Bristol to take its name from a make of racing bike gears, this is one of only a handful of authentic Italian pizzerias in town. You won't find any stuffed crusts in here, Mr Inglese.

CASA MEXICANA
Zetland Road
Tel: 924 3901 • www.casamexicana.co.uk
This place was the first Mexican restaurant in Bristol, and is now more than 20 years old. It has prospered largely because of the commitment of the owners Kevin and Lesley Duff. Even the national press have got down with their Mexican way.

FALAFEL KING
6 Cotham Hill
Tel: 329 4476
Tremendous value, great food, laid back surroundings, Falafel King serves some of the best Middle Eastern dishes in town. Try the home-made flatbreads. All the food is veggie or vegan.

FLINTY RED
34 Cotham Hill
Tel: 923 8755 • www.flintyred.co.uk
Set up by wine merchants Dominic Harman and Rachel Higgens of Corks of Cotham and chefs Matthew Williamson and Claire Thomson, Flinty Red offers fine dining with a Mediterranean/French twist and some unusual flavour combinations – braised octopus with fresh salted turnip and green olive, for example. Hosts regular wine tasting events.

KEBAB HOUSE
6 St Michael's Hill
Tel: 921 1958
It's been here longer than anyone can remember. It's small, out-of-way, friendly, atmospheric and the mezze menu is very good. What more could you ask for?

JUNIPER
21 Cotham Road South
Tel: 942 1744 • juniperrestaurant.co.uk
One of Bristol's best-known neighbourhood restaurants, Juniper is testament to the vision of owner Nick Kleiner. The à la carte menu offers mostly modern and traditional British and European fare, such as roast lamb or homemade bread and butter pudding.

HAVANA COFFEE
37a Cotham Hill
Tel: 973 3020 • www.havanacoffee.net
Why is it that it's always Che Guevara and not Fidel Castro that hangs from the walls of cafes like this? If you are happy having a coffee instead of a revolution then this South American-themed bubble offers all-day breakfasts, sandwiches, pancakes, fairtrade coffees and a Latin-jazz soundtrack. Now on Clifton Down Road next to WH Smith as well.

MOREISH
6 Chandos Road, Redland
Tel: 970 6078 • moreishrestaurant.co.uk
The first solo project of Tim Moores, Moreish

Eating out

Listings

occupies a prime corner spot right in the middle of Chandos Road. Cafe by day and restaurant by night, it offers the best of both worlds. Inside it is all wooden tables and floor boards and piles of cakes on plates, while outside, the terrace offers a sunny spot on this quiet road. It's an unpretentious spot, offering good food.

ZORBAS
7 Cotham Hill
Tel: 973 1469
Genuine Greek restaurants are a rarity in Bristol and Zorbas is as close as you can get to a traditional taverna without hopping on a plane to Athens. Sophisticated it ain't, but if you want to wash down a kebab or two with a few shots of ouzo, this is the place to come.

Montpelier, Easton, St Werburgh's BS2, BS5

BELL'S DINER
1 York Road, Montpelier
Tel: 924 0357 • www.bellsdiner.co.uk
A popular and long-established half-hidden favourite located in an ex-cornershop at the bottom of York Road, Bell's offers the perfect blend of fine contemporary cuisine in an informal setting. 'Eat, drink, da bells, da bells,' as their press ad almost says.

THE BRISTOLIAN
2 Picton Street, Montpelier
This is the place where the Montpelier counter-culture gathers for breakfast, a roll-up and a cup of tea. There's nothing too fancy about the Bristolian in its latest guise but the Turkish breakfast is definitely a winner. The toilets have been decorated by Ghostboy and his work has drawn somewhat unflattering, but highly amusing, comments on the walls.

CAFE MAITREYA
89 St Mark's Road, Easton
Tel: 951 0100 • www.cafemaitreya.co.uk
Because it's situated right at the heart of the busy St Mark's Road, it's no surprise to find Cafe Maitreya more like a chill-out zone than a hectic diner. The veggie and vegan menu always uses seasonal produce.

CASBAH CAFE
96 St Mark's Road, Easton
Tel: 939 8804 • www.lacasbah.co.uk
Tagines, couscous and all things Moroccan are on offer at this popular restaurant. The lamb tagine comes particularly recommended as does the couscous with seven vegetables. Downstairs there's a Moroccan bazaar selling hand-made merchandise.

ONE STOP THALI
12 York Road, Montpelier
Tel: 942 6687
1 William Street, Totterdown
Tel: 933 2955
64-66 St Marks Road, Easton
Tel: 951 4979
1 Regent Street, Clifton
Tel: 974 3793
www.thethalicafe.co.uk
From humble beginnings in Montpelier, this rulebook-ripping adventure into the heart of Asian cuisine has grown into something of a phenomenon. And they make it look so easy. Their secret? Fresh, tasty, home-cooked exotica served on steel plates at reasonable prices. Join their tiffin club.

ST WERBURGH'S CITY FARM CAFE
Watercress Road
Tel: 908 0798
The cafe was built in the late 1980s by a group of self-confessed hippies called the Bristol Gnomes who would carve materials with chainsaws and virtually sculpt buildings giving them a Gaudi or Gnomemade flavour. So the surroundings are unusual and the food is good quality, but it's expensive. Don't expect much change from £45 for a light lunch and drinks for a family of four.

TEOH'S
28 Lower Ashley Road
Tel: 907 1191
Old Tobacco Factory, Southville
Tel: 902 1122 • www.teohs.net
The original Teoh's has managed to thrive despite being located half way between the busy St Paul's junction and the M32. No-one does Malaysian and Thai food so cheaply. Crispy duck, chicken satay and beef rendang we know. But what on earth is Penang fried ho fun? There's also a Teoh's next to the Tobacco Factory in Southville.

South Of The River BS3/BS4

AL'S TIKKA GRILL
33 Ashton Road
Tel: 953 5950
BYO curry bistro near the Bristol City ground that is a South Bristol institution. This is a great greasy spoon by day and a BYO Indian restaurant and take-away in the evenings. They now have a Hot and Spicy version in North Street too (966 9008).

ASILAH
Wells Road
Tel: 07816 202827
Belly dancing and flamenco guitar evenings are just two of the regular attractions for diners at this neighbourly Moroccan eaterie. Wide-ranging menu of soups, fish, tagines and couscous with reasonable veggie options. It's BYO so you're not going to break the bank. If you want a laugh, ask the owner, Bridget, about when she hired a male belly dancer.

A CAPELLA
184c Wells Road
Tel: 971 3377 • www.acappellas.co.uk
Neighbourhood cafe with a small selection of deli stuff. Cafe by day and fancy pizza joint (including take-away) by night.

BOCABAR
Paintworks, Arnos Vale
Tel: 972 8838 • www.bocabar.co.uk
Large bar with outdoor seating serving salads, paninis and a wide selection of mains - the Bocaburger is recommended. Busy with mums, babies and office folk during the day. At 6pm the lights go down, the music is turned up, the menu turns to pizza and Bocabar transforms into a 'happening' nitespot.

CAFE GROUNDED
66-68 Bedminster Parade, Bedminster
Tel: 923 1000 • www.cafegrounded.co.uk
Independent, stylish cafe/bar with a strong emphasis on community and accessibility, so kids are welcome and the cafe was designed with disabled access in mind. Daytime menu for breakfast and lunch, pizza and tapas in the evening. Nice cakes. There's another Grounded on Church Road in Redfield..

CAFFE SAZZ
232 North Street, Southville
Tel: 963 3334 • www.caffesazz.co.uk
Before they took over the next door shop this used to be a tiny Turkish cafe renowned for its party atmosphere, particularly at weekends when there's often live music and belly dancing. Since they expanded they may offer a wider breakfast and daytime menu, but Sazz has lost some of its intimacy.

EL RINCON
298 North Street, Southville
Tel: 939 3457 • elrincon.moonfruit.com
Characterful Spanish bar/restaurant offering a range of tapas, raciones, specials and paella on Sundays. Wine tastings and Spanish language classes also on offer. Open evenings only apart from Sunday. Booking recommended.

LOUNGE
227 North Street, Southville
Tel: 963 7340
107 Wells Road, Totterdown
Tel: 908 6010
From the people who run Byzantium, Lounge is one of the new breed of Bristol bars-cum-restaurants. The atmosphere is pleasant without being too trendy and the range of food is good, most of it for under £7. In 2006, the Totterdown branch on Wells Road opened offering Totterdown locals somewhere central to drink and get a bite to eat.

SOUK KITCHEN
277 North Street, Southville
Tel: 966 6880 • www.soukkitchen.co.uk
Fabulous menu of Middle Eastern dishes in pleasant surroundings with big windows so you can watch the North Street world go by. The food here is excellent and the breakfasts are outstanding. Many people rate Souk as one of the best restaurants in town. The Turkish sausage and beans is certainly one of the finest breakfasts in Bristol. Loads of veggie options. Mixes a fine gin and tonic too, though not recommended for breakfast.

TOBACCO FACTORY
Raleigh Road, Southville
Tel: 902 0060 • www.tobaccofactory.com
If you want an insight into why North Street, Stokes Croft and other areas of Bristol are so staunchly independent and anti-chain bar and franchise food outlets, look no further than the

Eating out

Listings

success of George Ferguson's Tobacco Factory project. The idea is to regenerate run-down areas by attracting like-minded independent businesses around a flagship project. The Tobacco Factory has done this and is now firmly established as one of Bristol's best cafe bars. The menu is Mediterranean based with tapas, mezze plus a range of main meals. The beer is brewed about 50 yards away at Bristol Beer Factory and the bread is made even closer at Mark's Bread, just across the road. Tobacco Factory has a large outdoor area, and a Green Room that tends to be used by families. The bar also hosts art exhibitions and regular events.

RIVERSIDE GARDEN CENTRE CAFE

Clift House Road, Ashton
Tel: 966 7535 • riversidegardencentre.com
Veggie menu which includes organic, fairtrade and locally sourced ingredients. A lovely spot to eat outside and there's a small play area for the nippers.

WINDMILL HILL CITY FARM CAFE

City Farm, Philip Street, Bedminster
Tel: 963 3252
www.windmillhillcityfarm.org.uk
Famous for its hearty meat and veggie breakfasts, they also do a full lunch menu, cakes and snacks. The courtyard garden is a joy in the summer. The farm is an great place to bring the kids too (see Children's Bristol).

Other Areas

BEESES RIVERSIDE TEA GARDENS & CONHAM FERRY

Wyndham Crescent, Conham
Tel: 977 7412 • www.beeses.co.uk
Visiting Beeses can be quite an adventure when you take the most direct route – boat. If you've got your own vessel make your way up the Avon till you see Beeses on the starboard side. Or you can get the Conham Ferry across the river. Driving and parking up on the Brislington side of the Avon is the least interesting approach. This part of the Avon used to be the home of heavy industry such as the sprawling St Anne's Board Mills and Butler's Tar Works and it is relatively recently that the derelict factories have been replaced by houses. Beeses has been there since 1846 and now offers a menu of cream teas with home-made jams, burgers, baguettes, salads and baked potatoes. Once a month there's a gourmet fish supper evening which sells out ages in advance. Regular entertainment includes quizzes, music nights and spoken word events.

KONDI BRASSERIE

105 Henleaze Road, Henleaze
Tel: 962 8230 • www.kondibrasserie.co.uk
Hidden away and nestled between shops on Henleaze Road, lies a little café that sells fabulous cakes by day and transforms into a restaurant by night. The menu fairly traditional English dishes and there's a 2 for 1 deal on all meals every Wednesday. Kondi has a smart, vintage appearance, yet it still musters a homely feel and warmth. Attached to the cafe is a little shop selling the likes of hand-made bath bombs and Scrabble tea towels.

CASA MIA

38 High Street, Westbury-on-Trym
Tel: 959 2884 • casamiarestaurant.co.uk
Casa Mia was always a very good 'modern Italian' Michelin Star rated restaurant, then in 2010 it won Gordon Ramsay's Best Restaurant C4 series and it has become impossible to get a table. Apparently even Gordon Ramsay's mum couldn't get in once. Oh well, maybe by the time you read this, things will have calmed down a bit or they will have opened up their much mooted second restaurant in the city.

BRISTOL'S TOP TAKE-AWAYS

A TEAM OF 15 TAKE-AWAY CONNOISSEURS NOMINATED THEIR FAVOURITE SPOTS...

AHMED'S CURRY CAFE
1e Chandos Road, Redland
Tel: 946 6466
The best curry take out ever! Also a nice but cramped restaurant.

AL'S TIKKA GRILL
33 Ashton Road, Southville
Tel: 985 3016
Still the best take-away curry in town after all these years.

ALWAHA
12 High Street Easton, 147 Wells Road
The best chicken shawarma in town says our correspondent. Falafel is good too.

BRISTOL SAUSAGE SHOP
St Nicholas Market
Tel: 747 8302
Speciality sausages in either sandwich form or a take-away. Always a queue. The best.

CIAO BURGERS
207a Gloucester Road
Tel: 942 6228
Why would you go to McDonalds or Burger King when you can come here? Garlic, chilli, American style. And thin fries to go.

CHARCOAL GRILL
236 Gloucester Road
Tel: 942 8888
Don't be fooled by the unassuming facade, this place serves the finest kebabs in Bristol.

FALAFEL KING
The Centre
The best veggie take-away option in town. Also at Cotham Hill.

GRECIAN KEBAB HOUSE
2 Cromwell Road, St Andrews
Tel: 942 3456
Quality kebabs with all the trimmings. Cheesey chips are impressive.

KATHMANDU
Colston Tower, Colston Street
Tel: 929 4455
The Kancha Kukhura Special (Tandoori chicken cooked in Nepalese spices) is the most popular dish according to a customer poll. The veg and fish dishes are also fantastic.

LA CUISINE
392 Gloucester Road
Tel: 907 6534
Exotic name disguises a ludicrously wide-ranging menu with excellent kebabs.

LA RUCA
89 Gloucester Road
Tel: 944 6810
Selection of home-made treats. The veggie chimichanga with guacamole or falafels is brilliant.

MAGIC ROLL
3 Queens Row, Triangle, Thomas Lane, St Thomas
Seriously gorgeous food. From homemade muesli and hot porridge to fantastic wraps.

MELA
19 York Road, Montpelier
Tel: 924 9272
The thalis are great value and if you fancy a pint in The Beaufort next door, they'll come and get you when the curry is ready. What a nice bunch.

ROYCE ROLLS
St Nicholas Market
Homemade bread bagels, pasties and more. Lots of veggie stuff.

PORTUGUESE TASTE
St Nicholas Market
The stews are excellent and you can treat yourself to real-deal Portuguese cakes – pastel de nata.

Listings **Shopping**

Although Bristol can't claim to have anywhere near the clout of London, or the nook-and-cranny appeal of its near-neighbour Bath, it does register an above-average score as a post-globalisation retail centre. Okay, the Gloucester Road isn't quite Portobello Road, and Broadmead is even further away from Knightsbridge, but we do have two enormous shopping super-centres.

Despite being Broadmead-with-a-roof, and fewer beggars, Cabot Circus and The Mall at Cribbs Causeway are extremely popular. A case of never mind the quality, or the variety, just feel the width? Of course. But that's not Bristol's fault, it's Britain's. The city has managed to hang onto a decent number of independent shops but has lost just as many to the ruthlessness of 'the market'.

There are, for now anyway, some alternatives to Mall life. We won't bother telling you about Gap, Top Man, HMV or Next because you know more than you need to about them already. This guide tries to get under the skin of Bristol's retail experience. We will point you in the direction of the most cutting-edge record shops, the most radical second-hand stockists, the best places to pick up contemporary home design and the whereabouts of the most essential bookstores. Go forth, spend money – support your local shop.

Fashion

50:50
8 Park Street
Tel: 930 4990 • www.5050store.com
The spirit of Dogtown and the Z-Boys lives on here. 'Skateboarder owned and operated' reads the shop slogan and this total commitment to four-wheeled radicalism means the hipper of Bristol's teenagers come here before heading off down to College Green. Cutting-edge range of skate-inspired and urban fashion.

BEAST
224 Cheltenham Road • Tel: 942 8200
St Nicholas Market • Tel: 927 9535
www.beast-clothing.com
Beast is so much more than a cool clothes shop, it's a worldwide cultural ambassador for Bristol. But Beast doesn't spread the word about the city through fancy websites and multi-million pound marketing campaigns, it uses T-shirts bearing Bristolian phrases such as 'ark at ee', 'gert lush', 'theyz me daps mind', 'Mint innit' and 'cheers drive' which are proudly borne on chests around the world. The Bristolian community in Sydney is particularly fond of them. Lucy Wheeler and Andy Keith-Smith produced their first Bristol T-shirt ('gert lush') at the beginning of 2004 and now have a huge number in the range. 'We love Bristol, we're very proud of it,' says Lucy. 'The T-shirts convey a positive image of Bristol using phrases we used when we were kids and which you still hear in the city today.'

BILLIE JEAN
208 Gloucester Road
Tel: 944 5353
If you laid out all the velvet they stock in Billie Jean, it would cover an area approximately the size of Kent. Are they expecting a bulk order of smoking jackets from the ghost of Oscar Wilde or something?

BISHOPSTON TRADING COMPANY
193 Gloucester Road
Tel: 924 5598 • bishopstontrading.co.uk
Fairtrade is all well and good in principle, but surely no-one in their right mind can expect us

to wear clothes made out of hemp? Well, not quite. This fairtrade workers' co-operative was set up in 1985 to create employment in the South Indian village of K.V. Kuppam and offers simple but quality clothing for all – babies through to adults.

BS8
34 Park Street
Tel: 930 4836
A whole arcade displaying the work of young Bristol designers in addition to all manner of other left-of-centre club chic. Split over three levels, it's the ideal place to visit if you want something new to throw on that evening. You can pick up anything from skimpy throw-a-way tops and cool hats to elegant evening wear and *Sopranos* T-shirts. This is a shopping haven for those who like a rummage.

COOSHTI
57 Park Street
Tel: 929 0850
Bristol's only credible designer store. You'll find names such as Duffer of St George, Replay, Hope & Glory, Firetrap and Red or Dead scattered through every section.

CUSTARD HOUSE CLOTHING
St Nicholas Market
Tel: 07880 736054
www.custardhouseclothing.co.uk
Vintage clothing and hand-made clobber. Janine Chisholm studied Theatre Design specialising in Costume in a London College eighteen years ago, completed a Post Graduate in Innovative Pattern Cutting at St Martins College of Fashion and worked in professional theatre and television so the clothes here are a bit special.

HANDMADE SHOE COMPANY
64 Colston Street
Tel: 921 4247 • www.shoe-craft.co.uk
Handmade shoes that look like they've been designed by druids who live near a rainbow. Another gloriously stylistic offering bought to you by the people who gave us sandals.

KBK SHOES
203 Cheltenham Road
Tel: 924 3707
Boots. Made for walking. For nearly 100 years, this place has sold nothing that doesn't come with an air sole underneath. One of the largest

RETAIL HEAVEN: THREE CLASSIC SHOPS

1. 20TH CENTURY FLICKS
3 Richmond Terrace
Tel: 974 2570
www.20thcenturyflicks.co.uk
If only all video shops were made this way. It's not just that there are 10,000 titles to choose from, nor that every single conceivable genre of film is covered. What makes movie buffs really fall in love with 20th Century Flicks is the fact that the staff really know and care about films. They'll offer advice, discuss scripts, give on-the-spot reviews, suggest possible alternatives and come out with comments such as: 'It's the best sci-fi thriller of the mid 1980s' when you least expect it. You don't get that in Blockbuster. Do you?

2. REPSYCHO
85 Gloucester Road
Tel: 983 0007
Andy Minter knows a decent pair of whacked-out 1972 men's slacks when he sees them. His long-standing second-hand clothing emporium on Gloucester Road has everything you could want. Authentic clobber is what it's all about but you'll also find T-shirts bearing brand legends like Moog. Apparently, Linter trawls car boot sales as well as Europe's clothes markets to find his stock. Upstairs is full of moulded nu-plastic furniture. Downstairs is Prime Cuts, a 1960s pysch-beat and soul record shop.

3. BRISTOL SWEET MART
80 St Mark's Road
Tel: 951 2257
www.sweetmart.co.uk
A bit of a legend, not just in Easton, not just in Bristol, but all over the world. Take a few minutes to wander around the shop and you'll realise that their success is built on two equally vital factors: organisation and love. Lots of wondrous food stuffs you've never heard of from right across the known universe. This is the place to go for fresh herbs and it also sells Hobbs House bread from the Chipping Sodbury master bakers.

stockists of Dr Marten shoes and boots in Britain, the staff have Masters Degrees in DM Studies and attract shoe fanatics from all over.

MARCRUSS ARMY SURPLUS STORE
177-181 Hotwell Road
Tel: 929 7427
They made a mint when Echo & The Bunnymen made it fashionable to go out looking as if you were on a military manoeuvre. They cashed in on the 1990s trend for combats. And now they're doing a roaring trade in gas masks for paranoid people.

NAFF CLOTHING
13 Cotham Hill, Cotham
Tel: 973 7458
'This place is the perfect antidote to bland, high street clothes stores,' says a friend. Perhaps, but there are rather too many hippie sacks and horribly pleated 1980s jackets among the more interesting stuff.

PINK SODA
59 Gloucester Road
Tel: 942 0420
Be careful out there girls: there's some really quite adventurous independent design happening in Pink Soda. They have cute 1950s dress stylings and socks with fingers and so much more. This is wobbly hippie chic at its best. It looks like Pink Soda are just not afraid to love all our pasts.

RAG TRADE BOUTIQUE
2 Upper Maudlin Street
Tel: 376 3085 • ragtradeboutique.co.uk
Designer recycling. Take in your old fancy togs and Rag Trade sell them on at a commission. The emphasis here is on classy designer wear.

RECESSION
8 Jacobs Wells Road
www. recessionshop.webs.com
Brilliant name for a vintage/second-hand clothes shop. Excellent supply of retro clothes and accessories.

REPSYCHO
85 Gloucester Road
Tel: 983 0007
Legendary vintage clothing boutique with record store downstairs. See p223.

SEVEN 7
60 Park Row
Tel: 929 8898
Designer T-shirts, vintage and import trainers, jewellery and accessories, as well as exhibitions and artwork.

SHOP
19 Christmas Steps
Tel: 316 9421 • www.shoptheshop.co.uk
This is more like a fashion and ancient board game museum than a vintage clothes shop, such is the care with which everything is presented. Shop is a not-for-profit outfit committed to supporting community arts. It's a lovely place with sound politics and a huge amount of taste.

SHOP DUTTY
116 Cheltenham Road
Tel: 924 9990 • www.shopdutty.com
Vintage clothing and a platform for some of the city's fresh new designers. Shop Dutty is committed to recycling clothes, so many of the new designs use second-hand clothes. One of the city's coolest clothes retailers.

UNCLE SAM'S
54a Park Street
Tel: 929 8404
Considering that 1950s Americana hasn't been fashionable since, ooh, 1984, Uncle Sam's has done well to still be open after all these years. It specialises in T-shirts, shirts, jackets, jeans and huge amounts of leather.

Books

AREA 51
230 Gloucester Road
Tel: 942 4655 • www.area51online.co.uk
Abandon any hope of ever meeting girls all ye who enter here. As its name suggests, this is the sort of place that attracts blokes who fantasise about being trapped inside a UFO with the ginger half of the X-Files. In stark opposition to the proud celebration of geekdom that is Forbidden Planet, this is very much on the dark and moody end of the spectrum. Area 51 lurks in the shadows of Gloucester Road, keeping its head down and not talking to anyone. Still, with its range of card, board and role-playing games, not to mention the seemingly infinite supply of old

comics, this is one of the best (only) choices in Bristol if you're looking for that sort of thing.

ARNOLFINI BOOK SHOP
16 Narrow Quay
Tel: 917 2304 • www.arnolfini.org.uk
This outstanding specialist arts bookshop also stocks magazines on art, design, literature and film as well as posters, cards and gift wrap.

AVON BOOKS
4 Waterloo Street, Clifton
Tel: 973 9848
There's an interesting selection of second-hand books here with a strong local section and a decent antiquarian choice.

BEWARE OF THE LEOPARD
St Nicholas Market
Tel: 925 7277 • www.bishopstonbooks.com
Fabulous selection of rare and second-hand books and a name that alludes to a line from the *Hitchiker's Guide To The Galaxy*. Give yourself plenty of time to browse the many, many sections in two units at St Nick's Market.

BISHOPSTON BOOKS
259 Gloucester Road
Tel: 944 5303 · www.bishopstonbooks.com
A proper second-hand bookshop with shelves creaking under the weight of words. Owner Bill Singleton has increasingly moved his business online, but there's still an impressive selection on offer in the shop with a good choice of local books.

BLOOM & CURLL
74 Colston Street
www.bloomandcurll.co.uk
One of the new breed of Bristol second-hand bookshops with a fantastic selection of modern classics, politics and philosophy among everything else. Expect to find unusual editions of Orwell, TS Elliot, Dylan Thomas and Auden. Free cake for visitors and there's usually a game of chess on the go.

BOOKS FOR AMNESTY
103 Gloucester Road
Tel: 942 2969
www.booksforamnestybristol.org.uk
This superb shop stocks a vast array of second-hand novels and academia and is the kind of place where it's easy to lose an hour.

BOOTY
82 Colston Street
Tel: 933 0909
www.amazon.co.uk/shops/bootybristol
Another of the new Bristol second-hand bookshops, Booty has a wide, but carefully chosen selection of novels, art books, classics and more. Also sells second-hand records and CDs, cards and headwear.

BLACKWELL
89 Park Street
Tel: 927 6602
www.blackwell.co.uk
Most of Blackwell is now Jamie's Italian restaurant, which is hard to take for those who remember it as George's Bookshop, Bristol's own book store. Now occupying much reduced floor space, Blackwell is still a fabulous bookshop which seems to have benefited from a more focused stocking policy made necessary by less space.

BRISTOL BOOK MARKET
Wine Street
First Sunday of the month, alongside the Slow Food market. The Book Market won an award for best new market in the South West just a couple of months after starting up in 2010 and it's easy to see why. There are usually ten or so traders here selling new and second-hand books that range from politics and philosophy to classics and children's books.

BRISTOL GUILD
68 - 70 Park Street
Tel: 926 5548 • www.bristolguild.co.uk
Better known for tasteful gifts, furniture and cookware, the Guild also carries a good selection of local books

CITY MUSEUM
Queen's Road, Clifton
Tel: 922 3571 • www.bristol-city.gov.uk
Wide selection of local interest books, including pamphlets from Bristol Radical History Group and others that you will be hard pressed to find anywhere else.

DESTINATION BRISTOL
Bordeaux Quay, Harbourside
www.visitbristol.co.uk
Good selection of books about Bristol and surrounding area from local and national publishers.

Listings

DURDHAM DOWN BOOKSHOP
39 North View, Westbury Park
Tel: 973 9095
There's an old-fashioned decency about the shops on North View, typified by this charming bookshop with helpful staff. Let's hope it doesn't go the same way as some other recent losses in the area.

FORBIDDEN PLANET
Units 4&5 Clifton Heights, Triangle West
Tel: 929 7767 · www.forbiddenplanet.com
A little daunting even to hardened nerds, but the incredible (albeit frightening) range of sci-fi and cult comics, DVDs and assorted memorabilia makes this an unrivalled hotspot for all your geeky needs. Things to keep in mind: always enter with a clear objective to avoid wallet-draining impulse purchases. And remember to assure yourself that it is highly unlikely that you are the most hopeless case in the shop (applies even when there's only one other person there).

FOYLES
6 Quakers Friars, Cabot Circus
Tel: 376 3975 · www.foyles.co.uk
At precisely the time when high street bookselling in Bristol seemed at its lowest ebb – Borders gone bust, Blackwell downsizing, Waterstone's close University branch – in come Foyles to open their first store outside London and breathe new life into Bristol's book scene. Hugely knowledgeable staff and a carefully chosen selection of new writing and classics. Event space upstairs.

M SHED
Wapping Road, Princes Wharf
Tel: 352 6600 · www.mshed.org
Like the City Museum, M Shed boasts a wide selection of local books some of which you will struggle to find elsewhere.

RISE
70 Queen's Road, Clifton
Tel: 929 7511 · www.rise-music.co.uk
Impressive selection of music books, biographies, local books, cult classics, bestsellers and more all at bargain prices.

STANFORDS
29 Corn Street
Tel: 929 9966 · www.stanfords.co.uk
You can lose yourself in a world of travel adventure just by looking at the maps in Stanfords. This specialist travel bookshop has a staggering collection of books, globes, atlases and travel paraphernalia. The staff know what the hell they are talking about too. Which makes a change from many other bookshops.

TANGENT BOOKS
www.tangentbooks.co.uk
Online store run by the publishers of this very guide. Independent publishers can't take on the multi-national bookselling monster that is Amazon, but Tangent can offer limited edition and signed copies and books that are hard to find anywhere else. Stocks a selection of books, pamphlets, prints and music by up-and-coming Bristol authors and artists.

WATERSTONES
Galleries, Broadmead
Tel: 925 2274
Cribbs Causeway
Tel: 950 9813
www.waterstones.co.uk
The biggest selection of books in town. Vast array of fiction, travel, history and art books. If you can't find the book you want here, it probably doesn't exist.

Interiors & Gifts

BRISTOL GUILD
68-70 Park Street
Tel: 926 5548 · www.bristolguild.co.uk
Basically, this is pottery's way of telling you you've got too much money. The Guild sells a huge range of ornaments, gadgets, jewellery, kitchenware, toys and arty stuff for middle-class tastes.

DUSK TIL DAWN
188 Cheltenham Road
Tel: 944 2388
As its name suggests, this store sells a full range of contemporary beds and equally original furniture. Mass produced it isn't.

FIG.1
51 St Luke's Road, Totterdown
Tel: 330 8167 · www.fig1.co.uk
Home and gift shop full of lovely stuff and unusual items from small producers. Fig.1 stocks lots of cards, books and prints by local artists and is one of the focal points for the

flourishing Totterdown art and craft scene. Owners Mark and Luke also have a strong ethical policy, so expect to find many fairly traded and recycled goods. Fig.1 is also a thriving internet business, so if you can't make it to the shop, check them out online.

FIRED EARTH

65a Whiteladies Road
Tel: 973 7400 • www.firedearth.co.uk
If you've been to B&Q and didn't like any of their tiles or paint colours, Fired Earth could be your saviour. They offer a huge range of off-beat tiles and shades of paint that you won't find anywhere else.

IKEA

Eastgate Shopping Centre, Eastville
Tel: 0845 355 2264 • www.ikea.com
Anyone who moans about IKEA is not seeing the flat-packed wood for the self-assembly trees. The multi-storied, aggressively modernist, persistently cheap Scandinavian superstore is not so much a furniture retailer as a utopian revolutionary of interior design. So what if they have clogged up a little stretch of the M32, it was never the most picturesque of places anyhow. What IKEA have done is make good taste in furniture design accessible to all. Sofas with angles, bathroom cabinets for the price of a Terence Conran soap dish and coolish retro lamps for under £2? What more do you want!

INCA

Clifton Down, Whiteladies Road
Tel: 317 9758
Card and gift shop with a cool range of silver jewellery. Notable for its wide selection of Banksy cards.

IOTA

167 Gloucester Road
Tel: 924 4911 • www.iotabristol.com
A real rarity in these days of the homogenised high street, IOTA actually trades on its quirky originality. Owner Meibh O'Conner Morse stocks products she likes and this makes for an eclectic mix of 1950s lunchboxes, retro clocks, sleek kitchen utensils and some great post-modern vases.

KITCHENS

167 Whiteladies Road
Tel: 973 9614
A hangar-sized store devoted entirely to, you guessed it, kitchens. From Le Creuset saucepans to giant wooden chopping boards, they have everything and more for cooks who mean business.

LOVE FROM RANDOM

34 Park Street
Tel: 904 2725 • lovefromrandom.co.uk
A combination of kitsch, bizarre and good taste. All goods are selected by owner Mitch and include all manner of things for the home, plus, mugs, prints, cards, toys, books – anything Mitch fancies really.

SOFA MAGIC

121 Coldharbour Road
Tel: 924 8282
www.sofamagic.co.uk
If you're going to spend a large part of your life sitting on something, you really ought to sit on something that won't give way at the first sign of your fat auntie Rene's arse. Sofa Magic make made-to-measure settees that fit your lifestyle.

Specialist shops

20TH CENTURY FLICKS

3 Richmond Terrace, Clifton
Tel: 974 2570 • 20thcenturyflicks.co.uk
Legendary Bristol video store that has survived and thrived in the digital age thanks to its loyal customer base. (See Retail Heaven, 223)

BIRDS OF BALDWIN STREET

35 Baldwin Street
Tel: 927 3676
Nothing is more idiotic than laisse-faire capitalism on the high street and the UK is the biggest idiot in all of Europe. Here's why: If you want a packet of cigarettes in France, you have to go to a compact little independent shop called a tabac. You can't get fags anywhere else. Result? Small businesses are allowed to flourish, profits shared across the board, everyone is happy. Not here. By the year 2015, there could be just one shop left and its name will be Tesco. Do something, act now, vote with your lungs, get down to Birds and shop like you used to. This must be one of the city's

last surviving specialist shops. 20 Chesterfield s'il vous plait.

BRISTOL TICKET SHOP
12 The Arcade, Broadmead
Tel: 0870 4444 400
www.bristolticketshop.co.uk
An excellent little ticket seller in Broadmead that covers just about every event in the area and beyond.

CHRISTMAS STEPS COSTUME HIRE AND JOKE SHOP
47 Colston Street
Tel: 926 4703
They've been selling silly moustaches and crazy wigs at the top of Christmas Steps for over 50 years and now stock more than 2,000 fancy dress costumes on three floors. Do people really still hold fancy dress parties?

FOCUS ON THE PAST
25 Waterloo Street, Clifton
Tel: 973 8080
An eclectic range of antique goodies over two well-stocked floors. Make sure you have an hour or two spare for browsing.

HEALTH UNLIMITED
248 North Street, Southville
Tel: 902 0622 • www.silver-gecko.com
Unusual shop with an eclectic range of nutritional supplements, cards, wrapping paper and gifts. The perfect place to go if you're getting stressed looking for a birthday present. You could emerge with an Onya backpack, some ear candles, a birthday card, nice wrapping paper and some soothing geranium shower gel.

HEAVEN ON EARTH
18 Upper Maudlin Street
Tel: 926 4999
www.heavenonearthbristol.co.uk
Probably the country's only design your own life and death shop. Heaven on Earth are funeral arrangers who make chests for storing things in when you're alive that double up as a coffin when you need one. Apparently the plan was to open a coffee shop, but Simon Dorgan misheard co-owner Paula Rainey Crofts and though she said 'coffin shop'. Banksy reputedly painted the coffin of legendary Bristol club promoter Lez Hutchings which was supplied by Heaven on Earth. Heaven on

Earth is also a gift shop and is handily placed opposite the Bristol Royal Infirmary for those in need of their coffins.

KITESTORE
39a Cotham Hill
Tel: 974 5010 • www.kitestore.co.uk
Who'd have thought that anyone could make a decent living out of owning a shop selling kites. Martin and Avril Baker have. But when they opened one of the UK's only specialist kite stores, they surely did it for the love of standing in the wind with a plastic bag on the end of a piece of 60-foot string. One day they'll fly away, you know.

LA MAISON DU ZIGOU DAM
336 Gloucester Road
Tel: 944 2111
This fairtrade shop is run by Cameroonians and specialises in clothes, art, books, music and videos from Central Africa. It's also the base for the Zigou Dam dance group which works mainly with schools and covers everything from traditional to contemporary African dance and hip-hop.

MEMORIES
St Nicholas Market
Tel: 977 5488
Memories is a treasure trove of a stall. It stocks a remarkable selection of pictures of old Bristol, from the Centre to little local parks. Lots of the pictures are from family collections, so you can turn up some really unusual snaps of families in excellent olde outfits. Most of the prints are a fiver, which is a total bargain.

NEAL'S YARD REMEDIES
126 Whiteladies Road
Tel: 946 6034
www.nealsyardremedies.com
Winner of many awards for its natural health and beauty products, Neal's Yard also has therapy rooms and runs lectures and courses. 'We believe real health is generated from inside,' they say.

PACK OF CARDS
77 Henleaze Road, Henleaze
Tel: 962 3000
Pleasant cafe, homeware and gift shop catering for the homeware and gift tastes of Henleaze.

Shopping

POPPERS PARTY SHOP
151 Gloucester Road
Tel: 949 9001 • poppersthepartyshop.co.uk
Need some false moustaches, helium balloons and false breasts to get in the party mood? Look no further.

RICHER SOUNDS
143 Whiteladies Road
Tel: 973 4397 • www.richersounds.com
Forget about those hi-fi centres up at the Mall, there's only one place to go when you want to update your sound system. You'll have to queue but the deals are well worth it.

ROMANTICA
139 and 309 Gloucester Road
There's a bizarre quality to Romantica. OK it's only a card, poster and gift shop, but you'll probably leave wondering who shops at Romantica and feel slightly concerned when you realise it's YOU.

TANGY GIFTS
286 Stapleton Road
Tel: 951 2202
www.tangygifts.co.uk
This is, um, like, Bristol's Head Shop, yeah? They've got skins, bongs, pipes, seeds, tins, scales, books, funky cards, hats and, um, some other stuff about blow and that.

Music shops

BRISTOL ARCHIVE RECORDS
www.bristolarchiverecords.com
Mike Darby has been championing Bristol music for more than 30 years and during that time he's developed contacts with just about anyone from the city who has set foot in a recording studio. For the past few years he's been remastering forgotten tracks for download from bristolarchiverecords.com by local bands stretching back to the likes of the Electric Guitars, Vice Squad and Essential Bop from the late 70s. But it was the release of his Bristol Reggae Explosion collection (vinyl, CD and download) that really caught the popular imagination. Mike followed up this success with compilations from Bristol reggae heavyweights Talisman and Black Roots and there seems no end to the appetite for Bristol reggae classics from yesteryear. There are a huge number of artists at Bristol Archive

Records, it's a living museum of Bristol's post-punk musical history – the digital music equivalent of M Shed, but without the squeaky chairs in the cafe or the funding.

BRISTOL MUSIC SHOP
30 College Green
Tel: 929 0390
If you want to buy a brass or woodwind instrument, then this is the place to go. Centrally located right on College Green, you'll find lots of students and teens and other wannabe musicians searching out their favourite guitar tabs.

DRUM BANK MUSIC
203 Gloucester Road
Tel: 975 5366
www.drumbankmusic.co.uk
Bang, crash, wallop, thump, clatter, crack, boom, etc. It's amazing that this shop devoted mainly to percussion is still standing considering the sonic battering it gets.

FOPP
27-29 College Green
Tel: 937 7110
Stepping into Fopp is a Bermuda triangle experience. You intend to pick up one album and, before you know it, four hours have disappeared and you approach the counter looking like a contestant who's just done well on an alt.culture version of *The Generation Game*. Everything you meant to buy when it came out but never got around to it, and most of it under a tenner.

HOBGOBLIN
36 Park Street
Tel: 929 0902
www.hobgoblin.com/bristol/
Used to based at the back of the Bristol Music Shop just down the road, but now Hobgoblin has its own store packed with instruments and all the things you need to play them. Much frequented by Bristol's growing acoustic and folk community.

IDLE HANDS
74 Stokes Croft
www.idlehandsbristol.com
Rose from the ashes of Rooted Records. Quality selection of underground tunes and the place to go to keep up to speed with local dance music scene activity.

Listings

MICKLEBURGH
1-9 Stokes Croft
Tel: 924 4158
www.mickleburgh.co.uk
Sprawling, elegant musical instrument stockist whose range of pianos, guitars, keyboards, drums and amps are spread sparsely over a vast floor space. If Stan Getz was a Bristolian, he'd probably shop here.

PLASTIC WAX
222 Cheltenham Road
Tel: 942 7368 • plasticwaxrecords.com
Plastic Wax must have been selling second-hand music since the invention of vinyl but they have never got round to tidying up. This is what your bedroom would look like if you'd kept all the music you'd ever bought and your mum had never made you tidy up. You'll need to invest some time in understanding the 'system' but it's worth it.

PRIME CUTS
85 Gloucester Road
Tel: 983 0007
Prime Cuts resides below the RePsycho second-hand clothes shop (p223) and deals purely in second-hand vinyl including a great selection of rare and imported music. Check out the second-hand videos, most of which you've never heard of, and some of which are worth buying on comedy value alone.

RISE
70 Queen's Road, Clifton
Tel: 929 7511 • www.rise-music.co.uk
Voted the UK's Best Independent Music Retailer at the 2010 Music Week Awards, Rise boasts a staggering selection of CDs at bargain prices, but also stocks a cool choice of limited edition vinyl and CDs.

WANTED RECORDS
Unit 1, St Nicholas Market
Tel: 929 0524 • www.wantedrecords.co.uk
John Stapleton has been close to pretty much everything good that's come out of Bristol music for the last two decades. Although he is most associated with reggae and dance music in its many guises as Dr Jam, Blowpop, Go Go Children and various other club nights and DJ monikers, Stapleton is a walking encyclopedia of all forms of modern music. Found a collection of obscure prog rock from the 70s? Stumbled across a stash of 60s dancehall

vinyl in the attic? Head for Wanted Records to convert your vinyl treasure trove into cash and maybe pick up some new tunes from the awesome collection at St Nick's Market.

Art

ART WAREHOUSE & FRAMING FACTORY
Wapping Wharf
Tel: 929 8089
www.artwarehouse.co.uk
This Harbourside home to a large, yet often unusual, selection of sculptures, cards, original work and limited edition prints, is a refreshingly odd establishment.

BRISTOL BLUE GLASS
St. Catherine's Trading Estate, Bedminster
Tel: 01179 636 900 • bristolblueglass.com
Bristol has been the home of blue glassware for almost 400 years and the industry is still thriving in the city today. The distinctive blue colour is apparently created by adding cobalt oxide to the molten glass. Recently, the company provided the time rotor (which sits in the centre of the re-designed TARDIS console) for the *Doctor Who*, starring Matt Smith as the Doctor..

CREATIVITY
7-9 Worrall Road
Tel: 973 1710
Well-stocked, friendly arts and crafts store for grown-ups and children. Great place to browse – or ask the helpful staff if you're in a hurry.

FRAMERS' WORKSHOP
269 Gloucester Road
Tel: 944 6355
Whether it's Matisse or your kids' potato prints, art needs a frame almost as much as frames need art. This busy, independently-owned shop has every style and material for frames your walls can handle.

HAROLD HOCKEY
170-174 Whiteladies Road
Tel: 973 5988
Stationery and artists' materials specialists based in a wonderfully sprawling shop. Whether you want a pencil sharpener or a Winsor & Newton Bristol easel, this is the place to come.

NICHE FRAMES
26 Stokes Croft
Tel: 942 2213 • www.nicheframes.co.uk
Gallery, framer, Giclee printer and shop very
much in favour with the Stokes Croft art
crowd. Niche is a family-run, friendly business
that has been custom-framing since 1985. Also
stocks a large selection of prints and cards by
local artists.

SKY BLUE GALLERY
27 North View, Westbury Park
Tel: 973 3995 • www.skybluegallery.co.uk
Tiny gallery and framing shop that holds
regular exhibitions. Decent selection of prints
and cards.

Food & Drink

ASHTON FRUIT SHOP
269 North Street, Southville
Tel: 966 6838
A strong emphasis on local and seasonal
fruit and veg and a good organic selection.
Probably the best place in Bristol to get Seville
Oranges for marmalade-making in February.

BETTER FOOD COMPANY
Sevier Street, St Werburgh's • 935 1725
94 Whiteladies Road • 946 6957
www.betterfood.co.uk
Phil Haughton's organic supermarket is the
ragamuffin cousin of Clifton's posh delis.
Situated on a roundabout on the Montpelier,
St Paul's, St Werburgh's borders, the original
BFC brought locally produced, organic food to
the inner city. And now Clifton has embraced
the scruffy urchin of ethical food production,
scrubbed its face, given it a smart centre
parting and welcomed it to Whiteladies Road.

THE BREAD STORE
45 Gloucester Road
Tel: 9421 654
Whisper it gently, but a growing number of
'bread heads' reckon this place is even better
than Herbert's and Hobbs House. There's a
huge selection of speciality breads alongside
the standards.

BRISTANBUL
137 Gloucester Road
Tel: 924 0003 • www.bristanbul.co.uk
Not only is Bristanbul one of the best names

for a shop in Bristol, it's also one of the best
food shops in the city. All manner of Turkish
breads, pizzas and cakes are produced on
the premises, with a woman making the flat
breads in the corner of the shop. The filled
breads are fantastic and all the prices are
more than reasonable. Almost everything is
vegetarian and any meat is halal.

BRISTOL CIDER SHOP
7 Christmas Steps
Tel: 382 1679 • bristolcidershop.co.uk
A shop full of cider is obviously a good thing,
but this tiny outlet on Christmas Steps raises
the bar considerably. The 80 or so ciders
usually available are beautifully presented.
There are bottled offerings from all the leading
craft cider producers within a 50-mile radius
of Bristol, plus an ever-changing selection of
draught cider to take away straight from the
barrel. If you are lucky, you might find much
sought after offerings from Bristol craft cider
makers Ciderworks, Totterdown Press and
Bristol Cider. Regular events include visits to
cider festivals and producers, and make your
own cider days. Check the website for all
manner of cider-related malarkey.

BRISTOL SAUSAGE SHOP
Glass Arcade, St Nicholas Market
Tel: 07817 478302
www.bristolsausageshop.co.uk
Boasting more than 20 sorts of sausage all
made from locally-sourced produce where
possible, this is heaven for banger lovers.
Remember, never prick a Bristol sausage.
The natural casings are designed to keep the
yummy flavours in, so they take a bit longer
to cook and need to rest for a few minutes
before scoffing.

BRISTOL SWEET MART
80 St Marks Road, Easton
Tel: 951 2257 • www.sweetmart.co.uk
Kassam Ismail Majothi arrived penniless as a
refugee from Uganda in 1972 and founded the
Sweet Mart in 1978. Since then, it has become
the major supplier of ethnic foods, spices and
more in the south west. Sweet Mart is at the
centre of the regeneration of St Mark's Road
which is one of the most interesting shopping
streets in Bristol. Wandering around this
wonderful shop is a great experience, one that
inspires you to explore new flavours.

Shopping

Listings

CHARLES SAUNDERS
Albert Road, St Philips
Tel: 971 5454 • www.charles-saunders.com
You can buy anything from live lobsters to frozen Spotted Dick at Charles Saunders. The wholesaler is a major supplier of fresh fish to the South West catering trade and also has a staggering range of frozen meals which it supplies to restaurants. The choice of fresh fish is easily the biggest you'll find anywhere in the whole of Bristol and, although Charles Saunders is mainly a wholesale business, members of the public can also buy directly from the St Philip's premises as long as they spend a minimum of £20.

COOK
3 St John's Court, Whiteladies Road
Tel: 317 9748 • www.cookfood.net
Tasty home-cooked frozen meals at a reasonable price. This seems like a cosy, local set-up until you realise that 'home' is an industrial estate in Kent and there are scores of Cook franchises around the country, but mainly in the affluent South-East.

CORKS OF COTHAM
54 Cotham Hill
Tel: 973 1620 • www.corksof.com
One of a rare breed of independent off-licenses on the high street, Corks is driven by a passion for wine and providing unusual specialities such as French Grey Goose vodka.

DIG IN
229 Church Road, Redfield
Tel: 329 8773
Fresh fruit and veg reaches Redfield at last thanks to the friendly folk at Dig In which also does wholefoods.

EARTHBOUND
8 Abbotsford Road, Cotham
Tel: 904 2260
There was such an enthusiastic review of Earthbound on the *Vegan Guide to Bristol* website that we thought we'd reprint a bit of it. Here it is: 'Rammed full of the best quality organic fruit and veg, with fresh deliveries daily. Great selection of hummus including San Amvrosia and Natural Vitality, plus smoothies, juices, hemp oil and a first rate selection of vegan chocolate, as well as the Sikelia range of exotic Sicilian pestos.' Earthbound is a must-visit experience if you value your food.

ESSENTIAL TRADING
Unit 3, Lodge Causeway Trading Estate
Tel: 958 3550 • essential-trading.coop
Essential is an organic and ethical wholesale food co-operative which carries more than 6,000 product lines. Apart from supplying the retail and catering trade, you can also buy direct if you join or form a food co-operative.

FARMERS' MARKETS
There are several Farmers' Markets in the Bristol area, but the main one takes place every Wednesday morning in Corn Street

FOOD FOR ALL
Hartcliffe Food Co-op, Gatehouse Centre, Hareclive Road, Hartcliffe
Tel: 946 5285 • www.hheag.org.uk
Run by the Hartcliffe Health and Environmental Action Group (HHEAG), Food For All is a workers' co-op selling a wide range of Essential Trading products and vegetables brought by bike trailer from Hartcliffe Community Market Gardens. Free-range eggs, meat, bread and more. Anyone can shop at Food for All but they offer a 10% discount for co-op members.

HARVEST
11 Gloucester Road
Tel: 942 5997 • www.harvest-bristol.coop
Harvest is the retail outlet of the Essential Trading Co-operative (above) and, as such, is one of the longest established wholefood co-ops in the west. The philosophy here is to support ethical, organic, vegan, vegetarian and fairtrade products so there's a huge range of carefully-selected produce. There's a small deli counter too selling yummy quiche, wraps and spicy things.

HERBERTS
Wellington Avenue, Montpelier
Tel: 924 7713 • www.herbertsbakery.co.uk
Though no longer owned by the Herberts (who run Hobbs House – see below) this Bristol bakery still makes excellent bread. Don't leave Montpelier without a loaf or two.

HOBBS HOUSE BAKERY
39 High Street, Chipping Sodbury
Tel: 01454 317525
www.hobbshousebakery.co.uk
This Chipping Sodbury-based family business has a closely interwoven history with Herberts

Bakery (see above). When the Herberts, who had been baking quality bread since the 1960s, opened a Sodbury branch, they re-named it Hobbs House Bakery (after the original owner of the shop, which had previously been a butchers). Hobbs now has four different branches, plus a butchery next to the Sodbury branch. Still run by the Herberts, they famously provide a £25 loaf for Prince Charles, and their bread is available at selected outlets throughout Bristol, including Chandos Deli and Bristol Sweet Mart. Check the website for full details.

KALAHARI MOON

The Covered Market, St Nicholas Market
Tel: 07886 887 523 • kalaharimoon.co.uk
South African food and drink specialists. What exactly is sliced biltong?

KIN YIP HON

16a St Thomas Street, St Thomas
Tel: 929 9098
Next to the Dynasty Chinese restaurant (see Eating Out Listings), the sprawling Kin Yip Hon is a treasure trove of fresh, frozen and tinned ingredients from fish to dim sum and fresh oriental vegetables.

LA RUCA

83 Gloucester Road
Tel: 944 6810
Well-stocked wholefood shop run by a Chilean family with many fairtrade products. There's always a good selection of well-made deli snacks on offer.

LICATA

36 Picton Street •Tel: 924 7725
332 Gloucester Road • Tel: 924 7718
www.licata.co.uk
Brilliant Italian deli and grocery shop run by what seems to be several generations of the same family. Licata's has been in Picton Street for as long as anyone can remember. The quality of the food and drink is excellent.

MARK'S BREAD

291 North Street
Tel: 07910 979384 • marksbread.co.uk
There's a reassuring simplicity about Mark's Bread. The shop consists of a baker, an oven a till and a few tables. That's all you need to make, display and sell fantastic organic bread. Deliveries to local shops are made by bicycle.

LOCAL BEER PRODUCERS

1. BRISTOL BEER FACTORY

www.bristolbeerfactory.co.uk
George Ferguson, architect of Tobacco Factory fame and champion of independent businesses in Bristol, bought the old brewery in Ashton in 2004. He teamed up with production manager Simon Bartlett and head brewer Chris Thurgeson to resume making beer on the site where Thomas Baynton originally started brewing in 1840. In 2006, the Brunale Milk Stout (brewed to celebrate the 200th anniversary of Brunel's birth) was named Overall Winner from the 100-plus ales at the CAMRA Bristol Beer Festival. Other brews include Red, No. 7, Sunrise and Gold which are available at an ever-growing number of pubs in the city.

2. BATH ALES

www.bathales.com
Formed in 1995 and based in Warmley between Bath and Bristol, Bath Ales are as well-liked for their pubs as they are for the beers. There's no such thing as a bad Bath Ales pub, y'see. The Hare on the Hill in Kingsdown, The Wellington on Horfield Common, The Bridge in St Thomas and The Merchants Arms in Hotwells were the four Bath Ales boozers in Bristol at the time of writing with the promise of more to come. There are six Bath Ales brews and not a drop of lager in sight.

3. ZERODEGREES

www.zerodegrees.co.uk
The first branch of Zerodegrees opened in August 2000 in Blackheath in South East London. Obviously a success because they opened the Bristol version back in 2004. The distinctive Black Lager, Wheat Ale, Pilsner and Pale Ale are all brewed on-site at the microbrewery. The health conscious among you will be pleased to hear that Zerodegrees don't sterile filter their beer. This basically means that all their beer is unpasteurised, free of additives and colouring, which can't be bad. Sat on two floors on Colston Street, Zerodegrees is also a good Italian-style restaurant.

Listings

ORGANIQUE
172 Wells Road, Totterdown
Tel: 971 7932 • www.shoporganique.co.uk
Natural grocery store full of things fairly-traded, organic and ethically sourced. Good range of chocolate. Does Ecover refills.

PAK BUTCHERS
4 Roman Road
Tel: 951 8057 • www.pakbutchers.co.uk
Abdul Malik started out at Pak as a work experience youngster in 1990. He now runs the show and has built the business into the South West's main supplier of Halal meat and poultry. Pak also sells fish.

PAPADELI
84 Alma Road
Tel: 973 6569 • www.papadeli.co.uk
'If it's delicious and handmade, we sell it', is the philosophy at Papadeli. This well-stocked deli and cafe has an excellent selection of take-away food and you can order hampers online or over the phone.

RADFORD MILL FARM SHOP
41 Picton Street
Tel: 942 6644
On the site of the old One Planet shop, this community-based wholefood shop has a good selection of fruit and veg, tinned and dried organic food, plus deli counter and cafe.

RARE BUTCHERS
250 North Street, Southville
Tel: 966 3593
This used to be Bob Wherlock's butcher's shop, famous for its Saturday morning queue of carnivores stretching out of the door. But after 35 years in North Street, Bob and his team retired and the shop reopened in 2011 as Rare. The owners have a good selection of free range meat and claim that livestock welfare is one of the criteria for choosing suppliers.

REAL OLIVE COMPANY
Princess Wharf, Harbourside
Tel: 925 1762
123 Gloucester Road, Bishopston
Tel: 924 0572
www.therealolivecompany.co.uk
Built on the philosophy that 'a day without olives is like a day without sunshine' the Real Olive Company deli is a celebration of Mediterranean food. There's an impressive range of grilled vegetables, speciality stuffed olives, peppers, cheeses, vinegars and much more. The stuffed vine leaves are tops. Attached to the Harbourside deli is the great Olive Shed restaurant (see Eating Out Listings) which offers excellent food and view over the Harbourside.

REG THE VEG
6 Boyces Avenue, Clifton
Tel: 07890152628
Excellent vegetable shop on this popular cul-de-sac in Clifton, opposite the Primrose Cafe. Scotch bonnets on the counter is a good sign of a quality greengrocer.

SCOOPAWAY
113 Gloucester Road
Tel: 987 2199
There aren't many shops that require the customers to help themselves by employing that well-known gathering action, the scoop. Here you'll find yourself diving into a range of organic and fairtrade options and saving all that packaging and marketing money through your exertions.

SCRUMPTIOUSLY SWEET
83 Gloucester Road
Tel: 986 4414
www.scrumptiouslysweet.moonfruit.com
A nice and nostalgic little sweet shop that has been the delight of Bristol's children since it materialised. There is an excellent and varied selection ranging from cardboard boxes of Drumstick lollipops in the corners to big pots of ye olde fudge and bonbons on the high shelves. The pick and mix is a veritable wonderland, there's a good selection of liquorice and the staff are friendly and helpful. This is the kind of place that might make you pretend to have children to save face. But don't be ashamed, reverting to a state of infantile gluttony is the norm here. You won't be judged. Much.

SHEEPDROVE ORGANIC BUTCHERS
3 Lower Redland Road
Tel: 973 4643 • www.sheepdrove.com
The only completely organic butcher in Bristol. The meat is sourced from Peter and Juliet Kindersley's Sheepdrove organic farm in Berkshire, the shop also sells organic honey, wine, flour and more.

Shopping

SLOW FOOD MARKET
Corn Street
www.slowfoodbristol.org
Slow food is an Italian-inspired philosophy that is the antithesis of fast food – you take time to grow, create and make food. The Bristol market was the first of its kind in Britain and features some really good producers – the chicken from Exmoor is fabulous. Other highlights include a craft cider stall run by cider masters Tom Oliver and Keith Orchard.

SOUTHVILLE DELI
262 North Street
Tel: 966 4507 • www.southvilledeli.com
Neighbourhood deli and café specialising in organic, fairtrade and locally produced food and wine.

STONEGROUND
5 The Mall, Clifton
Tel: 974 1260
There's a good range of organic, healthfood and fairtrade produce at Stoneground and a modest deli selection plus some interesting alcohol choices. The quiche is lovely.

TART
16 The Promenade, Gloucester Road
Tel: 924 7628 • www.lovelytart.com
A favourite of the ever increasing tribe of Gloucester Road yummy mummies, Tart is a slightly better class of your naughty but nice.

T&P MURRAY BUTCHERS
153 Gloucester Road
Tel: 942 4025
This well-established butchers is a good source of organic and free range meat. There's also a host of salami, preserves pickles and cheeses in the deli. The sausages, including The Bishopston, are made on site. There's often a pavement barbecue on which the aforementioned sausages sizzle.

TASTE DELICATESSEN
Lakeside, Barrow Gurney
Tel: 01275 474586 • www.taste.gb.com
Situated towards Bristol Airport, Taste specialises in British seafood and locally-reared organic meat and game as well as the deli regulars. It can be particularly good for wild food and is the only place we've heard of that sometimes sells squirrel.

TEOHS
28-34 Lower Ashley Road
Tel: 902 1122
Pretty much all the ingredients and accessories you need to create a far-eastern feast are available at Teohs. The staff are always happy to give recipe advice.

THATCHERS CIDER SHOP
Myrtle Farm, Sandford, Somerset
www.thatcherscider.co.uk
Head out past the airport on the A38 and you'll soon be in Thatchers Cider country. Apparently if you put all the apples that Thatchers pressed in 2009 in a line, it would stretch from Somerset to Indonesia. The shop stocks all of the many Thatchers ciders and other locally produced products. While you're out there, take a stroll down the Strawberry Line footpath which takes you through some of the orchards.

TOBACCO FACTORY MARKET
Tobacco Factory, Southville
Sunday morning market that has come of age in recent years because you can do a full week's food shop without having to trouble the Tescos of this world. Good quality, meat, fruit and veg, fish and bread plus soups, soap, records, books and more. Don't leave without trying a at least one Jamaican pattie from the Agnes Spencer stall.

TONY'S CARIBBEAN FOOD
128 Grosvenor Road
Tel: 941 4266
If you need a matokie and some cho-cho to go with your sweet yam and ackee, you need look no further.

TOVEYS
198-200 Stapleton Road
Tel: 951 0987 • www.toveys.co.uk
It's often an experience visiting Toveys seafood shop which was established in Bristol in 1935. It's a lively, bustling place full of banter, wisecracks and lots of fish, as fresh as it comes. The staff are knowledgeable and will help you decide what you want. Toveys also stocks a wide range of frozen food. Make sure you ask for your fish to be descaled, watching the descaler in action is worth the trip alone. Don't forget to take a ticket or you'll never get served.

Shopping

Listings

TRETHOWAN'S DAIRY SHOP

The Glass Arcade, St Nicholas Market
Tel: 902 0332 • trethowansdairy.co.uk
Famous for its Trethowan's Gorwydd Caerphilly
– a mature Caerphilly made to a traditional
recipe using raw (unpasteurised) milk.

TWO DAY COFFEE ROASTERS

135 St Michael's Hill
Tel: 929 9191 • www.twodaycoffee.com
Caffeine nirvana. There's a huge selection of
quality (and usually ethically sourced) coffee
here, plus all the gubbins required to make
and ingest it. Tell them how you like your
coffee and they'll make you your own blend.

VALLEY SMOKEHOUSE

Elton Farm, Dundry
Tel: 0870 747 0850
www.valleysmokehouse.com
A traditional smokehouse specialising in
poultry, ducks, cheese, fish, meat, garlic and
more. The trout is locally caught and if you
phone up, you can arrange to take your
own food to be smoked. There's also a great
delicatessen on site.

WAI YEE HONG SUPERMARKET

Eastgate Oriental City, Eastville
Tel: 0845 873 3388 • www.waiyeehong.com
Family-run Chinese supermarket and cash and
carry that used to be based round the back of
Montpelier Station, now in the 'Oriental City'
round the back of Ikea. Established in 1981
and now the largest supplier of Chinese goods
in the South West.

WILD OATS NATURAL FOODS

9-11 Lower Redland Road
Tel: 973 1967 • www.woats.co.uk
Wild Oats has a huge selection of natural
foods from organic breads to chilled and
frozen foods, organic wines and beers and
lots of deli fodder. There's also a big range of
food supplements, skin care products, herbs,
homoeopathic remedies and aromatherapy.
It's run by people who are passionate about
food and can provide a wide range of advice
on everything from Feldenkrais technique to
Japanese cookery and oriental medicine.

WINDMILL HILL CITY FARM SHOP

Philip Street, Bedminster
Tel: 963 3252
www.windmillhillcityfarm.org.uk
There's every possibility that you've seen the
bacon you buy here before – when it was
in the pig sty with the brothers and sisters
you've already eaten. If that puts you off
eating meat (the shop also sells lamb, beef,
chicken and occasionally goat), the bantam,
hen, duck and goose eggs are collected daily
from the farmyard and they sometimes have
their own goats' milk. For vegans, there is a
great selection of organic vegetables from the
extensive farm allotments.

Cheap shops

POUNDLAND

82-92 Horsefair, Broadmead,
42-46 East Street, Bedminster
www.poundland.co.uk
An afternoon on East Street could involve
a pint of Cheddar Valley luminous orange
cider in the Apple Tree, a shopping spree at
Poundland and tea from the Codfather chippy
opposite. Don't knock it if you haven't tried it.

THE POUND STORE

334 Gloucester Road, Horfield
Tel: 942 0147
Don't make the same mistake I did in here
when I picked up something and turned to the
assistant and asked 'How much is this, please?'
'Everything in here is a quid'. 'Everything'. 'Yes'.
Even the 24-piece solid silver cutlery set.

EMMAUS

Barton Manor, St Phillips and
72 Bedminster Parade, Bedminster
Tel: 954 0886 • www.emmausbristol.org.uk
Self-styled Second-hand Furniture Superstore,
there are some real bargains to be had at
homeless charity Emmaus shops. Because
turn-around is so quick there are new items
in most days, some really nice stuff rubs
shoulders with the purely functional.

RAJANI SUPERSTORE

Maggs Lane, Speedwell
Tel: 958 6448 • www.rajanis.co.uk
If Aladdin had the most out-there suppliers
in the world, his cave would still look half-

empty when compared with this place. Spread over two jam-packed floors in a litter-strewn Fishponds business park, Rajani stocks a kaleidoscopic array of products, from the familiar to the never-seen-in your-life-before. Luggage, mirrors, kitchenware, three-foot high red Indian ornaments, electrical goods, toys, towering dead-eyed china dolls, bins, blah-blah-blah.

TK MAXX
The Galleries, Broadmead
Tel: 930 4404 • www.tkmaxx.com
Tempts you inside with the promise of cheap designer clothing. If you have a few hours spare, you might actually find some.

WILKINSON
Union Street, Broadmead; Broadwalk, Knowle; The Triangle, Clifton; East Street, Bedminster; Kings Chase, Kingswood
www.wilkinsonplus.com
Yes, you read it correctly, there's a Wilkinson in Clifton. It's on the site of the former Borders store on the Triangle, which was once the home of Maggs and Dingles, Clifton's very own Grace Brothers style department stores. For those people in Clifton who aren't familiar with the sort of shops you find in Bedminster and Knowle, Wilkinson is very much a belt-and-braces type of hardware store, Wilko's is big on functionality and even bigger on low prices. Comments like: 'Surely dishwasher powder ought to be more expensive than that!' and 'Remarkable! Just £1.14 for a mop and bucket!' are common.

Charity shops

GLOUCESTER ROAD
The Gloucester Road is a goldmine for the stylish but impecunious; you could spend all day working your way up it and probably replenish your entire wardrobe, if you had a mind to. You may find Sapphire adorning the window of the Marie Curie shop, which has a range of records, furniture and electrical goods as well as the inevitable clothes and books. The depths of the Amnesty Bookshop are well worth exploring, and its prices are very good. CLIC Sargent's new 'Shop' takes aim at the vintage clothing end of the market, but could do with making its size labelling a bit more obvious. Once you've climbed Pigsty Hill, the

second wave of charity shops begins. Take a big bag.

CLIFTON VILLAGE
If the opulence of Clifton Village is getting a bit much for you, the price labels at the St Peter's Hospice shop on Boyce's Avenue offer some welcome comic relief. How much for a second-hand Primark skirt? There's a bit more realism (and bargainous greetings cards) at Save the Children on Regent Street, and there are comfy chairs in the Oxfam Bookshop from which to roadtest a potential purchase.

COTHAM HILL
Cotham Hill probably has more charity shops per square yard than any other street in Bristol, and they are all gooduns. If the Gloucester Road could take you all day, you could probably give Cotham Hill a thorough going-over in under two hours. There are two St Peter's Hospice shops (one specialising in women's clothes, the other reputed to be very good for men's formal wear except just after Bristol University's Freshers' Week) and two Oxfam shops (one is a bookshop).

FISHPONDS ROAD
Trendy it isn't, but Fishponds has a great range of charity shops from the corner of Hinton Road to Straits Parade, selling clothes, books and bric-a-brac. Barnardo's usually has some great stuff at surprisingly modest prices.

ST JAMES BARTON
A small but significant rash of charity shops (so far: Peter's Hospice, Tenovus and DebRA) is appearing along the south-east side of the St James Barton roundabout, perhaps as a credit crunch counterbalance to Cabot Circus. The DebRA shop sells furniture in addition to the usual charity shop fare.

OTHERS
If you're after a clothes bargain, the Salvation Army shop on Cheltenham Road, the Methodist shop on Midland Road and the St Patrick's shop in Redfield are all worth a visit. The YMCA shop in Bedminster is recommended for furniture and old LPs. The various shops supporting cat sanctuaries are usually at the low end of the pricing spectrum, but a rather off-putting smell would sometimes seem to go with the territory.

Shopping

Listings **Culture**

One long-established theatre, a couple of very credible art schools, the highest concentration of patient Plasticine botherers in the UK and an unusually high percentage of hippies and post-hippies all add up to give Bristol an arty, creative public image. Compared to, say, Leicester or Carlisle, Bristol is like San Francisco c.1968.

True, improvisational theatre has never really taken off in Knowle West or Stockwood but you shouldn't have too much trouble finding a freely expressive amateur dramatic society in Montpelier or St Werburgh's. Someone, somewhere in the city, is always pursuing art for art's sake. It could be a beat poetry evening at the Cube, a South West scriptwriters work-in-progress play at the Macready Rooms, an electrical installation art at the Arnolfini or an afternoon of 13th-Century embroidery instruction at the Folk House.

Of course, if we used the broad definition of the word 'culture' here, we'd have to include karaoke nights in Kingswood, illegal car rallies at the Showcase Cinema and hen night city centre pub crawls; all are valid cultural happenings. But to make things simpler, this is where you'll find a selection of art, theatre, cinema and animation offerings.

Art Galleries

3D GALLERY
13 Perry Road, Park Row
Tel: 929 1363
Contemporary ceramics, sculpture, jewellery, painting, abstract and figurative art.

ALEXANDER GALLERY
122 Whiteladies Road
Tel: 973 4692/9582
www.alexander-gallery.co.uk
One of Bristol's leading fine art galleries and Beryl Cook's publishers since 1977. The gallery specialises in Cook limited editions at www.berylcookprints.co.uk.

ANTLERS
www.antlersgallery.com
Nomadic gallery that hosts temporary shows around town. Check the website for details.

ARNOLFINI
Narrow Quay
Tel: 929 9191 • www.arnolfini.org.uk
One of only a handful of Arts Council-funded galleries in the country, the Arnolfini is host to the most contemporary and most challenging national and international artists around. It reopened in September 2005 after massive re-development and expansion.

BRISTOL CITY MUSEUM AND ART GALLERY
Queens Road
Tel: 922 3571
From Old Masters to contemporary fine, applied and oriental art, the old museum may be a bit dustier than your average showroom but it's still a great place to walk around for an hour or two. And it's free to get in. Check out the old maps of Bristol on the balcony on the first floor. Fascinating.

BRISTOL GALLERY
Millennium Promenade, Harbourside
Tel: 930 0005 • www.thebristolgallery.com
Large, bright gallery space with an impressive roll call of exhibitions since opening in 2009. Highlights include a show of 75 original Henri Matisse lithographs, prints from Picasso, Salvador Dali and Peter Blake.

Culture

CREATE CENTRE
Smeaton Road
Tel: 925 0505
www.bristol-city.gov.uk/create
You just can't miss the size of this thing. It is one of those huge red buildings out near the Cumberland Basin. It has a few levels, usually hosting community projects and exhibitions over three rooms.

CUBE GALLERY
12 Perry Road
Tel: 377 1470
www.cube-gallery.co.uk
Since 2002, the Cube Gallery have been promoting work by established artists from the local area. They have moved to bigger premises so things are obviously going well.

GRANT BRADLEY GALLERY
1 St Peter's Court, Bedminster Parade
Tel: 963 7673
www.grantbradleygallery.co.uk
This pleasant, uncluttered gallery space with mezzanine has set itself the challenge of bringing culture to Bedminster. The Gallery is dedicated to the memory of Peter Bradley, Rev Gregory Grant's former business partner and co-founder of the The Grant Bradley Charitable Trust. The mission statement aims include: to promote the values and ideals of The Kingdom of God through art and education; to promote dialogue and understanding of different cultures and religious beliefs through the appreciation of art; to promote education through art for people of all ages; to be a centre for cultural exchange of art and ideas; to bring world-class art to local communities and to promote the work of local artists.

HERE GALLERY
108 Stokes Croft
Tel: 942 2222 • www.thingsfromhere.co.uk
The gallery opened back in 2003, originally to house an 'From The West Coast To The West Country' exhibition. A bunch of brave and enthusiastic souls then fought to keep the gallery open. What you have now is an exciting gallery, showcasing local and international artists. There is also a quirky little shop selling anything from underground art to wonderful hand-made clothing.

INNOCENT FINE ART
7a Boyce's Avenue, Clifton
Tel: 973 2614
www.innocentfineart.co.uk
Specialises in contemporary artists from the South West with particular emphasis on the Cornish School. The gallery includes paintings, ceramics, sculpture and glassware.

KING OF PAINT
9a Haymarket Walk
www.kopaint.org
Just off the Bearpit at the Stokes Croft roundabout, King of Paint holds regular exhibitions and sells urban art books and clothing, but as the name suggests its main function is to supply cans of aerosol paint to hooded youth.

LIME TREE GALLERY
84 Hotwell Road, Hotwells
Tel: 07879 475462 • limetreegallery.com
Specialises in contemporary fine art and glass. Seems to have a thing about Scottish artists.

OFF-CENTRE GALLERY
13 Cotswold Road, Windmill Hill
Tel: 987 2647
Contemporary international art from as far afield as Japan, Russia and the Ukraine. Be warned, it is only open by arrangement, day or evening. But well worth the trek.

PEOPLE'S REPUBLIC OF STOKES CROFT
35 Jamaica Street, Stokes Croft
Tel: 944 4540
www.sellinggallery.wordpress.com
The PRSC HQ and the hub for the huge amount of creativity in this historically neglected strip of road is the Selling Gallery next to Jamaica Street studios. Anyone with any interest in art should pay a visit because you won't find anywhere else like it. The gallery operates a Dutch Auction pricing policy so you bid what you think a piece is worth based on prices set by the artist. Typically the art stays on display for two weeks so you have an ever-changing collection by local artists. Given the nature of the gallery, there are few themes other than the art being varied and local. Next door on the ground floor of the studios, there's a reclaimed furniture showroom and a pottery specialising in excellent Stokes Croft china mugs and more.

Culture

Listings

ROYAL WEST OF ENGLAND ACADEMY
Queens Road, Clifton
Tel: 973 5129 • www.rwa.org.uk
Much-respected old school of art that seamlessly embraces classic art and the modern age with exhibits such as Jacqueline Pennel's multi-media installations. The Crimes of Passion Bristol street art show in 2010 was its most successful exhibition for years and has helped raise the RWA's national profile and no doubt helped attract a Damien Hirst installation of his work Charity on the front of the building. The RWA used to have something of the feel of a private members' club but has been spruced up and now has a Papadeli Cafe.

SOMA
Clifton Arcade, 1a Boyces Avenue
Tel: 973 9838
www.somagallery.co.uk
Soma is a gallery space and shop which opened in swanky Clifton Village in 2004. Showcasing artists from the UK with a focus on those from Bristol and the South West.

SPIKE ISLAND
133 Cumberland Road
Tel: 929 2266 • www.spikeisland.org.uk
Spike Island is all about producing and displaying contemporary art and design. There are 70 working spaces for artists in the former tea-packing factory and a rolling programme of exhibitions in the large gallery space. Spike Island is also home to the Spike Print Studio project. For more information, take a look at www.spikeprintstudio.org.

THREENINE
www.threenine.eu
Online gallery featuring the work of some of Bristol's leading urban artists and many from further afield.

UPFEST
198 North Street, Southville
Tel: 07725 231 878 • www.upfest.co.uk
Urban art gallery with regular shows by artists from Bristol and beyond. Upfest is also a free annual urban art paint festival based down the road at Tobacco Factory which features more than 250 artists and graffiti writers from around the world.

VIEW
159-161 Hotwell Road, Hotwells
Tel: 05603 116753 • viewartgallery.co.uk
Contemporary art gallery split into zones over two floors. A mix of media includes paintings, sculpture, photography, ceramics, and a dedicated room for video and installations.

WATERSHED MEDIA CENTRE
1 Canons Road
Tel: 927 5100
www.watershed.co.uk
Still the city's most versatile art space, it offers contemporary photography exhibitions, cinemas, darkrooms, media events and multimedia exhibits.

WEAPON OF CHOICE
8b Park Street
weaponofchoicegallery.blogspot.com
The gallery at the heart of Bristol's urban art scene. Entrance down the steps next to the 50:50 skate shop. Owners Sam and street artist Cheba have established WoC as a focal point for Bristol street art and opening nights are usually packed with old school writers and up-and-coming artists. Prices tend to be ludicrously reasonable and if you want something by a Bristol urban artist that isn't in stock, chances are that they will rustle it up in a few days.

Theatre and Circus

ALBANY CENTRE
Shaftesbury Avenue, Montpelier
Tel: 954 2154
New-age fringe venue with an emphasis on ethnic, political and feminist shows.

ALMA TAVERN AND THEATRE
18-20 Alma Vale Road, Clifton
Tel: 973 5171 • almataverntheatre.co.uk
This theatre above the Alma Vale Tavern has been going strong since it opened in 1997.

BRISTOL OLD VIC
King Street
Tel: 987 7877
www.bristol-old-vic.co.uk
The Theatre Royal was built in 1766 and has been home to the Bristol Old Vic since 1946.

Culture

CIRCOMEDIA
St Paul's Church, Portland Square
Tel: 924 7615 • www.circomedia.com
In the excellent photographic book of New Circus in Bristol Flying High, Circomedia Artistic Director Bim Mason explores the roots of New Circus and explains why Bristol has become the world capital of the artform. It all started in St Paul's in the 1980s so it's entirely appropriate that Circomedia's home is now in St Paul's (with another centre in Kingswood). Circomedia is essentially a circus school that runs Foundation Degrees in Contemporary Circus and Physical Performance and a variety of other courses and workshops.

HIPPODROME
St Augustines Parade,
Box Office: 0870 6077500
www.bristol-hippodrome.co.uk
Vast 2,000-seater theatre that has been a fixture in the city centre for a very long time. Specialises in often quite well-known musicals and pantomimes.

INVISIBLE CIRCUS
Jackdaw Studios, Paintworks, Arnos Vale
www.invisiblecircus.co.uk
Famous for their sell-out Carneyville shows in which Invisible Circus create a parallel universe of Victorian surrealism.

REDGRAVE THEATRE
8 Percival Road, Clifton
Tel: 315 7601
As soon as Sir Michael Redgrave declared it open in 1966, this theatre established itself as one of the most desirable venues in town.

TOBACCO FACTORY
Raleigh Road, Southville
Tel: 902 0344
www.tobaccofactory.com
Happening stage space and bar that has revitalised what was once a dark and dingy corner of South Bristol. The drama ranges from the Shakespearean to the experimental.

QEH THEATRE
Jacobs Wells Road
Box Office: 930 3082
www.qehtheatre.com
Vibrant venue that showcases a wide-ranging programme of theatrical happenings.

BRISTOL ARENA

There are two things that Bristol seems to have a mental block about – building a big swimming pool and a decent concert arena. Every so often the great Bristol public poses the question: why not build a stadium that Rovers, City and Bristol Rugby can share, use it as a concert venue and chuck in a swimming pool while you're about it? Such suggestions are met with a mildly confused expression by the city authorities who carry on blithely giving bits of planning permission for the Memorial Stadium and Ashton Gate, talking about redeveloping the Colston Hall and closing the occasional neighbourhood swimming pool.

Against this background, it's hardly surprising that the £100 million Bristol Arena scheme for land between Temple Meads and the Wells Road fell through. By the summer of 2006, plans had not been submitted and there wasn't a developer on board, yet the completion date for the arena was still officially 2008. Outline plans for the arena, a casino and 10-storey flats that had appeared in the local press were met with a wave of hostility by local residents appalled at the lack of ambition. They showed a 500-space car park for the 10,500-capacity arena, poor public transport links and confused pedestrian, car and cycle access.

Yet there is general agreement that Bristol needs an arena. The city has missed out on the touring bands and other events that are too big for the Colston Hall so our friends across the bridge in Newport and Cardiff have taken the Bristol pound by providing such facilities.

By 2007, the City Council and South West Regional Development Agency were forced to admit they had blown £15 million of public money on clearing the Arena site and courting developers without any serious interest from the private sector. Then in 2011, just as Bristol was getting used to the area around Temple Meads still looking like a bomb site, David Cameron turned up and lent his support to plans to redevelop the old Post Office sorting office site behind Cattle Market Road. It should be done by 2015. Let's see...

Culture

BRISFEST

BRISTOL'S BIGGEST AND BEST WEEKEND OFFERS LOCAL TALENT THE CHANCE TO GET SEEN

☀ Once upon a time Bristol had a famous free festival on the leafy lawns of the Ashton Court estate, a culmination of different circumstances meant that it went bust in 2007. In its wake a new festival was born called the 'Bristol Festival' and then later 'Brisfest'. Although based in the city centre Brisfest still retains a festival feel with a dance music stage, a rave tent, Mr Wolf's local music stage, an acoustic stage, a metal showcase, a kids area, arts and crafts, a garden area with a chill out area and bars. Although the city has lost a legendary festival, something new has arisen which may prove to be equally legendary in the fullness of time.

Bristolian Poppy Stephenson was a volunteer at Ashton Court and became one of the driving forces behind Brisfest. Here she explains what makes Brisfest special and why Bristol is a 'festival city'.

'After Ashton Court went bankrupt there was a meeting in a pub for people who wanted to keep the festival alive. Lots of people at the meeting were promoters and volunteers. Some commercial guys also came in – this really focused everyone's attention on what they wanted the new festival to be – which was something community run, with the profits going back into the festival and to local artists.'

So passion and community beat commercial interests?
'Some people were putting so much energy into it that they lost their jobs and broke up with their partners, I was sleeping 3-4 hours a night and working all the time. Everything came from the public in the first instance and promoters like Mr Wolf, people just came forward saying 'we can help, what do you want?'.

What makes Brisfest different from the old Ashton Court festival?
One of the things we have changed is to put a focus on training and volunteering. So people can learn about festival Health and Safety and Event Management, we have lost a lot of crew to London and to other jobs over the years, but training is part of what we do now.

We are in a different landscape to Ashton Court. They had a tradition of being a free festival, which you can't do now. You can't let people pee in the woods anymore. People expect to be safe and for there to be recycling facilities and those things need to be paid for. All 'free festivals' are paid for, by the tax payer or by sponsorship, so the idea of a 'free festival' is a bit of a myth.

You are planning a big year for 2012. What is on the cards?
We all got involved in the first place to bring Ashton Court back, so we are going to try and do that in 2012 by moving Brisfest up to Ashton Court.

Do you think Bristol is a 'festival city'?
Definitely, there are so many people here who have get up and go, who don't wait to be told whether they can do something or not. They just get up and do it. This is what makes Bristol special. Festivals are good value for money that introduce people to lots of new things. So everything from Upfest to streets parties (which Bristol also has the most of) are all part of that.

Are we in danger of having too many?
I don't think so, I think it is great. We are working more closely with other festivals in the city to avoid clashes and to encourage collaboration. The organic food fair and a music festival have very different audiences, about a 90% difference I'd say. But also we could do things like bring more people into the city to experience the festivals or push some of our better known brands out of the city and share what we have.

Interview with Poppy Stephenson by Marc Leverton

Culture

WICKHAM THEATRE
University of Bristol, Woodland Road
Bookings: 987 7877
This is the stage for the Bristol University Drama Department. Most productions are put on by students and are usually of an extremely high standard.

Cinemas

ARNOLFINI
Narrow Quay
Tel: 917 2300 • www.arnolfini.org.uk
When it first opened years ago, Arnolfini was a much-needed, no-apologies, art house cinema specialising in the latest European releases and re-runs of American classics. Now it still shows interesting films, but the programming is a liitle sparse.

CINEWORLD
Hengrove Park
Tel: 0871 220 8000 • www.cineworld.co.uk
Enormous out-of-town 14-screener multiplex complete with comfortable seats, totally overpriced refreshments and all the latest crap Hollywood blockbusters. Oh, they do a kids show on a Saturday morning too.

CUBE CINEMA
4 Princess Row, Kingsdown
Tel: 907 4190 • www.cubecinema.com
This is easily the most vibrant, challenging, non-funded counter-cultural art and media alternative in the West.

IMAX THEATRE, AT-BRISTOL
Harbourside
Tel: 0845 3451235 • at-bristol.org.uk
Now part of the Bristol Aquarium showing 3D films mainly about sharks. Because the Imax screen is 21 metres wide and 15 metres tall, it makes you feel like you are actually there. Shame about the standard of films though.

MY VUE
The Venue, Cribbs Causeway & Aspects Leisure Park, Longwell Green
Tel: 08712 240 240 • www.myvue.com
These out-of-town-in-the-middle-of-nowhere multiplexes has 12 screens, digital stereo surround sound and premiere size screens. You'll also find a couple of inauthentic multi-national eateries here.

ODEON
Union Street, Broadmead
Tel: 0871 22 44 007 • www.odeon.co.uk
Fading, pre-multiplex city centre picture house that runs a handful of major releases. Kids' Club on Saturdays and Sundays.

ORPHEUS HENLEAZE
Northumbria Drive, Henleaze
Tel: 0845 1662381
Admirable three-screen independent that runs the most popular films for longer than anybody else does.

SHOWCASE CINEMA
Bath Road, Avon Meads
Tel: 0871 220 1000
www.showcasecinemas.co.uk
This is the sort of place that puts the big into big screen. The complex has 1,500 car parking spaces, 14 screens and no less than 3,600 reclining armchair seats.

SHOWCASE DELUX
Glass House, Cabot Circus
Tel: 0871 220 1000
www.showcasecinemas.co.uk
Like the Showcase, but in Cabot Circus and Delux.

WATERSHED
Cannons Road, Bristol
Tel: 927 5100
www.watershed.co.uk
Two screens offer intelligently selected left-of-centre mainstream, arthouse and retrospective seasons. You can almost overlook the uncomfortable seats and lack of popcorn. They also offer interesting talks and meetings and, of course, the cool Watershed bar where you can have a pint by the water before your film.

Culture

Listings **Local Media**

Television, film, newspapers, magazines, books, radio, Internet. PR, advertising, marketing, design, video production. Bristol is now home to a multi-faceted array of media companies all jostling for so-called 'creative' space. The unprecedented growth of this sector has done much to raise the overall quality of the output with many organisations operating on a national, not just local level. But for every adventurous new art scene web mag, there is a dreary and irrelevant parochial yawn that passes for a free newspaper. You'll find both good and bad media here. We've concentrated on media that the public knows, as a list of creative digital communications agencies in Bristol would need a phone directory of its own. If you do produce a bi-monthly pamphlet on red squirrel activity in the Withywood area, we must apologise for missing you out.

Television

BBC WEST
www.bbc.co.uk/pointswest
'Hello and welcome to Pointless West.' The flagship show of the Bristol arm of the BBC's nationwide network suffers from an extreme case of 'local media syndrome'. It's cosy, superficial, its presenters wink at you from their sofa, the weatherman tells you about primary school fayres he is opening in lovely Minchinhampton.

ITV WEST
www.itvregions.com/west
This undistinguished lump of Brislington concrete is the commercial wing of the local television experience. It has been the perfect place to pump out an endless stream of toe-curlingly embarrassing programmes over the years, most of them fronted by the world's unfunniest man, Jon Monie. Every single leisure-type HTV show has been appalling but *Trip in the Cosmic Buggy* must be the worst.

ENDEMOL WEST
www.endemoluk.com
Based in a not-so-hip Bath Road industrial estate, this is the South West branch of the company that brought you *Big Brother*, *The Games*, and, somewhat surprisingly, BBC2's *Restoration*. Endemol employs up to 800 people in London, Bristol and Glasgow and is part of the international Endemol Group; a worldwide network of production companies spanning 22 countries. Endemol is owned by Spanish telecoms and media giant Telefonica – the largest provider of telecom and internet services in the Spanish and Portuguese language world with more than 62 million customers. Keep an eye open for adverts in the local press and you could end up in the studio audience for Noel Edmonds' *Deal Or No Deal* show which is filmed at Paintworks.

SKINS
Teen drama with beautiful young things often in a state of distress and undress. From a locals point of view, they often find interesting locations off the normal locations circuit.

THE RESTAURANT
Reality cooking competition where couples battle it out for the opportunity to go into business with Raymond Blanc. Cameraman Tom Swindell finds beauty in the most mundane of Bristolian locations and has won awards for his work.

MISTRESSES
Two-timing thirty-somethings try to work out their relationship dramas In some of the series Bristol looms large, almost as a character in itself, but sadly not any more. Apparently production is moving to Cardiff, and most people probably won't notice the difference.

Media

CASUALTY

Bristol's TV presence, to the extent that Bristolians saw the series as 'theirs'. But then the BBC realised it could save money by moving it to Cardiff, cue lots of uproar, outrage and local rag campaigning. All to no avail, we've still got Holby for the time being but who watches that?

DEAL OR NO DEAL

Game show credited with bringing Noel Edmonds back from obscurity. Contestants battle with the mysterious banker who can only be reached on a 1920s telephone. It's crap, but it is entertaining and addictive crap which has a loyal audience who arrive at Paintworks in Bristol in their droves, dressed all in black and looking like they have arrived for secret cult meetings with a self-styled demi god.

BEING HUMAN

BBC3's cult classic of three supernatural housemates sharing a place in Totterdown. Despite the success of the show and the brilliant use of locations such as the General Hospital it seems that even vampires and werewolves prefer Cardiff. It must be the new shopping centre they have there.

NATURAL HISTORY UNIT

The BBC department off Whiteladies Road is world renowned for its nature documentaries, which bring a wealth of creative talent to the city to form the backbone of the Wildscreen Festival in @Bristol.

Animation

AARDMAN ANIMATIONS
www.aardman.com
Can anyone smell burning plasticine? Well Morph and his cohorts may have starred in an impromptu version of the *Towering Inferno* when Aardman's St Phillip's warehouse burned down in 2005 but not even a charred cast of thousands has stopped Nick Park's ever-expanding animation empire from swelling ever wider.

BOLEX BROTHERS
www.bolexbrothers.co.uk
Perverse pixel-warping short film terrorists who debuted with the grotesque *Secret Adventures of Tom Thumb* in 1993. Deformed

---

TYPICAL POINTS WEST NEWS STORIES

1. WESTLAND HELICOPTERS
If a nut is done up too tight or a rotary blade out of synch, they wheel out Malcolm Frith for a 17-minute piece-to-camera lead story. Even the helicopters fall asleep.

2. BRIDGWATER CARNIVAL
Every year *Points West* descend on masse to the Bridgwater carnival. From the building of the floats, to the odd light bulb crisis, costume dilemmas to music selection, every aspect of this oh-so-thrilling 4-mile-an-hour drive-by is covered. The by far more interesting Ashton Court Festival, on the other hand, barely got a mention.

3. CAKES
If the bakery is closed for good, what are they going to do with all the cakes? Don't worry, Chris 'hello' Vacher and friends will save the day by donating all the pastry excess to a charitable organisation of their choice. That's a lead story if ever I saw one!

4. THE RED ARROWS
For what feels like 3,000 years, *Points West* has covered the bloody Red Arrows whenever and wherever they've been in flight. Listen, the Red Arrows were crap in 1973, they are worse than soddin' balloons. Every year it's the same: 'Oh look balloons', 'oh look the Red Arrows'. Enough is enough.

5. CONCORDE
Remembering it. Coming over all sad about its demise. Falling out over the museum version of it. *Points West* loves Concorde so much, it made a video of its life story. More than a thousand pensioners queued for two days to get their hands on a copy.

6. WHATEVER IS IN THE EVENING POST
Save yourself the cost of buying an evening paper, put your feet up with a cup of tea and have that nice Chris Vacher read it out to you. Sometimes 'newsgathering' on local television news seems to involve nipping down the newsagents.

Media

infants, ravenous insects and a hatful of surreal obsessions have been their themes ever since. David Cronenberg surely approves.

Radio

BBC RADIO BRISTOL
www.bbc.co.uk/bristol
If it's funny stories about making tea in Fishponds you're after, don't touch that dial. Hosted by John Turner and a few other blokes who sound like John Turner, this is radio circa 1961; yokel, pedestrian, coming live from flower shows in Melksham. To be fair Radio Bristol has a strong sense of community and John Turner's phone-ins are occasionally priceless. Is Steve Yabsley serious or as surrealist as Geoff Twentyman's moustache? Keith Warmington is good as well. Actually, we listen to it quite a lot.

BCFM
www.bcfm.org.uk
Bristol's community radio station, presumably for everyone else that isn't listening to Ujima. Some great stuff that wouldn't find airplay on any other station rubs shoulders with some appalling stuff that wouldn't get airplay on any other station. Guess you can't have one without the other.

BURST
www.burstradio.org.uk
Bristol University's official radio station is a lively mix of national and local news bulletins, special reports, arts and sports and a music policy that is just about on the right side of decent... most of the time. We agree that it is fantastic idea for the university to have its own station, but James Blunt? Come on guys! Are you for real?

JACK
www.jackbristol.com
So while all the ladies are driving around in their cars listening to Heart the men are all tuned in to Jack with its 'Playing what we want' music policy. Classic rock music is the order of the day here, RoxyFreeMadnessColdplay etc.

HEART
www.heart.co.uk/bristol
Here is an interesting thing, a station for the ladies. So what do ladies like? Pop music

according to Heart. Abba, Kylie, Katy Perry... you get the picture.

THE HUB
www.uwesu.net/thehub
UWE's much hipper take on the official uni radio station is based in Bower Ashton and encourages student involvement at every turn. 'Hey, we are always on the look out for new DJs to put more funk in our trunk!!' enthuses the website, embarrassingly. Right, where is that gaffer tape?

UJIMA
www.ujimaradio.com
'Bristol's No1 urban station' is a community run outfit primarily for people in the Easton and St Paul's areas of the city. Celebrating diversity and the cultural mix that can be found in both of these areas guarantees that Ujima is never predictable.

Newspapers, Magazines & Websites

EVENING POST
www.epost.co.uk
Okay, so it's half way between the *Daily Mail* and the *Yorkshire Post* but you have to admit it improved a hell of a lot under the editorship of Mike Lowe, even though sales fell dramatically. Then owners Northcliffe announced major redundancies in Bristol. According to insiders, bullying and backstabbing became a way of life at the *Post* and *Press* as some people who wanted redundancy were refused it and some who wanted to stay put were shown the door. Mike Lowe and his deputy Stan 'The Man' Szecowka left when Mike Norton was appointed as managing editor of the *Post* and *Western Daily Press*. With morale at the *Post* said to be the lowest ever, it's hardly surprising that the quality of the paper declined rapidly as more and more redundancies were made leaving the Post with only a skeleton staff of sub-editors. In the late 1980s, the circulation was about 110,000 a day. Sales at the beginning of 2011 had plummeted to just under 40,000 and Northcliffe took the decision to demolish the press hall next to the Post building in Old Market. The paper was being printed in Didcot along with other Northcliffe titles and shipped into Bristol. There is now

Media

only one edition a day meaning that the Post is completely unable to react to breaking news. The Stokes Croft riots that started at about 9pm on a Thursday were not reported by the *Post* until the Saturday. It's a tough time for all regional papers, but the *Post* seems to have been particularly badly managed. For years it has been out of touch with what is going on in Bristol and with the circulation continuing to fall it's conceivable that Bristol could become the first major UK city not to have an evening newspaper.

WESTERN DAILY PRESS
www.westpress.co.uk
As everyone frets about the health of the *Evening Post*, the *Western Daily Press* puts some coal on the fire and prepares to chug around the station for a while. The WDP is the rural morning paper covering the whole of the South West from the Cotswolds to Dorset. It's an old fashioned Tory workhorse, traditionally staffed by former Fleet Street hacks. Despite its *Daily Mail* tendencies, it's a well produced paper and seems to know its readership far better than the *Post*. With circulation falling to 29,000 per day, production was moved to Plymouth in 2011 leading to speculation that the WDP will eventually be merged with the Plymouth Morning News.

VENUE/FOLIO
www.venue.co.uk
Without doubt, the finest regional listings magazine in the country. *Venue* began as a kind of *City Limits* for Bristol under the visionary stewardship of the relentlessly single-minded Dave Higgett and the idiosyncratically entrepreneurial Dougal Templeton. It is now owned by Northcliffe but is still the only magazine to buy if you want to know what is going on in Bristol. In the Spring of 2011 a combination of falling circulation and decreasing ad revenue meant *Venue* was threatened with closure by its owners Northcliffe. A public outcry ensued and Venue was combined with sister title *Folio* to become a monthly listings magazine given away free. The closure threat confirmed many people's suspicions that the *Venue*/Northcliffe relationship was an uneasy one – it's never been easy for traditional *Venue* readers to reconcile themselves with the fact that they are buying a title from the publishers of the *Daily Mail*. But Northcliffe's problems with

regional titles go far beyond *Venue* and the company seems to be incapable of reacting to the digital age by producing a decent website. The *Venue* one has never been that good (though there was a revamp in 2011) and the *Evening Post's* thisisbristol web presence is truly terrible.

ORIGIN PUBLISHING
www.originpublishing.co.uk
A Future Publishing off-shoot (and now part of BBC Worldwide), Origin snatched all the hairdressing, sewing and fishing titles and relocated to a 1970s tower block near The Bierkeller. Doesn't sound very glamorous does it? But having an annual turnover of £21m proves there's gold in dull hobby magazines.

TRADE-IT
www.trade-it.co.uk
Published every Wednesday, Friday and Sunday, *Trade-It* is a free ads publication covering Bristol, Bath, Swindon, Gloucester, and the surrounding areas, offering 50,000 ads in categories ranging from computers to holiday homes. The Free to Collector section always contains some very weird stuff. Half-a-tonne of pebbledash for nothing? Now, that's a bargain.

THE SPARK
www.thespark.co.uk
What does *The Spark* tell us about Bristol? Well, it's the only city in the country that can sustain a free 33,000 circulation quarterly newspaper devoted to alternative therapy, psychotherapy, counselling and healing. John Dawson founded *The Spark* in 1993 and since then it has become the focus for the alternative community in the South West. In 2010 journalist Darryl Bullock bought the title and gave it a sympathetic Spring clean and increased distribution. *The Spark* is based on the free newspaper principle of advertising paying the wages and production costs and is eagerly awaited every quarter by those with an interest in the content and those who enjoy a look at the alternative world. It's easy to poke fun at *The Spark*, and they are not beyond a touch of self-deprecation, but how can you disagree with a mission statement that begins: 'Our aim is to keep you in touch with locally-based creative solutions for a changing world and to help you get the best out of life.'

Media

Listings

BRISTOL REVIEW
www.bristolreview.com
It's difficult to imagine the scene at the birth of this particular magazine. 'Right, we'll sell about 40-odd pages of adverts and fill in the remaining half-a-dozen with some shabby first-person 'reviews' of a few pubs, restaurants and clubs. Any questions?' It is not a guide to the city. It isn't really a magazine.

BRISTOL REVIEW OF BOOKS
www.bristolbooksandpublishers.co.uk
An ambitious team of independent Bristol publishers have put their competitiveness to one side and banded together to produce this rather good quarterly magazine about Bristol's publishing heritage. Despite being produced on a shoestring budget, *BRB* appears on a regular basis and is easily the city's most intelligent magazine. It is mainly distributed through bookshops and libraries, but copies disappear quickly. If you want to make sure of getting a copy, you can subscribe for just £15 a year at www.tangentbooks.co.uk.

BRISTOL INDYMEDIA
www.bristolindymedia.org
This is an essential source of alternative news and views plus details of local protests, demos and campaigns as well as national and international issues. The site is updated daily and has a policy of not editing comments and views unless they are malicious. There is a huge archive of Bristol's non-aligned political activity and good links to subverting sites and more. This is one of the few sources of information in Bristol and around that isn't controlled by that giant Northcliffe propaganda machine.

SUIT YOURSELF
www.suityourselfmagazine.co.uk
Free, independent quarterly aimed at all the young fashionable things in Bristol. A bit like *Venue* used to be.

BRISTOL MAGAZINE
www.thebristolmagazine.co.uk
Irritating middle aged, middle-class, middle of the road magazine which arrives through your door if you live in a posh area, but the rest of you might find a copy in a bar.

CLIFTON LIFE
www.cliftonlifemag.co.uk
When husband and wife publishing supremos Greg and Jane Ingham quit Future Publishing in Bath with zillions of shares between them, they bought Surf Media and established MediaClash in late 2006. The Clash bit is a reference to Greg Ingham's favourite band. Among other publishing and online ventures they produce the Life series of titles for Cardiff, Wells, Frome, Tetbury and other areas. Clifton Life is a well-produced, topical title with high production values, as you would expect from any title that benefits from the Inghams huge magazine experience. There are noticably more listings and a sparkier editorial approach since *Venue* was threatened with closure.

Media

Media

Listings **Nights Out**

Mention Bristol to anyone north of Cheltenham or south of Bath and it won't be long before their eyes widen and they start banging on about the city's club scene. The thing is, it's all true: Bristol is a clubbing city. Anything that's happened in the last two or three decades has happened within earshot of a bruising rhythm and a throbbing bass. Punk rock came and had reggae at its side. Some of us even spent Live Aid in a St Paul's blues club. We began going to the Dugout a few times a week, absorbing reggae, disco and early hip-hop beats. It was in and around independent black clubs like this that the hybrid Bristol sound was born.

Although you never felt the hand of history on your shoulder in the Dugout, it was easily the most vibrant club the city has ever seen. You shuffled along the corridor, pushed your entrance fee under the glass into the hand of the always unfazed Max or Chips, stumbled down a flight of stairs and felt your shoes stick to whatever the substance was that covered the dance floor.

So, is there any room for places like the Dugout these days? Well, one of the last remaining 'alternative' club venues, Easton Community Centre, is no more. The free party scene seems to have run out of hiding places too. But all is not lost to the crazy gods of pointless noise. Big Chill, Lakota, Cosies, Bank of Stokes Croft, the Black Swan, and The Croft aren't afraid of stepping over the boundary ropes and help keep some swagger in the famous Bristol groove. Tomorrow, by the way, probably belongs to Motion, the radical rock revolution at The Croft and the warped electroclash mayhem of Metal Disko. Try dancing to that in a pair of sensible shoes!

ANSON ROOMS
Queens Road, Clifton
Tel: 954 5800 • www.ubu.org.uk
This cavernous room on the first floor of the bleak 1960s-built Student Union building is the largest standing venue in Bristol. The Anson Rooms sadly suffers from a stupidly restricted guestlist policy, too many idiot door staff in rugby shirts and the atmosphere of a school assembly hall.

BANK OF STOKES CROFT
84 Stokes Croft
Tel: 9232565
www.thebankofstokescroft.wordpress.com
From the same team at the Big Chill, The Bank has regular club nights Thurs-Sat featuring a wide range of tunes from hip-hop to soul, disco and boogie.

BIERKELLER
All Saints Lane, The Pithay
Tel: 926 8514 • www.bristolbierkeller.co.uk
Without doubt, Bristol's most miserable live venue. Dingy and unfriendly, this oompah house is characterised by Newcastle Brown Ale, people playing pool while the band is on and flooded toilets. They only book around one decent band every two years. Friday night sees the Phuct! DJs playing metal and there's free entry to 'anyone in a Mankini, Swimsuit, Bikini or Budgie Smugglers'. Saturday night is worse.

BIG CHILL BAR
15 Small Street
Tel: 930 4217 • www.bigchill.net
First Big Cill outside London was an immediate success thanks to nice surroundings, friendly staff and an intelligent music policy that

Nights out

combines big name national DJs with local stars and occasional appearances by the likes of Grant from Massive Attack, Queen B and DJ Derek. Wanted Records have a regular Thursday night slot.

BLACK SWAN
438 Stapleton Road, Easton
Tel: 939 3334
Heavyweight Drum 'n' Bass and Hardcore hangout. Mental.

BLUE MOUNTAIN CLUB
2 Stokes Croft
The Blue Mountain might not be as famous as it thinks it is, but it is one of the more challenging sonic spaces around. Keeps threatening to revive the vibe of the mid 90s when it was one of the best club's in town, but never seems to quite make it..

BRISTOL 02 ACADEMY
Frogmore Street
Tel: 0970 771 2000 • bristol-academy.co.uk
Soulless, functional venue for big names when they visit Bristol, as well as other live music and club nights.

THE BUNKER
78 Queen's Road
Tel: 930 4604 • www.thebunkerbristol.com
Student hangout that promises 'frolicking mayhem'. Jeeez!

COLSTON HALL
Colston Street
Tel: 922 3686 • www.colstonhall.org
Gene Pitney, Status Quo, the Polish National Symphony Orchestra, the Chippendales, Sing-A-Long-A-Abba… if you were being cruel you could describe the Colston Hall's booking policy as 'anything as long as it's crap'. But let's not forget that The Clash played here once. Massive Attack refuse to play here because of the association with slave trader Edward Colston. In January 2006, Bristol City Council approved a £20 million redevelopment of this part of Bristol history and the result is the Colston Hall Foyer, a large and airy event space and cafe/bar that all works rather well.

COOLER
4 Park Street
Tel: 945 0999 • www.clubcooler.com
Bristol's old indie clubs never die, they just take their copies of James' *Sit Down* around town. Cooler is a rubbish name for a dance club, let alone an alternative one, and is a long way from being progressive, but the reports have been good. Mr Rotten used to sneer from the Cum flyposters and that is never a bad thing.

COSIES
34 Portland Square, St Paul's
Tel: 942 4110 • www.cosies.co.uk
Hidden away in a stylish Georgian square best known for parking and prostitution, Cosies is a mild-mannered wine bar for office workers by day and a furious miss-mash of leftfield reggae beats in the evening.

THE CROFT,
117 Stokes Croft
Tel: 903 0796 • www.the-croft.com
An institution in Bristol. Nobody has a music policy quite as switched on as The Croft's. Anticipating the death of the dreary dance scene, they have grabbed the approaching new dawn of diversity with both hands and mix dub, mangled electro synthcore and radical alt. rock nights.

DOJO LOUNGE
12-16 Park Row
Tel: 925 1177
Owned by former England fast bowler Syd Lawrence, Dojo has the knack of being one of the most relaxed, as well as one of most ambitious, clubs in Bristol. The weekend nights are all about the hip-hop favourites Slosh and Payback.

FIDDLERS
Willway Street, Bedminster
Tel: 987 3403 • www.fiddlers.co.uk
Tucked away down a sidestreet off a sidestreet south of the river, this unlikely family-owned success story has carved out a niche for itself by offering mainly earthy blues and roots with a raw live appeal. Simply finding the place is a bit of an adventure.

FLEECE AND FIRKIN
12 St Thomas Street, St Thomas
Tel: 945 0996 • www.thefleece.co.uk
Not too long ago, The Fleece was Bristol's foremost gig venue but then reverted to counterfeit Stones, pretend Blondies and several Whole Lotta Led Zeps to fill the week, while very average soul covers get the Blues

Nights out

Listings

Brothers parties going at weekends. Then Blue Aeroplanes bass player Chris Sharp took over the Fleece and returned it to its former glory with an imaginative programme of new music and by telling the tribute acts to fake off.

THE HATCHET
27 Frogmore Street
Tel: 929 4118
The upstairs bar at 'Bristol's oldest pub' has been home to many a rock night over the years and continues to deliver.

LA ROCCA
Triangle South
Tel: 926 0924 • www.laroccabristol.co.uk
With its original disco seating and groovy circular wall holes, La Rocca can be a cool place when the music is right. Sadly, inconsistency is the tune you're most likely to hear.

LAKOTA
6 Upper York Street, St Paul's
www.lakota.co.uk
The once mighty Lakota was pulling punters from all over when the rest of Bristol's upstart club venues were empty warehouses. Lakota's status may have faded but it still comes up with the occasional surprise.

LIZARD LOUNGE
66 Queen's Road
Tel: 949 7778 • lizardloungebristol.co.uk
Caters for students in the good old fashioned pissed-off-their-heads-dancing-to-*Club-Tropicana* sense of the word. Cocktail nights, salsa nights, mad-for-it nights, cheap pints on Tuesday nights. This is student heaven right on the Triangle.

THE LOUISIANA
Wapping Road
Tel: 926 5978 • thelouisiana.net
It might be the size of an average toilet and have a curb instead of a proper stage, but this hasn't stopped the Louisiana from pulling in some of the biggest names on the indie scene over the years. It has always been and still is one of the coolest gig venues in town. Let's just pray that the owners the Schillacis don't book the Polyphonic Spree.

MBARGO
38-40 Triangle West
Tel: 925 3256 • www.mbargobristol.co.uk
Reinforcing the Triangle's reputation for being a touch more sophisticated than the clubs 'down the hill', Mbargo boasts a decent wine list, cocktails and imported beer.

MOTION
74-78 Avon Street, St Phillips
www.motionbristol.com
Warehouse-style party venue round the back of Temple Meads hosting a wide range of dance styles from Drum 'n' Bass to Rave, Techno and Hardcore. There's even an occasional Roller Disco.

MR WOLF'S
33 St Stephens Street
Tel: 927 3221 • www.mrwolfs.com
A very chilled out little bar in the centre of town where you can get a lovely bowl of noodles. At its best, it acts as a lively pre- or post-club bar. On the downside, the live music can dominate, so unless you really want to see the band, it's best to come early or late.

Nights out

CONCERT HALLS

ST GEORGE'S
Great George Street, off Park Street
(0845 40 24 001)
www.stgeorgesbristol.co.uk
From Lloyd Cole to the London Fortepiano Trio, Shostakovich's Piano Sonata No 1 to I Don't Want To Go To Chelsea, St George's is a venue that suits them all. Built in 1823 by Sir Robert Smirke, it is known nationwide for its quite exceptional acoustics. In terms of sound quality, this is one of the UK's most highly rated concert halls, it offers the sort of up-close-and-personal sonic intimacy that even ambient perfectionist Brian Eno himself would approve of.

COLSTON HALL
www.bristol-city.gov.uk
Bristol City Council spent £20 million on the new foyer, but the old hall still looks like the lightbulbs haven't been changed since 1955. This is not necessarily a bad thing.

OCEANA
South Buildings, Canons Road
Tel: 927 9203 • www.oceanaclubs.com
This is the most super of super-clubs in Bristol (and we mean super in size, not quality). Its slogan brags five bars, two nightclubs and dining in one destination. It sounds like a meat market to us. And you have to wear proper shoes to get in.

PLATFORM 1
Clifton Down Station
Tel: 973 4388 • www.platform1club.com
The sort of place where ladies on hen nights get off with Bristol Rovers reserve team players.

PRIVÉ
13-15 King Street
Tel: 930 4603 • www.privebristol.com
Targets the more cultivated clubbing clientele, so painted everything purple and gold. Book a table and find out if they've succeeded.

POLISH CLUB
50 St Paul's Road, Clifton
Tel: 973 6244
Okay, so it's not really a club in the traditional sense of the word and is generally a private party and members-only establishment. But anywhere that hangs a photo of the legendary 1982 Polish World Cup side behind the bar deserves to get a mention. And it is the most fantastically friendly club in Bristol.

PO NA NA
67 Queens Road
Tel: 925 6225 • www.bristolponana.com
Po Na Na's subterranean halls are famously popular with students. Removed from the melee of the town clubs, it's a classy joint with a music policy that includes classic Motown, funk and disco.

THE PROM
The Promenade, Gloucester Road
Tel: 942 7319 • www.theprom.co.uk
The transformation of the old wine bar into a Mediterranean-flavoured cafe-blues bar has been like a breath of sunshine for the lower Gloucester Road area. Friendly, not bothered by fashion and home to the longest-running Tuesday night pop quiz on Planet Earth.

THEKLA
The Grove, Harbourside
Tel: 929 3301 • www.theklabristol.co.uk
Bristol's legendary floating nightclub has always been the choice of clubbers who don't really like going to clubs. Downstairs is suitably dark and dingy so that regulars like Zoology and Wobble can thrive.

THE THUNDERBOLT
Bath Road, Totterdown
www.thethunderbolt.net
An eclectic mix of music, spoken word, film and community events is what makes The Thunderbolt special. Somehow Dave and Sophie McDonald manage to tempt the likes of The Christians, Wayne Hussey, Dr Feelgood, Jerry Dammers and The Stranglers to play a small south Bristol pub. The 'Bolt' also has a policy of supporting new local acts as well as squeezing middle-aged blokes onto the stage.

TIMBUK2
22 Small Street
www.tb2.co.uk
Underground arches rock to breaks, house, electronica and drum 'n' bass.

WEDGIES
48 Park Street
www.wedgies.co.uk
The Wedge... The Big Wedge... Wedgies... Whatever you want to call it, this is Bristol's greatest and cheesiest student club night. With sports teams, members, VIP cards (apparently you have to strip on a podium to get one), this is more than just a club night, it's a way of life. Best get hammered before you go in. Not the place to enter sober!

Nights out

Listings **Sport**

Bristol is the biggest regional city in England not to have had a football team in the top division in the last 30 or so years. In fact, we've never had a team in the Premier League since its inception in 1992. Think about it – Liverpool, Manchester, London, Birmingham, Newcastle, Portsmouth, Bolton, Blackburn, Blackpool, Norwich, Reading and Wigan are all famous for having top-flight football in recent years. The last time a Bristol team was in the top division was when City were in Division One between 1976 and 1980. And after getting relegated, they fell straight through the divisions in successive seasons before landing bankrupt at the bottom of Division Four with one almighty thump. This resulted in the entry into Bristol folklore of the "Ashton Gate Eight" – eight players who tore up their well-paid long-term contracts to save the club from financial meltdown.

There are probably deep sociological reasons why Bristol football is as bad as it is, but the reason you'll hear trotted out most is that it's because rugby and cricket are the dominant sports. Sadly, this theory is rubbish. Although egg chasing is a popular West Country pastime, so is cheese rolling and Bristol Rugby Club have suffered poor fortunes since the advent of professionalism, while Gloucestershire County Cricket Club is hardly among the modern game's pacesetters. Besides, have you ever heard anyone argue that football in Manchester has suffered because of the success of Lancashire CC or Sale Rugby Union?

Professional Sport

BRISTOL ROVERS
Memorial Stadium, Filton Avenue, Horfield
Tel: 909 6648 • www.bristolrovers.co.uk
Nicknamed the Pirates, Rovers have been stuck in the 3rd and 4th tiers of the football pyramid for years. Their highest finish was when they came within four points of promotion to the top league (then Division One) in the 1955-56 season. They finished sixth in Division Two that year… a feat they repeated in 1958-59. So long ago… oh, the pain. Rovers self imploded in 2010/11 sacking manager Paul Trollope and getting relegated to the bottom division.

BRISTOL CITY
Ashton Gate, Ashton
Tel: 963 0630 • www.bcfc.co.uk
City have enjoyed slightly more success than Rovers in recent years, earning promotion to the Championship (the second highest tier) in the 2006-07 season and almost reaching the Premier League in their first year (losing the play-off final to Hull City). Since then they have been a constant in the country's second tier, though Rovers fans will argue that they experience more excitement than City thanks to various promotions and relegations. Their highest ever finish was in 1907, when they finished runners-up in Division One. They also reached the FA Cup Final in 1909, losing to Man United.

GLOUCESTERSHIRE CC
County Ground, Neville Road, Bishopston
Tel: 910 8000 • www.gloscricket.co.uk

BRISTOL RUGBY CLUB
Memorial Stadium, Filton Avenue, Horfield
Tel: 0871 208 2234 • bristolrugby.co.uk

Sports Centres/Pools

BISHOPSWORTH POOL
Whitchurch Lane • Tel: 903 1600

BRISTOL SOUTH POOL
Dean Lane, Bedminister • Tel: 966 3131

DAVID LLOYD CLUB
Ashton Road, Nr Long Ashton
Tel: 953 1010 • davidlloydleisure.co.uk

EASTON LEISURE CENTRE/POOL
Thrissell Street, Easton
Tel: 955 8840 Gym: 903 8000

HENBURY LEISURE CENTRE
Avonmouth Way, Henbury
Tel: 353 2555 Gym: 353 2554

HENLEAZE SWIMMING CLUB
Henleaze Lake, Lake Road, Henleaze
www.bristolhenleazesc.org.uk
This is a fabulous members-only lake with high diving boards. This is a perfect spot for a day out in the summer. Get signed in by a member if you want to try it out. Sadly, the waiting list for membership is about two years long, but worth putting your name down for.

HORFIELD LEISURE CENTRE
Dorian Road, Horfield
Tel: 903 1643 Gym: 353 2540

JUBILEE POOL
Jubilee Road, Knowle • Tel: 903 1607

KINGSWOOD LEISURE CENTRE
Church Road, Staple Hill Tel: 01454 865701

ST PAUL'S COMMUNITY SPORTS ACADEMY
Newfoundland Road, St Paul's
Tel: 377 3405 • Gym: 377 3405

WHITCHURCH SPORTS CENTRE
Bamfield, Whitchurch
Tel: 01275 833 911

Other Sports

CLIMBING
Undercover Rock, Bristol Climbing Centre, St Werburghs Church, Mina Road
Tel: 941 3489
www.bristolclimbingcentre.com
Learn how not to get stuck halfway up the Avon Gorge. Bristol Climbing Centre is a ludicrously popular place with both kids and adults. There is a 12-metre high wall with pillar, fins, overhangs and arches, and a bouldering area. Undercover Rock runs a whole host of courses, works with children from local schools and also offers corporate 'team dynamics' stuff, all based around climbing.

ATHLETICS
Bristol and West Athletics Club
www.bristolandwestac.org.uk
Holds regular training sessions at the Whitchurch and Filton track as well as hill training all around Bristol and training runs at Ashton Court. The club competes in a number of national competitions at all levels.

FENCING
Bristol Fencing Club
www.bristolfencingclub.com
Long-established fencing club based at Redland High School. Organises the Bristol Fencing Open annual event and runs coaching sessions for adults and juniors.

TENNIS
Bristol Lawn Tennis & Squash Club
Redland Green, Redland
Tel: 973 1139
www.bltsc.co.uk
Bristol used to be the last UK grass court tournament before Wimbledon, so loads of top players visited Bristol for the Lambert & Butler Championship. The pre-Wimbledon week has long since gone, but the club remains a top regional tennis centre.

Sport

Listings **Events**

January

BRISTOL ACOUSTIC FESTIVAL
www.stgeorgesbristol.co.uk
Not so much unplugged as plugless at one of the cities' first music festivals of the year. However, this ensures a good turnout… just be prepared to freeze your socks off in the midwinter chill. Now held at St. George's.

SLAPSTICK SILENT COMEDY FILM FESTIVAL
www.slapstick.org.uk
Laurel and Hardy, Harold Lloyd, Charlie Chaplin and Buster Keaton blowout at various venues. Usually third weekend in January.

February

STORYTELLING FESTIVAL
www.bristolstoryfest.co.uk
Held during national Storytelling week in February, this festival is made up of a series of events during which accomplished storytellers share their experiences, stories and ideas with audiences which vary from families to other authors. Worth turning up to – the thrill of a good story beckons.

March

FAIRTRADE FORTNIGHT
www.bristolfairtradenetwork.org.uk
Bristol is an active fairtrade city so watch out for promotions, exhibitions, speakers, films and other events for two weeks in mid March.

BRISTOL BEER FESTIVAL
www.camrabristol.org.uk
Now settled into a long-term venue at the Brunel Passenger Shed at Temple Meads station, the Bristol Beer Festival is usually held on the last weekend in March. At the last count it features more than 125 real ales and about 40 ciders. Shame you can't try them all. Or can you? Tickets go on sale in December and are often all gone in a couple of weeks.

May

STOKES CROFT STREETFEST
www.stokescroftstreetfest.wordpress.com
The Stokes Croft community and its admirers turns out in force to enjoy live music, street theatre, DJs, cabaret and the ever-popular Crofts Dog Show. The hated Tesco shop is closed to avoid being trashed by revellers.

BRISTOL ANARCHIST BOOKFAIR
www.bristolanarchistbookfair.org
After trying various locations, the Anarchist Bookfair now seeems settled at Hamilton House in the People's Republic of Stokes Croft. It is now established as the biggest anarchist bookfair in the UK outside London.

FOLK FESTIVAL
www.bristolfolkfestival.com
Thanks to tireless work and campaigning from festival fans, this event was held for the first time in 32 years in 2011. Housed at the Colston Hall, it takes place in the first full week of May.

MODEL RAILWAY EXHIBITION
www.bristolmodrailex.co.uk
One of the biggest and widely attended model railway exhibitions in the country, the Bristol show has been held since 1968. It takes place on the Friday, Saturday and Sunday before the May day bank holiday at Thornbury Leisure Centre. Among the notable visitors to have graced the exhibitions' floors over the years is devilish pop supremo and steam locomotive owner Pete Waterman.

JACK IN THE GREEN
home.freeuk.net/bristoljack
Pagan frivolity featuring a procession of musicians and dancers dawdling behind Jack from the Harbourside to Horfield Common in a celebration of summer. Expect Morris dancers. Held on the first Saturday in May.

REDLAND MAY FAIR
www.rcas.org.uk
A village fete affair on Redland Green with loads of stalls which has been going since the

mid 1970s. So busy you have to push your way through the crowds of teenagers trying to look cool by the coconut shies and cake stands. Surreal fun.

CHEESE ROLLING

www.cheese-rolling.co.uk
In a tradition that dates back to the 1700s, country folk congregate at Coopers Hill near Brockworth between Cheltenham and Stroud and chase a bloody great big Double Gloucester down the hill. The event takes place on Whit Bank Holiday Monday despite annual health and safety attempts to prevent it.

June

UPFEST URBAN PAINT FESTIVAL

www.upfest.co.uk
Europe's largest (free) urban paint (in other words, graffiti) festival is firmly established on the calendars of street art lovers everywhere. Based at the Tobacco factory and spreading out into Southville, it is annually held on the first weekend in June. It's a massive celebration of urban art that you won't want to miss.

FESTIVAL OF NATURE

www.festivalofnature.org
Centred around the At-Bristol complex, the festival is organised by the Bristol Natural History Consortium and features talks, walks, animal encounters, cookery, real food, green markets, books, art and much more. A great day out for all the family. Usually the first weekend in June.

BIKE FEST

www.bike-fest.com
Increasingly popular bike racing event at Ashton Court. Second weekend in June.

ARCHITECTURE WEEK

www.architectureweek.co.uk
Bristol usually comes up with an impressive range of lectures, tours and other events in National Architecture Week in late June

BRISTOL VEGETARIAN FAYRE

www.yaoh.co.uk
One of the world's biggest vegetarian/vegan events usually takes place around the L-Shed at Princes Wharf on the second weekend of June.

REFUGEE WEEK BIG FUN DAY

www.refugee-action.org.uk
Free festival of dance, music, art and food in Queen Square celebrating the contribution to Bristol's community of asylum seekers and refugees. Usually the third Sunday of June and the start of a week of special events.

BRISTOL'S BIGGEST BIKE RIDE

www.bristol-city.gov.uk
Thousands of Bristol cyclists set off from town on a mass cycle ride on a variety of routes. Usually the last Sunday in June.

ST GEORGE'S MIGRATIONS

www.stgeorgesbristol.co.uk
Migrations is a unique festival celebrating world music and the role that the migration of people has had in enriching Bristol's musical language. It also explores the whole idea of migration and culture through films at Watershed, talks, debates, events and a festival "chill" day in June.

July

ST PAUL'S CARNIVAL

www.bristolurban.org.uk
Legendary street fun in the multi-cultural heart of Bristol. Floats, PA battles, lots of food, drink and nocturnal liveliness. First Saturday of July.

SIKH MELA

www.visitbristol.co.uk
Mela is Punjabi for 'festival'. This one is held in Eastville Park on the first weekend in July and showcases the art, music, culture and food of the city's South Asian community.

PRIDDY FOLK FESTIVAL

www.priddyfolk.org
Mendip folk festival usually held early July.

ST WERBURGHS CITY FARM SUMMER FAIR

www.stwerburghs.org
Music, craft workshops, carnival procession. Big fun. Usually early July.

JAMAICA STREET STUDIOS OPEN DAY

www.jamaicastreetartists.co.uk
This Stokes Croft studio with a big reputation throws open its doors in July.

Events

Listings

SOUTHMEAD CELEBRATION
www.visitbristol.co.uk
Community carnival, usually held mid July.

BRISTOL HARBOUR FESTIVAL
www.bristol-city.gov.uk/harbourfestival
After years of expansion, the Harbour Festival was scaled down in 2011 and the traditional Saturday night firework extravaganza was scrapped. Still a huge event, but it increasingly seems to have less to do with boats and more to do with drinking in Queen's Square and going shopping.

PARK ARTS FESTIVAL
www.friendsofstandrewspark.ning.com
This one-day event is held in St Andrew's Park, and features acoustic music, poetry readings and other various entertainment for fans of the arts. Held every two years in July.

PRIDE
www.pridebristol.org
Gay and lesbian festival that finally seems to have established itself after several false starts.

August

AMNESTY INTERNATIONAL GARDEN PARTY
www.bristol.amnesty.org.uk
A wonderful and rare opportunity to explore the grounds of Goldney House, one of Bristol's best preserved 18th-Century houses, famous for its grotto. Usually held on the first Sunday in August. Hope for sun!

BRISTOL BALLOON FIESTA
www.bristolballoonfiesta.co.uk
If the tacky cynicism of the funfair and the squawkings of the wannabe 'pop' acts don't appeal, go instead to the Avon Gorge Hotel's patio bar and watch Europe's finest hot-air balloons drift majestically by. Mid August at the Ashton Court Estate

BRISTOL JAZZ FESTIVAL
www.bristoljazzsoc.co.uk
Whether a stage between the Old Duke and Llandoger Trow in King's Street constitutes a festival is debatable. But let's not be mean spirited. This is a fun event held over the August bank holiday.

BRISLINGTON BUS RALLY
www.bvbg.org.uk
If riding around in colourful vintage buses that should have been retired years ago is your idea of a fun day out, then this is the event for you. Based at Brislington Park-and-Ride, the annual event is held in conjunction with Avon Valley railway. It is held every August, and also includes a running event.

TREEFEST
www.forestry.gov.uk
Replacing the Westonbirt's now-defunct "Festival of the Tree", this four-day event takes more of a focus on family fun, with an exciting line-up which includes live music, food, workshops and crafts. It is still held at Westonbirt and features a line-up of intricately made wood carvings which were the main event of the "Festival of the Tree" for so many years. Environmentalist bliss.

September

SOIL ASSOCIATION ORGANIC FOOD FESTIVAL
www.soilassociation.org
This is a huge Harbourside celebration of all things organic and green organised by the Bristol-based Soil Association. The event is so big and popular, it even has its own Fringe Festival where you might find the likes of the Vienna Vegetable Orchestra. It is usually held the first weekend in September.

INTERNATIONAL KITE FESTIVAL
www.kite-festival.org
Huge variety of specialist kites and paraphernalia on display in the sublime kite-flying environment that is Ashton Court. First weekend in September.

BRISFEST
www.brisfest.co.uk
More than 500 bands, DJs, comedians, cabaret and circus performers over three days and nights on the harbourside.

DOORS OPEN DAY
www.bristoldoorsopenday.org
Popular event in which the finer private, closed and inaccessible buildings and spaces of Bristol are opened to the public in early September.

Events

BRISTOL POETRY FESTIVAL
www.poetrycan.co.uk
Couplets, ballads, rhymes, blank verse, conceits, elegies, enjambment and maybe even some iambic pentameter. You'll find it all at this 10-day festival in mid September.

BRISTOL HALF MARATHON
www.runbristol.com
13-mile jog which is sometimes sponsored by BUPA but which costs the NHS a fortune in ferrying out-of-breath, blistered people to hospital and treating them. Mid-September.

REDFEST
www.facebook.com/redfestbristol
Held in Redfield, this annual arts festival includes music, art, kids stuff, circus performances and theatre.

THE BRISTOL DO
www.thebristoldo.com
Very laid back gathering outside Circomedia HQ in Portland Square with the emphasis on circus, cabaret and street theatre.

October

FESTIVAL OF LITERATURE
This celebration of literature happens around mid-October. A new addition to Bristol authors' calendars, it promises to inspire audiences with works that range from fiction to poetry to scripts. Aspiring authors, take note.

ROYAL WEST OF ENGLAND ACADEMY AUTUMN EXHIBITION
www.rwa.org.uk
There are exhibitions here all year, but one of the highlights is the annual Autumn Exhibition between October and December when more than 600 works of painting, printmaking, sculpture and architecture are selected by open submission.

WILDSCREEN
www.wildscreenfestival.org
Filmfest for the wildlife media industry usually starts mid October.

CAJUN AND ZYDECO FESTIVAL
www.bristolcajunfestival.com
A weekend of Louisiana-style music, dance, food and drink at the Folk House. Started in 2004 and seems to have selected a mid October regular date.

BRISTOL HARMONICA FESTIVAL
www.harmonica.co.uk
Cupped hands and blowing at the Folk House in Park Street.

November

ENCOUNTERS SHORT FILM FESTIVAL
www.encounters-festival.org.uk
Showcases the best in UK and international short filmmaking. Cool scene for aspiring industry types, schmoozers and blaggers. Held at the Watershed usually towards the end of November.

FRONT ROOM ART TRAIL, TOTTERDOWN
www.frontroom.org.uk
Go and look at art in people's front rooms, in their cellars, in their kitchens and even in the pub. The Totterdown trail was the first one, now just about every area of Bristol has followed suit. Usually held the third weekend in November.

December

CREATE CHRISTMAS FAYRE
www.visitbristol.co.uk
Ecological Christmas gifts that won't cost the earth (geddit). Very popular. Usually second weekend in December.

CAROL SINGING AT BRISTOL ZOO
www.bristolzoo.org.uk
It's something of a tradition for many Bristolians to stand round the bonfire, cupping some mulled wine and singing along with gusto to Good King Wenceslas and the rest.

MARSHFIELD MUMMERS
This ancient mystery play is performed on Boxing Day (unless it's a Sunday) by Marshfield villagers wearing costumes made from torn up newspaper. There's carol singing at 10.30am before the Mummers perform the play four times at different points in the village and then adjourn to the Catherine Wheel.

Events

Listings **Gay Bristol**

P eople are often disparaging about Bristol's provincial gay scene, but comparing gay life in Bristol to the nation's capital is about as sensible as comparing Dr Scholl to Manolo Blahnik. It might be small, but Bristol's gay scene is perfectly formed, and with football and rugby teams, book groups, cinema clubs, walking groups, networking evenings, supper clubs, the annual gay film festival at the Watershed and more there is so much going on outside of the traditional pub and club circuit that only those with chemically-enhanced levels of stamina could hope to keep up.

Gay life in Bristol has changed beyond all recognition in recent years: such is the transient nature of the scene no doubt by the time you read this it will have altered again. In the last five years we have said hello to the Bristol Bear Bar, Flamingos, the Lounge, the Old Castle Green, OMG and the Palace but have waved goodbye

to Castro's, Club 46, the Elephant, the Griffin, Prague and Vibes. We've also, after years of bitter infighting, behind the scenes wrangling and the occasional organiser skipping town, finally got a full-on Pride (www.pridebristol.org), a week of celebrations which culminates in a day-long party in Castle Park attended, in 2010, by 20,000 people.

The major boast for Bristol's gay scene is that it's more relaxed, more friendly and a damn sight less cliquey than those of London, Manchester and Brighton. Being split over two opposite ends of town – Old Market, Bristol's gay village, and the Frogmore Street 'strip' – can make a night of club hopping a bit of a chore, but both sides have their fans and their own identity. You can keep the bright lights of Soho; I'd rather have a pint of 6X in the Old Market Tavern, thank you very much.
Darryl W Bullock

Pubs & Bars

Flamingos crowd who seem to like their booze to be neon coloured.

BRISTOL BEAR BAR
2-3 West Street, Old Market
Tel: 955 1967 · www.bristolbearbar.co.uk
Britain's first bespoke Bear bar is a small, one-room affair which aims to cater for older, hairier guys, although you're just as likely to bump into the odd (and, being Bristol, they will be odd) drag queen or two.

THE LOUNGE
53 Old Market Street
Tel: 0117 922 1224
One-room corridor of a bar, the Lounge hosts regular karaoke nights and often has cheap drinks offers to entice the younger, pre-

OLD CASTLE GREEN
46 Gloucester Lane, Old Market
Tel: 330 9140 · www.oldcastlegreen.com
Traditional pub with erratic opening hours, but licensed until 4am at the weekend – later than any other pub in Old Market. Regular Sunday afternoon barbecues during the summer.

OLD MARKET TAVERN
29 Old Market Street, Bristol BS2 0HB
TEL: 922 6123 · www.omtbristol.co.uk
The good-value lunch menu, friendly atmosphere, fantastic sun trap of a garden and cracking Sunday roast makes the OMT popular with a mixed crowd of office workers, local

Gay

business people and gay men and women who aren't sold on the endless campery other venues offer. The only gay pub in Bristol that serves real ale.

THE PALACE
1 West Street, Old Market
With entertainment most nights of the week the Palace may have a glitzy surface but don't scratch too deep, as often what you'll find is a bunch of pissed-up straight men and screeching women plastered in fake tan heckling a fat bloke in a frock.

THE PINEAPPLE
St George's Road, Bristol BS1 5UU
Tel: 316 9938 • thepineapplebristol.com
One of the longest-serving gay pubs in the city has had a chequered career, but it's still very popular with students, lesbians and others after a reasonably-priced drink before heading off to the Queenshilling or OMG.

THE RETREAT
16 West Street, Old Market
Busy feeder bar for Flamingos (well, it is owned by the same people) set over two floors, with a popular weekly quiz and the occasional theme night.

Clubs

CLUB O
7 Lawrence Hill
Tel: 955 6448 • www.clubobristol.co.uk
Members-only club (membership is free, but must be applied for in advance), Club O's opening hours are erratic at best, but it's currently the only club in the city which specialises in events for the fetish crowd and the TV/TS community.

COME TO DADDY
www.cometodaddyclub.co.uk
Come to Daddy is the UK's premier, travelling men only night, providing a totally attitude-free space for men of all ages, shapes and sizes. The longest-running men-only club night in Bristol, it's usually held on the second Saturday of the month at the Old Castle Green.

FLAMINGOS
23-25 West Street, Old Market
Tel: 955 9269 • www.flamingosbristol.com
The biggest gay club in the south west has two distinct sections, with more party-hearty, serious clubbing events taking place in Arena Two whilst the main room keeps the camper customers happy with regular live PAs and theme nights.

LIBERTY
Toto's Bar, 125 Redcliffe Street
www.libertybristol.co.uk
The city's only regular women-only club night, organised exclusively by women for women, with guest DJs and live performances.

OMG
Frog Lane, Frogmore Street
www.omgbristol.com
Bristol's newest gay nightclub took over the building that for many years housed Vibes. Just the place for you if your idea of fun is shaking your sequinned booty to Lady Gaga, at the time of writing the owners were about to launch a new bar on the opposite side of the road.

QUEENSHILLING
9 Frogmore Street
www.queenshilling.com
After two changes of ownership in less than six months the Queenshilling reopened in April 2011 with a new look and a new attitude. The Shilling's basement toilets were the stars of the recent short film *Fucked*, fact fans.

WONKY
www.clubwonky.com
Bristol's biggest – and longest running - alternative gay club night is aimed squarely at homos who hate hard house. With a mix of indie, electro, 80s pop, vintage house and disco, Wonky is currently held on the first Saturday of the month at Basement 45 in Frogmore Street.

Gay

Listings

Shops

NICE AND NAUGHTY
45 Colston Street
Tel: 929 7666
Formerly Clone Zone, Nice and Naughty offers a range of Ann Summers-esque sex toys, 18-rated DVDs, magazines, fetish wear, 'room aromas' and related tat.

THE PACKAGE
29 The Arcade, Broadmead
www.thepackage.co.uk
The place to buy your designer underpants: online ordering is available for those who can't face the embarrassment of calling into the Broadmead shop and coughing up £20 plus for a pair of skivvies.

THE VILLAGE SAUNA
19-21 West Street, Old Market
Tel: 330 7719 • www.villagesauna.com
Bristol's only gay sauna, with TV and cinema lounges, sauna, steam room, hot tub, dark rooms, private cubicles and something called a 'suckatorium' (your guess is as good as mine)!

Contacts

BRISTOL BISONS RFC
Tel: 07971 239504 • www.bisonsrfc.co.uk
Real men play rugby, and the Bisons are no exception. Bristol's gay and gay-friendly rugby team, established in 2005, welcomes new players and supporters.

BRISTOL LESBIAN AND GAY SWITCHBOARD (BLAGS)
Helpline 922 1328 • bristolblags.org.uk
Continually running since 1975, BLAGS is the second-oldest gay switchboard in the UK. Confidential support and information for LGBT people and for others concerned about issues relating to sexuality. Currently open Tues, Weds & Thurs 8-10pm, new volunteers are always welcome.

BRISTOL LGBT FORUM
Create Centre, Smeaton Road
Tel: 352 5633 • bristol-lgb-forum.org.uk
A Registered Charity fighting for, and educating about, equality; partly funded by Bristol City Council.

BRISTOL PANTHERS FC
bristolpanthersfc@hotmail.co.uk
www.bristolpanthers.co.uk
Bristol's gay and gay-friendly football team, originally formed in 2000, welcomes new players.

EACH
Freephone helpline: 0808 100 0143
(Mon-Fri 9am-4.30pm)
www.eachaction.org.uk
Charity providing support to individuals affected by homophobia and training to organisations committed to realising an equal and safe environment for all, regardless of sexuality, age, ethnicity or ability.

FREEDOM YOUTH
Tel: 377 3677 • www.freedomyouth.co.uk
Bristol-based LGB youth project, including a weekly drop-in for LGB youth 25 and under offering information, advice and guidance.

GAY WEST
PO Box 586, Bath BA1 2YQ.
0870 811 1990 • www.gaywest.org.uk
Social group for LGB people in the South West whose roots stretch back as far as 1971 and the establishment of the Bath Gay Awareness Group. The group holds a café/drop-in in Bath every Saturday afternoon and a monthly social in Bristol.

Gay

Gay

Bristol at-a-glance

Get to know Bristol with a quick guide to language, population and some other useful stuff

A note on the lingo

Don't be alarmed the first time you encounter somebody talking in a broad Bristolian accent. The speaker will not harm you. Probably. As with all accents, there are subtle variations across the city, the most obvious one being between a Gloucestershire accent (North and East of the city) and a Somerset burr (South Bristol).

The main linguistic features of the great Bristolian accent include:
The post-vocalic 'R': Pronouncing the R where it occurs after a vowel as in CaRt, PaRty, alaRm, neveR. Asder (ASDA)

The add-on 'er': Most commonly heard in lover (love), slider (playground slide).

Rising intonation: When a statement is made to sound like a question.

The Bristol 'L': Adding an L to the end of words that end in an unstressed vowel as in Australial (Australia), ideal (idea) and areal (area). Also sometimes heard in the middle of words as in drawling (drawing).

For years, speaking in a Bristolian accent was regarded as a sign of simplicity. Indeed, there have been several stories over the years of Bristol footballers having to leave teams from outside Bristol because they or their partners and families got the piss taken out of their accent so badly. But, all that has changed, thankfully. The three main champions of the Bristolian accent are football manager Ian Holloway, *Little Britain's* Vicky Pollard character and clothing shop Beast, whose Bristolian T-shirts are spreading the word across the world.

Five phrases...
In Bristolian

1 Cheers drive
Thank you bus driver for a safe and pleasant journey.

2 Gert lush
Absolutely wonderful.

3 Awright me babber/lover
Hello.

4 Ark at ee
Listen or look at that.

5 Where's ee to?
Do you by chance know the whereabouts of...?

For further help with the Bristol dialect, see *A Dictionary of Bristle*, available from all good book shops and at www.tangentbooks.co.uk

Flower of Bristol

The Scarlet Lychnis (Lychnis Chalcedonica) or Nonsuch has been associated with Bristol since the Middle Ages when it was known as the Flower of Bristowe. It is thought the flower is native to the Middle East and was imported to Bristol by sea traders, or possibly by returning crusaders. The association of the flower with the city is recognised by Bristol University in the choice of its distinctive colour for academic hoods.

Coat of Arms

Until 1569, the Bristol Coat of Arms was only the shield. The coat of arms with the unicorns and crest was granted to Bristol in 1569 by the College of Arms. The background to the shield is red with a golden ship sailing on blue waves out of a silver castle which stands on a green mound – all signifying Bristol's huge importance as a major port.

Above the shield is a silver helmet, a red wreath and two crossed arms holding a green serpent and golden scales representing wisdom and justice. The unicorns are a symbol of extreme courage, virtue and strength. The motto translates as: 'By virtue and industry'.

VIRTUTE·ET·INDUSTRIA

Bristol figures

393,400 Bristol population – 2004 estimate

188,200 Males	193,500 Females
80,100 0-17 years	79,900 18-29
166,000 30-64	55,600 65 and over

8.2% are from black or ethnic minority groups

33% of households are single-person

Fallen Comrades

Our tribute to places we liked that have departed since the publication of the first edition of *The Naked Guide to Bristol.*

The Albert Inn, Bedminster; The Old Fox, Easton; **Ashton Court Festival;** Hand of God stencil on Totterdown Bridge; **Mixu The Chicken, Totterdown;** Bristol Books, Stokes Croft; **Replay Records, Park Street and Bedminster;** House of Darts, Gloucester Road; **Soup Etc, Hotwells;** The view over Bristol from Park Row blotted out by the Zerodegrees bar; **Eat The Beat, St Nick's Market;** Alterior Clothing, Park Street; **Greenleaf Bookshop, Colston Avenue;** Smiles, Colston Avenue; **Level, Park Row;** Imperial Music, Park Street; **Last floodlight from Eastville Stadium, Eastville;** Bristol North Baths, Gloucester Road; **Old Possums Wine Bar, Redland;** The Bristolian paper; **Clifton Bookshop;** York Cafe; **Rooted Records,** Bag 'O Nails

Phew! it's gone

It took six months to demolish, but Tollgate House has gone. The huge, horrendous tower block at the bottom of the M32 was a grim welcome sign for Bristol. It must have been a strong sense of irony that persuaded the Department of the Environment to move into such a monstrous blot on the landscape. Tollgate House was dismantled to make way for Cabot Circus.

Bibliography

Bibliography

Bristol Review of Books
Keep up to date bout all the new books about Bristol and new titles from local publishes by subscribing to the *Bristol Review of Books* at *www.tangentbooks.co.uk*. Bristol Review of Books is also available free of charge at local libraries and book shops. Some of the books listed below are now out of print, but you should be able to find a second-hand copy easily enough.

A Celebration of the Avon New Cut
Various contributors
Fiducia, £7

A Dictionary of Bristle
Harry Stoke and Vinny Green
Tangent Books, £5.95
www.tangentbooks.co.uk

Art & Sound of the Bristol Underground
Chris Burton and Gary Thompson
Tangent Books, £10
www.tangentbooks.co.uk

Banksy's Bristol: Home Sweet Home
Steve Wright
Tangent Books, £12
www.tangentbooks.co.uk

Bristol's 100 Best Buildings
Mike Jenner
Redcliffe Press, £17.95

Bristol Beyond the Bridge
Michael Manson
Past and Present Press, £8.95

Bristol: Ethnic Minorities and the City, 1000-2001
Madge Dresser, Peter Fleming
Phillimore & Co, £14.99

Bristol Radical History Group Pamphlets
£3.50 each
www.tangentbooks.co.uk

Bristol Treasure Island Trail
Long John Silver Trust
Broadcast Books, £4.95

Brunel's Bristol
Angus Buchanan
Redcliffe Press, £9.95

Children of the Can: 25 Years of Bristol Graffiti
Felix Braun
Tangent Books, £25
www.tangentbooks.co.uk

Children's Bristol
Edited by John Sansom
Redcliffe Press, £8.50

Court in the Act: Ashton Court Festival 1974-1992
£10
www.tangentbooks.co.uk

Eating Out West
Venue Publishing, £4.99
www.tangentbooks.co.uk

Flying High: New Circus in Bristol
Monica Connell
Tangent Books, £14.99
www.tangentbooks.co.uk

From Gothic to Romantic: Thomas Chatterton's Bristol
Alistair Heys
Redcliffe Press, £14.95

LINK TO THE NAKED GUIDE WEBSITE

If you want a reciprocal link between **www.tangentbooks.co.uk** and your site, email us through our website.

Granary Club
Al Read
Broadcast Books, £14.50
www.tangentbooks.co.uk

Hidden History of St Andrew's
Mike Manson
Past & Present Press, £12
www.tangentbooks.co.uk

Let's Have Coffee: The Tao of Ian Holloway
Alex Murphy
Toilet Books, £4.50
www.tangentbooks.co.uk

Naked Guide to Bath
Gideon Kibblewhite
Tangent Books, £9.95
www.tangentbooks.co.uk

Naked Guide to Cider
James Russell
Tangent Books, £9.95
www.tangentbooks.co.uk

Pevsner Architectural Guide to Bristol
Andrew Foyle
Yale University Press, £9.99

Pirates and Privateers Out of Bristol
Ken Griffiths, Mark Steeds, Roy Gallop
Fiducia, £10

Politics & Protest
Pete Maginnis
Tangent Books, £12
www.tangentbooks.co.uk

Recollections of Jazz in Bristol
Dave Hibberd
Fiducia, £12.50

Riot! The Bristol Bridge Riot
Michael Manson
Past and Present Press, £8.95
www.tangentbooks.co.uk

Secret Underground Bristol
Sally Watson
Broadcast Books, £14.95

Slavery Obscured: The Social History of the Slave Trade in Bristol
Madge Dresser
Redcliffe Press, £14.99

Straight Outa Bristol
Phil Johnson
Hodder & Stoughton, £9.99

The Street Names of Bristol: Their Meanings and Origins
Veronica Smith
Broadcast Books, £11.95

Trenches to Trams
Clive Burlton
Tangent Books, £14.99
www.tangentbooks.co.uk

Wall and Piece
Banksy
Century, £20

Wild Dayz
Photos by Beezer
Tangent Books, £15
www.tangentbooks.co.uk

Index

Index

NG NAKED GUIDES

Enjoyed The Naked Guide to Bristol? Then why not visit **www.tangentbooks.co.uk** where you can find out more about our books and buy them online. We also publish The Naked Guide to Bath, The Naked Guide to Cider and plan to release The Naked Guide to Cardiff. Just as soon as we've written it.

THE NAKED GUIDE TO **BATH**
BY GIDEON KIBBLEWHITE

OUT NOW!

Not all guide books are the same...

The Naked Guide to Bath:
Discover the delights (and horrors) of the World Heritage City of Bath, a city designed for pleasure.

"Bath stripped bare"
The Bath Chronicle

"Devilishly honest"
Bristol Evening Post